FRONTIS-PISS.

Frontis-Piss, by William Hogarth (1763)

Witchcraft and
Its Transformations
c.1650–c.1750

IAN BOSTRIDGE

CLARENDON PRESS · OXFORD
1997

Oxford University Press, Great Clarendon Street, Oxford OX2 6DP
Oxford New York
Athens Auckland Bangkok Bogota Bombay
Buenos Aires Calcutta Cape Town Dar es Salaam
Delhi Florence Hong Kong Istanbul Karachi
Kuala Lumpur Madras Madrid Melbourne
Mexico City Nairobi Paris Singapore
Tapei Tokyo Toronto
and associated companies in
Berlin Ibadan

Oxford is a trade mark of Oxford University Press

Published in the United States
by Oxford University Press Inc., New York

British Library Cataloguing in Publication Data
Data available

Library of Congress Cataloging in Publication Data
Data applied for

ISBN 0-19-820653-4

1 3 5 7 9 10 8 6 4 2

Typeset by Graphicraft Typesetters Ltd., Hong Kong
Printed in Great Britain
on acid-free paper by
Bookcraft Ltd., Midsomer Norton, Somerset

For Lucasta

[The] Antient System . . . [is] broken up, the Vessel of Sorcery shipwreckt and only some shattered planks and pieces disjoyned floating and scattered on the Ocean of the human Activity and Bustle.

(Ezra Stiles, pastor at Newport, Rhode Island, later president of Yale College, diary entry, June 1773)

Acknowledgements

OVER the long gestation period of this book, which started life as a doctoral thesis, I have accumulated many debts. Simon Schaffer first suggested that I work on witchcraft. Robin Briggs was one of the examiners of the thesis and has been a great help since. Above all I have to thank Keith Thomas, whose *Religion and the Decline of Magic*, to which this volume forms some sort of footnote, I first read on a cross-channel ferry some fifteen years ago. As my tutor, supervisor, and editor, and the head of my college, his kindness and intellectual example have sustained me.

Other help of various kinds has come from: Jonathan Barry; Alexander Bird; Jonathan Clark; Stuart Clark; David Ekserdjian; Mark Goldie; Penny Gouk; Clive Holmes; James Howard-Johnston; Michael Hunter; John Hyman; Joanna Innes; Mark Jenner; Peter Laslett; Roy Park; Aileen Ribeiro; Lyndal Roper; Alessandro Schiesaro; Nigel Smith; John Spurr; Daniel Szechi; and Penry Williams.

St John's College, Oxford, my undergraduate college, helped me out in my early years of graduate research; the British Academy has been a patient benefactor, both in my time as a graduate and as a postdoctoral research fellow. For my last three years as an academic, I have enjoyed being part of Corpus Christi College in Oxford; as I now leave the academic world, I realize that I could not have been in a nicer place, or with more congenial and stimulating colleagues. The staffs of the British Library, the London Library, the Cambridge University Library, and above all the Bodleian Library have been great enablers.

On a personal note I would like to thank David Cook, Ross McKibbin, Peter Southern, and Malcolm Vale for teaching me; Annette Allen, Peter Bloor, and Robert Rattray for (perhaps unwittingly) nursing me through the last stages of production, and giving me the confidence to finish; my brother, Mark, for introducing me to the study of history; my parents and my stepmother, Paulyne, for countless reasons; and Lucasta Miller, to whom this book is dedicated.

Contents

List of Illustrations

Abbreviations

BJHS	*British Journal for the History of Science.*
BL	British Library, London.
BM, *Sat.*	British Museum, *Catalogue of . . . Political and Personal Satires.*
CUL	Cambridge University Library.
DNB	*Dictionary of National Biography.*
EHR	*English Historical Review.*
HJ	*Historical Journal.*
HMC	Historical Manuscripts Commission, Reports.
HS	*History of Science.*
JBS	*Journal of British Studies.*
JEH	*Journal of Ecclesiastical History.*
JHI	*Journal of the History of Ideas.*
Locke Correspondence	John Locke, *Correspondence*, ed. E. S. de Beer.
OED	*Oxford English Dictionary.*
P & P	*Past and Present.*
Defoe, *Review*	*Defoe's 'Review'*, ed. A. W. Secord.
SHR	*Scottish Historical Review.*
SRO	Scottish Record Office.
State Trials	Cobbett, Howell, *et al.*, *Cobbett's . . . State Trials.*
Thomas, *RDM*	Keith Thomas, *Religion and the Decline of Magic.*
TRHS	*Transactions of the Royal Historical Society.*

1. *Ducking a Witch*, by G. M. Brighty (1815); appears in 1819 edition of Defoe's *Political History of the Devil*

Introduction

Maggie with deepening colour went without hesitation to Mr Riley's elbow and looked over the book, eagerly seizing one corner and tossing back her mane, while she said,

'O, I'll tell you what that means. It's a dreadful picture, isn't it? But I can't help looking at it. That old woman in the water's a witch—they've put her in, to find out whether she's a witch or no, and if she swims she's a witch, and if she's drowned—and killed, you know,—she's innocent, and not a witch, but only a poor silly old woman. But what good would it do her then, you know, when she was drowned? Only, I suppose she'd go to heaven, and God would make it up to her. And this dreadful blacksmith with his arms akimbo, laughing—oh, isn't he ugly?—I'll tell you what he is. He's the devil really'

(here Maggie's voice became louder and more emphatic)

'and not a right blacksmith; for the devil takes the shape of wicked men and walks about and sets people doing wicked things, and he's oftener in the shape of a bad man than any other, because, you know, if people saw he was the devil, and he roared at 'em, they'd run away, and he couldn't make 'em do what he pleased.'

Mr Tulliver had listened to this exposition of Maggie's with petrifying wonder.

'Why, what book is it the wench has got hold on?' he burst out, at last.

' "The History of the Devil", by Daniel Defoe; not quite the right book for a little girl,' said Mr Riley. 'How came it among your books, Tulliver?'[1]

This scene is from George Eliot's novel *The Mill on the Floss*, published in 1860. Seventy years after the French Revolution, some thirty years after Catholic Emancipation and the Great Reform Act: this was a world remote from witch-hunts, religious persecution, and England's *ancien régime*. Intellectual transformation was in the air. James Clerk Maxwell was conjuring an ethereal realm into existence, trembling not with occult forces, devils, and witches, but with mathematically abstract electromagnetic lines of force. Of more direct interest to the biologically-minded

---

[1] George Eliot, *The Mill on the Floss* (1860; Harmondsworth, 1979), 66–7.

George Eliot, Darwin's *Origin of Species* was published just a year before. The modern world is coming into being.

Dorlcote Mill and the valley of the Floss, however, are part of a past rustically imagined, suffused with the old ways and populated with 'people of the old school', as Mr Riley ('a gentleman with a waxen complexion and fat hands, rather highly educated for an auctioneer and appraiser') condescendingly observes. The unassisted intellects of these 'simple country acquaintances' of the late 1820s are all afever with Old Harry (the Devil), and with visions of a country prey to Papists and Radicals, having only just suffered betrayal by the Duke of Wellington on the issue of Catholic Emancipation. Mr Tulliver's embarrassment is patent. The collision of Maggie's irrepressible enthusiasm, Mr Riley's patronizing gentility, and Tulliver's 'petrifying wonder' generates the comedy. It also points to something about the position of witchcraft and demonology in George Eliot's imaginary world, around the time of the dissolution of the old regime. For someone like Tulliver, poised between politeness and country ways, the possession of books about witchcraft was not quite right; it was something which might betray a lack of breeding or some sort of backwardness.

Mr Tulliver, we are told, bought Defoe's book in a bundle with some seventeenth-century sermons. This book will set out to explain how belief in witchcraft moved from the respectability of sermons and treatises, via the ambivalent satire of Defoe, to nineteenth-century embarrassment. It looks beneath politeness to its roots in politics. It is striking that witchcraft should remain a queasy issue at Dorlcote Mill; not necessarily generating profound debate, but touching a nerve. That such nervousness and sensitivity went together with an addiction to the old political settlement is no coincidence. Marian Evans treasured her own childhood copy of Bunyan, and of Defoe's history of the Devil, reprinted with those bewitching illustrations in 1819. In however peripheral a way, Eliot's reflections on her childhood, refracted through Maggie, encapsulate something of the ideological trajectory of witchcraft theory, and its hitherto secret history.

The argument of this book differs in two essential regards from previous treatments of the subject. It suggests that witchcraft theory had a serious constituency well beyond 1700; and that the reasons for its loss of credibility were at least partly political. Over the period covered by this book, I will argue that witchcraft theory—centred upon the notion that men and women could covenant with the Devil to do harm to their communities, thus setting themselves up against the divine and social order—lost its mainstream ideological roots and was expelled from the world-view of the polite classes in England. I set out to discover when witchcraft theory ceased to be credible; when it became ridiculous; when it was so marginalized as to be neither argued for nor argued against within polite society. This is the moment at which witchcraft theory was expelled from the public domain. It was from here on that the modern attitude towards witchcraft, that of George Eliot and her readers, developed.

Though there were no witch 'crazes' in England comparable in ferocity to those which occurred in parts of continental Europe, there were phases of relatively intense persecution which can be related to particular political stresses or disordered social conditions. But these 'epidemics' punctuated long periods of what one might call 'endemic' prosecution, at a much lower, often almost negligible level. Witchcraft theory could thrive in periods of low-level prosecution; the disruptions of intense persecution were, indeed, often more threatening to educated acceptance of the existence of witchcraft. It could also lie low, an unquestioned assumption whose relative quiescence did not necessarily imply that it was moribund.

The persecutory zeal which accompanied the disorders of the English civil wars was followed by an era of endemic prosecution. The customary interpretation of this period has been that witchcraft theory was in retreat. Prosecution was falling, after all, and the last execution for witchcraft in England took place in 1685. These assumptions need to be challenged. Witchcraft remained a crime; levels of prosecution had fallen to very low levels before, in the 1630s; and it is only in retrospect that the 1685 execution could be recognized as the last. Some authors and lawyers may have been sceptical; others, quite clearly, were not. The assumption of decline has affected the perception of witchcraft theory in the period between the end of the Civil War and the repeal of the laws against witchcraft in 1736. It has discouraged historians from gathering together the fugitive materials which are available to construct a history of educated witchcraft theory in this period; and it has skewed the reading of some of the vital texts in this history. Too often, these have either been ignored or read too cursorily, on the assumption of the triumph, by the 1680s, of a fundamental educated scepticism.

Educated scepticism did exist, but it had done so from the start. Moreover, the sceptical arguments offered by Francis Hutchinson in 1718 were much the same as those of Reginald Scot in 1584 or Thomas Ady in 1656. Hutchinson's work entered the mainstream straight away; Scot and Ady were part of the radical fringe. It is only by looking outside

the purely rational content of sceptical works, and recognizing the political appeal which such books offered, and the ideological context in which
they operated, that we can understand why the same arguments were
received in such different ways.

The demise of witchcraft theory was not simply, in the classic scientific
fashion, the discovery of a previously unrecognized, if commonsensical,
truth. Because natural philosophers in the seventeenth century were
fascinated by the phenomena of witchcraft, we have come to look for
solutions to the question of the demise of witchcraft theory in the domain
of science. While witchcraft theory had its roots in a way of seeing the
natural world—a world full of spirits and wonders—which we have come
to reject, it was as much a social, political, and theological theory as a
natural one. Witchcraft theory, as we shall see in the course of this book,
told the ruling classes of seventeenth-century England much about the
nature of the divine order, and reinforced certain notions of the relationship between the secular and the spiritual realms. The disintegration of
witchcraft theory was as much to do with changes in these conceptions as
with the development of the new natural philosophy. The mechanical
philosophy left too much of the old world of spirits and wonders intact to
have acted as reason's exorcist in the casting-out of witchcraft.

The intellectual demise of the concept of witchcraft has rarely been
studied to symmetrical effect. Proponents and opponents of witchcraft
belief have not been treated as equal and opposite for the purposes of
historical study. Such even-handedness is arguably a necessary feature of
historical explanation. One would not explain the triumph of Newtonian
mechanics by asserting that Newton was right, if only because he was not.
Historical explanation of beliefs should struggle towards neutrality as
regards the truth-content of rival positions. For, unless we attempt to be
symmetrical, we fail to come to terms with the motives, prejudices, and
dispositions of historical actors. An asymmetrical history of ideas amounts
to a history of truth; an ideal, Platonic process, removed from time and
only imperfectly acted out in the real, messy business of history.

Concentrating on the function which the notion of the witch played
within the ideologies of the educated élite, this book examines the historical relationship between the fortunes of witchcraft theory and the ideologies with which it had become associated, or for which it had a particular
affinity. Chapter 1 assesses the ideological significance of the covenantal
demonology espoused by the Puritan theologian William Perkins at the
end of the sixteenth century and still current at the time of England's
last witch-craze in the 1640s. It goes on to decipher the countervailing

political interests which motivated the Royalist theorist Sir Robert Filmer in his opposition to witch-hunting early in the following decade. The chapter ends by tracing the persistence of the covenant tradition in Scotland, and the political uses of the language of covenantal demonology there, into the 1690s and beyond.

1

Contract

the Devil is Gods Ape, and one that faines to imit[a]te him though
in contrary ways. And therefore as God makes a Covenant of Grace
with his: so does the Devil with his a Covenant of death.

(John Gaule, *Select Cases of Conscience* (1646))

WILLIAM PERKINS

The political context of beliefs about witchcraft in the seventeenth century has been, on the whole, ignored. The ideological function of witch
beliefs among the English élite has remained largely unexplored. An
attempt to relate witchcraft and high politics, Reginald Trevor Davies's
Four Centuries of Witch-Beliefs, was published nearly fifty years ago, but,
since then, the two subjects have been kept in separate compartments.
This is unsurprising given Davies's eccentric, even monomaniac, conclusions. Arguing that the Pilgrim Fathers set sail because their desire to
hunt witches was being frustrated by lax government, Davies saw the
conflict between King and Commons in the 1640s not as a matter of taxa-
tion, foreign policy, or theological dispute, but as something which arose
from concern about the persecution of witches; Oliver Cromwell took
issue with his king because of his religious convictions, to be sure, but
that these 'were affronted by Charles I's protection of witches is in a high
degree probable, although no word of his can be quoted to this effect'.
Easy ridicule should not, however, allow us to bypass the basic proposition which Davies advances: that the belief in witchcraft was rooted in
political and ideological debate.

Subsequent historians, like John Teall for England, or E. W. Monter for Geneva, dismissed any systematic correlation between Calvinism and demonology.[1] To prove his case, Teall pointed to the variety of beliefs which three men he categorized as Calvinists held about witchcraft, from the outright scepticism of Reginald Scot through the moderate belief of George Gifford to the persecutory enthusiasm of William Perkins. If all these men were Calvinists, yet varied so much in their response to witch-craft, how could Calvinism and witch belief be so bound together?

These three men were, however, hardly theological allies. Scot was highly unorthodox, and has been variously defined as a sceptical Sadducee or a crypto-familist; while Gifford's Calvinism cannot be assimilated to the contractarian casuistry which Perkins subsequently developed.[2] Any-way, the lack of a cut-and-dried equation between Calvinism and witch-craft beliefs is surely not the same thing as the absence of any affinity whatsoever between the two. The special features of Calvinist doctrine, and notably the emphasis on predestination, were certainly compatible with the belief in witchcraft. The Calvinist insistence on the depravity of man made the diabolical alliance a plausible one.[3] More than this, how-ever, the federal theology increasingly favoured in England had a parti-cular affinity with witch theory. The restriction of the miraculous which Protestant theology introduced necessitated a shift from much of the scheme laid out in the *Malleus Maleficarum*, and put an increased empha-sis upon the diabolical compact. This was a development especially well suited to the language of the sort of English Calvinism represented by Perkins. Tempering predestination with the alloy of the covenant—both resisting the anarchic tendency towards antinomianism and allowing for lay initiative and involvement—English Calvinists put a divine compact

[1] John L. Teall, 'Witchcraft and Calvinism in Elizabethan England: Divine Power and Human Agency', *JHI* 23 (1962); E. W. Monter, *Witchcraft in France and Switzerland: The Borderlands during the Reformation* (Ithaca, NY, 1976).

[2] For these versions of Scot, see Sydney Anglo, 'Reginald Scot's *Discoverie of Witchcraft*: Scepticism and Sadduceeism', in Anglo (ed.), *The Damned Art: Essays in the Literature of Witchcraft* (1977), and David Wootton, 'Reginald Scot' (paper at Birkbeck College London early modern history seminar, 199?). For George Gifford, see his *A Dialogue concerning Witches* (1593) and *A Discourse of the Subtill Practises of Devilles by Witches and Sorcerers* (1587).

[3] Although the witch as enemy of human society was no particular invention of Geneva; and, as Monter has pointed out, the plenitude of divine justice, the inadequacy of the human variety, might rather have suggested that severity, in as doubtful and complex a crime as witchcraft, should be reined in: E. W. Monter, 'The Historiography of European Witchcraft: Progress and Prospects', *Journal of Interdisciplinary History*, 2 (1972).

at the centre of their theology. That their anti-theology should come to emphasize a diabolical covenant is hardly surprising.[4]

William Perkins, author of *A Discourse of the Damned Art of Witchcraft*, was also the most eminent exponent of English Calvinism, and one of the most widely read of English writers.[5] His classic work of theology, *Armilla Aurea*, appeared at Cambridge in 1590, and was translated the following year as *A Golden Chain . . . containing the Order of the Causes of Salvation and Damnation*. Predestination, double and absolute in Perkins's sense (though not necessarily supralapsarian, dating election before the fall, as Perkins did), was arguably the prevalent doctrine of grace in the Church of England at the accession of Charles I.[6] This was the doctrine against which Arminius wrote in the fullest account of his doctrine, the posthumous *Examen Modestum* of 1612.[7] For some historians, this ideological division between Arminianism and Calvinism should be seen as the engine of civil war, with either Arminians or Calvinists as unsettling innovators.[8] Questions of grace, election, and free will, all the complex issues raised by predestination, were certainly a focus for intellectual discussion and dissension prior to the Civil War. These doctrines and debates were also, to a large extent, discredited in the course of the 1640s and 1650s. Fruitless speculation, as some saw it, had led some towards sectarianism and, ultimately, the horrors of antinomianism.[9]

Particular elements in English Calvinism distinguished it from its Genevan parent, notably the idea of the covenant between God and man. Perkins held that 'the stipulation of the couenant of Grace is the substance of the gospel'.[10] Before the 1590s, this contract had been largely conceived

---

[4] On federal theology and its transplantation from Heidelberg to England, see R. T. Kendall, *Calvin and English Calvinism to 1649* (Oxford, 1979), ch. 2 and *passim*; David Zaret, *The Heavenly Contract: Ideology and Organization in Pre-Revolutionary Puritanism* (Chicago, 1985).

[5] According to Nicholas Tyacke, *Anti-Calvinists: The Rise of English Arminianism* (Oxford, 1987), 29.

[6] See e.g. William Perkins, *Workes* (2 vols.; Cambridge, 1609), i. *A Golden Chaine*, 'To the Christian Reader', 9.

[7] Jacobus Arminius, *Examen Modestum* (Leiden, 1612).

[8] See e.g. Tyacke, *Anti-Calvinists*.

[9] See e.g. Thomas Hobbes, *Behemoth* (1679); Samuel Butler, *Hudibras* (1663); Meric Casaubon's introduction to John Dee, *A True and Faithful Relation of what passed for many years between Dr John Dee . . . and Some Spirits* (1659); or William Dugdale, *A Short View of the Late Troubles in England* (Oxford, 1681).

[10] Cited in Zaret, *Heavenly Contract*, 152. For the American historian Perry Miller, the covenant of grace was, famously, the 'marrow of puritan divinity'. Perry Miller, 'The Marrow of Puritan Divinity', *Publications of the Colonial Society of Massachusetts*, 32 (1935). For one of Perkins's successors, Nicholas Byfield, it was part of *The Marrow of the Oracles of God* (1640).

of as unilateral in form, combating radical heresy and separatist tendencies within the English church: the heavenly contract was an inheritance, a generous gift from God, which separatists should not refuse to the sinful multitude. George Gifford, for one, defended the English church on the basis of a unilateral covenant, all Christians being 'from antient discent within the covenant'.[11]

As attention shifted increasingly from ecclesiological to pastoral issues, a new and bilateral conception of the covenant came to the fore. It seemed ever more necessary to strike a balance between hope and despair in the assurance of grace, to avoid either the despondent torpor of the pessimist or the optimist's breezy self-satisfaction. 'Now', wrote John Downame to this purpose, 'the meanes to be in this Couenant with God, is to performe the condition of Faith'.[12] Yet faith itself was a gift of God through the aid of grace—a duty and a gift. So Richard Sibbes could assure his readers that 'the covenant of grace is so called because God is so gracious to enable us to perform on our part'.[13]

A flexible Puritan casuistry developed out of these sorts of considera-tion, one which asserted that introspection could bring retrospective knowl-edge of election. The godly were led to search for evidence of the contract. One major source of such theorizing was William Perkins, who consist-ently advocated an ambiguous blend of activism and determinism in the pursuit and enjoyment of grace. The activities of the church, including what had once been sacraments, were to be interpreted within such a framework. Baptism was 'the seal of the covenant of grace', the Eucharist an ongoing symbol of consent. In this pragmatic scheme of things, an election to grace, located in the past, became a conditional offer to believ-ers in the present. Sermons were part of this scheme too, and were even more essential since 'the preaching of his word . . . is the Couenant of grace'.[14] This covenant is, then, the theoretical solution to the psychologi-cal tension which Max Weber identified in his account of the 'Protestant ethic': the productive resolution of salvation anxiety. The heavenly con-tract was proclaimed by preaching, and offered redemption to all on condition of faith. If this condition was fulfilled, salvation was guaran-teed; but only the elect were actually able to believe and repent.

---

[11] According to Henry Barrow, 'A Refutation of Mr Giffard's Reasons' (1590/1) in *The Writings of Henry Barrow*, ed. L. H. Carlson (1966), 337.

[12] John Downame, *A Treatise of Securitie* (1622), 98.

[13] R. Sibbes, 'Bowels Opened' (1639), in *Works*, ed. A. B. Grosart (Edinburgh, 1862), ii. 183, from the 20th sermon, use 3.

[14] John Downame, *The Christian Warfare* (1634), 117.

The process of perdition seems to have been reflexive in the same
way, within this all-embracing predestinarian framework. As we learn in
a witchcraft tract of the 1650s, as much an expression of current theological trends as of demonology itself, 'we may see much of the Justice
of God . . . that those that will rebelliously harden their hearts against
God, shall be judicially hardned by him'. These implacable sinners are
chosen from the very beginning, and 'what a madness rests in the sons
of men, to think they can repent when they will'.[15] God's promise of
saving grace is for the elect, 'not . . . the wicked, because the Couvenant
is not made with them, by reason they agree not to the Condition of
becoming God's people'.[16] The bilateral nature of the contract is strikingly clear. God 'hath bound himselfe to performe what he hath said . . . we
should learne thus to importune God; tell him, *Lord*, I have a sure
promise'.[17]

Thus the Genevan idiom of Calvinism, with its emphasis on man's
depravity by nature, on free grace and predestination, was modified by
the contract, which came to infuse all Puritan theology. This was a direct
affront to the Arminian party which came to prominence under Charles
I, especially after Laud became Archbishop of Canterbury in 1633. In
particular, Puritan dualism was directly opposed to the sacramentalism of
the Laudians. Baptism and the Eucharist were not seals of a covenant for
the Arminians, but efficacious outpourings of mysterious grace, available to
all men. Laud set out to limit the teaching of covenant theology, and, for
instance, had charts depicting the sacraments in covenantal terms removed
from several London churches by his authority as Bishop of London.[18]
William Perkins's immersion in the soon-to-be contentious doctrine of
the covenant is vitally relevant to his work on witches; and the Arminian
Sir Robert Filmer's particular attention to him in his *Advertisement to the
Jury-Men of England, Touching Witches* (1653) was, I shall argue, a function of the political and religious debates of the 1640s and 1650s.

The rationale for the severity of the punishment meted out to the
convicted witch and the particular noxiousness of the crime lay, for

---

[15] Edmond Bower, *Doctor Lamb Revived, or, Witchcraft condemn'd in Anne Bodenham*
(1653), 42.
[16] Daniel Dyke, *Two Treatises: the one of repentance; the other of Christs Temptations*
(1618), 88, cited in Zaret, *Heavenly Contract*, 157.
[17] John Preston, *The Breast-Plate of Faith and Love*, 4th edn., (1634), 81 f. Cf. James
Hogg, *Confessions of a Justified Sinner* (1824; Oxford, 1969), 99: 'I cited his own words
against him, and endeavoured to hold him at his promise'.
[18] See Zaret, *Heavenly Contract*, 143.

Perkins, in the overt rejection of the covenant and its seals.[19] Since witches 'covenant to use . . . [the Devil's] helpe for the working of wonders', they are not only rejecting the generous covenant of God, but also binding themselves to an anti-contract which, for Perkins, is the essence of witch-craft, and in precise counterpoint to the theology of covenant. The posi-tive vision of salvation is dramatized by the anathematization of its mirror-image. Within Perkins's scheme witchcraft fulfils a specific func-tion as the inversion of orthodox soteriology. That which makes a witch is that which makes a Puritan saint, namely 'the yeelding of consent upon covenant'.[20]

This implication is drawn out in the epistle to Perkins's book on witches, written by Thomas Pickering and addressed to the Lord Chief Justice, Sir Edward Coke. The Devil, it is said,

composeth his course . . . by way of counterfait and imitation, not of the actions and dealings of men, but of the order of Gods owne proceeding with his Church; holding it a sure principle in policie, That actions will be much more effectuall, when they be framed unto the best presidents, then when they are suted to the direction of meaner examples. To this purpose, as God hath made a Couenant with his Church, binding himselfe by promise to be their God, and requiring of them the condition of faith and obedience; so doth Satan indent with his Subiects by mutuall confederacie, either solemnly or secretly; whereby they bind them-selves on the one part to observe his Rules, and he on the other to accomplish their desires.

The inversion of covenant theology is exact—'as God hath made a Couen-ant . . . so doth Satan indent with his subiects by *mutuall* confederacie'. The comparison extends to embrace ceremonies and the word, all this being contrived by the arch-deceiver to 'maintaine his owne principalitie'.[21] For Perkins, the 'soveraigne preservative' against the onslaught of the Devil and his human servants was 'to be within the covenant of grace'. Like is fought with like, one covenant with another.[22]

In dealing with the question of why all witches are not speedily de-tected, Perkins presents the Devil as God's instrument—the lesson of the book of Job—and emphasizes the absolute nature of predestination. That

---

[19] 'They renounce the Lord that made them, they make no more account of his favour and protection, they doe quite cut themselves of[f] from the covenant made with him in Baptism, from the Communion of Saints, from the true worship and service of God.' Perkins, *A Discourse of the Damned Art of Witchcraft; So farre forth as it is reuealed in the Scriptures, and manifest by true experience* (Cambridge, 1608), 170.
[20] Ibid. 183, 170.   [21] Ibid. preface.   [22] Ibid. 220.

is, he momentarily presses the balance of covenant theology *away* from free will of a sort, towards determinism, in order to maintain the equilibrium of the whole work. As ever, the paradoxes of covenant theology are resolved by a continual flux of shifting emphases. So, one reason for the failure to discover all witches speedily is that some of them may be elect. Moving in his mysterious way, God may allow them to be held 'in the snares of Satan', though finally 'in mercie he reclaimes them'. In the mean time he does not allow the Devil 'to exercise the depth of his malice in discovering them to their confusion'.

Thus witches, those covenanters with the Devil, may none the less be elect, by God's mercy; witchcraft is heinous sin only for the reprobate— '*There is no condemnation to them that are in Christ*, Rom. 8. 1. because no sinne is imputed unto them'. Yet so too may the reprobate be sunk further into their witchcraft by the justice of the Lord. He will allow them to live on undisclosed, so that 'they may live to fill up the measure of their iniquities, and thereby be made finally inexcusable, that they may receive their iuster condemnation.'[23]

Witchcraft is a sort of lesson for the meaning of predestination as a whole—it is not enough to be a good person in the eyes of the world. A traitor who helps his neighbour is nevertheless 'by the law of Nations, no better than a dead man, because he betraies his Soueraigne'.[24]

For Perkins, witchcraft belief was part of a larger system, witchcraft itself a feature of the divine economy. This is why the *Discourse* is as much pastoral guide and theological treatise as a textbook on witchcraft.[25] It is, however, also important to recognize that, enshrining as it did a particular version of godliness (as all theories of witchcraft did), Perkins's work was ideologically committed and open to ideological attack.

Perkins was an influential writer and his system of witchcraft belief was widely disseminated. John Gaule in his *Select Cases of Conscience* (1646) followed Perkins almost exactly on these issues. He remarks 'how utterly opposite the diabolicall Covenant is, to the Covenant of Grace' and is insistent upon the covenantal nature of witchcraft: 'The formall cause of a Witch, is the Covenant, Compact, Contract, Confoederation, League, societie, familiarity with the Devill.' The nature of witchcraft as a sort of upside-down godliness is reiterated:

---

[23] Ibid. 217.   [24] Ibid. 184
[25] Stuart Clark, 'Protestant Demonology: Sin, Superstition, and Society (*c.*1520–*c.*1630)', in Bengt Ankarloo and Gustav Henningsen (eds.), *Early Modern European Witchcraft: Centres and Peripheries* (Oxford, 1990).

Besides the Devil is Gods Ape, and one that faines to imit[a]te him though in contrary wayes. And therefore as God makes a Covenant of Grace with his: so does the Devil with his a Covenant of death.[26]

SIR ROBERT FILMER

Sir Robert Filmer, author of the notorious absolutist text *Patriarcha*, associate of prominent English Arminians, also wrote on witchcraft. His brief tract formed part of a general attack on Calvinism as he conceived it, in both its covenantal and its original forms. First, in the 1640s, came his questioning of Calvin's own account of the blasphemy against the Holy Ghost; then an attack on witchcraft theory in the 1650s which undermined the foundations of the newfangled covenant theology.

Filmer published his *Advertisement to the Jury-Men of England, Touching Witches* in 1653, the year of his death. He came out against the equation made between the Hebrew witch and the English, and argued for a large dose of caution and scepticism. On its own 'the publique faith of the present Age', fallen as it is, 'is none of the best evidence'. For certainty on such matters as witchcraft one would need the concurrence of the 'universality of Elder times', which cannot be assumed. His attitude to witchcraft is tinged from the outset with his characteristic irony, and a lament for a kingdom fallen on evil times. The doctrines of witchcraft, spawned by 'ignorance in the times of darknesse', have been continued by 'credulity in these dayes of light'.[27]

The immediate occasion of the work was the 'late execution of Witches at the Summer Assizes in Kent', on 30 July 1652, before Peter Warburton, at Maidstone. One of the supposed witches had been taken before a justice of the peace by soldiers of one Colonel Humfrey's regiment.[28] Filmer's motives are not entirely clear, but one may surmise that, having suffered imprisonment and intimidation at the hands of Parliament men, he would not have welcomed their busybodying interest in witchcraft in

---

[26] John Gaule, *Select Cases of Conscience* (1646), 100, 55 f., 68 f. Cf. John Smith (d.1652), *Select Discourses* (1660), 479 f.; Alexander Roberts, *A Treatise of Witchcraft* (1616), esp. 26–31; Thomas Cooper, *The Mystery of Witchcraft* (1617), 90: 'She must be covenanted solemnly in to the house of God . . . renouncing all *former covenants* with the Lord.'

[27] Robert Filmer, *An Advertisement to the Jury-Men of England Touching Witches. Together with a difference between an English and Hebrew witch* (1653), preface.

[28] On this trial see C. L'E. Ewen, *Witchcraft and Demonialism* (1933), 321 f. Humfrey does not appear in C. H. Firth assisted by G. Davies, *The Regimental History of Cromwell's Army* (2 vols.; Oxford, 1940).

his county.[29] Kent was a notoriously divided region in the Civil War, disputed between a controlling minority of Parliamentarians, and a grumbling majority of Royalists who rebelled, with near decisiveness, on two occasions.[30] We can gather from his manuscript treatise 'Theologie: Or Diuinity' that Filmer had previously subscribed to orthodox witchcraft beliefs.[31] What seems decisive to the political context of the *Advertisement*, in view of the circumstances of the trial and the tone of the opening passages, is its concern to attack the views of William Perkins, the doyen of godly theorists, that 'great *Rabby*', as Filmer calls him. The *Advertisement* was ideologically motivated to a large degree, setting out to confound the self-styled godly at the apogee of their power.

Filmer had launched his first attack on Calvinist '*Rabbys*' in his tract *Of the Blasphemie against the Holy Ghost*, published in 1646.[32] He complains of those Reformed theologians who, following their own '*zealous conceits*', go about 'perplexing . . . the tender consciences of weake Christians'.[33] A case in point, Calvin's doctrine of the blasphemy against the Holy Ghost is 'perplexing' in its very definition of that sin: 'They sinne against the Holy-ghost, who of determined malice resist the known truth of God, to the end onely to resist.'[34] This is impossible; as if a man could at one and the same time believe and 'unbeleeve' something. Calvin's sin against the Holy Ghost is such 'as no man possibly can commit', but at the same time such 'as no man living but commits'. Such heady doctrines are a current danger given the 'dangerous inferences weak consciences' may draw from such an 'unbridled and unlimited proposition'.[35] This sort of theology undermines Christian order and ends in the spiritual anarchy of the sects. Filmer condemns the whole Calvinist system, full as it is of such unsettling paradoxes (notably, the fragile suspension between the certainty of depravity and the assurance of grace). It entails 'unbridled, unlimited' perils—reprobate licence and the antinomianism of the self-styled saints—which were all too much in evidence in 1646.

---

[29] See entry on Filmer in *DNB*.

[30] See Alan Everitt, *The Community of Kent and the Great Rebellion, 1640–1660* (Leicester, 1966).

[31] In the possession of Dr Peter Laslett of Trinity College, Cambridge. The *Advertisement* was published in the year of Filmer's death; the manuscript predates it. For further discussion of its contents see below pp. 18–19.

[32] Anonymously, and mistakenly attributed to John Hales in a collection of 1677. Draft MS in the possession of Dr Peter Laslett. See Robert Filmer, *Patriarcha and other political works*, ed. P. Laslett, (Oxford, 1949), intro.; and G. Schochet, 'Sir Robert Filmer: Some New Bibliographical Discoveries', *Transactions of the Bibliographical Society*, 5th ser. 26 (1971).

[33] [Robert Filmer], *Of the Blasphemie against the Holy Ghost* (1646), 1 f.

[34] Ibid. 14 f.   [35] Ibid. 17 ff.

THE *ADVERTISEMENT*

Filmer's *Advertisement to the Jury-Men of England, Touching Witches* was the second instalment of the political-cum-religious polemic he had started in *Of the Blasphemie against the Holy Ghost*. Filmer had made an authentically Protestant complaint against Calvin in the latter work: that the Genevan theologian had 'started aside from . . . Scripture'. The *Advertisement* accuses those who had elaborated witchcraft theory of the same oversight, offering, on its title-page, the prospect of an explanation of 'the difference between an English and Hebrew witch'. The witches of biblical times cannot be identified with the supposed witches of seventeenth-century England; and scriptural laws about them cannot be used as the basis for modern laws about malevolent old women of reduced circumstances. Just as in the case of the blasphemy against the Holy Ghost, Filmer's opponents were following their own '*zealous conceits*' rather than the Scripture they claimed to adhere to; and this in a period of civil conflict in which the ill-effects of such conceits were quite clear.

If this scriptural concern forms an appendix to the book, the core of the book sets out to refute the author of English Calvinism, and another 'Rabby', William Perkins. In his central task of destroying Perkins's covenantal theory of witchcraft, Filmer also undermines the fundamentals of covenantal theology itself.

It is important to recognize that Filmer does not always have the best arguments, or present the most reasonable front. Questioning Perkins's analysis of the means of discovering witches, he ridicules the distinctions Perkins wants to make between presumptions and proofs. Here Filmer sets himself against legal tradition, within which presumptions lead to arraignment and proofs to conviction. Within the framework of a trial, the relationship between the two, and the customary legal procedure, was usually clear. Filmer also misrepresents Perkins on the issue of confession; a bare confession is not held to be sufficient by Perkins, as Filmer would have us believe, but only one 'after due examination taken upon pregnant presumptions'.[36]

Filmer's attack on Perkins's arguments for the case when the accused witch refuses to confess seems at first sight more apt. The requirement for two witnesses to the diabolical compact is all very well, but since the league is 'closely made' it is very difficult for proof of its occurrence to

---

[36] Perkins, *Discourse*, 212.

emerge.[37] Perkins's answer is that 'Satan endeavoreth the discovery, and useth all meanes to disclose witches'.[38] Yet, as Filmer points out, no proof is offered for this view—and how can we seriously accept the testimony of a Devil whom Perkins has manifestly discredited? By pointing to the Devil's untrustworthiness, and the complexities of agency, Filmer nevertheless underscores Perkins's very reasonable case. Since the Devil is God's agent, to be used 'as shall be expedient for their [the elect's] good and salvation' and, apparently, to punish the reprobate, Satan's endeavour to uncover the witch, which seems a logical flaw, is in fact part of the providential plan. God's justice will not be frustrated. As long as we proceed cautiously, using presumptions and proofs in tandem, injustice will not triumph. Perkins stresses the need to preserve innocent blood. One should not proceed by presumption alone. But he also recognizes the biblical injunction relating to witches, and the requirements of equity— the innocent should not suffer, but neither must the guilty go scot-free.[39]

On the central ground of the diabolical compact, Filmer denies the indispensability of contract to the crime of witchcraft, nicely citing one Puritan divine, Henry Ainsworth, against another, Perkins.[40] As an alternative to the diabolical contract, Filmer asks us to focus on *maleficia*, the evil actions of witches. He dismisses the problem of a witchcraft statute defined around the diabolical pact, by citing the actual practice of the courts. They interpret the Jacobean legislation as if the punishment were being directed against the commission of diabolical crimes, rather than the diabolical pact *per se*:

Although the Statute runs altogether in the disjunctive *Or*, and so makes every single crime capitall, yet the Judges usually by a favourable interpretation take the disjunctive *Or* for the copulative *And*; and therefore ordinarily condemne none for Witches, unless they be charged with the Murdering of some person.[41]

Filmer goes on to use this judicial notion of witchcraft as essentially *maleficium* to debunk prosecution entirely, with a typically precisian approach to terminology. With the centrality of the pact dismissed, the crime of *maleficium* is shown to be incoherent. Witchcraft must be the witch's art, not the Devil's, for it to be her crime, and yet 'It is confessed on all hands that the Witch doth not worke the wonder, but the Devill

---

[37] Insider deals in the contemporary world of finance are also closely made; they put similar pressure on the legal system to loosen standards of evidence.

[38] Filmer, *Advertisement*, 14.

[39] Perkins, *Discourse*, preface: 'The Lawe of Moses, the equitie whereof is perpetuall.'

[40] Filmer, *Advertisement*, 4, where Mr Ainsworth is 'as great a *Rabby* as Mr Perkins.'

[41] Ibid. 2. For an account of the various English statutes see Thomas, *RDM* 525–7.

onely'. How can the witch be exercising a craft, then, if her only skill is to command another to act? This is one of the cruxes, if an apparently bizarre one:

how can the *accessary* . . . be *duely and lawfully convicted and attainted* according as our Statute requires, unless the Devill who is the Principall be first convicted, or at least outlawed, which cannot be, because the Devill can never be lawfully summoned according to the rules of our Common-law.[42]

Here Filmer is not only ridiculing Perkins but also, perhaps, the earnest pursuits of common-law theorists to whom he was so opposed.[43]

Yet it is the earlier stage of Filmer's argument that must attract our attention, with its concern to construe the diabolical pact as unintelligible. The pact is denied scriptural warrant, with ironic applause for King James, who at least admitted as much, since '[he] doth not medle with it at all, but takes it for granted that if there be Witches, there must needs be a Covenant, and so leaves it without further proof'. The same is true of William Perkins, who in producing only one supporting text that 'intimateth' the covenantal nature of witchcraft, seems to assume that witchcraft implies covenant. The key to Filmer's argument is not Scripture at this point, however, but a simple consideration of the logical or legal cogency of such a contract. Filmer's denial of viability to the diabolical covenant effectively impugns, in the scheme of Perkins and his followers, that heavenly compact in whose image it is constructed. The problem as far as Filmer is concerned is that 'they call [it] a Covenant, and yet neither of the parties are any way bound to performe their part, and the devill without doubt notwithstanding all his craft hath far the worst part of the bargaine'. The covenantal theory of grace is revealed in all its contradictions, since the witch, if he 'have so much grace as to repent', can avoid fulfilment; moreover, if the witch requires what God will not allow the Devil to do, 'the Devill may lose his credit, and give occasion of repentance'.[44]

All these arguments fail to engage with the ambiguities of covenantal theory. They draw its strands apart, unravel them, and isolate contradictions by the application of a robust common sense. Subtlety is not allowed. Filmer taunts Perkins throughout the book by blithely comparing

---

[42] Filmer, *Advertisement*, 7.

[43] For the common-law tradition and its opponents see J. G. A. Pocock, *The Ancient Constitution and the Feudal Law: A Study of English Historical Thought in the Seventeenth Century. A Reissue with a Retrospect* (Cambridge, 1987).

[44] Filmer, *Advertisement*, 4–6.

him to the Papist Delrio; the process reaches its apogee with discussion of the contract, which for Delrio means the denial of 'Faith, and Christianisme, and Obedience to God, and reject[ion of] the patronage of the Virgin *Mary*'. The juxtaposition of Delrio's Catholicism with Perkins's Puritan conception of the diabolical contract as a renunciation of God and of the baptismal seal is meant to be as subversive as the prints of the 1640s which show Jesuit wolves in Puritan sheep's clothing. Witchcraft is a Roman concept which Protestants should be wary of. Filmer then moves from Romanism to another contradiction in the Devil's pact: surely only Christians can become witches if it involves renunciation of the baptismal seal? How, then, should we understand reports of witchcraft in 'Heathenish Nations'?[45]

In a later passage, Filmer highlights the conflict in covenantal theology between arbitrarily offered grace and freely chosen contract, by considering the Satanic inversion of that very conflict. On the one hand, the Devil's motive is to secure the soul and body of the witch, to persuade a human agent to contract; on the other, according to Filmer's version of Perkins: 'the Precepts of Witchcraft are not delivered indifferently to every Man, but to his owne Subjects the wicked; and not to them all, but to speciall and tried ones.' Thus the aim seems to be 'not to gaine *Novices* for new subjects, but to make use of old ones to serve his turne'. Of what utility then is the covenant, diabolical or divine? It becomes an idling wheel in the scheme of things. It is otiose, obsolete, an affront to the elegant majesty of God. Another ambiguity in the demonological account has obvious implications for soteriology. For, if 'by vertue of the pre-contract, the Devill is cock-sure of his instrument', it is also true that 'though he have good hope of them . . . some by the Mercy of God have bin . . . freed from his Covenant'.[46]

Filmer's earlier manuscript treatise on 'Theologie: Or Diuinity' deals, in the sixth chapter of a section on the ten commandments, with 'the doctrine of the first precept'. Here, Filmer moves from hatred to fear in general, and thence to forms of false fear. In particular, he discusses idolatry, apostasy, and witchcraft. As regards the last, his position is strikingly different from that he adopted in the 1650s. 'Witchcrafte is an arte; powerfull by faith in a covenant: formal or open . . . made with Sathan.' Here at least, Filmer seeks to save the phenomenon of witchcraft by stripping it of dangerous Manichaean tendencies, and strictly limiting the Devil's power. All Satan's wonders are to be explained either naturally,

---

[45] Ibid. 6.   [46] Ibid. 8 f., 14.

by virtue of his great knowledge of nature; rhetorically, in that he is given to 'speakinge doubtfully'; by his knowledge of 'politique causes'; or 'by vertue of his Speciall Commission' from God, as in the case of Job. Emphatically, 'he cannott, worke a miracle as beinge actually damned'.

This approach is pursued in examining several cruxes in Scripture, taking a shot at Puritanical and Popish manipulation of spirits on the way: 'the Jewes caste out Sathan: not by miraculous authority: Nor by fastinge and praier . . . but by magicall consent.'[47] Witchcraft is then divided into theoretical and practical branches; but the pivotal remark concerns conviction and punishment:

Witches are to be convicted either by their owne witnesse, voluntary, or extorted by the rack: *or by the witnesse of others yt can prove theire league with sathan*: or Supernaturall operations. They shall be punished with death: *not for their hurte, but for theire League.* [my emphases]

Peter Laslett cited this passage in a seminal article on Filmer published in 1948.[48] His omission of the phrases in emphasis has, however, allowed a misinterpretation of Filmer's position before and after the Maidstone trial. It is Laslett's notion that the trial of witches which Filmer attended at Maidstone in 1652 produced a *volte face* on his part, leading to the composition of the *Advertisement*, Filmer's recantation and his swansong. This reading was based on Filmer's supposed rejection of self-incrimination, or uncorroborated confession, in witch trials. Having seen in court the tawdry hysteria of confession, the only form of proof, Filmer turned. This is the story. Yet he had, as we see in the full quotation, already accepted the witness of others in witch trials, and the centrality of the league. He had been prepared to confirm both the reality of the contract with the Devil, and the possibility of admissible evidence over and above bare confession. His belief in witchcraft had not been based solely upon the fragile assumption that what people admit must be true; and the rejection of the diabolical compact in the *Advertisement* represents a real intellectual shift.

An examination of the political and religious publications of Sir Robert Filmer provides an explanation of his change of mind on the witchcraft issue which, while not rejecting the Maidstone trial as a plausible occasion for publication, runs deeper than emotional trauma. One of Filmer's

---

[47] Canon 72 of the church canons of 1604 forbade the casting out of devils 'by fasting and prayer' without episcopal licence. Apparently, no such licence was ever issued. See Thomas, *RDM* 579.

[48] Peter Laslett, 'Sir Robert Filmer: The Man versus the Whig Myth', *William and Mary Quarterly*, 3rd ser. 5/4 (1948).

primary aims in the *Advertisement* was to throw doubt on the Puritan
theology of covenant by demolishing its demonological counterpart; he
had attacked another, related, godly doctrine in his tract on the blasphemy against the Holy Ghost, but in the years of civil disorder covenant
had evidently come to the fore. His mockery of presumptuous and fantastical covenants in the *Advertisement* goes hand in hand with his theory of
sovereignty.

The conceptual congruity of covenant theory in divinity and government evoked a broad response from Filmer in the decade after the Solemn League and Covenant. Many of the remarks he devoted to Hobbes
echo the witchcraft pamphlet, or apply common lessons. Thus, 'For a
man to give up his right to one that never covenants to protect'—and
does not the Devil do all in his power to discover his agents, is his credit
not empty?—'is a great folly'. In God's natural sovereignty over man,
with grace freely available via mysterious sacraments, the Devil cannot
intrude to seek allegiance: 'if a contract be the mutual transferring of
right, I would know what right a people can have to transfer to God by
contract'.[49]

This goes headlong against the mutuality of covenant theology, and
undermines that of consensual theories of sovereignty.[50] It sets up a
notion of contract which demonological accounts of witchcraft can barely
satisfy. Covenant and witchcraft theory place too much emphasis on the
breaking of the seal, and do not properly engage with the phenomenology
of sin—the very point we saw Filmer arguing in the tract on the blasphemy against the Holy Ghost, 'as if the beginning only of a rebellion
were an unjust act, and the continuance of it none at all'.[51] *Patriarcha* also
evinces a concern for the technicalities of covenanting in considering the
Oaths of Kings:

Let it be supposed for truth that Kings do swear to observe all the laws of their
kingdoms, yet no man can think it reason that Kings should be more bound by
their voluntary oaths than common persons are by theirs. If a private person make
a contract either with oath or without oath he is no further bound than the equity
and justice of the contract ties him.[52]

Contract is too fragile a creature on which to build a polity. Contracts
operate within kingdoms, whether human or divine, not as regulative

    [49] Robert Filmer, 'Observations on Mr Hobbes's Leviathan' (1652) in *Patriarcha*, 244, 248.
    [50] Cf. 'it was not in their power to choose whether God should be their God, yea, or nay:
for it is confessed He reigned naturally over all by his might', Ibid. 248.
    [51] Ibid. 247.   [52] Filmer, *Patriarcha*, 104.

principles between subject and god, be he mortal or otherwise. Filmer's interest in covenant is most plausibly a reaction to the religious and political events of the 1640s, and a thoroughgoing reaction at that, one which touched his demonology as much as his theology or his ideas on government.[53]

SCOTLAND

In the neighbouring kingdom of Scotland, the notion of covenant remained, through all the turbulence of the 1630s, up to the 1680s and beyond, a vital part of political theory and theology. Calvinist federal theology, stigmatized in England, was an enduring feature of Scottish religion. Consider the importance of specific covenants to Scottish history and political tradition. The National Covenant of 1638 was directed against the Laudian prayer book imposed by Charles I, while the Solemn League and Covenant of 1643 pledged Scots and Englishmen alike to preserve and extend the Presbyterian allegiance. Covenanting after the Restoration meant a stand against English perfidy; against the restoration of episcopal establishments in both England and Scotland; against the abrogation of the Solemn League; against temporizing and free-thinking tendencies. The covenants themselves were declared illegal in 1662, but their impact (rather like the influence of the nonjurors in the Anglican Church after 1689) persisted. Even after the revolution of 1688 had restored Presbyterian orthodoxy north of the border, English treachery remained a Scottish anxiety, among moderates as well as firebrands. The covenants were binding, as James Stewart, future lord advocate, had put it in 1669, 'so long as *Scotland* is *Scotland*'.[54]

Theological and political covenants were bound together, and reinforced each other. We can see this in a contemporary pamphlet, lambasting what it calls the 'Scotch Presbyterian Eloquence'. A compilation of 1692, discovering 'the foolishness of their teaching . . . from their books, sermons, and prayers', it is a treasure-house of covenantal rhetoric.[55] The

[53] See also Filmer's remarks in his treatise 'In Praise of the Vertuous Wife' [Laslett MS]: 'If she be accused in the gates of *Judgment*, either for *witchcraft* or *whoredome*, or be molested in suites of lawe defend her by declaring her former innocencye. Use. 1. *Deedes doubtfull* are charitably to be interpreted according to the former integrityе. Use. 2. Children must defend their parents in warre, and lawe, As heere, and in *Psalme* 127.5.'

[54] [James Stewart of Goodtrees], *Jus Populi Vindicatum* (1669), 5.

[55] [Gilbert Crocket and John Monro?], *The Scotch Presbyterian Eloquence* (1692), title-page. For the identity of the authors see T. Maxwell, 'The Scotch Presbyterian Eloquence: a Post-Restoration Pamphlet', *Records of the Scottish Church History Society*, 8 (1944).

sources are various, many of them anonymous. An emphatic equation is made between the abrogation of covenants and the crime of witchcraft. One 'arch-prelate' was accused by the Presbyterians of 'Perfidy, Perjuries, Apostacies, *Sorceries*, Villanies, and Murders'.[56] Indeed the episcopalians are said to 'imitate the Devil himself' and, 'When their Hierarchy was restored, the Devil, who seemed to be bound sometime before, was let loose, the Flood-gates of all Impiety and Wickedness were set open; and Hell did triumph in its Conquests over the Nation'. The Scotch gentry and clergy who follow episcopacy 'are Godless Miscreants, of the true Ægyptian brood, infamous parricides, *Sorcerers*, and incestuous Apostates . . . the Devil's Instruments'.[57] The compilers' ironic marginalium tells us how the Devil's 'Drudgery on Earth is to be performed by his Covenanted Agents', capturing the promiscuous Presbyterian circulation of language, in which bishops are witches and vice versa. All the actions of the Presbyterians' enemies are subsumed, by Presbyterians, into a covenantal and diabolical context. 'The *Scotch* covenants' are compared to the 'Covenant of Grace', while 'the breaking of the Covenant is the most Heinous of all Sins'. Paying taxes to an episcopal regime is to supply 'that Party of the Dragon's legions, in their War against Prince *Michael* and his Angels'. This is a 'sacrifice' to the Devil—again, the parallel with true religion— working towards his 'absolute Dominion in the Nation'. These 'black Meals' are paid by his 'Vassals' in recognition of his 'Sovereignty'.[58]

So covenant-breaking is condemned and associated with diabolical forces. Toleration of covenant-breakers is seen, explicitly, as a diabolical form of covenant-making, since 'To engage in Bonds of living peaceably, is to engage in Bonds of Iniquity; they are Covenants of Peace with God's Enemies, whom we should count our Enemies.' This is manifest witchcraft, and '*What peace, so long as the whoredoms of thy mother Jezabel, and her witchcrafts are so many?*' As the compilers remark, it was such considerations that led the 'late Assembly' of the Kirk to refuse 'to receive the Episcopal Party into any terms of Peace or Communion'. Indeed, the episcopal party was for these men 'the Mother of Harlots and Witchcrafts'.[59]

The issue of covenant continued to form an obstacle to better Anglo-Scottish relations, and an objection to renewed plans for union, into the

---

[56] Namely, James Sharp, murdered by the conventiclers in May 1679, *Scotch Presbyterian Eloquence*, 50, my emphasis.

[57] Ibid. 66 f., my emphasis.   [58] Ibid. 45 f., 59 f.

[59] Ibid. 58 and margin. For further parallels between divine and diabolical practice see e.g. ibid. 100 and 107.

eighteenth century.[60] While the Scots were 'obliged [by the Covenant] to endeavour that Justice be done upon such as oppose the Peace and Union between the Kingdoms', Charles II and his successor had broken that covenant, and thus had 'destroy'd and annull'd that which was the Bond of these Kingdoms Union, *viz.* the Solemn League and Covenant'.[61] The breaking of such a holy covenant was itself an act of covenanting with the Devil. Anxiety about broken covenants is heightened into anxiety about witchcraft. As so often, witchcraft theory indicates a trauma about the relationship between the secular and the divine order, and the religious constitution of the state. In England, as I shall argue in the next chapter, this meant that much of the writing about witchcraft after the Restoration was concerned with the restoration of a unified Christian community, and the recovery of a lost idyll of togetherness usefully defined by the negative symbol of the witch, with little room for the discredited rhetoric of covenants, divine or diabolical. In Scotland, concern for political correctness and religious cleansing associated itself with the idea of a covenant; with anxieties about the abrogation of a holy covenant, and subscription to diabolical ones. Who then should be surprised if, to give the screw one final turn, the English doubted the very reality of witchcraft; if the Devil incited his agents, 'sagacious and nice conjurers themselves', to look after his own.[62] From the establishment of the Presbyterian Kirk in Scotland in 1690, up to and beyond the union of 1707, members of that Kirk attacked a medley of loose morals, deistical opinions, Episcopal pretensions, and English pollution, all of which were associated with diabolical covenant-making and witchcraft. The remainder of this chapter will explore exactly how these themes played themselves out in the 1690s; but throughout one should recall the grounding of the language of witchcraft in the Scottish idiom of covenant-making and covenant-breaking.[63]

[60] See e.g. *Memoirs of the Life of Sir John Clerk of Penicuik*, ed. J. M. Gray (Publications of the Scottish Historical Society, 13; Edinburgh, 1892), 65: 'as the security of the church of England was to follow . . . [as] consequence [of the union], many of the clergy of Scotland grew jealous of their neighbouring clergy, and endeavoured to instill notions in their Bretheren that such a security given to the church of England was contrary to the principles of their forefathers, who had strenuously supported the Solemn League and Covenant.'

[61] [Crocket and Monro], *Scotch Presbyterian Eloquence*, 55.

[62] On diabolical rule cf. Alexander Shields, *A Hind let loose* (n.p., 1687), 330, 368; Edward Gee, *The divine right and original of the civill magistrate from God* (1658), 220–4. The final phrase is from a letter of Robert Wylie, discussed below.

[63] Cf. the procession at Linlithgow on the anniversary of the Restoration in 1661. A Royalist pageant included the burning of an arch adorned with pictures and inscriptions. On top of the arch the Devil was to be seen exhorting his followers to 'stand to the cause', while on the arch itself was a version of the biblical injunction, 'Rebellion is the mother of witchcraft', and a picture of an old hag holding the covenant. For this inversion of covenanting

Presbyterian concern for moral order was expressed in a series of Acts during the 1690s. In 1697, the General Assembly of the Kirk answered 'His Majesty's gracious Letter' to them, by lamenting 'the abounding of impiety and profanity in this land'. They went on to issue an 'Act against Profaneness' which complained of 'mocking of piety and religion, and the exercises thereof, fornication, adultery, drunkenness, excess tippling, Deism, blasphemy, and other gross abominable sins'. Witchcraft was both a target, the grossest example of disobedience, and also a tool with which to teach the Deists and their debauched pupils, a palpable proof of the existence of spirits in the world. In 1699 and in 1708, at this time of moral panic and in the immediate wake of union, the General Assembly made specific Acts against witchcraft.[64]

The notorious Renfrew witch trial of 1697, which resulted in the burning of seven of those convicted, was part of this moral panic. Much of the material surrounding the case also, however, speaks the language of national self-determination. James Hutchisone, for instance, who preached before the commissioners of justiciary appointed for the trial, presented the Scots as a godly people, despite the 'great evil' in 'such a place as the west of Scotland where the gospell of christ has been purely preacht'. The Scots people are God's own people, a 'national church'. This church has the 'power of the sword committed to them', to determine and execute justice. It is an exclusive power, not to be interfered with. It is not to be committed to others; 'we need not insist upon this To whom it is directed'.[65]

This last enigmatic hint can be followed through in a letter which, shortly after the trial, Robert Wylie, Presbyterian minister and covenanter, wrote to William Hamilton, Laird of Wishaw and renowned antiquary. Wylie connected the witch case with another issue of public morals, in which Scottish jurisprudence was also being called into question, that of an Edinburgh student, Thomas Aikenhead.[66] Aikenhead had been executed

rhetoric see J. Kirkton, *The Secret and True History of the Church of Scotland from the Restoration to the Year 1678*, ed. C. K. Sharpe (Edinburgh, 1817), 126 f.

[64] T. Pitcairn *et al.* (eds.), *Acts of the General Assembly of the Church of Scotland 1638–1842* (Edinburgh, 1843), 258, 261.

[65] Printed in *SHR* 7 (1910).

[66] On the Aikenhead trial, see *State Trials*, xiii. 917–40; and Michael Hunter, '"Aikenhead the Atheist": The Context and Consequences of Articulate Irreligion in the Late Seventeenth Century', in M. Hunter and D. Wootton (eds.), *Atheism from the Reformation to the Enlightenment* (Oxford, 1992). A copy of Wylie's letter is Bodleian MS Locke b4 f107, part of a collection of materials concerning the Aikenhead case sent to Locke by his friend James Johnstoun, for which see his letter to Locke, in *Locke Correspondence*, vi. 17. For the identification of the correspondents, see David Laing in *Proceedings of the Society of Antiquaries of Scotland*, 11 (1876), 438. The original of the letter is in the Scottish Record Office, SRO GD103/2/3/17/1, dated 16 June 1697.

for blasphemy. Wylie's letter is a forceful repudiation of foreign, specifically English, slurs upon Scottish actions. The 'pious & charitable Witts at London and elsewhere' who have passed censure 'upon the Governmt' in the case of 'Aikenhead the Atheist' have misunderstood Scottish law, 'the ground of that wretches Sentence'. Wylie wonders if those who have condemned the sentence 'are capable of thinking or understanding any thing but a bold sparkish Jest'. This was a 'mistake of the case & matter of fact'. Blasphemy, 'a perverse malicious railing against the adorable object of Christian worship', has been confused with heresy or something similar, which is an 'errour of the Judgment'. While the latter can be 'retracted', the former 'simply inferrs death'. 'Witty Criticks' would do well to consider 'that Reason Common Sense and good manners (their own Trinity) do require that no man should in the face of a people spitefully revile & insult the object of their adoration'. The implication is that deistical tendencies, even denial of the Trinity proper, are the inspiration behind these 'pleadings against Aikenheads condemnation'. Certainly, the denial of the Trinity was a central feature of the young man's crime; and, as so often with witchcraft, the denial of the guilt of the accused is made tantamount to the crime itself.

Wylie continued his defence with a piece of relativism remarkable from a man of his party and sentiments: 'a Christian could not be innocent who should raile at or curse Mahomet at Constantinople.' The minister's outrage seems particularly directed towards foreign, more specifically English, misunderstanding of Scottish law; a perverse misunderstanding which tried to appropriate 'Reason Common Sense and good manners' for itself. This reading makes more sense than one which views the letter as a formulaic outburst of religious bigotry. Such an interpretation cannot satisfactorily account for the actual content of Wylie's diatribe, the distinction between blasphemy and heresy, the legal terminology, and the comparison drawn with Constantinople. It cannot make proper sense of his target, *English* wits, either. We know that at least one eminent Scotsman, James Johnstoun, objected to the sentence. 'Laws long in dessuetude', he wrote to Locke, 'should be gently put in Execution and the first example made of one in circumstances that deserve no compassion, whereas here ther is youth, Levity, docility, and no designe upon others.'[67] And surely there can have been no shortage of native wit to attack. The choice of London in particular is the key to the political context of these remarks, centring on the question of Anglo-Scottish relations.

Similar xenophobic perceptions attached to the issue of witchcraft.

---

[67] In Johnstoun's covering letter to Locke, *Locke Correspondence*, vi. 17.

The execution of Aikenhead coincided with that of seven Renfrew witches in the case of the afflicted Christian Shaw, but this was no mere coincidence. The two issues were closely linked. In his farewell epistle, for instance, Aikenhead did not deny the main substance of the charges against him; he only denied, in parting from his friends, that he had 'practised magick and conversed with devils'.[68] This association between blasphemy and witchcraft, both seen as diabolical practices, is also reflected in Wylie's letter, as it moves from Aikenhead's case to that of the witches of Renfrew. He clearly thought that the Aikenhead affair should have been enough to silence English wits and critics. 'After all this', he suggested, such people should surely 'be more sparing and cautious'. In view of the 'distance' and 'such uncertainty of report' these same scoffers ought to avoid making 'little rash Judgments'. Again, the opposition comes from Londoners, too far away to be proper judges of the affair. And, again, these unworthy aspersions are being cast upon 'the late proceeding of this *Government*'. This is unwarranted interference by the subjects of a neighbouring kingdom. These cosmopolitan types are given another blast of punning, sarcastic abuse, reviled as '*Esprits* forts . . . Sagacious & nice *conjurers* themselves'. 'I see not', writes Wylie, 'with what modesty or good manners The proceedings of the Government in another Nation can be Judged & Censured.'

Throughout the remainder of his letter, Wylie lays the responsibility for action against the witches upon the government, who will take further 'measures', and whom 'your Sparks at London blame . . . of severity', while 'there are some here no less apt to complain of their remissness'. He is at pains to insist that the process was 'exceeding wary' and to show his own moderation, both by pointing to those who blamed the government for laxity, and by adding, in parenthesis, that 'many Stories that pass in the Country I do not regard'. But in general the witnesses are 'credible', the confessions 'exactly agreeing in circumstances'. Indeed, 'I am as much for waryness & caution as any in such dark & abstruse matters where the vulgar is easily imprest by Superstitious fears, and the Devil mingles fables', as opposed to 'well attested narrative', in order 'to conceal or discredit truth'. Those who deny the existence of spirits or witches have 'renounced humanity as well as Religion' and they go against an express 'Scripture Law'. Any not convinced by a full account of the trial must have, like witches, 'harden[ed] themselves against all conviction'.

For Wylie, the problem was not merely that of 'Atheism and Sadducism';

---

[68] *State Trials*, 934.

it was that of atheism, sadducism, and irreverent wit embodied in an English culture which threatened Scots independence and Scots rectitude. It was the government's responsibility to act against the diabolical assault; it was Scottish self-government which the London *cognoscenti* deprecated; and witchcraft prosecution was an assertion of that right to national government, an assertion of Scottish propriety and identity in the face of English scoffing. Wylie's sensitivity to the issue of Scottish rights was later displayed in the memorial of grievance he sent to the Revd Thomas Linning in 1714. In his covering letter, Wylie recalled two things which had 'especially in King William's reign, done us much hurt'. One was the failure to 'use that freedom we might and should have done in laying before his Majesty the nature and rights of our constitution', a failure to keep Scots matters independent of English interference. The other related problem was that the Presbyterians had relied too much on their fellows about the king who, contrary to expectation, 'valued themselves upon keeping Church matters, in an Erastian dependence upon the Court'.[69]

In an earlier letter to the Duke of Hamilton, in 1693, Wylie was already worrying about these problems, and the need for ministers to act in concert to preserve the liberties of the church.[70] In the 1714 memorial we see how much further he had moved away from the 'extream of moderation', as one contemporary commentator put it, towards 'the other side'.[71] Wylie positively seethes about the 'strange treatment of a legally established and secured national Church'. What was, despite the Union, 'the Legislature of another nation', had taken upon themselves 'to determine what was or was not agreeable to Scots Presbyterian principles'. This only a general assembly was fit to judge. Such behaviour was 'more like the usage of a conquered than a united people'. Wylie calls the union 'a very nice point', which is nevertheless 'an universal grievance to the nation' and, what is more, 'a heavy yoke wreathed upon their unwilling necks', something which they were 'wheedled into'.[72] Wylie's response to the Aikenhead and Renfrew trials can be seen as part of the progression he was making from moderation via wounded sensibility to outraged national pride. The question is not whether Wylie was responding to real

---

[69] *The Correspondence of the Rev. Robert Wodrow* (Edinburgh, 1842), i. 592 ff.

[70] Letter of 11 Dec. 1693, in HMC, *Supplementary Report on the MSS of the Duke of Hamilton* (1932), 129 f.

[71] Letter from Robert Wodrow to James Wallace at London, 8 Mar. 1701, in *Early Letters of Robert Wodrow 1698–1709* (Publications of the Scottish Historical Society, 3rd ser. 24; Edinburgh, 1937), 154.

[72] *Correspondence of Wodrow*, i. 592 ff. On the wooing of clerical opposition to the union, see also *Memoirs of Clerk of Penicuik*, 64 f.

English infidelity. It is rather that, anxious about English encroachment, he blends fears of witchcraft, infidelity, and national subordination into one heady, discursive brew.

Wylie's vision of the witch trial and of the Aikenhead case was shared by the author of *Sadducismus Debellatus*, published in 1698. This book advances the notion that the Devil may be constrained to make 'stupendious Appearances against his Will' in order to supply a 'visible Testimony superadded to the greater *Gospel* proofs' that there are spirits. Aikenhead's denial of this is mentioned, with the rider that 'he died in full Conviction of it', and the implication that the Devil appeared to Aikenhead himself. The effect of the passage is once more to associate these two incidents, the blasphemy of Aikenhead, and the great apostasy of the Renfrew witches (as the very title does).[73]

The author's vision of the state of religion in the two neighbouring kingdoms is an extreme and derogatory one. Britain should be called the 'Unfortunate Island . . . *Africk* never having been more fertile in the production of *Monsters*'. Indeed 'its observ'd, that through all the Successions of Men, there was never before any Society, or Collective Body of *Atheists* till these dreggs of time'. The author takes his stand on sense, and attacks the critical literature in a passage which could have been penned by Robert Wylie:

Seeing Devils take so much pains to contract for the Souls of Witches; the Saducee's tho judicially blinded in their Reason, are hereby rendred inexcusable by very sense; ill Books, which corrupt and ensnare curious Fancies, who are seldom endow'd with accurate Judgments, ought to be restrain'd: As also such ridiculous Pamphlets, as no doubt by the Instigation of Satan, have lately been sent abroad, designedly to frustrat any good use which might be made of such extraordinary Providences as these contained in the ensueing Narrative. The Authors of those Pamphlets having either forged other subjects or disguised this.[74]

---

[73] A whole variety of sins 'pav[e] the way' to witchcraft, including malice, envy, and sinful curiosity. The use of charms, often motivated by such feelings, is an open invitation for the Devil to step in. See Stuart Clark, 'Protestant Demonology', in Ankarloo and Henningsen, *Early Modern Witchcraft*.

[74] *Sadducismus Debellatus: Or a True Narrative of the Sorceries and Witchcrafts Exercis'd by the Devil and his Instruments upon Mrs Christian Shaw* (1698), preface. The British Library catalogue attributes this to Francis Grant, Lord Cullen (1658–1726), a Scottish judge, 'living library . . . of great piety and devotion' (Wodrow) and author of, among others, *A discourse concerning the Execution of the Laws made against Prophaneness* (1700) and *An Essay for Peace by Union in Judgment: About Church-Government in Scotland* (1703). See his entry in *DNB*. *A Relation of the Diabolical Practices of above Twenty Wizards and Witches of the Sheriffdom of Renfrew in the Kingdom of Scotland* (1697) preceded this book, published by the same house. The theme of Providence is a well-worn one in Presbyterian and dissenting circles, e.g. Cotton Mather, Robert Wodrow (with whom Mather corresponded), and Richard Baxter. See also Samuel Petto, *A Faithful Narrative of the Wonderful and Extraordinary Fits*

The language used is that of a common-sense empiricism—*seeing, sense, fancies* without *judgement*. Like witches themselves, the critics are 'judicially blinded', and act 'by the Instigation of Satan'.[75] These pamphlets 'sent abroad' are pinned down later in the book, there being 'scarce any need to take notice of a late Scurrilous Pamphlet, that has been printed in England, *pretending* to give an account of those proceedings'. This contained 'neither good Language, Sense, nor Truth' in it. It is not extant, but the xenophobic response to English infidelity may well have led men to seize on the rumour of such a book, or the conviction that one must, surely, have been produced.[76]

Sadducismus Debellatus follows the pattern of Wylie's letter. It rejects foreign reports of the proceedings—they only 'pretend' to give an account —and evinces a studied moderation. The trial was undertaken with 'Tenderness and Moderation' and even the prosecution showed no 'Byass of Partys' but rather 'shewed an equal Concern to have the accused Persons absolved, if it could be found compatible with Justice'. The latter part of the pamphlet is largely concerned with matters of law, and the proper procedure relative to the admission of evidence in this '*Excepted Crime*'. James VI is cited as premier authority, since 'as a Prince he is to be credited about *the Law of His own Country*; and as a King has determined any doubt that might have remained'. Witchcraft is as much an excepted crime, with its own special procedures, as 'Treason and . . . Falshood'.[77]

The fear of English subversion as regards witchcraft may have been more to do with Scottish political perceptions than real English beliefs. Such perceptions were long-standing, judging from the most thoroughgoing episode, before the eighteenth century, of Scottish subordination to the English state, the Cromwellian 1650s. 'There is much witcherie up and downe our land, though the English be but too spareing to try it, yet some they execute', declared Robert Baillie in 1659. When the Protectorate came to an end, the limbo in which Scottish law was left made the situation even worse for those concerned about witchcraft: 'Becaus the laws ar now silent, this sin becomes daylie more frequent', declared the Earl of Haddington. In the first sixteen months of the Restoration regime,

---

under which Mr Tho. Spatchet . . . was under by Witchcraft: Or, A Mysterious Providence in his even Unparallel'd Fits (1693).

[75] *Sadducismus Debellatus*, preface.　　[76] Ibid. 46, my emphasis.

[77] Ibid. 46, 52 ff., my emphasis. See Christina Larner's essay on witchcraft as a *crimen exceptum*, 'The Crime of Witchcraft in Europe', in her *Witchcraft and Religion* (Oxford, 1984). On James and witchcraft, Larner, *Witchcraft and Religion*, 3–22, 'James VI and I and Witchcraft'; and Stuart Clark, 'King James's *Daemonologie*: Witchcraft and Kingship', in Anglo, *Damned Art*.

660 public accusations of witchcraft were made, and perhaps 150 executions took place. A backlog was being cleared.[78]

Another correspondent does show us quite how difficult the business of witchcraft was in the context of Anglo-Scottish relations during the 1690s. James Johnstoun, former Scottish secretary of state, wrote to his former colleague, Lord Polwarth, about Aikenhead and the witch trial on 1 April 1697.[79] The blushing tone of this letter shows an embarrassed Johnstoun caught between Scottish affiliation and his own more freethinking propensities. It opens with an expression of gratitude. Polwarth had graciously refused to believe some ill reports relating to Johnstoun's conduct out of office. The latter explains further: 'As to the government I absolutely abstain from medling, in so much that I have not written to nor heard from some of those with you in Scotland, whom you reckon my best friends, these six moneths, and its not verry credible that I who have been Secretary will be a litle agent.' Johnstoun's pride rebuts any accusation that, having lost power, he is scheming against the government. He also denies that any criticisms he may have made were the issue of pique: 'As to talking, I have said nothing since I was out but what I said when I was in.' He vindicates his behaviour as honourable. He has not plotted or masqueraded. He is a man of integrity, of consistent principles. 'The truth is I have the same thoughts of men and things that I ever had.' These accusations were spread around because of what Johnstoun had 'said in my speech to your friends against the businesse of Aikenhead, and your share in it', presumably in the Privy Council. This was one thing, to speak thus 'to your friends, and Scotch ones'. With friends, and with fellow countrymen, he could be openly critical. With those of the neighbouring kingdom, circumspection was necessary, and 'To the English ones, I made the best defence [of the Aikenhead judgement] I could' (though Johnstoun had not scrupled to complain to one English correspondent, John Locke).

The remainder of this section of the letter is concerned with the current Presbyterian campaign against infidelity, which Johnstoun considered to be ill-conceived. The 'blow' that this has given the Presbyterians is not 'in the opinion [merely] of libertins but [more generally] of the body of this [English] nation'.

---

[78] Brian P. Levack, 'The Great Scottish Witch Hunt of 1661–1662', *JBS* 20 (1980), 92 ff. But note, in Baillie's remark, the distinction between being 'spareing', as the English were, and not executing witches at all, which they could not be accused of.

[79] HMC, 14th report, app. iii, 132, item 177.

A wyfe thats jealoused most shun even the most innocent appearances. They are accused by their enemies of a bitter persecuting spirit and suspected by their friends of it. The libells and clamour of the outed clergy [i.e. the episcopalians] have hightened those thoughts of them so the least appearances passe for a proofe even amongst their friends. Should I tell you matter of fact you could not believe it. The wisdom of the serpent is recommended as well as the innocency of the dove.[80]

The prosecution of witches was a central part of this campaign. As in Wylie's letter, witchcraft and the Aikenhead case are yoked together; and again, Johnstoun cloaks himself in ambiguity:

So as to witches that there may be such I have no doubt, nor never had, it is a matter of fact that I was never judge of. But the parliaments of France and other judicatories who are perswaded of the being of witches never try them now because of the experience they have had that its impossible to distinguish possession from nature in disorder, and they chuse rather to let the guilty escape than to punish the innocent. If indeed there be malifics, they punish those malifics according to the laws and the nature of them, without respect to the principalls whence they proceed.

Presbyterian campaigns against witchcraft, infidelity, and the episcopal church in Scotland, so recently disestablished, are all part of a single movement which is seen, south of the border, as the product of 'a bitter persecuting spirit'. On the peripheral issue of witchcraft itself, the letter speaks for itself, with its pragmatic scepticism and refusal to judge.[81] Johnstoun's letter is most valuable for showing us the pressures at work in Scotland of the 1690s: the recognition of English power, combined with the desire of some to escape its influence and assert Scottish versions of godliness; the difficulties of a cosmopolitan figure like James Johnstoun, treading on eggshells and faced by what he saw as Presbyterian extremism liable to alienate English opinion. These were the same pressures which would be manifested in the later debate over union. They sprang from a blend of uncomfortable political and economic realities, and the union under one crown of two very different church establishments.

[80] On the new Scottish settlement of religion in 1690, and its aftermath, see P. J. Riley, *The Union of England and Scotland* (Manchester, 1978), 9 f. Zealots 'purge[d] the church by devious and underhand means'. The routine method of the opposition was 'to approach the English tory ministers to stigmatize the Scottish court as "presbyterian bigots" and "hot men" alienating the loyalty of the episcopalians'.

[81] Cf. Thomas's reading in *RDM* 686. On the work of the *parlement* see Robert Mandrou, *Magistrats et sorciers en France au XVIIe siècle* (Paris, 1968), esp. 313–63. For a corrective view, see Alfred Soman, 'The Parlement of Paris and the Great Witch Hunt (1565–1640)', *Sixteenth Century Journal*, 9/2 (July 1978), and Ch. 9 below.

Reports in the English newspapers of the time hardly indicate a raging spirit of incredulity at large, or any condemnation of Scottish barbarism. Of course, the reports were received from Scottish correspondents; but any editorial interpolations were in favour of the rooting-out of this devilish 'crew', and abhorred the diabolical practices described.[82] The *Flying Post* for 23 January 1696/7 noted that the Scottish Privy Council had received certificates from Glasgow relating to the Renfrew case, and had ordered the sheriff, and some others, to investigate.[83] The lead story in *Lloyd's News* for 26 January was much the same, referring to the evidence supplied by 'divers Ministers and other Persons of Credit and Reputation', and reporting that the Privy Council had given 'Orders for the Trying of several Witches'.[84] The next issue of the *Flying Post* referred back to the Aikenhead affair which had been, it complained, 'much exclaimed against and aggravated by the *Deists, Socinians, Debauchees*, and others who bear no good-will to the Kingdom of Scotland'.[85] The *Protestant Mercury* mentioned the witchcraft case in the early part of the year, noting the 'plain proof' against the accused, and again in early March, announcing the adjournment of 'the Trying of the Witches in the West'.[86] Richard Baxter's *The Certainty of the Worlds of Spirits* was being advertised in a new edition in numbers of the *Flying Post* for March and April.[87] The interest continued into April and May in both *Flying Post* and *Protestant Mercury*. The *Flying Post* expressed sympathy for the victims. It was an 'Infernal Tragedy' and 'a lamentable Instance of Satan's Fury and Witches Malice'. The paper made its own position clear:

This passage will no doubt be flouted at by many Persons as incredible; to whom we shall only say, That they have it as it is Transmitted to us, and we doubt not in a little time, to give them an Account of the Particular Trials of the Witches concerned in this Affair, of their own Confessions, and the Evidence against them.

Exaggerated accounts of the fates of the victims and the numbers of witches followed, but the *Protestant Mercury*'s laconic report in its 19 May issue seems to mark a tailing-off in interest: '7 of the Witches were Convicted and Sentenced to be Burned.'[88] Another paper, the *Foreign*

---

[82] On the press in this period, see L. Hanson, *Government and the Press 1695–1763* (Oxford, 1936).
[83] *Flying Post*, 23–6 Jan. 1697, no. 266, f451b.
[84] *Lloyd's News*, 26 Jan. 1697, no. 64, f452a.
[85] *Flying Post*, 26–8 Jan. 1697, no. 267, f455b.
[86] *Protestant Mercury*, 19–24 Feb. 1697, no. 137, f498b; 5–10 Mar. 1697, no. 141, f514b.
[87] *Flying Post* nos. 283, 285, and 297.
[88] Ibid. 8 Apr. 1697, no. 297, f547a; also no. 308. *Protestant Mercury*, 19–21 May 1697, no. 162, f604a; also nos. 149, 150, 153, and 154. Also *Post Boy* for 6–9 Feb. 1697, no. 275.

Post for 2 June, showed no more sympathy for the condemned or incredulity as to the reports than its fellow journals. The length of consideration by both judges and jury was noted; the evidence was 'as convincing proved . . . as the Nature of the Crime would be imagined to allow'; and the criminals were referred to as 'that Infernal Crew', a 'gang'. There is little or no evidence of widespread English outrage or incredulity, only of Scottish defensiveness, and of a threat which they saw coming from the neighbouring kingdom.[89]

There is, however, even after the Union, evidence of English concern about covenantal attitudes which suggests that, rather than rejecting demonology out of hand, English writers were prepared to turn it against their Scottish brethren. The author of a pamphlet entitled *The Church of England's Late Conflict with, and Triumph over, the Spirit of Fanaticism*, published at the height of the rage of party in 1710, painted Scottish attitudes as thoroughly diabolical:

And to confirm both to us and others, that there is no Salvation own'd by them to be out of the *Pail of their Kirk*, they always baptize their Infants into the *Solemn League* and *Covenant* and *Westminster Confession* of *Faith*; that *Covenant* being injoin'd at Baptism as if the same Consequence with the *Covenant of Grace* it self; and instead of renouncing the *Devil*, the *World* and *Sin*, renounce *Monarchy* and *Episcopacy*, are baptiz'd to *Rebellion* and *Schism*.

This Englishman clearly shares a political language with his Scottish enemies. As much as they see the Covenant as a holy league, the abrogation of which was a diabolical act, he sees the Covenant itself as a diabolical league, making the biblical elision between rebellion and the sin of witchcraft literal. These Scotsmen and their allies are 'whatever *Pretences* to *pure* and *undefil'd Religion*, they make . . . *even before others, in the Gall of Bitterness and Bond of Iniquity*'. What name could be better for them than '*Tools of the restless Enemy*'?[90]

These sorts of attacks did not go unnoticed north of the border. In a letter of 1711 to a Glasgow merchant, Robert Wodrow commented on an offensive sermon which Edmond Archer had made before the Lower

[89] *Foreign Post*, 2–4 June 1697, no. 9, f635ab. Though see also *Letters . . . to the Duke of Shrewsbury by James Vernon, Esq., Secretary of State*, ed. G. P. R. James (3 vols.; 1841), ii. 300 f., 6 June 1699: 'I have the honour of your Grace's letter of the 3rd. I think the noise of witches breaks out like a plague in several places at distant times. If these miserable creatures are in haste to die by other people's hands, and will confess they know not what, they will be served as they are in Scotland, where the judges tell them they don't believe them, and yet sentence them to be burnt.'

[90] P[atrick] D[rewe], *The Church of England's Late Conflict with, and Triumph over, the Spirit of Fanaticism* (1710), 28 f., 30, 51.

House of Convocation in England in the midst of the 'rage of party'. Wodrow reports Archer as having said that 'the old Spirit, that is, Satan, keeps the Dissenters in a slavish bondage, under the stubborn obligation of the odious League and Covenant'. The imputation of Satanism to the true covenant was an inversion which aroused Wodrow's anger, since 'to attribute that to the influence of Satan, which was so much owned from heaven, comes near . . . the sin against the Holy Ghost'.[91]

Moderate Englishmen, those in power seeking to promote Anglo-Scottish amity for whatever reasons, were well aware of how offensive English vituperation could be, how much Scots were aware of English opinion, and how easy it was for misunderstanding to arise. Profoundly cautious English attitudes towards Scottish witchcraft are reflected in the lengthy gestation of one of the great works of English scepticism, Francis Hutchinson's *Historical Essay*, published in 1718. Hutchinson was, from 1692, vicar of St James's, Bury St Edmunds, one of the centres of witchhunting activity in the mid-seventeenth century. By the early years of the new century he was planning a book about witchcraft, which he had circulated to his friends. Dubourdieu, French minister at the Savoy, had told him, Hutchinson wrote in a letter to Sir Hans Sloane in 1706, that the book had Sloane's 'Approbation, & he [Dubourdieu] believed the Publication would be of service to the World'. All in all, responses were favourable, and Hutchinson decided to send his papers on witchcraft to Rogers, a bookseller. Unfortunately they were taken by someone 'who went directly to ye Bishop of Norwich', John Moore. This untrustworthy emissary 'being deep in the other Notions' of witchcraft—a believer, in other words—represented Hutchinson's case and his book 'with no favourable Character'.[92] The effect of this unwarranted intrusion was that Hutchinson was 'advised to stop the Press till the Archbishop had had the perusal of them'. The archbishop's answer was a piece of studied

---

[91] *The Correspondence of Wodrow*, i. 203, 19 Feb. 1711. Archer was Archdeacon of Wells and a fellow of St John's College, Oxford. His sermon was, as was usual for the occasion, published: *A Sermon preach'd . . . Before the Reverend Clergy of the Lower House of Convocation: Being the Anniversary of the Martyrdom of King Charles the 1st* (1711). He talks of the dissenters' 'sullen Contempt of this solemn Fast . . . By this peevish morose Non-compliance with the Commands of their Superiors, one cannot help thinking, that the *old Spirit* still *works in these Children of Disobedience*, and that he still keeps them in a slavish Bondage, under the stubborn Obligation of the odious *League and Covenant. Wherefore ye be witnesses to your selves, that ye are children of them which killed the Prophets*, Matt. xxiii.31 [17].'

[92] There is in fact some ambiguity as to whether Norwich or the go-between was 'deep in the other Notions'. It seems, syntactically, more likely to be the latter. Also John Moore had no particular interest in witchcraft, as far as one can tell from his *Sermons on several Subjects*, ed. S. Clarke (2 vols.; 1715, 1716).

evasion.[93] 'What', Hutchinson asked Sloane, 'must be done to prepare
. . . [the book's] way'? The intervention of the church hierarchy was quite
in earnest, and 'till that restraint be taken off I must by no means venture,
neither dare I do any thing towards the removing of it'. By 1712,
Hutchinson was again considering publication, but remained concerned,
'unwilling to venture any such censures as I should meet with from some'
and anxious to 'submit all to your [Sloane's] prudence & judgment',
ready to 'either send my papers up or forbear according as you advise'.
Hutchinson's papers were finally published in 1718, and entered the
canon of the early English enlightenment.

The striking thing about this minor episode in speculative bibliogra-
phy is not only the behaviour of Hutchinson's go-between—who thought
the matter of witchcraft serious enough to rat on his friend—or the
seriousness of a church hierarchy which still bothered to concern itself
with witch beliefs twenty years after the last English execution. There is
the vital matter of the the archbishop's motivation. Without discounting
the continuing vitality of witchcraft as part of English élite culture around
this time, or assuming the progressive moribundity of demonology—
issues we shall deal with in subsequent chapters—we can see that it is a
matter of politics and, moreover, a Scottish one which comes to the fore.
Fear of Scottish reactions drives the English hierarchy's caution. 'Perhaps', Hutchinson writes, 'when the Scotch union is settled the Season
may be more proper.' The English government, as represented by the
primate of the English church, is concerned that the publication of a book
by a prominent churchman, dismantling witch beliefs, regardless of the
general pertinence or impertinence of such a book, could give the wrong
impression to Scottish observers suspicious of English deistical tendencies,
and anxious about the prospects for godliness under the forthcoming
union of kingdoms. There could be no more convincing demonstration
that the issue of witchcraft remained a touchy part of Anglo-Scottish
relations; and that while Scots accused the English of witch advocacy, the
English remained sensitive to the charge.[94]

[93] 'the Answer that I had through his [the go-between's] hand was that the Archbishop
was not for the printing of them or not for the printing them yet I could not well tell which
he meant.' The archbishop was Thomas Tenison (1636–1715), whose views on witchcraft
can be garnered in all their ambiguity from his *The Creed of Mr Hobbes Examined* (1670),
62 f.: 'such, as publickly deny Witch-craft, are sawcy affronters of the Law'. For further
discussion, see the following chapter.
[94] 'I am sure', Hutchinson continued, 'it will be most needfull to guard against those kind
of notions that one may have the benefit of their strength & assistance without the influence
of their superstitions. Our people are very apt to receive these strong impressions.' Letters of
F. Hutchinson, BL Sloane MSS 4040, f302; 4043, f38.

Statistics do not play a large role in this book. It has been my contention, from the outset, that the numbers of executions for witchcraft, and
the virulency, currency, or significance of witchcraft belief are two different things. A decline in prosecutions cannot be equated with a weakening
of belief; it cannot in any simple, self-evident way explain it, or be
explained by it. Patterns of prosecution may, nevertheless, tell us something, inasmuch as they are embedded within the context of a wider
story.[95] In the context of the ideological connotations of witchcraft in
post-Restoration Scotland, the statistics of Scottish witchcraft prosecution in this period are telling. This is not a matter of tracing the ebb and
flow of large-scale persecution, of the 'witch-craze', but rather of looking
at the tiny number of prosecutions during periods of endemic witch
prosecution. Taking decennial figures, the 1680s saw twenty-seven prosecutions, the 1690s twenty-five, while the decade of the Scots union
could count forty-four. Prosecutions continued after 1707, if at a lesser
rate: one in 1707, two in 1715, and the last known Scottish execution
(under irregular procedure) in 1727. The initiation of some prosecutions
within the soon-to-be-abolished Privy Council lends an added political
significance to the trial of witches. Remember that for Wylie the Aikenhead
trial had been, ultimately, 'the late proceeding of this *Government*'. It
might be worth noting the execution of two male witches in July 1706,
proceeded against in Privy Council in the very year before union. We
might argue that this supports the contention that the Scottish élite still
took witchcraft seriously in the early eighteenth century; and that the
prosecution of witchcraft in Scotland had some sort of political function,
even perhaps as an assertion of Scottish identity in the years leading up
to the union. An analysis of the opposition to the repeal of English and
Scottish witchcraft legislation under the aegis of that union, attempted in
Chapter 8 below, amplifies and confirms this conclusion.

In both Scotland and England, theories about witchcraft, and consequently beliefs about witchcraft, were bound up with politics and religion. This is not surprising since they were creatures of ideology. We
have outlined the contract theory of witchcraft as it emerged in English
Calvinism, and seen how its rootedness in ideology informed opposition

---

[95] In other words, we cannot say belief must have been in decline because prosecution
was. We recognize the different possible conjunctions—low-level belief, high-level prosecution; high-level belief, low-level prosecution; low-level belief, low-level prosecution; high-
level belief, high-level prosecution—all of them at least *possible* (although the first would
need some explaining), and assess them for both their inherent plausibility and how they
match the evidence.

to it in the 1650s. While ideology is not necessarily the whole story of the *Advertisement*, Robert Filmer's writing against witchcraft can no longer be seen as uncomplicated scepticism or straightforward humanitarian impulse. We shall see in Chapter 3 what sort of theory of witchcraft emerged from the 1650s in England, and why; but in Scotland contract demonology came out of the 1650s intact or even reinforced. This was precisely because it became part of a complex of beliefs, attitudes, and activities which defined a Scottishness out of the reach of England's condescension or assimilation, England 'o'regrown with Briars and Thorns' all set to 'o'rgang *Scotland*'.[96] The Scottish case shows how a sophisticated political culture could maintain witchcraft beliefs into the eighteenth century because they retained an ideological role. The question then becomes, when and how did they lose such a function in England?

---

[96] A satirical picture of Scottish fanaticism, from Archibald Pitcairne's *The Assembly, A Comedy, By a Scots Gentleman* (1722), 20. See, conversely, the complaints about English 'superstition' in an anonymous pre-union pamphlet, *To the Loyal and Religious Hearts in Parliament* (1706).

2

Thomas Hobbes

In the second chapter of his *Leviathan*, 'Of Imagination', Thomas Hobbes makes an apparently fleeting reference to the subject of witchcraft. Many historians have noted this but, in their apparent fancifulness, Hobbes's words have been left virtually unanalysed. Fancy, he suggests, can lead 'even they that be perfectly awake, if they be timorous, and supperstitious, possessed with fearfull tales, and alone in the dark . . . [to] believe they see spirits and dead mens Ghosts walking in Church-yards'. Upon such dispositions, and an inability to distinguish fancy from sense—since sense itself is an externally provoked phantasm—Hobbes believes, the edifice of pagan theology, the 'Religion of the Gentiles', was built. And that religion, of 'Satyres, Fawnes, Nymphs and the like' is juxtaposed to current beliefs of 'rude people' in 'Fayries, Ghosts and Goblins', and 'the power of Witches': 'For as for Witches, I think not that their witchcraft is any reall power; but yet that they are justly punished, for the false beliefe they have, that they can do such mischeife, joyned with their purpose to do it if they can.' This was the much the same view as that taken by Hobbes's friend John Selden, recorded in his *Table Talk*. Its force in *Leviathan* is quite clear: social norms have to be enforced. Rather than making witchcraft a mere delusion, it allows it to be a living practice among 'rude people', and one which is grounded upon and issues in malice. Hobbes says more than this, however, maintaining that the 'trade' of witches is 'neerer to a new Religion, than to a Craft or Science'—a remark which, in its very cursoriness and mystery, invites closer analysis.[1]

Another well-known Hobbesian dictum on witchcraft was recorded by Margaret Cavendish in her life of her husband (William Cavendish, duke

---

[1] Thomas Hobbes, *Leviathan* (1651), ed. Richard Tuck (Cambridge, 1991), 18. John Selden, *Table Talk* (Oxford, 1892), section cl, 195. On sense as phantasm see *Leviathan*, chs. 1 and 13–14.

of Newcastle, poet, playwright, and Royalist), published in 1667. Two exchanges are set down; they are, perhaps, Hobbes's own recollections of conversations with his friend and patron. Both occurred in Paris. While one concerned the feasibility of man-powered flight, the other considered a not unrelated issue, the powers and nature of witchcraft:

> . . . they falling into a discourse concerning witches, Mr Hobbes said, that though he could not rationally believe there were witches, yet he could not be fully satisfied to believe there were none, by reason they would themselves confess it, if strictly examined.[2]

If we strictly examine Hobbes's opinion itself, we can draw out the tension between rational belief on the one hand, and empirical procedures on the other. This is fully consonant with Hobbes's approach. He had prior grounds for doubting the real power and thus, perhaps, the very existence of witchcraft. In the same way, he disputed the cogency of the notion of vacuum, from first principles.[3] Yet, in the case of witchcraft, empirical evidence gave him some cause for doubt, if not sufficient utterly to undermine his confidence in the initial belief. It was Cavendish who filled in the gap between reason and evidence. His first response was to reject the metaphysical, with a flourish, since 'for his part he cared not whether there were witches or no'; in other words, he did not see that confession necessarily had any relevance to the putative reality of witchcraft itself. Instead he maintained a scepticism founded upon indifference. The occurrence of confession was then examined in a religious and psychological light:

> the confession of witches, and their suffering for it, proceeded from an erroneous belief, viz., that they had made a contract with the devil to serve him for such rewards as were in his power to give them; and that it was their religion to worship and adore him; in which religion they had such a firm and constant belief, that if anything came to pass according to their desire, they believed the devil had heard their prayers, and granted their requests, for which they gave him thanks; but if things fell out contrary to their prayers and desires, then they were troubled at it, fearing they had offended him, or not served him as they ought, and asked him forgiveness for their offences.

This is the religious part of the phenomenon. The trappings of covenant theology's version of witchcraft are here, and the inversion of true religion, but *without* the reality of demonic intercourse of any kind. God is

---

[2] Margaret Cavendish, *The Life of William Cavendish*, ed. C. L. Firth (1886), 198 f.

[3] See Thomas Hobbes, 'Dialogus Physicus', tr. S. Schaffer, in S. Shapin and S. Schaffer, *Leviathan and the Air-Pump* (Princeton, 1985).

mocked in the prayer for forgiveness, and in the pretence of a diabolical providence. The psychological account is eminently Hobbesian:

Also . . . they imagine that their dreams are real exterior actions; for example, if they dream they fly in the air, or out of the chimney top, or that they are turned into several shapes, they believe no otherwise, but that it is really so. And this wicked opinion makes them industrious to perform such ceremonies to the devil, that they adore and worship him as their god, and choose to live and die for him.

The religious theme is recapitulated and its centrality to the definition of witchcraft is reaffirmed.

This, then, was Cavendish's view 'which Mr Hobbes was also pleased to insert in his fore-mentioned book', *Leviathan*. Hobbes's laconic reference to the witch's 'trade' in *Leviathan* stands for an interpretation of witchcraft as a social and religious category which Cavendish gives us in full. Assimilating Hobbes to Cavendish, it will be seen that this line on witchcraft meshes well with Hobbes's wider outlook on belief and idolatry in a Christian commonwealth. On the metaphysical issue, however, he and Cavendish clearly differed, within a common framework which made a distinction between essentials and inessentials in religious doctrine. Cavendish 'doth not count this opinion of his so universal as if there were none but imaginary witches; for he doth not speak but of such a sort of witches as make it their religion to worship the devil in the manner aforesaid'. Cavendish pulls back from a radically sceptical account. His opinion is one that applies not universally, but to specific types of witchcraft. He suspends judgement in a matter indifferent:

Nor doth he think it a crime to entertain what opinion seems most probable to him, in things indifferent; for in such cases men may discourse and argue as they please, to exercise their wit, and may change and alter their opinions upon more probable grounds and reasons; whereas in fundamental matters, both of Church and State, he is so strict an adherent to them, that he will never maintain or defend such opinions which are in the least prejudicial to either.

Such deference to authority in Church and State is the hallmark of a true Hobbesian. The difference between Hobbes and his noble pupil on the issue of the power of witchcraft was that while the latter 'cared not', Hobbes thought the question a material one to the constitution of Church and State. Witchcraft beliefs of a traditional kind were grounded in a metaphysical doctrine of separated essences which was 'prejudicial to' the proper relationship between Church and State. Equally, Hobbes's understanding of witchcraft, as actually practised, can be seen as a function of the leading thread of his theology, his unyielding voluntarism in regard to the nature of God, as well as his conception of what religion, properly speaking, is. These issues will be dealt with in turn.[4]

Hobbes's opposition to reasoning upon spirits as a distinct substance, and his refusal to admit the existence of immaterial substance, were set out early in his career. The discourse on 'Human Nature', written in 1640, and published as part of the *Elements of Law* in 1650, has as its eleventh chapter a discussion of the supernatural, 'forasmuch as we give names not only to things natural, but also to *supernatural*; and by all names we ought to have some meaning and conception'. Subsequent paragraphs treat of God, the virtues attributed to him, and the proper conception of spirit, of good or bad angels. God himself is defined in a resolutely voluntarist sense. His will is his primary attribute rather than his intellect; and, given his omnipotence, he is consequently both morally and, ultimately, rationally inscrutable. The existence of God is assured by our knowledge of a first cause. The attributes we erect on the basis of this bare existential statement 'are such as *signify* either *our incapacity* or our reverence'.[5] Later remarks, in *Leviathan*, and in the various replies Hobbes made to the outraged criticism of Bishop Bramhall, make it clear that, nevertheless, God is conceived of as material.[6] When we apply the term *immaterial substance* to him, it signifies an incapacity to conceive of the divinity, whom we therefore designate infinite, omnipotent, and ineffable; and our desire to do him reverence. In itself, or as part of a proposition, *immaterial substance* cannot be construed. The adjective 'immaterial' cannot be brought to bear upon the noun it qualifies, 'substance', in any rationally definable sense. It is a contradiction in terms, and while 'men may put together words of contradictory signification, as *Spirit*, and *Incorporeall*; yet they can never have the imagination of any thing answering to them'. If the title 'incorporeall Spirit' is given to God, this is done not '*Dogmatically*, to make the Divine Nature understood; but *Piously*, to honour him with attributes, of significations, as remote as they can from the grossenesse of Bodies Visible'.[7] Yet elsewhere, Hobbes makes it clear

---

[4] Cavendish, *Life*, 198 f.

[5] 'forasmuch as God Almighty is *incomprehensible*, it followeth, that we can have *no* conception or *image* of the *Deity*, and consequently, all *his attributes* signify our *inability* and defect of power to *conceive* any thing concerning his nature, and not any conception of the same, excepting only this, that *there is a God*'. Hobbes, 'Human Nature' (1650; written 1640), in *English Works*, ed. W. Molesworth (11 vols.; 1839–45), iv. 59 f.

[6] Thomas Hobbes, 'An Answer to Bishop Bramhall's Book' (1682; written *c*.1668), in Hobbes, *English Works*, iv.; and *Leviathan*, chs. 12 and 34.

[7] *Leviathan*, 77 f.

that God's location, the fact that he has place, vouched for in Scripture, together with his metaphysical nature as first cause, ensures his materiality, as a 'most simple corporeal spirit'.[8]

Hence Hobbes moves on, in 'Human Nature', to spirits in general. First, the definition. A spirit is something 'of such *subtilty*, that it worketh not upon the senses; but . . . filleth up the place which the image of a visible body might fill up'. Our notion of spirit conforms to an image of figure without colour; not, as the Schoolmen had asserted, substance without dimension, which is literally inconceivable. It is the same with spirits as with God, in that 'it is not *possible* by *natural* means only, to come to *knowledge* of so much, as that *there are such* things'. This is then embroidered, as Hobbes admits the existence of good and evil angels as part of Christian doctrine but denies the possibility of a *science* of demonology. Science requires 'natural evidence' which can only come through the senses; 'And *spirits* we suppose to be those substances which work *not* upon the *sense*.'[9]

In *Leviathan*, Hobbes preserves a very strict voluntarism, emphasizing God's arbitrary will and absolute power, and is thus compelled to maintain that, formally at least, 'there is no doubt, but God can make unnaturall Apparitions'; but he goes on to say that scriptural references to spirits coming, descending, going, and dwelling, imply locality, and thus dimension and body, however subtle. The overarching conclusion is firm: Scripture favours the corporeality of angels and of spirits. The central point is, however, that spirits, be they considered as corporeal or incorporeal, are not available to sense, and are, consequently, no fit subject for natural philosophy. Demonology is not a science.[10]

The implications of this are various, but Hobbes himself explicitly raised the issue of interests: *cui bono?* If we can know nothing of spirits except by revelation, why have the schoolmen erected, dogmatically, their doctrines of incorporeal substance and separated essences?

this doctrine of *Separated Essences* built on the Vain Philosophy of Aristotle, would fright . . . [men] from Obeying the Laws of their Countrey; as men fright Birds from the Corn with an empty doublet, a hat, and a crooked stick. For it is upon this ground, that when a Man is dead and buried, they say his Soule (that is his Life) can walk separated from his Body, and is seen by night amongst the graves. Upon the same ground they say, that the Figure, and Colour, and Tast of

---

[8] Hobbes, 'An Answer', 306. On some of these issues, see Arrigo Pacchi, 'Hobbes and the Problem of God', in G. A. J. Rogers and A. Ryan (eds.), *Perspectives on Thomas Hobbes* (Oxford, 1988).

[9] 'Human Nature', 60 f.   [10] *Leviathan*, 19.

a peece of Bread, has a being, there where they say there is no Bread: And upon the same ground they say, that Faith, and Wisdome, and other Vertues are sometimes *poured* into a man, sometimes *blown* into him from Heaven; as if the Vertuous, and their Vertues could be asunder; and a great many other things that serve to lessen the dependance of Subjects on the Soveraign Power of their Countrey.

Whom can this benefit? Only those who oppose the laws, or those who seek to set up power in opposition to the sovereign:

For who will endeavour to obey the Laws, if he expect Obedience to be Poured or Blown into him? Or who will not obey a Priest that can make God, rather than his Soveraign; nay than God himselfe? Or who, that is in fear of Ghosts, will not bear great respect to those that can make the Holy Water, that drives them from him?[11]

The learned belief in witchcraft, and its demonological foundations, depended on the same central resource, and collaborated to the same destabilizing effect. Hobbes dismantles possession and exorcism in particular, and demonology in general, as 'Remaines of Gentilisme' like those which his friend John Aubrey was later to catalogue.[12] Priests wield this metaphysical weapon, being a caste of pseudo-experts who construct their own 'science' to bolster a counterfeit prestige. 'By their demonology, and the use of exorcism, and other things appertaining thereto, they keep, or think they keep, the people in awe of their power' and thus intend 'to lessen the dependance of subjects on the Soveraign Power'.[13]

It is difficult to overestimate the importance of this double strain, both anti-metaphysical and anticlerical, in Hobbes's thought. In his 'Six Lessons to the Professors' of 1656, he identifies the occasion of *Leviathan*, and one of its major tasks, as the consideration 'of what the ministers before, and in the beginning of, the civil war, by their preaching and writing did contribute thereunto'.[14] Papists are especially condemned in *Leviathan*; in this sense, its discourse on superstition and demonology is in the tradition set out by Reginald Scot, and continued by Thomas Ady.[15] The perpetrators of superstition themselves constitute the true

[11] Ibid. 465.

[12] John Aubrey, 'Remaines of Gentilisme and Judaisme', in *Three Prose Works* (Fontwell, 1972).

[13] *Leviathan*, 477, 465.

[14] 'Six Lessons to the Savilian Professors of the Mathematics', in Hobbes, *English Works*, vii. 181–356; 335.

[15] Reginald Scot, *The Discoverie of Witchcraft* (1584); Thomas Ady, *A Candle in the Dark* (1656). Followed also by John Wagstaffe in his *The Question of Witchcraft Debated* (1669), for which see ch. 3, below.

kingdom of darkness. The fourth part of *Leviathan* is, significantly, entitled 'Of the Kingdome of Darknesse'.

Presbyterians are enemies too, and semi-papistical in their assertion of an independent spiritual jurisdiction.[16] In *Behemoth*, his history of the civil wars, Hobbes again stresses the important contribution of 'metaphysical doctrines' and 'like points' to the outbreak of hostilities; these were 'the study of the curious, and the cause of all our late mischief'.[17] As this relates to witchcraft, we have a sort of secularized version of Thomas Ady's vision in *A Candle in the Dark* (1656), which presented the war as a punishment for the nation's sins, the shedding of the innocent blood of witches crying out for vengeance. For Hobbes, the war was the outcome of the adoption of a pernicious politico-theology, of which witchcraft theory was but a part. Witchcraft is not central to *Leviathan* in the way it is to *A Candle in the Dark*, but it evidently forms part of a complex of obnoxious doctrines which are set out as early as chapter 2. They are moreover given a whole chapter in, and determine the title of, part 4.

Much of chapter 45 of *Leviathan*, 'Of Daemonologie', is addressed directly to the subjects discussed by witchcraft tracts. Christ's being led into the wilderness 'in the spirit', for instance, something we can find in witchcraft treatises over the whole period from the sixteenth to the eighteenth centuries, is glossed in a way which avoids the possibility of real spiritual or demonic possession. Spiritual possession falls victim, first, to a version of orthodox theology: 'Christ and the Holy Ghost, are but one and the same substance'. The phrase 'in the spirit' must indicate a visionary experience. Temptation by the Devil in the wilderness is also deconstructed. No mountain in the world could have been high enough for Satan to show Christ all the kingdoms of the world in a physical sense. The possibility of possession by the Devil in this account is denied. Here a Hobbesian rule comes into play—if part of the story is to be read metaphorically, all of it must be so read. No enthusiasm, no diabolism.[18]

Hobbes also forms part of the sceptical tradition of witchcraft writing in one of his definitions of the biblical crime of witchcraft, which is 'the worship of [idols] with Divine Honour . . . that which is in the Scripture called Idolatry, and Rebellion against God'.[19] This amounts to an oblique

---

[16] For a different view of Hobbes's motives, see Noel Malcolm's piece on 'Hobbes and the Royal Society' in Rogers and Ryan, *Perspectives on Thomas Hobbes*.

[17] *Behemoth* (1679; written 1670), in Hobbes, *English Works*, vi. 232.

[18] Cf. John Bramhall, *Castigations of Mr Hobbes . . . [&] The Catching of Leviathan Or the great Whale* (1658), 488: 'He fancieth that all those devils which our Saviour did cast out, were phrensies, and all *daemoniacks* (or persons possessed) *no other than mad-men.*'

[19] *Leviathan*, 446.

reference to witchcraft, since 'rebellion is as the sin of witchcraft'. Passages in part 3, 'Of a Christian Common-wealth', are also of distinct relevance to the debate. The chapter 'Of the WORD OF GOD, and of PROPH-ETS' demolishes the sort of apocalyptic scheme favoured by writers like Nathaniel Homes in his *Daemonologie, or the character of the Crying Evils of the Present Times: In which, Beside the transcendent wicked practises of Men that never sipt of Religion: and the unparallel'd impious Principles of Hypocrites degenerated from their Profession of Religion, whether SEEKERS, SHAKERS, FAMILISTS, RANTERS, ADAMITES &c Are handled the DOCTRINES OF DEVILS* (1650). Homes presents such horrors as the 'idioms and proper markes of the LAST DAYES'. Hobbes is clear that the doctrines of devils 'signifieth not the Words of any Devill, but the Doctrine of Heathen men concerning *Daemons*, and those Phantasms which they worshipped as Gods'.[20]

The famous story of the witch of Endor, from 1 Samuel 28, another favourite with writers about witchcraft, is given a thoroughly naturalistic gloss, one which yet again spurns either diabolical or divine intervention. She raised only a 'phantasme' of Samuel and had no 'science' of prophecy or spirit-raising. God merely intended 'that Imposture to be a means of Sauls terror', to effect his discomfiture and contribute to his fall.[21]

Chapter 37, 'Of MIRACLES, and their Use', discusses the feats per-formed by the magicians of Egypt in response to Moses: how could these heathen have produced such apparently miraculous effects? Hobbes makes a distinction between pretended, lying wonders, often called 'Enchant-ment', and true wonders or miracles, which belong to God alone. Hence, enchantment, like the work of Pharaoh's magi, is 'Imposture, and delu-sion, wrought by ordinary means; and so far from supernaturall, as the Impostors need not study so much as of naturall causes, but the ordinary ignorance, stupidity, and superstition of mankind, to doe them'. Overall, Hobbes concludes, 'those texts, that seem to countenance the power of magick, Witchcraft, and Enchantment, must needs have another sense, than at first sight they seem to bear.'[22]

In the course of *Leviathan*, the denial of 'any reall power' to witches takes on a new aspect, and derives polemical force, from the denunciation of a priestly ontology, and the unveiling of imposture. The assertions of demonology are part of a nonsensical and pernicious philosophy: non-sensical because founded on an incoherent doctrine of separated essences; pernicious because tending to divide power in the commonwealth between

[20] Ibid. 288.   [21] Ibid. 291 f.   [22] Ibid. 304.

a spiritual and a secular or material order, personated respectively by the clergy and the laity.

The concept *witchcraft* is broken up, and its fragments variously re-apportioned in Hobbes's work. Demonology is false. Any wonders that are currently on offer—ranging from those of the village conjuror to those of the Roman priest—are the legacy of ignorance, or the issue of cunning, high and low. The witchcraft condemned in the book of Samuel is idolatry, no more, no less. The witches of current human experience are, as we would expect, denied efficacy or 'reall power'. Like the witch of Endor, they have no 'science'—they work no wonders by the devil's aid or by nature. They have no craft, and are to be distinguished from village conjurors, who are nothing if not crafty. In adhering to a 'new Religion', they are manifestly idolatrous. Cavendish sets out the details which Hobbes neglects to do.

Hobbes manages to dispose of the metaphysical portion of witchcraft belief, rejecting dangerous doctrines and striking a blow against overt and clandestine Popery, against sacerdotalism in all its forms. Yet at the same time he manages to maintain the anti-devotional and anti-social core of the crime of witchcraft. This is at the heart of my argument here. Even Hobbes, who rejects so many of the trappings of demonology, retains a place for witchcraft as a crime in his highly articulated system of politics. His belief in the justice with which this crime is punished should not be dismissed as an airy piece of irony. It could be so construed when witchcraft had ceased to be a matter for serious debate; at a time when it was deadly serious, this seems unlikely. It was a vital issue for Hobbes, and a capital one for the law. Hobbes, in fact, constructs a system of witchcraft belief purged of accrued antique debris, such as real *maleficium* or the contract with the Devil. He reduces witchcraft to the essentials of purpose and belief: a rebellion against God, and the desire to cause harm. All this can be placed within the wider context of Hobbes's voluntarist theology, and related to the covenant theology tradition sketched in the previous chapter.

First, however, look at a couple of contemporary reactions to Hobbes's demonology. The absence of the Devil in Hobbes's theology clearly worried John Bramhall, who sarcastically acclaimed him for killing 'the great infernal devil, and all his black Angels', leaving 'no devils to be feared, but devils incarnate, that is wicked men'.[23] Thomas Tenison, examining 'the creed of Mr Hobbes', upbraids his opponent most severely on the

---

[23] Bramhall, *Castigations*, 488.

issue of what the law, as promulgated by the sovereign, actually is. Those who

publickly deny Witch-craft, are sawcy affronters of the Law and therefore, for their opinion, which rather establisheth irreligion, than subverts the faith, they ought to be chastiz'd from those Chairs of Justice, which they have reproachfully stain'd with the bloud of many innocent and misperswaded people.

Tenison is almost as dismissive of the Hobbesian notion of punishing witches justly for thinking themselves witches, a position which would equally disable the law by allowing it 'to be accused of unreasonable severity'. Such thinking witches 'ought rather to be provided for in *Bedlam*, than executed at *Tyburn*'. Tenison ends with a final excoriation of Hobbes. Even if we could grant the execution of Hobbes's deluded witches to be just, 'yet would that evasion be too thin to shelter those from the censure of the Law, who . . . do most insolently revile it, by denying all real confederacy with *Daemons*', a confederacy which is confirmed in the Jacobean witchcraft legislation, which the future archbishop cites. 'The making Covenants with some evil and wicked Spirit' is, as Tenison cites the statute, 'a practice granted and notorious'.[24] This is orthodoxy from the pen of a rising star in the ecclesiastical hierarchy, *circa* 1670. When it comes to nailing Hobbes it is notable, however, that Tenison cannot catch him on the public denial of witchcraft (for which, see Hobbes's remark on witchcraft in his *Dialogue on the Common Laws*, discussed below), but only on misconstrual of the statute; of its provisions and of its definition of witchcraft. It is Hobbes's denial of confederacy with demons, of covenant-making with the Devil, of diabolical intercourse, that is given centre-stage. Hobbes himself was always very careful not to deny that there was, at law and in justice, a crime of witchcraft, and this needs explaining.

Hobbes's voluntarism has been characterized in detail by several authors, who have set out his relation to the theology of his day.[25] It has been shown that John Bramhall attacked Hobbes with the traditional weapons of anti-Calvinist polemic. The arguments over *Leviathan* can be seen duplicated in Bramhall's attack upon William Twisse, for instance,

---

[24] [Thomas Tenison], *The Creed of Mr Hobbes Examined; In a feigned conference between him, and a student in divinity* (1670), 62 ff.

[25] See esp. Noel Malcolm, 'Thomas Hobbes and Voluntarist Theology', Cambridge Ph.D. thesis (1983). Also Pacchi, 'Hobbes and the Problem of God', and Leopold Damrosch, Jr., 'Hobbes as Reformation Theologian: Implications of the Free-Will Controversy', *JHI* 40 (1979).

who published a restatement of English Calvinist orthodoxy in the 1640s.[26]
When Bramhall writes of those who 'father their own fancies upon God,
and when they cannot justify them by reason . . . plead His omnipotence',
he could as well be talking about Twisse, Hobbes, or the wilder sectarians.[27]
Bramhall and his allies preferred to rely upon an ethical intuition which
made God's will subservient to his essential goodness. After 1660, their
doctrines caught on. Hobbes emphasized instead God's arbitrary will and
absolute power. This voluntarism, anti-essentialist in its emphasis, was
one of the strongest determinants of his intellectual isolation after the
Restoration.[28] Thomas Pierce was one author who used Hobbes as a whip
for predestinarians in general, 'Mr *Hobbs*' being 'as able a *Calvinist* (as to
these points) as their party had'.[29]

Hobbes went further than Twisse, however, who had defended a doctrine of sin as a privation of being, which was consequently unattributable
to God. For Hobbes this made no sense, and his emphasis on the arbitrary justice of God's will was thoroughgoing. God's actions cannot be
measured by 'pacts and covenants', and 'that which he does, is made just
by his doing it'. Or, in the words of the book of Job, '*Where wert thou
when I laid the foundations of the earth?*', which Hobbes glosses: '*Power
irresistible justifies all actions, really and properly*, in whomsoever it be
found.'[30]

That reference to pacts and covenants in Hobbes's definition of divine
power is to be seen in the context of the covenant theology of the pre-
Civil War era, and the covenanting of the 1640s. This is clear from
Leviathan:

. . . whereas some men have pretended for their disobedience to their Sovereign,
a new Covenant, made, not with men, but with God; this also is unjust: for there
is no Covenant with God, but by mediation of some body that representeth Gods
Person; which none doth but Gods Lieutenant, who hath the Soveraignty under
God.

Hobbes drives this point home, speaking of the 'pretence of Covenant
with God' as the action of not only 'an unjust, but also of a vile, and

---

[26] William Twisse, *The Riches of Gods Love unto the Vessells of Mercy Consistent with His
Absolute Hatred or Reprobation of the Vessells of Wrath* (Oxford, 1653).

[27] John Bramhall, *Works*, ed. A.W.H. (5 vols.; Oxford, 1842–5), iv. 76.

[28] See I. C. Bostridge, 'Jurisprudence and Natural Philosophy: Matthew Hale and Thomas
Hobbes', Cambridge M.Phil. thesis (1987).

[29] Thomas Pierce, αυτοκατακρισις or *Self-Condemnation* (1658), cited in Malcolm,
'Thomas Hobbes and Voluntarist Theology', 105.

[30] Hobbes, *English Works*, iv. 249 f., 'Of Liberty and Necessity'.

unmanly disposition'.[31] He utterly denies the logic of a truly divine covenant, paralleling Filmer's refusal of intelligibility to the diabolical pact; and, indeed, the reality of one reflects on that of the other. The Old Testament covenant was made by the prophet Moses, personating God, with divine authority, and representing Israel. No bilateral contract[32] existed between Israel and either God himself, or Moses. This was a deliberate echo of the authorization process in civil government. The new covenant of the New Testament was made by Christ, as a man vested with the Father's authority, and representing the people of God, the elect, by virtue of his humanity. The 'marrow of Puritan divinity' is anathema to such a scheme. A *bilateral* contract, in which we can sue God 'on his own bond', derogates from God's majesty, and can hardly be reconciled with the idea of his 'power irresistible'. Hobbes's extreme position on the issue of divine will and sovereign inscrutability destroys the reality of the divine covenant proper and thus, symmetrically, makes the real diabolical covenant redundant.

This is only half the story, however. Hobbes insists on calling the witch's trade a 'new religion', and thus in some sense preserves the social reality of the witch's own beliefs. It is Hobbes's notion of religion as law that is vital to further understanding here. In his history of the Civil War, *Behemoth*, Hobbes condemns 'the design of drawing religion into an art, whereas it ought to be a law'. The nature of religion has, according to Hobbes, been mistaken; it has been 'taken for the same thing with divinity to the great advantage of the clergy'. The problem has been, more specifically the 'mingling our religion with points of philosophy', things like free will, incorporeal substances, and the like, 'which the people understand not, nor will ever care for'. Religion as Hobbes saw it 'admits no controversy. It is a law of the kingdom and ought not to be disputed.'[33]

The dictum on witchcraft with which this chapter started declares, similarly, that witchcraft is not an art, a craft, or a science, but a matter of religion, and thus of law. In Hobbes's work religion and witchcraft are related as type and antitype, law and rebellion. Religion is not to be equated with divinity, with all its supernatural mumbo-jumbo. It is about law and odedience. The inversion of religion is witchcraft, a crime of disobedience; and witchcraft, similarly, is not defined around spirits and incorporeal substance.

---

[31] *Leviathan*, 122. Hobbes cites this very passage in 'Considerations upon the Reputation, Loyalty, Manners, and Religion of Thomas Hobbes', in *English Works*, iv. 434.

[32] 'the mutuall transferring of Right', *Leviathan*, 94.

[33] Hobbes, *Behemoth*, 235 ff., 276.

How is the crime of witchcraft related to that of heresy, that other premier offence against religion? In his 'Historical Narration concerning Heresy', Hobbes writes that heresy is 'no more than a private opinion' to be punished by the 'ordinary censures . . . of the church'. No doctrine is heretical unless 'declared and published' as such by civil authority or the first four councils of the church. His argument is that the laws of England, as set down since the reign of Elizabeth, have repudiated all former heresy laws, and provide no details as to the punishment of heresies left defined by the early church councils. Yet, men are so 'fierce . . . where either their learning or power is debated, that they never think of the laws, but as soon as they are offended, they cry out, *crucifige*'. Hobbes's complaint is a bitter and a personal one. That which can be punished is a matter of law and religion; heresy in itself, as a private opinion, is not punishable. The corollary is that witchcraft is punishable by law not only as an act of malice (belief *joined with* purpose, as in *Leviathan*, chapter 2), but also as a rebellion against established religion.[34]

In Hobbes's *Dialogue* on the English common law, a passage on witchcraft is significantly juxtaposed to the section which deals with heresy, and itself forms part of the consideration of capital crimes. The opinions expressed are just as difficult to unpick, just as ambiguous and shrouded in caution, as those in Cavendish's *Life*. Hobbes's lawyer in the dialogue talks of 'Conjuration, Witchcraft, Sorcery and Inchantment', which are undeniably capital crimes by statute. His companion, a philosopher, displays a healthy indifference, desiring 'not to discourse of that Subject'. The point being made by this rhetorical gesture is that we should not bandy divinity words in a matter of religion and law. While doubtless 'there is some great Wickedness signified by those Crimes', the philosopher finds himself 'too dull to conceive the nature of them, or how the Devil hath power to do many things which Witches have been accused of'.[35] Hobbes is not maintaining any sort of principled scepticism here. The ironic tone does suggest the implausibility of many accusations, but the philosopher does not conclude that, as a consequence, the laws on the matter should be expunged. This is of a piece with the other passages examined in the course of this chapter. Hobbes, of course, had a problem whenever he disagreed with sovereign-made law, since the whole coherence of his world-view was founded on the word of the sovereign. The

---

[34] 'An Historical Narration concerning Heresy, and the Punishment thereof', in *English Works*, iv. 387, 406 f.

[35] Thomas Hobbes, *A Dialogue between a Philosopher and a Student of the Common Laws of England* (1681), ed. J. Cropsey (Chicago, 1971), 122.

consequence here seems to be, simultaneously, an attempt to redefine terms, and to avoid the issue.[36]

Having established the affinity of covenant theology with a particular and widespread understanding of witchcraft—as a detailed inversion of godly practices—and having set out the political relevance and topicality which this gave the witchcraft issue in Filmer's work, I have gone on to expand and explain Thomas Hobbes's numerous, but disparate, remarks on witchcraft. Most fundamental is the parallel between the ideas set out in the conversation recorded by Margaret Cavendish, and Hobbes's remarks on witchcraft in *Leviathan*.

More generally, Hobbes's theology and his Erastian anticlericalism encouraged him to deny the status of natural knowledge, or of expertise, to pneumatology and, consequently, to demonology. Only revelation tells us that spirits exist. We cannot reason upon this knowledge, and we have no sense-experience about spirits since, though material, they are, by definition, exceptionally subtle. Nothing is in the intellect, as the schoolmen had it, which has not been in the senses. The Hobbesian approach to miracles or wonders, in which there is not much difference between them, withdraws 'magical' actions altogether from the realm of reality, and completes the Protestant eschewal of the Catholic supernatural. Witchcraft theory shadows developments in theology. The holy and the demonic move in step. The paradoxes of the covenant theologians' version of witchcraft are thus variously resolved. The emphasis on the inversion of the holy as an act of *dérogeance*—Hobbes himself talks of the 'Leiturgy of Witches'—is extended so as to exclude the physical reality of *mira* and *maleficia*.[37] In the Latin version of *Leviathan*, carefully supervised by Hobbes, he does not use the latter term, but rather the phrase *mala facinora*—criminal, vicious evils.[38] His version of covenant forbids the systematic bilateral covenant of the likes of Perkins, in either the holy or the demonic spheres. In holding religion to be a matter of law established,

[36] Tenison (see above) may have thought he had caught Hobbes, in that the latter allowed *Leviathan* to be republished after 1660, when the legal position was much clearer, and more unfavourable to the opinions expressed in the book, but see below, n. 38.

[37] *Leviathan*, 78.

[38] Thomas Hobbes, *Latin Works*, ed. W. Molesworth (1839–45), iii. 13: 'Nam etsi sorcilegiam potentiam aliquam realem esse non putem, puto tamen sorcilegos puniri jure posse, cum mala facinora et facere posse credant, et conentur quantum possunt.' The Latin version introduces a negative conditional, changing 'I think not' into *nam etsi . . . non putem*, 'even if I did not think'. This may relate to Hobbes's anxiety to remain within the law. In 1651 the Interregnum gave greater scope for Hobbes to interpret the law constructively; by the 1670s it was clear, as Tenison pointed out, that the 1604 legislation on witchcraft was in force.

Hobbes maintained witchcraft as a crime, one of rebellion joined with malice. As we would expect, his ideas on witchcraft, the category which symbolizes the inversion of desirable values, reflect Hobbes's particular vision of human relations with God, and the place of religion in society. The subversion of the state by a charismatic individual, 'is plain rebellion; and may be resembled to the effects of witchcraft'; the enemies of society are compounded.[39] Rebellion as the sin of witchcraft, the scriptural analysis, makes particular sense within Hobbes's system. Rebellion against the sovereign is the same as rebellion against God because the sovereign, as sole public interpreter of religious experience, is the only mediator between God and the subject. He is the only representation of God that the subject can know.[40]

---

[39] *Leviathan*, 230. Cf. *De Cive*, English version, ed. H. Warrender (Oxford, 1983), 155 f.: 'So the common people through their folly (like the daughters of *Pelias*) desiring to renew the ancient government, being drawne away by the *eloquence* of ambitious men, as it were by the witchcraft of *Medea*, divided into *faction*, they consume it rather by those flames, then they reforme it.'

[40] For a parallel evaluation of Hobbes's 'farrago of Christian Atheism', as Henry Hammond called it, see Richard Tuck, 'The "Christian Atheism" of Thomas Hobbes', in Michael Hunter and David Wootton (eds.), *Atheism from the Reformation to the Enlightenment* (Oxford, 1992).

3

Witchcraft Restored

[A]s we see in the visible Administration of the World, or of any one Kingdom thereof, there is continual Diligence on one side by seditious turbulent minded Men to break the Peace of a Kingdom or City, or place, which is with much diligence, watchfulness, and vigilancy, attended and prevented by wise and good Men.

> Matthew Hale, *A meditation concerning the mercy of God, in preserving us from the malice and power of evil angels* (1693; written 1682).[1]

RESTORATION

For Robert Filmer, an avowed sceptic, witchcraft theory was none the less the 'Publique faith of the present age'. Even so radical a theorist as Hobbes found a place for witchcraft in his political ontology. Alive and well in the 1650s, where did witchcraft theory stand in 1660, as the political nation turned away from the excesses of Civil War and Interregnum? This chapter sets out to establish the nature of witchcraft theory in the wake of the Restoration. For the Royalist churchman Meric Casaubon, witchcraft belief was an intellectual tradition which could be deployed as part of a campaign to shore up the newly restored and sacralized political order. It was also a symbolic means of defining a Christian community against a diabolized outsider, thus asserting the unity of the Christian body after a period of threatening religious pluralism during the Civil War and Interregnum. Casaubon's concerns had a definite political purpose. Yet they were also avowedly and essentially non-partisan, setting up the image of

---

[1] *A Collection of modern relations of matter of fact, concerning witches and witchcraft upon the persons of people. To which is prefixed a meditation concerning the mercy of God, in preserving us from the malice and power of evil angels. Written by the late Lord Chief Justice Hale, upon occason of a tryal of several witches before him* (1693), 7.

a broad and unified Christian community, with assent grounded in a consensual intellectual order defined against its negative image, witchcraft. Those outside that order, witches and sceptics, were demonized. Witchcraft belief was, paradoxically, a way of unifying through exclusion. Witchcraft itself had always been conceived of as an inversion of positive religious and social values; in Casaubon's writings its prominence had a particular purpose as part of the process of the restoration of cherished values.

In this chapter, some other, very different, writers are examined in the light of these concerns of Casaubon's: the experimentalist clergyman Joseph Glanvill; the Peripatetic experimenter and judge Sir Matthew Hale; his friend, the English dissenting minister Richard Baxter; and the colonial congregationalist pastor Cotton Mather. The themes of unity and tradition identified in Casaubon's writings about witchcraft are seen to inform the work of these authors too, from churchman through to dissenter. Those who directly opposed witch beliefs in this period, including John Wagstaffe and John Webster, are shown to have been intellectually marginal and just as ideologically-motivated as their antagonists.

Witch beliefs were widely held after the Restoration. Witchcraft theory articulated a common anxiety to maintain the sacral nature of the state, and the acceptance of a model in which Church and secular society were somehow intertwined. The continued robustness of witchcraft theory lay in its capacity to express unity and, conversely, to avoid controversy. There was common ground on the witchcraft issue, somewhere between the extremes of Matthew Hopkins's fanaticism or Reginald Scot's freethinking; an intellectual space within which dissenters and churchmen could readily coexist and express their common anxiety about the splintering of Christian fellowship. Witchcraft was not the marginalized possession of fanatics after the Restoration, but common intellectual property; not interesting to all the people all of the time, but quite capable of marshalling wide support across parties and religious divisions. The reality of witchcraft was widely accepted in the 1680s. This intellectual position had an ideological rationale regardless of low levels of prosecution, and despite the ebb and flow of 'committed believers', or the tide of unbelief about which contemporaries so often complained.

Witchcraft theory partook of the restoration of values which occurred after 1660. The existence and relevance of witchcraft was accepted by a disparate range of intellectuals. Witchcraft theory had a common ideological core, centring on an identification between the spiritual and secular realms. Any questioning of this last assumption could threaten witchcraft's relevance and its ideological appeal.

ENTHUSIASM

In 1690 Sir William Temple, Jonathan Swift's future employer and a great admirer of Dutch religious moderation, delivered a characteristically urbane attack on enthusiasm.[2] A clear account of enthusiasm, and the related phenomenon of fascination, 'from their natural causes', might, Temple contended, with a politic emphasis which was to be repeated in subsequent decades, 'prevent many publick disorders, and save the Lifes of many innocent deluded People, who suffer so frequently upon Account of Witches and Wizards'. Temple was disappointed that such a project 'has not imployed the Pen of some Person of such excellent Wit and deep Thought and Learning as Casaubon'. In particular he remembered that author's 'curious and useful Treatise of *Enthusiasme*', which had 'discovered the hidden or mistaken Sources of that delusion'.[3]

Meric Casaubon (1599–1671), son of the great scholar Isaac Casaubon, was an Anglican divine, deprived in the Interregnum and restored at the Restoration. His *Treatise Concerning Enthusiasme, As It is an Effect of Nature: but is mistaken by many for either Divine Inspiration, or Diabolical Possession*, written in the 1650s, does promise in its very title a restriction of the domain of the supernatural. Medical explanations are to be offered for the supposed actions of spirits or devils in various forms of enthusiasm, from divination and philosophy, to rhetoric, poetry, and prayer. Casaubon's aim is to prevent men from 'embracing a Cloud, or a Fogge for a Deity', something that had been, in the preceding years of civil war and dissension, an all too common and 'foul mistake'.[4] The treatise stands alongside Henry More's *Enthusiasmus Triumphatus* as an attempt to depict the sects or fanatics of the 1650s as bad physicians in their diagnosis and manipulation of possession, men who required physic themselves in

---

[2] See his *Observations upon . . . the Netherlands* (1672). On witchcraft in Holland, see Ch. 4 and Conclusion below.

[3] Cited by George Williamson, 'The Restoration Revolt against Enthusiasm', *Studies in Philology*, 30 (1933), 582. Following Temple, Francis Hutchinson showed a similar concern to restrain the progress of witch-crazes and enthusiasm. See his *A Short View of the Pretended Spirit of Prophecy* (1708) and *An Historical Essay Concerning Witchcraft* (1718), esp. 181, 195–201. Recent historians have also linked the issues of enthusiasm and witchcraft together, seeing the disgrace of the one as the death-knell of the other. See Michael MacDonald, *Mystical Bedlam* (Cambridge, 1981), ch. 5; id., 'Religion, Social Change, and Psychological Healing in England 1600–1800' (*Studies in Church History*, 19; 1982), 101–25; and J. C. D. Clark, *English Society 1688–1832* (Cambridge, 1985), 169. On enthusiasm more generally, see also M. Heyd's review article, 'The Reaction to Enthusiasm in the Seventeenth Century: Towards an Integrative Approach', *Journal of Modern History*, 53 (1981).

[4] Meric Casaubon, *Treatise Concerning Enthusiasme*, 2nd ed. (1656), 'To the reader'.

the sheer lunacy of their precatory enthusiasm.[5] Casaubon ranges much wider than this, but his preface confirms this as the main subject, the spur, and the political motive. The irony is that, having written this anti-enthusiastic and essentially sceptical work, reining in the supernatural, Casaubon did indeed write about witchcraft, but to a very different purpose from that suggested by Temple.[6]

DR DEE'S BOOK

Casaubon's next work was an edition of the papers of John Dee, Elizabethan mathematician and magus, relating to his supposed commerce with the world of spirits.[7] Why should Casaubon have chosen to publish such a book in the late 1650s, dredging up a long-dead controversy and dwelling upon a supernatural realm he had only just fenced in? By writing about the past, he was hoping to avoid censorship; and by condemning Dee's unlicensed spiritual exercises he sought to blacken what he saw as the spiritual excesses of those fanatics at large in the unlicensed 1650s. This, in turn, would reflect discreditably upon any government which could permit such outrages.

Two letters are extant relating to the genesis of this book. One is from Nicholas Bernard, protégé of the Irish archbishop Ussher, chaplain and almoner to Oliver Cromwell, and disputant with the Arminian controversialist Peter Heylyn. The letter was intended to clear up a misunderstanding. Bernard confirmed that Ussher had indeed borrowed the manuscript from the great antiquary Sir Robert Cotton, in London, 'and

---

[5] [Henry More], *Enthusiasmus Triumphatus, or a Discourse of the Nature, Causes, Kinds, and Cure of Enthusiasme; written by Philophilus Parrasiastes, and prefixed to Alazonomastix his Observations and Reply* (1656).

[6] Note that even in the *Treatise Concerning Enthusiasme* Casaubon cautiously rejects the conclusion 'of particular cases, by generall Rules and Maximes' which is 'a principall cause of most strifes and confusions' ('To the reader'). His stance is not a simple, naturalistic, anti-enthusiastic one, even here. See John Webster, *The Displaying of Supposed Witchcraft* (1677), 8, for one interpretation of Casaubon's motivation: 'He [Casaubon] had before run in a manner (by labouring to make all that which he called Enthusiasm, to be nothing else but imposture or melancholy and depraved phantasie, arising from natural causes) into the censure of being a Sadducee or Atheist. To wash off which he thought nothing was so prevalent, as to leap into the other end of the balance (the mean is hard to be kept) to weigh the other down, by publishing some notorious Piece that might (as he thought) in an high degree manifest the existence of Spirits good and bad, and this he thought would effect it sufficiently, or at least wipe off the former imputation that he had contracted.'

[7] Meric Casaubon, *A True and Faithful Relation of what passed for many yeers between Dr John Dee (A Mathematician of Great Fame in Q. Eliz. and King James their Reignes) and Some Spirits. With a preface confirming the reality (as to the point of spirits) of this relation: and shewing the several good Uses that a sober christian may make of all* (1659).

each night I read a great part of it to him, and for my own satisfaction ran over the most part of it'. But Ussher had never, as some seemed to be saying, thought Dee's relation 'a dangerous book'; Bernard did 'not remember any such speech of his', and, if the archbishop were now alive, 'I have cause to believe . . . he would not discourage you the publishing of it.' Bernard himself was a little reserved about his own views, thinking the project 'worthy of advise in some particulars, which might be omitted', but there is no evidence that Casaubon took Bernard's advice.

Attached to Bernard's letter is a statement by John Cotton, the antiquarian Robert Cotton's grandson, vouchsafing that Ussher had thought Dee's relation 'an excellent book to convince atheists &c.' and 'wished it printed'.[8] This sort of controversial, religious use of the witchcraft theme, for the convincing of atheists, was to be central to the writings of the last generation of hag-ridden authors, like Glanvill, More, and Matthew Hale. It was stimulated as much by the practical atheism of the 1640s and 1650s, as by the theoretical and recherché materialism of Thomas Hobbes.

Casaubon's own aims for his edition of Dee are clearly stated in 'a letter written by Dr Casaubon and entred in a blank page before the Earl of Angleseas Copy'. The relevance of the work to Interregnum enthusiasm is evident from the first. Casaubon wanted to set out publicly the condition of those fanatics acted upon by 'pretended inspiration and special guidance of the Spirit'. Many, he declared, 'were really deluded'; and they acted under the misconception that in 'preaching and praying on, and in much shew of zeal, God must needes be here'.[9] This spiritual anarchy and factionalism was of deep concern to Casaubon, a concern further evinced in his *Vindication of the Lord's Prayer*, published the year after the Dee relation, in 1660. In this work, Casaubon defends the provision of prescribed prayers; but he also hints at the constraints under which he worked as an author before 'this blessed alteration' of 1660. If the book had been composed since the Restoration, rather than before, 'my expressions might have been fuller and plainer, in some places'.[10] In Casaubon's writings of the 1650s, cryptic phrasing of dangerous sentiments is to be expected. Publishing Dee's sixteenth-century manuscript as, effectively, a postscript to an editorial attack on religious fanaticism was certainly one way of trying to outwit the authorities. Casaubon's letter sets out how Dee's text relates to his own preface. Dee's is 'a miserable account of a Man deluded', of 'the preachings and prayings of

---

[8] *DNB*; Bodleian MS Ashm. 1788 f65 (1658).
[9] Bodleian MS Ashm. 1788 f65. Another copy in Bodleian MS Rawl. D 923 f205.
[10] Meric Casaubon, *A Vindication of the Lord's Prayer* (1660), 'To the Reader'.

Spirits (real devils) with shew of great devotion'. It is topical too, 'the very language of the tymes observable in many places'. Whereas in the 1656 treatise on enthusiasm certain forms of supposed divine and diabolical possession were shown to be natural; here, 'precatory enthusiasm', unlicensed and divisive religious devotion, is shown to be a form of traffic with the Devil. As for the details of Dee's story, Casaubon was hardly interested. The preface and the table of contents 'will give you a view of the whole Book, which otherwise is tedious and full of impertinent and confused stuff, much like, in many things, the canting language that was then in use'.

The book did attract political attention. Cromwell became aware of it and it was 'stopped at the press, and in question at the Councill table'. If the Protector had lived it would not have been printed, 'but upon his death . . . it was got out'.[11] Cromwell knew well the power of Casaubon's pedigree, as son of the greatest scholar of the age, Isaac Casaubon, whose very name carried an impressiveness hardly to be measured. The Lord Protector had tried to use that reputation for his own purposes, asking Meric Casaubon to write an impartial account of the Civil War. Casaubon preferred to compose covert attacks on the usurping power and its clients.[12]

Casaubon's *True and Faithful Relation* sets out, on its very title-page, the political consequences of spiritual anarchy. Dee's activities had threatened '*a General Alteration of most* STATES *and* KINGDOMES *in the World*'. Similar ambitions are credited to the 'Anabaptists', all-purpose religious anarchists, with whom the *Relation* continually compares the diabolical dupe John Dee. Dee, for example, had illusionary comforts 'such as the Saints . . . and *Schismaticks* of these and former times have ever been very prone to boast of, perswading themselves that they are the *effects* of Gods Blessed *Spirit*'. Such men 'become *Saints* before they know what it is to be *Christians*'. Dee's devils too were 'perswaders to Piety and godliness', and to a similarly pernicious end. The Devil is 'a notable Polititian' and 'can any man speak better than he doth by the mouth of Anabaptists and Schismaticks?'[13] For Casaubon, these enthusiasts, in their irregular conduct, their departure from custom and resistance to legitimate

---

[11] Bodleian MS Ashm. 1788, f65.

[12] See *DNB* and M. R. G. Spiller, *'Concerning Natural Experimental Philosophie': Meric Casaubon and the Royal Society* (The Hague, 1980).

[13] *A True and Faithful Relation*, 31, 34, 36. On the Devil as politician in the work of Defoe and others, cf. Ch. 5 below.

authority, are 'such men as can give no account of their calling'. When dealing with 'so great and weighty a business as the salvation of Souls', one must, for safety's sake if nothing else, 'use the means that God hath ordained'.[14]

As editor, Casaubon goes beyond mere noting of the similarities between Dee's practices and those of enthusiasts, and the insinuation of a common, if unwitting, diabolical involvement. Talking of Dee's spirits' 'confident and reiterated Addresses unto, and Attempts upon so many great men in Power and Authority', he asks us to 'consider it well . . . since *England* might have been over-run with Anabaptism . . . long before this'. Casaubon seems to be saying that Anabaptists are well on their way to power; if not in full and confirmed possession of it, they are at least in their 'first pretensions'. Appealing to 'all truly sober and Religious' men to pray for a deliverance from this, Casaubon implicitly condemns those who tolerate such outrages. Dee's spirits are implicated in an Anabaptist conspiracy; and the laxness of the English commonwealth is simultaneously condemned.[15]

William Perkins's theory held witchcraft to be the inversion of a divine order and liturgy, and consequently placed great emphasis upon the witch's contract with the Devil. This inversion of the divine compact acted as a reinforcement of contract theology.[16] Casaubon's strategy is a little different. Reclaiming the doctrine of witchcraft from the saints, he turns it around. An essentially imitative conception of the diabolical can be redirected against those who call themselves godly. 'The Divel we see can Pray and Preach . . . and talk of Sanctity and Mortification, as well as the best.' Casaubon's idea is not so much of inversion as of mimicry, 'as to outward appearance we mean'; something impossible to distinguish from the real thing without the sanction of established authority. Those 'enthusiasts' who 'can give no account of their calling' must be suspected of a league with the Devil or, at least, of acting under diabolical inspiration.[17]

Casaubon also uses the imitation of the divine order by the Devil to give a perverse sanction to his own ecclesiastical and social preferences.

[14] Ibid. 52.

[15] Ibid. 51. On toleration and liberty of conscience under the Cromwellian regime, see Blair Worden, 'Toleration and the Cromwellian Protectorate' (*Studies in Church History*, 21; 1984), 209 f.

[16] See also P. Stallybrass and A. White, *The Politics and Poetics of Transgression* (1986), 4–26, esp. 23–5.

[17] *A True and Faithful Relation*, 52.

'Holy furniture' is central to Dee's practices, what with 'the *Holy Table*' and 'this *personated* sanctuary'. Casaubon makes no question 'but the Divel in all these things had a respect to the Ceremonial Law especially', as we would expect from a good churchman.[18]

The preface to Dee's relation is, more generally, a source for Casaubon's demonology. The diagnosis of witchcraft is an expert science, but one rife with difficulties, 'very lyable to many mistakes and divers impostures'. Trials should preferably be conducted with the assistance of 'prudent Divines, and learned experienced Physicians'. Yet one or two instances of fraud do not entirely discredit the phenomenon, which would be 'as if a man should deny the power of herbs because a thousand things have been written of them of old, and are yet daily falsely and superstitiously'.[19] The practice of exorcism had generated many of the scandals and impostures associated with witchcraft and possession. Canon 72 of the 1604 canons effectively outlawed the casting out of devils without episcopal licence. Despite this, Casaubon defends a moderate, non-superstitious practice of exorcism. His safeguard is, as with witchcraft, expert opinion; a physician should always be in attendance at such undertakings.[20]

As far as Casaubon is concerned, the evidence for witchcraft cannot be discredited by scandal or reduced to a few spurious examples. It is corroborative, and well-distributed in time and space. He presents witchcraft, in fact, as singularly unproblematic, and his reasons for this are those that made the phenomenon a favourite weapon against atheism in the 1660s and 1670s: 'it is a Subject of that nature as doth not admit of many Arguments, such especially as may pretend to subtilty of Reason. Sight, Sense and Experience (upon which most Humane Knowledge is grounded) generally approved and certain, is our best argument'.[21]

---

[18] Ibid. 47, 49.

[19] Ibid. 13. Cf. Meric Casaubon, *A Treatise of Use and Custome* (1638), 186, with its warning, 'lest conforming to the vulgar in those things, hee himselfe become one of them'. Later in the century the battle was lost—effective therapies were discredited for the purposes of social demarcation and professional definition: Macdonald, *Mystical Bedlam*, esp. 226 f.

[20] *A True and Faithful Relation*, 21 f. See Thomas, *RDM* 579. For comparison see also Jean de Viguerie, 'Le Miracle dans la France du xviie siècle', *xviie Siècle*, 140 (1983), 313–31. On the political dangers of exorcism, see [N. Orchard], *The Doctrine of Devils proved to be the grand Apostasy of these later Times. An Essay tending to rectifie those Undue Notions and Apprehensions Men have about Daemons and Evil Spirits* (1676), 102: '. . . a rebellious Doctrine; some Exorcists upon the account of it, instigate to rebellion; we conquer Devils, can flesh and blood stand out?'

[21] *A True and Faithful Relation*, 16. Cf. J[ohn] W[agstaffe], *The Question of Witchcraft Debated*, 1st ed. (1669), 59: 'they are wont to wave arguments, and to cry out, this is a question not to be disputed on, in regard it is a matter of fact, and consequently the object of sense, not of reason'. Casaubon's is the sort of common-sense empiricism, absorbing

Casaubon also used the preface to set out the limits of the science of spirits, pneumatology, making basic definitions, but denying the pertinence of its more arcane details:

The very word *Spirit*, is a term of great Ambiguity; We understand by it, commonly, substances, that are altogether immaterial. Many of the ancient Fathers, it is well known, did not allow of any such at all, besides God: But we think that to have no visible Body, and to be purely immaterial, is all one: God knows how many degrees there may be between these, but we cannot know it, neither doth it concern our salvation.[22]

This is similar to the position taken by Henry Power, for whom 'the corporeal was allowed to merge imperceptibly into the incorporeal'; the same was true for the experimental judge Matthew Hale, and for his dissenting friend Richard Baxter. This continuum allowed the experimentalists Mayow, Hooke, Boyle, and the like to manipulate spirit in the laboratory to the confusion of ill-disciplined enthusiasts and empty-headed materialists alike. Witchcraft reports, as Boyle saw it, could form part of this programme.[23] In one sense Casaubon was a part of, even the precursor of, this trend. But he nevertheless criticized those who 'would reduce all learning, to natural experiments',[24] and, as far as pneumatology was concerned, was satisfied merely to postulate a hierarchy of spiritual agencies, good, bad, and indifferent.[25] He condemned anything more ambitious than this as the arrogance of natural philosophers, whose presumption vied with that of the sects.[26] Rejecting attempts to 'make all men wise, of one mind, good, religious' through experimental endeavour and reforming projects as 'Castles . . . built in the air', no more likely to succeed than if the heavens were 'battered with great guns', Casaubon's philosophy was conservative and sceptical, thoroughly removed from the cocksure tone,

tradition and textual authority, which Daniel Defoe was to adopt in relation to witchcraft, see Ch. 5 below. See also R. T., *The Opinion of Witchcraft Vindicated. In an Answer to a Book Intituled the Question of WITCHCRAFT Debated. Being a Letter to a Friend* (1670), 62, on the dangers of 'becom[ing] a Sceptick, and reject[ing] the Testimony of . . . [the] Senses'.

[22] *A True and Faithful Relation*, 42.

[23] Charles Webster, 'The Experimental Philosophy of Henry Power', *Ambix*, 14 (1967); Richard Baxter, *Of the Nature of Spirits* (1682); id., *Additional Notes of the Life and Death of Sir Matthew Hale* (1682); Simon Schaffer, 'Godly Men and Mechanical Philosophers: Souls and Spirits in Restoration Natural Philosophy', *Science in Context*, 1 (1987).

[24] *A True and Faithful Relation*, 33; Meric Casaubon, *Of Credulity and Incredulity in things Natural, Civil and Divine* (reissue of 1668 ed., 1672), 296.

[25] *A True and Faithful Relation*, 42; *Of Credulity*, 195.

[26] Compare *A True and Faithful Relation*, 33 with *Of Credulity*, 185: '. . . besides profest or secret *Atheism* and infidelity; there is not, among them that profess to believe . . . any greater cause of miscarrying, than *presumption*'.

as he saw it, of the Royal Society and its men, 'our great undertakers & reformers of Arts and Sciences'.[27] Yet it is striking that witchcraft remained on the agenda for both.

Any consideration of the spirit world in this period was bound to touch on the business of miracles. To what extent or in what sense could devils or other spirits perform such actions, especially considering the Protestant disinclination to recognize modern-day miracles?[28] How could the power of devils and spirits be compatible with the unconstrained omnipotence of God? As spirits, and creatures of long experience, Casaubon asserts, devils must have 'perfect knowledge of all natural things', and this gives them a power to perform actions which men consider wonders. Some might quarrel with this use of the term perfection, which should be God's prerogative, but Casaubon explains that he means relative perfection, 'incomparably greater than man is capable of'.[29] Despite the admitted occurrence of imposture, he believes in the possibility of 'supernatural things, as cures, &c . . . in every age, for which no reason can be given, which also for the strangenesse may be called Miracles'. Yet if we retreat to the strict definition of *miracula*, which must proceed from God alone, Casaubon is judicious: 'I shall not', he writes, 'be very ready to yield that many such Miracles are seen in these Dayes.'[30]

Such details of demonology and theology are fascinating, but Casaubon's political stance remains the key to the Dee relation's publication and

[27] *A True and Faithful Relation*, 33. On this essentially Baconian utopianism, see Charles Webster, *The Great Instauration* (1975). For Casaubon's campaign against the Royal Society, see his *Letter . . . to Peter du Moulin . . . Concerning Natural Experimental Philosophy* (1669).

[28] See e.g. [William Sherlock], *The Notes of The Church, As Laid down By Cardinal Bellarmin; Examined and Confuted* (1688), 252: 'We of the Reform'd Church, as we do not pretend to the working of Miracles in our Age, so if we did, we could pretend to prove nothing by them but what hath already been sufficiently prov'd by the Miracles of Christ and his Apostles.' But for another point of view see [John Gilbert], *Reflections on Dr Fleetwood's Essay upon Miracles: Shewing the Absurdity, Falshood, and Danger of his Notions. With a Supplement, Wherein is represented the Extent and Strength of the Evidence which Miracles give to Revealed Religion* (1706), 92 f.: 'the World supposes the Devil to have a Power to work Miracles, and that he may empower his Agents also. Whether the Devil's Power in this Case be his Natural Power that he was created with, or some Power given him for this particular Purpose, the World perhaps does not think it self concerned to enquire, neither knows any certain means of being satisfied . . . And this the World thinks to be the Difference between the Power of God, and the Power of the Devil in working Miracles; the one's Power is absolute and omnipotent, the other's finite, limited and restrained; and that consequently which appears restrained, the World supposes is not to be thought the Power of God.'

[29] *A True and Faithful Relation*, 38.

[30] Ibid. 18 f. The refusal to rule out miracles entirely may reflect a commitment to a view of Charles I as a sainted, and miracle-working, martyr, for which see below in this chapter, pp. 67–9.

preface. Calculated equilibrium is a persistent feature of Casaubon's writing. We see it in the structure of his books, and in the decision to publish the Dee relation, damning sectarians as diabolical, after the treatise on enthusiasm, which had refused to credit the sects' own claims to supernatural experience. In his moderation, Meric Casaubon was a model English churchman, as his book on the *Necessity of Reformation* confirms. It is the fierceness of many reformers, following the example of Luther and Calvin, that has hindered a true reformation. It should never be denied, Casaubon insists, that the church of Rome, despite its waywardness, is a true church. The Pope is Bishop of Rome, not Antichrist. Any other position is 'contrary to the judgment and declaration of the Church of England'. While moderating Protestant anti-Romanism, Casaubon is also anxious not to lose the opportunity to conscript Calvin himself, a 'rigid man' no doubt, yet 'godly pious' and someone who, 'had he lived in *England*, and had been better acquainted with the true state of businesses, he would have been of another mind, in many things'.[31]

There is a connection between this vapid entreaty, with its appeal to the better nature of the long dead, and Casaubon's anxiety about 'Scisme', which is 'the most horrid of crimes that can be committed by the wickedest of men'.[32] And there is in turn an affinity to be found between that concern about schism and division, and the apologetic for witchcraft theory set out by Casaubon in the preface to the Dee relation. Dee with his devils, and the fanatics whom Casaubon fulminated against, separated themselves from the body of Christian society, and rejected the voice of established authority. It was established authority which Casaubon was anxious to reaffirm, and schism in the widest sense which he hurried to disown; and witchcraft theory represented the casting out of illegitimacy, and the drawing together of all good Christians against a diabolical threat.

Casaubon's was a church which abhorred the schism of those outside its mantle, yet sought to evade responsibility for that schism, which put the scrupulosity of its opponents under the magnifying glass while turning a

---

[31] Meric Casaubon, *Of the Necessity of Reformation, in, and before Luther's time* (1664), 156. Laud called the Church of Rome a 'true' but not a 'right' church. See his *Conference with Fisher the Jesuit* (1639; 1901), 145–80. The thirty-nine articles refer to the bishop of Rome [xxxvii] and to the church of Rome having 'erred' [xix]. On Casaubon's father Isaac's career of principled moderation, standing between Rome and Geneva, see *DNB* and Frances Yates, *Giordano Bruno and the Hermetic Tradition* (1964), 398–431.

[32] Note that Casaubon uses the same sort of language he uses against witchcraft, *Necessity of Reformation*, 'To the Reader'. Cf. Henry Dodwell, *Separation of Churches from Episcopal Government, as practised by the present Non-Conformists, proved schismatical . . . The Sinfulness and Mischief of Scisme* (1679), esp. ch. 14, '*Separation* from the *Church* proved to be a *sin* against the *Holy Ghost*'.

blind eye to its own. 'Some course to beget a better union and composure in the minds of my Protestant subjects in matters of Religion'; this was the stated purpose of the 1668 bill for a comprehension. Some hoped that clemency and indulgence might wear out prejudices and reduce the dissenters to the unity of the Church. Others—often the very same people—worried that a comprehension would be 'a Toleration of the worst sort, as being seated not in the State only . . . but in the very bowells of the church'. How to maintain the unity of the church, understood as a divine community, with unity a necessary feature of the true way—this was the overriding anxiety of Restoration churchmen. 'How soon', wrote one, 'an offended God may *un-church* us', adding with striking emphasis, '*un-people* us'. Failing to woo those outside the church proper was perhaps schismatic; so too, however, was introducing dissension into the 'bowells' of the church. The paradoxes of the Restoration church were not to be resolved. They eventually dissolved, but in the mean time left patterns of seemingly conflicting clerical policy, irritability basking in the sunlight of its own supposed benevolence.[33] But witchcraft was one means of defining the legitimate community of the church by setting up its diabolical mirror image.

In Casaubon's case it is not so much the theological details and patterns of inversion which matter, as had been the case for Perkins, but rather the ecclesiological structure. The wickedest of schismatics are those who put themselves entirely in opposition to God's order, the enemies of God and man, the witches. No crime 'can be either more injurious to the Divine Majesty, or more pernicious to the community of men' than witchcraft.[34] By identifying a certain type of enthusiasm as tantamount to witchcraft, and, again, calling such men 'Saints . . . and *Schismaticks*', Casaubon is drawing the boundary within which the unity of Christ's church can be legitimately pursued, and diabolizing the excluded. The crime of witchcraft hedges the divine community, and binds together the community of men.[35] The relevance of witchcraft to what became, for some, the issue of comprehension, is manifested in Casaubon's work around the time of the Restoration. These matters acquired a particular

[33] Bodleian MS Tanner 40, f39, Bohun to Sancroft, 23 Jan. 1677; Adam Littleton, *Sixty One Sermons* (1680), 3 pts. in one vol. II. 237. See John Spurr, 'The Church of England, Comprehension and the Toleration Act of 1689', *EHR* 104 (1989), and id., *The Restoration Church of England, 1646–1689* (New Haven, 1991), esp. chs. 1–4.

[34] *Of Credulity*, 170.

[35] *A True and Faithful Relation*, 31. On comprehension, and Anglican approaches both to Presbyterians and Gallicans, see N. Sykes, *From Sheldon to Secker* (Cambridge, 1959), esp. chs. 3 and 4; id., *Church and State in the Eighteenth Century* (Cambridge, 1934), 18.

resonance in a period during which the unity of Christ's English church had been at least temporarily shattered. Such use of the witchcraft theme is to be found in later writers, right into the eighteenth century with authors like Daniel Defoe and Richard Boulton.[36] An analysis of Casaubon's work on witchcraft helps to define the bounds of possibility for witchcraft as ideology in a period in which the unity of the Christian community was endlessly contested, and a central feature of political debate.

CREDULITY AND CUSTOM

Casaubon's work on credulity was a contribution to an intellectual restoration intended to match that accomplished in the political sphere. It was one among many such projects. Traditional beliefs, like that in witchcraft, were to be rescued from sectarian hands. Moreover, a proper degree of credulity, and a belief in the operation of the supernatural and the marvellous, were essential to the continued security of the Royal state. This emerges from Casaubon's major work on witchcraft and the supernatural, *Of Credulity and Incredulity in things Natural, Civil, and Divine*, published in 1668. This publication was reissued posthumously in 1672 with a title which placed it firmly within the context of the burgeoning witchcraft debate, *A Treatise proving Spirits, Witches and Supernatural Operations*.

Casaubon's immediate target in *Of Credulity and Incredulity* is the threat of atheism. Those who refuse to believe in witches, devils, and the like, 'if not all Atheists themselves', are nevertheless helping to promote atheism, and are in turn aided by undoubted atheists.[37] Casaubon's avowed aim was to present witchcraft narratives as evidence to confute atheism, which was based on 'the not believing the existence of spiritual essences, whether good, or bad; separate, or united; subordinate to God, as to the supream, and original Cause of all; and by consequent the denying of supernatural operations'. But, *Of Credulity and Incredulity* should be seen not only as a blast against rampant philosophical atheism, but as a discourse on the grounds of belief in the wake of a severe disruption of social

---

[36] See Chs. 5 and 6 below.

[37] *Of Credulity*, 29. On the perceived threat of Hobbist atheism see Samuel Mintz, *The Hunting of Leviathan Seventeenth-Century Reactions to the Materialism and Moral Philosophy of Thomas Hobbes* (Cambridge, 1962); Daniel Scargill, *Recantation publickly made before the University of Cambridge (of which he was formerly a member)* (1669); Gilbert Burnet, *Some Passages of the life and death of . . . John earl of Rochester* (1680); Michael Hunter, 'The Witchcraft Controversy and the Nature of Free-Thought in Restoration England: John Wagstaffe's *The Question of Witchcraft Debated* (1669)', in *Science and the Shape of Orthodoxy* (Woodbridge, 1995). More generally, David Wootton, 'Lucien Febvre and the Problem of Unbelief in the Early Modern Period', *Journal of Modern History*, 60 (1988).

and constitutional order. This, surely, is why the work yokes together the
natural and the civil in its very organization.[38] It forms a sequel to
Casaubon's earlier work, the pre-war *Treatise of Use and Custome* (1638),
with its concern for custom as a foundation of true belief intensified by
the frightening innovations of the Civil War and Interregnum.[39]

In his preface to the reader, Casaubon apologizes for the delay in
producing *Of Credulity and Incredulity*, a work which he had first hinted
at in the preface to 'Doctor *Dee's* book'. The long gap between the two
(which were clearly associated in Casaubon's mind) was the result of
'other things, or cares, occasioned by that *miraculous* revolution of affairs
in this Kingdom'.[40] Casaubon even makes himself into an embodiment of
divine providence and of his own argument about wonders. A severe
illness had relented, allowing him to write something which would, he
wrote, 'be *incredible* unto many . . . I was unto my self, I am sure, a
wonder.'[41] From the very start the theme of miracles is established. The
works that had been published by Casaubon in the mean time, alongside
his renewed clerical duties, included the *Vindication of the Lord's Prayer*
(1660), and *Of the Necessity of Reformation* (1664), both of which had a
distinct political relevance. *Of Credulity and Incredulity* should be considered in the same light. The problems surrounding the doctrines of witchcraft after the Restoration were numerous. Prosecutions of the war years
had associated the persecution of witches with the Parliamentarian cause.[42]
The classic contractarian theory of witchcraft was set within the framework of an unmodish theology with dangerous affiliations.[43] Casaubon
had dealt with some of this in the preface to Dee's relation. What needed
more stressing, evidently, was the danger of incredulity, and the value of
customary belief. Thus, much of the work is a reworking of old arguments, with a new twist.

[38] *Of Credulity*, 7.

[39] Meric Casaubon, *A Treatise of Use and Custome* (1638). A note in the Bodleian Library's copy, Vet A2 e 295, says that the work was originally planned as 'A Treatise of Use
and Custome in things natural, civil and divine', presaging the title of Casaubon's later
book.

[40] My emphasis.

[41] *Of Credulity*, preface. Others, like the author of *The Doctrine of Devils*, were not so
sure, seeing instead 'some Old, Crazie-Brain'd, Doting, Melancholical, Hypochondriack
Dreamers in the Paroxysm of their Distempers', 178.

[42] See Samuel Butler, *Hudibras*, ed. J. Wilders (1663; Oxford, 1967), II. iii. 127–48 and
189–91; Zachary Grey in his edition of *Hudibras* (1744), II. 11; Francis Osborn, *Advice to a
Son* (1656), I. v. § 28, 176: '. . . and *Witches so abound*, as seems by their frequent Executions,
which makes me think the strongest Fascination is incircled within the *ignorance* of the
Judges, *malice* of the Witnesses, or *stupidity* of the poor Parties accused'.

[43] See discussion of Filmer in Ch. 1 above.

Casaubon's first argument in favour of belief in witchcraft reflects the purpose of the whole work. He admits that witchcraft accusations have been abused. A phenomenon is not to be jettisoned because of its abuse, however. This is 'a popular way indeed, and with vulgar judgments, of great force'. It is, nevertheless, 'the way to deny all *truth*, and to over-throw all government, and whatsoever is most holy among men'. Political epistemology is the keynote of the book and is allied with the notion of the *consensus generis humani*. Casaubon observes the value that this con-cept has already had to the confutation of atheism, used 'by ancient Heathens' and others 'to prove that there is a God'. The consent given has been wide, unpartisan, and material.

In the context of Restoration, consensus was a conservative argument, one which could be applied as much to kingship as to divinity. The links between a rational credulity in things natural, and allegiance to a consen-sual political order is made quite clear in the section which covers things civil. It is surely wondrous that 'a most godly religious Prince', Charles I, had been 'by his own Subjects . . . upon pretences of Justice and Reli-gion, massacred in cold bloud'. Having seen such a thing happen, how could anyone marvel at strange stories of cannibalism and parricide in faraway lands? One of the two recent martyrdoms of the English church—Laud's being the other—is to be given credit as a wonder, not rational-ized as an act of secular politics. Should we wonder at the miraculous nourishment of Romulus and Remus by wolves, when that martyr's own son, later to be Charles II, by a 'concatenation of providences' was 'lodged and fed in a Tree' preserving him for his own 'miraculous . . . *Restoration*'?[44]

Alongside the imperial swell of the comparison with Rome's founding fathers, the reader is being asked to assent to the myths that attend the restoration of order, as he must also assent to the existence of witches.[45] Regicide is as bad, and unbelievable, as cannibalism. The Boscobel oak is transformed into a nourishing she-wolf. The rhetoric works both ways. If you believe the Royal wonders, other wonders must be believed too; but

[44] Ibid. 165, 36, 199 f.
[45] Cf. John Evelyn, *Diary*, ed. E. S. de Beer (6 vols.; Oxford, 1955), iii. 246, entry for 29 May 1660, citing Psalm 118: 23: the Restoration is 'the lord's doing, *et mirabile in oculis nostris*'. The theme of witchcraft is also to be seen in a context of restoration in a pamphlet of 1660, *The English Devil: or, Cromwel and his monstrous witch discover'd at White-Hall: with the strange and damnable speech of this hellish monster, by way of revelation, touching king and kingdome; and a narrative of the infernal plots, inhumane actings, and barbarous conspiracies of this grand imposter, and most audacious rebel, that durst aspire from a brew-house to the throne, washing his accursed hands in the blood of his royal soveraign*. Restoration as divine miracle; Protectorate as conspiracy of diabolical intent and inspiration.

if you believe in supernatural wonders, the dynastic mythology deserves just as much reasonable credulity. Consensus helps general belief. For specific details of particular stories, Casaubon goes on to provide a set of rules, defining when one should be credulous, and when incredulous.[46]

This deployment of witchcraft belief in the service of a renewed political tradition, with Casaubon scorning 'that malignant humor of innovating', runs throughout *Of Credulity and Incredulity*. The whole repertoire is brought into play. Even the issue of God's permissiveness in relation to the commission of diabolical acts of witchcraft is given a political twist: 'How can they so much wonder at this, who know that God in all ages hath suffered, sometimes, as lately amongst us, eminently a wicked cause to prosper: and Godly men, his faithful Ministers and Servants; yea godly Kings and Princes (whereof our late most pious *Soveraign*, a rare example) to fall into the hands of the wicked?'[47]

Royal wonders are recounted again later in the book, with a more explicit reference to the grounds of belief. Casaubon tells of some 'extraordinary cures' effected by Charles I during his captivity on the Isle of Wight. These, if the stories are 'true, and certain' ought to be better known; and as the witnesses were 'persons of quality', Casaubon was 'apt to believe' them.[48] Yet, as with Christ himself, the proof is not in such individual miracles, but in the wonder of his whole life: 'We need no counterfeit miracles; his death, and his book [*Eikon Basilike*] are sufficient miracles to canonize him.' Part of the effect is to suggest the credibility of the miracles, since, if we need none, those we do report are unlikely to be concoctions. The parallel with Christ verges on the idolatrous—his death and his book, his word—and it is followed to its extreme:

they that could not, cannot yet be converted from their *rebellion* and *schism* (I may now add, *Atheism*) by *either*; I think I may say of them, that though one rose from the dead, or an Angel did appear unto them from Heaven, they would not be converted, or believe.

---

[46] *Of Credulity*, 199. See William Matthews (ed.), *Charles II's Escape from Worcester: A Collection of Narratives Assembled by Samuel Pepys* (Berkeley and Los Angeles, 1966). For the detailed rules, see *Of Credulity*, 159 ff., and note the summary, 172: 'it is the part of an intelligent reader . . . to consider the nature of the thing, and all the circumstances . . . [some] cannot be so thoroughly examined and searched . . . [while others are] not accompanied with convincing circumstances.' This is similar to what Casaubon says in the *Treatise Concerning Enthusiasme*, 'To the reader'.

[47] *Of Credulity*, 117 f.

[48] Ibid. 293 f. Cf. *A Miracle of Miracles: wrought by the Blood of King Charles the First, of happy memory, upon a Mayd at Detford foure miles from London, who . . . by making use of a piece of handkircher dipped in the Kings blood is recovered of her sight, etc.* (1649).

Atheism, schism, and rebellion are conflated as common enemies; and the definition of the proper bounds of credulity is a task performed in the defence of social order.[49]

From the late 1650s, through the Restoration and beyond, Meric Casaubon was concerned to reassert the claims of a sacral political order and cast out the schismatics who had disrupted the continuity of Church and State, and broken the bonds of Christian society. His publication of the Dee papers and his work on credulity were part of this campaign, which the Restoration only served to intensify. Witchcraft theory, both as a negative reinforcement of the good society, and as a relic of the old, divinely conceived political order, deserved its own restoration.

OPPOSITION

One of Casaubon's most ferocious opponents was John Wagstaffe, graduate of Oriel College, gentleman, and wit.[50] His *Question of Witchcraft Debated* starts out in resolutely political mode, with its opposition to standing armies, absolutism, and priestcraft. Witchcraft is a piece of deception practised upon the body of the people, not by poor old women but by men like Casaubon, 'wise Politicians, *famous in their Generations*, and very well experienced in the Nature of Man'. It is these people who have 'promoted these fears . . . and improved them for the designs of Government'.[51] There is a host of other ways in which Wagstaffe opposes everything that Casaubon stands for,[52] but it is his ideological reading of witchcraft theory that is most striking. In the second edition of his book, published in 1671, he makes a typically Hobbist query—'we ought chiefly to consider, *Cui bono*, that is for what end or advantage . . . [these things] were said and done.' He is insistent, as Temple was to be, upon the dangerous extremism, the enthusiastic passion of the subscribers to belief in witchcraft. Their doctrines are 'all bloody . . . full of dangerous consequence, unto the lives and safety of men'.[53]

Wagstaffe defends his book in its second edition as being 'agreeable to Scriptures, and in no wise contrarient to Church or State'. This Hobbesian

---

[49] *Of Credulity*, 294.

[50] On Wagstaffe, see Hunter, 'Witchcraft Controversy'.

[51] *The Question of Witchcraft*, 2, 70 f., my emphasis.

[52] He dismisses Plato, Casaubon's favourite philosopher ('who can read with patience, such notorious lies in Prose'), speaks irreverently of the 'notorious mistakes of our English [biblical] Translations', and refuses to accept the relevance of medical expertise in demonology, exposing 'want of knowledge in the Art of Physick' as one of the roots of the problem. See *The Question of Witchcraft*, 6, 66, and on Plato (2nd edn., 1671), 141.

[53] Ibid. (2nd edn.), 125, 147.

assurance is matched by his offering a parallel sort of witchcraft in state-craft, just like Hobbes's in *De Cive*, calling Calvin's reading of the prophet Nahum in evidence, Nahum who thought of witchcraft as a whole range of 'Plots and Arts which a great City useth to subdue her Neighbours'.[54]

In contrast to Casaubon, Wagstaffe was a ferocious critic of Popery. His first published work was an attack on the pretensions of the Roman Church, utterly divorced from Casaubon's healing efforts. The Papacy is construed as a demonic force. The Popes have 'possessed the minds of men' with 'notorious jugling'. Roman theology is 'aequivocal, and jugling . . . the *Cobweb subtilty of a wordy nothingnesse*'. Those who follow Rome are of a 'praepossessed understanding'.[55]

Wagstaffe redefines witchcraft as idolatry. In doing so he follows in a long tradition.[56] Assimilating the rhetoric of witchcraft theory to anti-Popery, his position is thus the mirror-image of Casaubon's. Casaubon uses witchcraft to support traditional authority, and to define a notion of Christian fellowship which can include Catholics and Protestants alike in the service of a true reformation. Wagstaffe exposes Casaubon's ideological stance and the political content of his plea for credulity. He has his own alternative ideological programme, and a use for the language of witchcraft, stripped of its superstitious accretions. The language and metaphors of witchcraft are to be redeployed against Popery, while, on a more literal plane, witchcraft is recategorized as exactly the sort of priestly imposture practised by the Roman Church he had attacked so vigorously in 1660, or even by Meric Casaubon himself. Wagstaffe's programme is rooted in heterodoxy; he inhabited what Michael Hunter has called a 'slightly risqué milieu'. Here was a Hobbist, an opponent of priestcraft and self-professed admirer of 'that thrice-renowned *Saracenical* Empire'. His opinions on witchcraft represent anything but the mainstream.[57]

Another opponent of Casaubon's was the radical physician John Webster. Webster and his *Displaying of Supposed Witchcraft* (1677) reveal the status of witchcraft theory after the Restoration in two distinct ways. First, like

[54] Ibid., preface and 27.

[55] John Wagstaffe, *Historical Reflections on the Bishop of Rome: chiefly discovering Those Events of Humane Affaires which most advanced THE PAPAL USURPATION* (1660), 4, 15, 26 f. In this book Wagstaffe also anticipates Henry Stubbe, another Hobbesian, in admiring 'the glorious proceedings, of that thrice renowned *Saracenical* Empire' (p. 38). Cf Casaubon's criticism of '*Enthusiastick Arabs*' in *Of Credulity*, 34. On Stubbe, see J. R. Jacob, *Henry Stubbe, Radical Protestantism and the Early Enlightenment* (Cambridge, 1983).

[56] Most recently, Thomas Ady, *A Candle in the Dark: Shewing The Divine Cause of the distractions of the whole Nation of ENGLAND, and of the Christian WORLD. That is, the Lord doth Avenge the blood of the Innocent upon the Inhabitants of the Earth* (1656).

[57] Hunter, 'The Witchcraft Controversy', 294 and Wagstaffe, *Historical Reflections*, 38.

Thomas Hobbes, and to an even greater extent, he shows us how 'sceptics' found it difficult utterly to discard the traditional categories of witch belief. However spiritualized, intercourse with the Devil remains part of Webster's world-view. Secondly, Webster's scepticism about witchcraft again rubs shoulders with marginalized heterodoxy. It is self-consciously a minority view, something which should alert us to the vigour of the theory of witchcraft in orthodox circles after the Restoration.

Webster's anti-papal polemic compares with Wagstaffe's. The subtext is, if anything, more subversive. Two 'beneficed Ministers' of the Church, namely Casaubon and Joseph Glanvill, have 'newly furbished up the old Weapons, and raked up the old arguments, forth of the Popish Sink and Dunghills'. There is an edge of radicalism to Webster's attack, pursued as it is 'without fear, or any great regard to . . . Titles, Places, or Worldly Dignities'. All in all, his approach seems to be in direct collision with Casaubon's. Where Casaubon uses witchcraft as part of a scheme of unity and restoration, Webster wants to reject witchcraft in a mood of truculence and a desire for further reformation.

If we ask who is the more mainstream of the two, the answer is quite clear. Webster is the mystic, the Grindletonian, he of the 'Familistical-Levelling-Magical' temper.[58] Belying the notion of experimental learning, he appears an alienated figure, having 'for many years last past lived a solitary and sedentary life' which involved 'more converse . . . with Books than with Men'. If Casaubon had been ejected in the 1640s and 1650s, Webster is now even more on the edge in the era of Restoration, having had 'a large portion of Trouble and Persecution in this outward world', being 'besmeered over with the envious dirt of malicious scandals', with 'the whole giddy Troop of barking Dogs, and ravenous Wolves . . . labour[ing] to devour me'. It is important in relation to Webster's writings on witchcraft to recognize this sense of isolation, far more intense than the rhetorical pose of the witchmongers who saw themselves fighting rampant atheism. 'The generality of an opinion,' Webster defensively maintains, 'or the numerousness of the persons that hold and maintain it, are not a safe and warrantable ground to receive it, or to adhere unto it.' Nor is it 'safe or rational to reject an opinion, because they are but few that do hold it, or the number but small that maintain it'.[59]

Yet the distance Webster is prepared to travel from orthodoxy—in a

---

[58] Christopher Hill, *The World Turned Upside Down* (Harmondsworth, 1975), 290, citing T. Hall, *Vindiciae Literarum* (1655).

[59] John Webster, *The Displaying of Supposed Witchcraft* (1677), the preface or introduction, epistle dedicatory, 13.

book refused an imprimatur by the ecclesiastical authorities but licensed
by the Royal Society—is ultimately very small. He does not dispute the
existence of witchcraft, but its nature. He cites Thomas Ady's notion of
witchcraft as idolatry with approval, but goes even further than him in
maintaining the formal aspects of witchcraft theory. Webster acknowl-
edges 'a spiritual and mental League betwixt the Witch and the Devil',
but 'other League or Covenant is there none'. This league is no mere
matter of form. Those who believe that the Devil acts for their benefit are
'fast bound' in a 'spiritual and implicit League'.[60] Witches are the Devil's
'Bond-slaves' and his children. There is no need for the farrago of a
visible contract since 'all those that are accounted Witches' are 'holden
fast enough by their own consents and corrupt wills'.[61] Yet Webster is
even prepared to admit that the spiritual league between witch and Devil
may be, 'in some respects and in some persons . . . an explicit League',
which is to say that the parties 'are or may be conscious of it'. Moreover
this is a crime 'wherein to free the guilty, and condemn the innocent, is
equally abominable to the Lord'.[62]

What then distinguishes Webster from the witchmongers, as he so
dismissively addresses them? He rubbishes the wilder stories, of 'carnal
copulation', the raising of tempests or transubstantiation into animal
form. But then, these are travellers' tales which many of the witchmongers
themselves disowned. The core of Webster's argument, as stated on the
title-page, is that there are 'many sorts of Deceivers and Impostors, and
Divers persons under a passive Delusion of Melancholy and Fancy'.
There is nothing new about this, or the recommendation to mercy. It is
very much the position taken by the sixteenth-century writer Johann
Weyer. In his account, Webster does make a clear distinction between
those who are imposters and cheats, 'active Deceivers', as he calls them,
and those who are merely under a 'passive delusion'. While the former
deserve to be punished, as witches, the latter need 'rather mere pity and
information'. Yet both appear to be, as far as Webster is concerned,
leaguers with the Devil.[63]

---

[60] Ibid. 67, 75. In a characteristic touch, Webster declares that 'under this spiritual
implicit League are also comprehended all those that are Witchmongers'.

[61] Ibid. 71, 76.   [62] Ibid. 73, epistle dedicatory.

[63] Ibid. 74: 'so all the several sorts of the Diviners or Witches mentioned in the Old
Testament, were under a spiritual League with the Devil, and did very well know, that what
they did, was not by the finger of God, but either by the help of Art, Nature, Leger-de-
main, Confederacy, or such like impostures and cheats'. The same is true for modern-day
conjurers, and there are others 'under this spiritual League, though implicitly, *as are all
those that we have granted to be passively deluded Witches*', my emphasis.

Webster's ultimate position is a radical breakdown of the traditional categories of criminal activity, positing 'an internal, mental, and spiritual League or Covenant betwixt the Devil and all wicked persons, such as are Thieves, Robbers, Murtherers, Impostors, and the like'. The criminal, tempted and allured by Satan, 'assent[s] and consent[s] unto the motions and counsels of the evil Spirit'. The implication here seems to be confusingly double-edged. Witchcraft is no special crime, but merely imposture instigated by the counsel of the Devil. On the other hand, all crime is witchcraft, in that all crime involves a league with the Devil. Webster's radicalism and his dangerous perfectionism are betrayed in this, 'for men are either the Temples of God, or the Temples of Satan and Antichrist'.

ALLIES?

The Civil War was not a turning-point for the intelligibility or plausibility of witchcraft theory. Political and ideological positions generated particular versions of credulity or scepticism: Filmer's broad-fronted opposition to contractarianism in theology, politics, and demonology, for instance. Witchcraft retained, all the while, a capacity to be reinvented, either radically as with Thomas Hobbes, or with more conservative intent for such as Meric Casaubon. The intellectual landscape had a place for witchcraft which it was difficult even for those of a sceptical disposition to eradicate. Even thinkers who rejected (often in perplexity) the metaphysical underpinnings of witchcraft theory needed some concept of witchcraft in social and religious theory. For Casaubon, both metaphysics and ideology demanded the reality of the witch. Traditional beliefs, refurbished, could come to the aid of a restored social and political order.

Casaubon's edition of Dee's relation was the first in a succession of books after the Restoration which vindicated witchcraft belief. The best-known is Joseph Glanvill's, successively enlarged from his initial *Philosophical Considerations touching Witches and Witchcraft* of 1666, through a variety of editions, like the fourth of 1668, entitled *A Blow at Modern Sadducism*, to the republication with additions by Henry More entitled *Saducismus Triumphatus*, which had in turn reached its third edition by 1700. Historians have analysed Glanvill's work in the context of the early Royal Society and the rise of the new science, Casaubon's bugbear, but it can also be seen as falling into much the same sort of defensive Restoration posture as Casaubon. Even on the issue of the new science, Glanvill and Casaubon are much closer than one might expect: for both the defender of the Royal Society and its arch-opponent, the key to a healthy natural philosophy is a due scepticism. Casaubon's main worry about the new philosophers is their sheer presumption, which he associates with the confident excesses of the civil war sects. It was one of Glanvill's primary aims to overturn such exuberant self-confidence, to oppose the '*proud and phantastick pretences* of many of the *conceited Melancholists* in this age', as he puts it in one place, or, in another, to make a vaunted 'Corrective of Enthusiasm'. From another direction this meant opposing the equally presumptuous 'Atheists, Debauchees, Buffoons', including 'Deriders of the belief of Witches and Apparitions' who had taken hold among 'the looser Gentry and the small pretenders to Philosophy and Wit'.[64]

Glanvill's works on natural philosophy, on the occult, and on religion were as much conditioned by the trauma of civil war as Casaubon's. Glanvill's response to the destruction of the 'Ancient Doctrine and Government' by fanatics and enthusiasts, and the subsequent assault by the irreligious, was to use the latest methods to restore it.[65] '*Mechanick Philosophy*', he wrote, 'yields no security to *irreligion*.'[66] In typical Anglican fashion, reason was to be loudly preserved, since nothing has done 'so much mischief to Christianity, as the disparagement of Reason, under pretence of respect, & favour to Religion'. But the method was to be that of 'Scepsis Scientifica: or, confest ignorance', a condemnation of the 'vanity of dogmatizing, and confident opinion'. The design of the new Royal Society was not 'to *cant* endlessly about *Materia*, and *Forma*', nor to 'hunt *Chimaera's*', nor to 'dress up *Ignorance* in words of *bulk* and *sound*'.[67] As Moody Prior has pointed out, Glanvill's commitment to the belief in witchcraft, paradoxical as it may seem, was part and parcel of this resolute scepticism, 'which took the form, not of the classical *epoché*— the suspension of belief—but the tentative suspension of disbelief'. An opposition to dogmatism led 'to an extreme of scientific skepticism that

---

[64] Joseph Glanvill, *Saducismus Triumphatus: or, full and plain evidence concerning witches and apparitions, the first part thereof containing philosophical considerations which defend their possibility. Whereunto is added, the true and genuine notion, and consistent explication of the nature of a spirit, for the more full confirmation of the possibility of their existence* (1681), preface, 48; [Joseph Glanvill], *The Zealous and Impartial Protestant, shewing some great, but less heeded dangers of Popery. In order to thorough and effectual security against it . . .* (1681), 44.

[65] Joseph Glanvill, 'Antifanatick theologie and free philosophy. [In a continuation of the New Atlantis]', in *Essays on several important subjects in philosophy and religion* (1676), 5.

[66] Joseph Glanvill, *Scepsis Scientifica: or, confest ignorance, the way to science; in an essay of the vanity of dogmatizing, and confident opinion* (1665), 'To the Royal Society'. He guards against the plebeian accent of 'mechanick' by stressing the efforts of the '*gentilely* learned and ingenious'.

[67] Ibid.

at times verged closely on credulity'. Glanvill and his associates were, according to Prior, willing to consider any hypothesis, treat any phenomenon seriously. Ruling anything out of scientific consideration was the vice of dogmatism.[68]

The ideological roots of this aversion to dogmatism can be traced back to the Civil War and Glanvill's reaction to the same anxiety as Casaubon. A multiplicity of over-confident opinionizers was, for both men, one of the great disasters of the years of civil discord. What is more, the content as well as the occasion of Glanvill's epistemology can also be seen in the same light as Casaubon's. 'Sight, Sense and Experience (upon which most Humane Knowledge is grounded) generally approved and certain, is our best argument'; this is the virtue of witchcraft as an argument for the existence of spiritual substance, and it is a virtue which Glanvill recognized and exploited.[69]

The anxiety about atheism and rejection of sectarianism fitted into a broader notion, for Glanvill as well as for Casaubon, of restoring order after a period of social and intellectual anarchy.[70] In the *Relation*, Casaubon had used witchcraft to define the outer boundaries of Christian society, diabolizing a major contemporary threat, enthusiasm, and its associated factionalism; in *Of Credulity* he had set up the intellectual markers for the restored order. Glanvill's image of the Christian community under threat comes at the very outset of *Saducismus Triumphatus*, and is one of walls, war, and exclusion. His aim is 'to secure some of the *Outworks* of *Religion*'. This makes explicit, if metaphorically so, exactly what we found in Casaubon: the use of witchcraft to define the outer boundaries of the Christian community. Men like Glanvill are concerned to 'maintain the Walls'. The sects have made breaches in them, and it is through these that atheism now enters 'by large strides', while they carry on 'venting their *Animosities* against each other'.[71] Much the same language was being used by Glanvill in the early 1680s, with a concomitant binding together of the civil and religious which witchcraft as an amphibious crime (prosecuted in the secular courts as a religious and civil offence against a

---

[68] Moody E. Prior, 'Joseph Glanvill, Witchcraft, and Seventeenth-century Science', *Modern Philology*, 30 (1932–3), esp. summary, 192 f. We must not, for instance, 'boldly . . . stint the powers of Creatures, whose natures and faculties we know not', *Saducismus Triumphatus*, 11.

[69] Casaubon, *A True and Faithful Relation*, 14. Sceptics about witchcraft 'are *both* best convinced by the proofs that come nearest the *sence*, which indeed strike our minds *fullest*, and leave the most *lasting* impressions'. The truth about witchcraft is to be known 'by Experiments that could not deceive', *Saducismus Triumphatus*, dedication, 1 f.

[70] *Saducismus Triumphatus*, preface.   [71] Ibid., dedication.

sacrally conceived state and society) itself implies. 'The Church of England is that which our Protestant Law-givers have erected . . . This is now twisted with our Monarchy, and the whole frame of our Civil Government: so that the overthrow of one, will be the destruction of both.' At this time of Popish plot and religious dissension, Parliament should be 'fasten[ing] our Foundations', and 'labouring to build up our almost ruined Walls, and to fortifie our Bulwarks'. A people had never been 'so Broken, so Divided'; and the great danger, the lure of Popery, was that it offered the image of a city like the psalmist's Jerusalem, 'that is at unity in it self'. Glanvill's solution is typical Restoration stuff: 'there is no way for us to come to any assurance against Popery, but by Union'.[72]

A few years later, across the Atlantic, and in the midst of the last outbreak of extensive witch-hunting in the English-speaking world, Cotton Mather resorted to the same sort of images as Joseph Glanvill. 'The Walls of the whole world are broken down,' he wrote. Mather's book *The Wonders of the Invisible World* consistently emphasizes the unity of Christians within the context of a besieged community, New England, 'once the *Devil's* Territories'. In this sense, its preface is less about witchcraft, and more about the need for Christian unity, even a meditation upon it. 'The Names of *Congregational, Presbyterian, Episcopalian*, or *Antipoedobaptist*,' he writes, 'are swallowed up in that of *Christians*.' The Devil's 'Hellish Design' is to bewitch and ruin the land, and 'all the Rules of Understanding Humane Affairs are at an end, if . . . we must not Believe the *main strokes* wherein those *Confessions* all agree'. The Devil and his witches are waging a 'War upon a people'; his business is 'Rooting out the Christian Religion from this Country'; the gravest problem is the '*Misunderstanding*, and so the *Animosity*, whereinto the *Witchcraft* now Raging, has Enchanted us'. Witchcraft is a purposely confusing business which creates dissension; for dissension is of its essence. Opposition to the effects of witchcraft, and to the Devil and his agents, means drawing together as Christians and as a people: ' 'Tis necessary that we unite in every thing.' The Devil's scheming is even construed by Mather in thoroughly political terms: 'the design of the Devil is to sink that Happy Settlement of Government, wherewith Almighty God has graciously enclined Their Majesties to favour us . . . Our Constitution . . . is attended with singular Privileges.'[73]

---

[72] Glanvill, *The Zealous and Impartial Protestant*, 2, 9, 24, 25, 26.
[73] Cf. Cotton Mather, *The Wonders of the Invisible World* (1692; New York, 1991), 67, 14, 12, 16, 18, 21, 24, 20.

Glanvill's concern with witchcraft has to be seen in the context of Restoration worries about intellectual order, the confusions of the past, and the lack of unity which is pulling the Christian order apart. In *Saducismus Triumphatus* itself, Glanvill finds himself 'astonisht sometimes to think into what a kind of *Age* we are fallen, in which some of the *greatest impieties* are accounted but *Bugs*, and *terrible Names*, *invisible Tittles*, Peccadillo's, or Chimera's'. The impieties he complains of, and binds together in one breath, are 'SACRILEDGE, REBELLION, and WITCHCRAFT'. The Devil, he writes, is a name 'for a *Body Politick*'; and when he observes that literally 'thousands in our own Nation have *suffered death* for their *vile compacts* with apostate spirits', he is implicitly referring back, yet again, to the dangers of civil war.[74]

This is by no means an exhaustive summary of Glanvill's ideological concerns and intellectual predispositions. It is instructive to look at his work on witchcraft in the light of Casaubon's, to identify a common genre, and confirm our idea of a refurbished witchcraft theory which could have taken part in a more general movement of intellectual restoration. With the emergence from a period of religious dissension and the splintering of authority, atheism is a major concern. Atheism was a complex business in the seventeenth century, not the simple speculative and detached intellectual position of the modern era.[75] With this in mind, it is striking to notice that for Glanvill atheists do not merely disbelieve in witchcraft, but are constructed of the very same stuff as witches. They are 'the common Foes, enemies not only to Religion, but to all Government, and Societies; to Mankind: and should be used as such'.[76]

EXPERIMENTAL KNOWLEDGE

By the early 1680s, Glanvill's attitude to the need for unity among Christians had become an unstable mixture of optimistic wooing and cussed anathemas. One dissenter whom he was prepared to praise, in particular for his 'excellent Catholick, healing indeavours', was the 'Reverend, Pious and Learned' Richard Baxter. Glanvill went so far as to see opposition to Baxter's healing endeavours as a diabolical plot, unable as he was 'to ascribe the ingaging of so many virulent pens against you, to any other

---

[74] *Saducismus Triumphatus*, preface, 35, 5.

[75] See e.g. the essays in Michael Hunter and David Wootton (eds.), *Atheism from the Reformation to the Enlightenment* (Oxford, 1992).

[76] Glanvill, *The Zealous and Impartial Protestant*, 44.

cause than the indeavours of Satan, [to] hinder the success which your powerful pen hath had against the Dark Kingdom'.[77] Baxter was the author of *The Certainty of the World of Spirits* (1691), whose format echoed *Saducismus Triumphatus*. Baxter's was an influential text in dissenting demonology.

Baxter agreed with Glanvill that the experimental route, in its widest sense, was the safest approach to knowledge. 'Experimentall knowledge only', he wrote, 'maketh truly wise', before waxing tautologically mystical, if still empiricist in emphasis: 'Only the Living know what Life is and only the Seeing know what Light and Sight are.' Similarly, he held that 'Experiences are contemptible to none but Atheists'.[78] The unwilling dissenter Baxter, for whom the Restoration settlement had ended in disappointment and exclusion from the established church, was none the less prepared to 'condescend' to the bishops for the sake of peace, and hoped for Christian unity via 'an Act for a larger Constitution of the Church of England'. In this he was at one with his very good friend Sir Matthew Hale.[79]

Baxter and Hale, Lord Chief Justice, were neighbours in Acton, and spent much of their time together discussing metaphysical issues. Above all, they debated the nature of spirit.[80] This is hardly surprising, given the tenor of Hale's extensive intellectual programme after the Restoration. Hale, in Dr Johnson's understatement, 'knew a great many other things' than law.[81] He was a prolific writer and a participant in some of the great

[77] *Mr J. Glanvil's Full Vindication of the late Reverend, Pious and Learned Mr Richard Baxter* (1691?).

[78] N. H. Keeble and Geoffrey F. Nuttall (eds.), *Calendar of the Correspondence of Richard Baxter* (2 vols.; Oxford, 1991), ii. 186, letter 994, Baxter to Hale, 2 May 1676; 161, 'To the Reader', Baxter's preface to Thomas Gouge, *The Surest and Safest Way of Thriving* (1676).

[79] Ibid., ii. 315, letter 1232, John Humfrey to Baxter. See also ii. 186, letter 994, Baxter to Hale, 2 May 1676: 'You go off the stage with more universall Love and honour than any man that English history ever mentioned that was no king'. Also Richard Baxter, *Additional Notes of the Life and Death of Sir Matthew Hale* (1682), 39: 'nor [should] Sects, Parties, or narrow Interests be set up against the common duty, and the publick interest and peace'. And Gilbert Burnet on Hale, *Life and Death of Sir Matthew Hale* (1682), 66: 'the *Heats* and *Contentions* which followed upon those *different Parties* and *Interests*, did take People off from the *Indispensable things* of Religion, and slackened the *Zeal* of other ways *Good men* . . . It also gave great advantages to *Atheists*'.

[80] 'We were oft together, and almost all our discourse was Philosophical, and especially about the Nature of Spirits and superiour Regions; and the Nature, Operations, and Immortality of man's Soul', Baxter, *Additional Notes*, 4 f. See also Richard Baxter, *Of the Nature of Spirits* (1682).

[81] James Boswell, *Boswell's Life of Johnson. Together with Boswell's Journal of a Tour to the Hebrides and Johnson's Diary of a Journey into North Wales*, ed. G. B. Hill and L. F. Powell (1791; Oxford, 6 vols.; 1934), ii. 158.

intellectual debates which followed the Civil War, in both political and philosophical thought. Once again, it is the business of restoration, of the renewal of order, which seems to have motivated him. He would have 'preferre[d] a Law by wch a Kingdome hath been happily governed four or five hundrd yeares' rather than 'to adventure the happiness and peace of a Kingdome upon Some new Theory of my owne', and this was a sentiment as relevant in natural philosophy as political theory.[82] The same is true of Hale's conviction that laws are 'the Production of long and Iterated Experience'.

Another subject of conversation at Acton was the philosophy of Aristotle,[83] whom Hale valued as a trusted authority and a guarantor of ideological order. Men of 'Wit and Parts', he thought, should not be 'too hasty or positive in exterminating the *Aristotelian* Philosophy, and entertaining new *hypotheses*, 'till they have fully and maturely considered, and *well looked about them*'.[84] The sense of looming intellectual anarchy, of civil disorder, is palpable. Hale was involved in experimental philosophy, opposing the Boylean solution of the Torricellian vacuum with a reformed Aristotelian model of fluid continuity;[85] in the natural history of man and the analysis of his immortal soul;[86] and in the composition of works of contemplative and practical divinity.[87] He was active in the campaign for a bill of comprehension in the 1660s. Most pertinent here, though linked to all these other activities, is his involvement in a witch trial of the early 1660s at Bury St Edmunds. The Bury trial is interesting both for the light it throws on how a witch trial could be conducted after the Restoration (especially in Bury, site of the notorious Hopkins trials in 1645); and for the forensic rhetoric which, under Hale's direction, it employed.

In many ways the 1662 case of Rose Cullender and Amy Duny in Bury St Edmunds was a model witch trial. Old women of low status were

---

[82] 'Reflections by the Lrd. Cheife Justice Hale on Mr Hobbes His Dialogue of the Lawe', in W. S. Holdsworth, *History of English Law* (1903–72), v. (1924), 504. For a 'rough draught', see BL Add. MS 18235.

[83] 'We neither of us approved of all in Aristotle; but he valued him more than I did.' *Additional Notes*, 'To the Reader'.

[84] Matthew Hale, *Difficiles Nugae; Or, Observations Touching the Torricellian Experiment* (1674), preface, my final emphasis.

[85] Ibid.; id., *An Essay Touching the Gravitation or Non-Gravitation of Fluid Bodies* (1673); id., *Observations touching the principles of natural motions* (1677).

[86] Matthew Hale, *The Primitive Origination of Mankind* (1677); id., 'The Secondary Origination of Man', BL Add. MS 9001, f21.

[87] e.g. *The Judgment of the late Lord Chief Justice Hale Of the Nature of True Religion* (1684), or his *Magnetismus Magnus* (1695), a divine meditation on magnetism.

abused, then accused by members of their local community.[88] Shortly
after the sentence had been read, most of the afflicted were relieved of
their ailments, textbook confirmation of the guilt of the convicted. Other
details were more theatrical. A toad in a blanket had exploded when
tossed in the grate; while a 'godly minister' sitting by one of the afflicted
girls 'suddenly felt a force pull one of the Hooks from his Breeches: And
while he looked, with wonder what was become of it, the Tormented Girl
Vomited it up out of her Mouth'.

In the course of the trial, the medical man Sir Thomas Browne, being
a 'Person of great knowledge', was 'desired to give his Opinion . . . and he
was clearly of Opinion that the persons were Bewitched . . . for he conceived that these swouning Fits were Natural . . . but only heightned to a
great excess by the subtilty of the Devil, co-operating with the Malice of
these which we term Witches, at whose Instance he doth these Villanies'.[89]
Like the expert whom Casaubon suggested ought to be present at witch
trials, Browne makes the necessary discrimination between natural and
supernatural.

Most striking, however, are the experiments upon which, as reported
in the pamphlet account of 1682, the trial centres. These involved the
witches in touching the girls, 'when they were in the midst of their Fitts,
to all Mens apprehension wholly deprived of all sense and understanding'. The result was that 'by the least touch of one of these supposed
Witches . . . they would suddenly shriek out opening their hands'. The
test was elaborated and the afflicted girls 'blinded with their own aprons'.
Then, however, an 'ingenious person' pointed out the possible experimental fallacy. Surely the children could have faked their movements,
guessing that the touch must be that of one of the witches?

Wherefore to avoid this scruple it was privately desired by the Judge, that the Lord
Cornwallis, Sir *Edmund Bacon*, and Mr Sergeant *Keeling*, and some other Gentlemen there in Court, would attend one of the Distempered persons in the farther

---

[88] See Thomas, *RDM*, ch. 16, 'The Making of a Witch', for the classic account.
[89] For Browne's views on demonology, see his *Religio Medici* (1642; Oxford, 1972), 32:
'I have ever believed (and do now know) that there are witches. They that doubt of these
do not only them but spirits, and are obliquely and upon consequence a sort, not of infidels,
but atheists', but, 'I do not credit these transformations of reasonable creatures into beasts,
or that the Devil hath a power to transpeciate a man into a horse, who tempted Christ—as
a trial of his divinity—to convert but stones into bread.' But see also the more cautious
remark in his commonplace book: 'We are noways doubtful that there are witches, but have
not always been satisfied in the application of their witchcrafts', cited in R. T. Davies, *Four
Centuries of Witch-Beliefs* (1947), 109.

part of the Hall . . . and *Amy Duny* was . . . brought to the Maid: they put an Apron before her Eyes, and then one other person touched her hand, which produced the same effect as the touch of the Witch did in the Court. Whereupon the Gentlemen returned, openly protesting, that they did believe the whole transaction of this business was a meer Imposture.

Hale spent much of his spare time in the 1660s conducting experiments to answer questions in pneumatics; here he was designing an *experimentum crucis* to solve a knotty problem in pneumatology, the science of spirits, the outcome of which 'put the Court and all persons into a stand'. The father of two of the victims, Mr Pacy, thought 'that possibly the Maid might be deceived by a suspition that the Witch touched her when she did not', an interpretation that 'was found to be true afterwards'. After her recovery, the young Miss Pacy asserted that she had understood the goings-on in court while apparently incapacitated. Thus, the victims, 'when they apprehend or understand by any means, that the persons who have done them wrong are near, or touch them . . . moved with rage . . . do use more violent gestures of their Bodies'. In fine, the experiment was 'rather a confirmation that the parties were really Bewitched, than otherwise'. As with so many experiments crucial to the experimental philosophy, the bare facts could construct various chains of plausible interpretation.[90]

One historian has seen the Bury St Edmunds trials as symptomatic not of a continuing belief in witchcraft, but rather of a Restoration crisis in the jurisprudence of witchcraft which heralded its demise. Barbara Shapiro's idea is that witches ceased to hang because of a new scepticism as to degrees of proof. She cites Hale's behaviour at the end of the trial in support of her thesis: 'the Judge in giving his direction to the Jury, told them, that he would not repeat the Evidence unto them, least by so doing he should wrong the Evidence on the one side or on the other.' According to Hale himself, in his *Pleas of the Crown*, a judge was bound to give the jury, 'in matters of fact . . . great light and assistance, by . . . weighing the evidence before them and observing where the knot of the Business lies; and by showing them his opinion even in matters of fact'. Why did Hale refuse to sum up in this witch trial? Did Hale's need to combat atheism

---

[90] *A Tryal of Witches Held at the Assizes held at Bury St. Edmunds* (1691), 42–8. For the underdetermination of theory by data, see e.g. Pierre Duhem, *The Aim and Structure of Physical Theory*, tr. Philip P. Wiener (1906; New York, 1962), ch. 6; and W. V. O. Quine, *From a Logical Point of View* (Cambridge, Mass., 1964), 42 ff.

overcome his 'commitment to the new methodology', creating a 'cognitive dissonance' which the refusal to sum up reflects?[91]

This seems unlikely. The pamphlet is clear that Hale was 'fully satisfied with the verdict'. It makes more sense to conclude that Hale refused to repeat the evidence and risk distortion precisely because the matters of fact themselves were so clear. Hale certainly recognized the problems in securing satisfactory evidence sufficient to convict, especially in the case of such crimes as witchcraft and, tellingly, rape 'wherein many times persons really are guilty. Yet such evidence as is satisfactory to prove it, can hardly be found'.[92] No sensible jurist considered rape an affair which should be immune from criminal proceedings. Why, given the belief in the possibility of bewitchment, should witchcraft have been any different? In the event of the submission of confusing evidence, where the knot of the business was too hard to unite, a weighing-up of evidence was necessary. Here, where the evidence was clear, where contradictory findings had been explained away, where witnesses were reputable, and where any network of collusion centring on the victims would have had to be almost unimaginably complex—in such circumstances, repetition of the evidence could be no more than mere repetition, a redundant exercise. Hale did in fact sum up, but not on matters of fact, which the community of the court had already legitimated through oath and witnessing; or on the bearing of those matters of fact as to a verdict, which was the jury's task; but on matters of belief and points of law. Hale's words made clear the prerogative and duty of the jurors:

they had Two things to enquire after. *First*, Whether or no these Children were Bewitched? *Secondly*, Whether the Prisoners at the Bar were Guilty of it? That there were such Creatures as *Witches* he made no doubt at all; For *First*, the Scriptures had affirmed so much. *Secondly*, The wisdom of all Nations had provided Laws against such Persons, which is an Argument of their confidence of such a Crime. And such hath been the judgment of this Kingdom, as appears by that Act of Parliament which hath provided Punishments proportionable to the quality of the Offence.[93]

[91] Barbara Shapiro, *Probability and Certainty in Seventeenth-Century England* (Princeton, 1983), 208. Francis Hutchinson is the source of this interpretation; see his *Historical Essay Concerning Witchcraft* (1718), 120; his notion was picked up later in the century, see memoir of George Onslow (1770), 14th Report of HMC, app., pt. ix, 480.

[92] See Matthew Hale, *The History of the Pleas of the Crown* (1734), 626–36 and Gilbert Geis, 'Lord Hale, Witches, and Rape', *British Journal of Law and Society*, 5 (1978), who also convincingly dates the trial to 1662.

[93] *A Tryal of Witches*, 58, 55 f.

The outcome of the trial was quite clear. As one writer put it at the beginning of the eighteenth century, the jury 'upon downright Testimony, and moral Demonstration of the Merit of their Case, brought them in guilty of Thirteen Indictments; and it must be very strange, if they could be mistaken in all'.[94]

Perhaps the most vital piece of evidence for Hale's attitude to the witch trial at Bury and, more importantly, for the place which that trial assumed in his intellectual programme, is the 'meditation' which he wrote after the trial, and which was published in 1693 as preface to a collection of witchcraft relations.[95] The purpose of this publication, according to its editor in the preface, was not 'to convince the Atheists and Sadducees of this Age', who if they are not convinced by other signs of divine providence, are already past saving; but rather, to gain 'a better Understanding of the Nature, Power, and Operations of these Spirits, of the Means by which they get Advantage against us, and of the Means whereby we may either prevent the same, or be relieved and extricated out of their Power', something which would be 'of no little Use and Benefit to Men'. The relation of the Bury trial, 'written by his [Hale's] Marshal . . . I suppose is very true, though to the best of my Memory, not so compleat, as to some observable Circumstances, as what he related to me at his return from that Circuit.' The editor himself points out that the composition of Hale's 'Meditation' immediately after the trial shows that he was 'well satisfied in it'.

Hale's mood in the piece is largely contemplative; his purpose is not to demonstrate the existence of evil angels, but to show that the exercise of their powers is limited by the admirable providence of God. In the language Hale chooses, and in his metaphors in particular, barely metaphors at all, we read the same sense of a Christian polity under threat as in Glanvill. The Devil threatens God's 'Invisible Oeconomy'. 'Impure Spirits' act as 'Rebels and Malefactors against their Lord'. This is just as it is in the secular world, where 'there is continual Diligence . . . by seditious turbulent minded Men to break the Peace of a Kingdom or City, or place.'[96] Witchcraft theory and political theory overlap and reinforce each other.

---

[94] Richard Boulton, *The Possibility and Reality of Magick, Sorcery, and Witchcraft, demonstrated, OR A Vindication of a Compleat History of Magick* (1722), 107.

[95] *A Collection of modern relations of matter of fact, concerning witches and witchcraft upon the persons of people.*

[96] Ibid. 5 f., 7.

For a wide variety of intellectuals after the Interregnum, witchcraft belief retained its vitality as a guarantee and definition of social, religious, and intellectual order. Witchcraft played well to a number of different audiences, and was a negative area of discourse upon which otherwise divided Christians could agree. 'It seems doubly grievous to me', wrote the Dutch Calvinist Balthasar Bekker in an examination of the religious economy of England, 'that the Protestant Church is split by such a thing as Nonconformism, yet finds itself at one in such inexcusable error.'[97] Perhaps only an outsider could properly recognize this aspect of Restoration witchcraft theory.

[97] Balthasar Bekker, *Engelsch verhaal van ontdekte tovery wederteid door Balthasar Bekker* (Amsterdam, 1689), 23 f. (a translation of and commentary on *Great News from the West of England* [1689]). Cited in Anna E. C. Simoni, 'Balthasar Bekker and the Beckington Witch', *Quarendo*, 9 (1979), 142.

4

Pandaemonium

Still the old Confederacy is kept up, tho under new Forms and Notions.

Richard Bovet, *Pandaemonium*, (1684)[1]

RESTORATION TO REVOLUTION

The last decades of the seventeenth century do not present a clear picture of a moribund witchcraft theory, gradually extinguished. Instead the usual mêlée of scepticism and advocacy is compounded by a sense of confusion. If some were, as the playwright Thomas Shadwell declared himself,[2] 'somewhat costive of belief', a determinate climate of opinion remains difficult to gauge. Some, like Joseph Glanvill, Richard Baxter, and Henry More, complained that witch beliefs were under threat, a state of affairs indicative of a more general undermining of the foundations of religious belief. Shadwell indicated, on the contrary, the activities of a 'prevailing party who take it ill that the power of the Devil should be lessened'.[3] In what sense was this party 'prevailing'? Whether or not it represented the majority of right-thinking people, it certainly included among its number figures of weight and distinction.[4]

---

[1] Richard Bovet, *Pandaemonium* (1684; repr. Aldington, Kent, 1951), 97.

[2] *c*.1642–92, member of Middle Temple; succeeded Dryden as poet laureate at the Revolution; Dryden's MacFlecknoe; a disciple of Ben Jonson's.

[3] Thomas Shadwell, *The Lancashire Witches* (1682), preface, in Thomas Shadwell, *The Complete Works of Thomas Shadwell*, ed. Montague Summers (1927), iv. 101.

[4] Further examples: Isaac Barrow, *Theological Works* (8 vols.; Oxford, 1830), iv. 480 ff.; George Hickes, letter to Samuel Pepys, in *Private Correspondence and Miscellaneous Papers of Samuel Pepys, 1679–1703*, ed. J. R. Tanner (2 vols.; 1926), i. 367–76; Pepys himself found Glanvill's work well-written if unconvincing; he thought the account of the Drummer of Tedworth worth reading, see Samuel Pepys, *The Diary of Samuel Pepys*, ed. R. C. Latham and W. Matthews (10 vols.; 1970–83), vii. 382 and viii. 589.

The Jacobean witchcraft statute of 1604 had entered into the body of the law, to be embroidered by the legal process. Robert Filmer's talk in his *Advertisement to Jury-Men* of the statute's 'favourable interpretation' at the hands of judges is an indication of how the practice of the law and the complexities of evidence necessitated that Parliament's Act be modified to accord with forensic reality. As one recent historian puts it, 'an indictment for witchcraft required either the death of the victim or proof of diabolical practices . . . an odd reading of the Jacobean legislation . . . but . . . one that had begun to be favoured in the 1630s, and which was revived after the peculiar circumstances of the Civil War and Interregnum cases.'[5] The problem of how to prove the crime of witchcraft worried legal minds. Legal approaches to witchcraft became, in this sense, more vexed in the course of the seventeenth century, although, intrinsically, the evidential problems offered by witchcraft were no more knotty than those of some rape cases.[6] This process had occurred quite early, however, with extremely low levels of conviction in the 1630s. These were only raised by the disruptions of the civil war period, which gave a jolt to the system of belief and law, and allowed for a relaxation of the laws of evidence.[7] Since the result was the manifest excesses of the Hopkins campaign in Essex, greater caution may well have been exercised after the 1650s; but it was exercised within the context of a thriving witchcraft theory.

There is much talk of the legal establishment's withdrawal from witchcraft prosecution as a key feature of decline. The example of Sir Matthew Hale, recognized even by his critics as the greatest lawyer of his generation,[8] was a powerful one to the contrary; having presided over the conviction of a witch in the 1660s, he was admired for his firm belief in witchcraft well into the eighteenth century. Against this, one might weigh the entrenched and influential scepticism of Sir John Holt, who tried cases in 1690, 1693, 1696, 1701, and seven others according to Francis

[5] Clive Holmes, 'Women: Witnesses and Witches', *P & P* 140 (1993), 50.

[6] *Pace* Gilbert Geis, 'Lord Hale on Witchcraft and Rape', *British Journal of Law and Society*, 5 (1978). In modern jurisprudence, insider dealing is similarly tricky in terms of evidence; as with witchcraft, the pact in question is 'closely made', and some legal authorities demand relaxation of the rules as to what is and is not admissible evidence.

[7] Particularly influential in the 1630s was the Lancashire outbreak of 1634, which ended in acquittals, see C. L'E. Ewen, *Witchcraft and Demonianism* (1933), 244–51.

[8] See e.g. Roger North, *The Lives of the Norths*, ed. A. Jessopp (3 vols.; 1890), i. §§ 80–98, for an account of this 'partial', 'demagogical', but 'very great lawyer'. Samuel Petto in *A Faithful Narrative of the Wonderful and Extraordinary Fits which Mr Tho. Spatchet . . . was under by Witchcraft* (1693) uses Hale, this 'Renowned, Cautious and Judicious Judge', as a witness for the reasonableness of witch beliefs, 'Epistle to the reader'.

Hutchinson, all of which resulted in acquittals.[9] Nevertheless, witches continued to be indicted and arraigned. Legal unanimity had yet to be secured.[10]

At a less exalted level of jurisprudence, consider the charge of a Surrey JP at the general quarter sessions at Dorking in 1692. Having dealt with crimes which are 'so frequently and so impudently perpetrated', Hugh Hare goes on to note others 'which may not improperly be ranked among the offences against Moral Justice'. These, however, are crimes whose proof is admittedly 'difficult' and which are, moreover, 'seldom practised'. Consequently Hare will 'but just put you in mind of them'. His outline of the attitude to the crime of witchraft is symptomatic and important. The jury is to 'enquire and present all Persons that have invocated, entertained or employed any wicked Spirit, or have used any Witchcraft, Charm, or Sorcery'. Such sins are 'of a very deep die', and punishable by death, both by 'the Law of God', and by the Jacobean statute. This straightforward instruction is modified by a demand for prudence. This is a matter in which 'full proof' is difficult to come by, and 'no Jury can be too cautious and tender in a prosecution of this Nature'. Nevertheless, 'where the evidence is clear and undeniable, you must proceed according to your Oaths'. While caution is crucial, while the crime itself is rare, it is, nevertheless, a crime by divine and human law, and must be rooted out whenever it is found.

Hare's words are an apt summary of the paradox that emerged: extremely infrequent prosecution, at or below the levels of the 1630s, accompanied by a robust, if contested, theory of witchcraft.[11] Witchcraft theory had been under assault since the sixteenth century; and, as Robert

---

[9] Sir Richard Rainsford, on the other hand, later to succeed Hale as Lord Chief Justice, presided over the conviction of Anne Tilling at Salisbury in 1672; see Ewen, *Witchcraft and Demonianism*, 356.

[10] See C. L'E. Ewen, *Witch Hunting and Witch Trials* (1929), 262 ff. and 43; id., *Witchcraft and Demonianism* (1933), considers the possible conviction and perhaps even execution of a witch in Northamptonshire in 1705, 381 ff. For issues of procedure, see *Witch Hunting and Witch Trials*, 52 ff. The final commitment was in 1717, at Leicester Assizes, a case thrown out by the Grand Jury, ibid. 44.

[11] *A Charge Given at the General Quarter Sessions of the Peace for the County of Surrey* (1692), 18 f. Hare's political persuasion seems to have been that of a solid churchman if nothing else, referring as he does to our 'Blessed Martyr K. *Charles*' (p. 26), and insisting that 'you are also to enquire and present all Persons that have depraved the Sacrament of the Body and Blood of our Blessed Lord and Saviour' (p. 19). In relation to those who swear and curse, Hare notes the forbearance of God in 'not consigning them . . . to that Devil whose Protection they so often invoke' (p. 7). His address was popular enough to be specially printed. For other, later, charges to grand juries, see Georges Lamoine (ed.), *Charges to the Grand Jury, 1689–1803*, Camden 4th ser. 43 (1992), 98, 358, 365, 377, 381.

Vilvain put it in an anti-sceptical work of the mid-1650s, 'the best is, only privat persons deny it: but al public Princes and Christian Common-wealths make strict Laws against it'.[12] Advice for those involved in trying witches continued to be offered in print. Richard Bernard's *Guide to Grand Jurymen* was reissued in 1680 and 1686; John Brinsley published *A Discovery of the Impositions of Witches and Astrologers* in 1680, virtually a reissue of Bernard; while Joseph Keble's *An Assistance to the Justices of the Peace* of 1683 repeated material from earlier authors like Lambard, Bernard, and Bolton without, moreover, any of their emphasis upon caution.

Even if we examine a familiar expression of the legal scepticism of the period, some ten years before Hare's jury charge, things are not quite as they had seemed. Francis North, Lord Chief Justice, writes to the Secretary of State, Leoline Jenkins:

Here [in Exeter] have been three old women condemned for witchcraft. Your curiosity will make you enquire of their circumstances. I shall only tell you what I had from my brother Raymond [Sir Thomas Raymond, his fellow judge on the circuit], before whom they were tried, that they were the most old, decrepid, despicable, miserable creatures that ever he saw. A painter would have chosen them out of the whole country for figures of that kind to have drawn by. The evidence against them was very full and fanciful, but their own confessions exceeded it. They appeared not only weary of their lives but to have a great deal of skill to convict themselves. Their descriptions of the sucking devils with saucer eyes were so natural that the jury could not choose but believe them.

The cocktail of melancholy delusions, superstitious fantasies, and miser-able decrepitude in North's tale is a common one in the sceptical litera-ture. There could not be a more compelling expression of what senior figures in the legal establishment were supposed to have been thinking about witchcraft by the 1680s. This sort of joshing ridicule was no doubt commonplace at the Inns of Court.

Nevertheless, North's further comments reveal a much more complex and tangled skein of political considerations. North was both judge and politician, the agent of a government pursuing a Tory campaign against the legacy of Whig opposition during the Exclusion Crisis. It is hardly surprising that in his tour of the South West, politics often came to the

---

[12] Robert Vilvain, physician, *Theoremata Theologica* (1654), 239, a passage attacking Hobbes's position on witchcraft in *Leviathan*, and citing in evidence 'Serjeant *Glyn* (who at last Lent Assises in *Cornwal*, condemned eight Witches upon pregnant presumptions and personal confessions) [and] can scientiously satisfy any Man, that ther be such impious confederats with Satan'.

fore.[13] With exquisite irony, he finds the county 'fully *possessed* against' the witches, and claims with politic determination that 'we cannot reprieve them without appearing to deny the very being of witches, which, as it is contrary to law, so I think it would be ill for his Majesty's service, for it may give the faction occasion to set afoot the old trade of witch finding, that may cost many innocent persons their lives, which this justice will prevent'.[14]

This complicated sentence conceals a complicated, perhaps not entirely coherent, train of thought. The tortured syntax reveals the dilemma which, for a start, denied an easy victory to the urbane ridicule of London lawyers: this is an account of a trial in which the witches were not released, but condemned and executed. If one were to unpick the threads of North's sentence, it would be to draw on three of them. First, when North says the denial of witchcraft '*as* it is contrary to law, *so* I think it would be ill for his Majesty's service, *for* it may give the faction occasion . . .', what does this succession of particles imply? They seem to point both towards a desire to stop any escalation of trouble, by yielding to popular superstition (North was involved in the prosecution of Jesuits during the Popish Plot, with similar purpose and to similar effect); and a suspicion that the abrogation of the law, in any area, by Crown authorities suspected of trying to stand above the law, might be exploited by the Whig opposition. As a Tory politician, North is presenting the machiavellian case for sticking to the law as it is, even when it is an ass. Secondly, there is an implied distinction between the denial of the very being of witches, an extreme position which North seems to distance himself from, and something else, namely the discovery of imposture. Confession, as in this case, does not allow for reasoned acquittal in the way that the investigation of supposed evidence does.[15] Finally, when North talks of saving the innocent lives of some, by sacrificing those of others, what does his reference to 'justice' really mean? Whether it is a nasty touch of irony, or a more unconscious piece of moral equivocation, it hardly suggests a clear-cut decline of witch beliefs in the 1680s.[16]

---

[13] Judges were 'as susceptible as others to the political passions of the early 1680s, when much of the 'justice' they dispensed was blatantly partisan', John Miller, 'The Late Stuart Monarchy' in J. R. Jones (ed.), *The Restored Monarchy* (1979), 43.

[14] *Calendar of State Papers, Domestic Series, 1682* (HMSO, 1932), 347, Aug. 19, Exeter: S.P. Dom., Car. II. 420, No. 24.

[15] e.g. North's displaying of imposture at a trial of a wizard at Taunton-Dean, *Lives of the Norths*, i. § 194. And cf. discussion of Filmer and confession in Ch. 1, above.

[16] The moral of North's story was tidied up in his brother Roger's biographical collections; the politics were left out. See ibid., §§ 191–3. See another version of North family witch-lore

North's fears that the 'faction' might use witchcraft to partisan political ends were not entirely fantastical. We can certainly find writers with Whig credentials embracing witch theory, and with political ends in mind. Scion of a radical Somerset family, Richard Bovet wrote *Pandaemonium* in 1684. In it, he uses witchcraft as a means to assault renascent Romanism, showing how acceptable and appealing witchcraft theory still was before the Revolution. For Bovet anti-popery is not a substitute for demonology; it is a special branch of it, and he compares 'the Idolatries of the Roman Church with those of the Ancients, and prove[s] by Natural Consequence, that Idol Worship is a Confederacy with Devils, and a practice necessarily promoting that detestable sin of Witchcraft'. Most of *Pandaemonium* is an attack on Romish superstition, at a time when Roman assault upon English godliness was daily expected through the offices of the Duke of York and his Jesuitical cronies. It is an assault on Romanism and its allies under another pretext; it presents itself as an attack on the sin of witchcraft. Popery is repeatedly assimilated to Devil-worship. It cannot be doubted 'that they who seek to the Devil in forbidden Images and Idols, will be ready to entertain him in a stricter Confederacy'. Priestcraft and diabolism are 'inseparable dependents one upon the other', and the empire of the Devil 'hath been *supported*, and *promoted* by the *Collusion* of his Priests, and the Reputation of the Priest hath been acquired by his converse, and intercourse with the Devil and his Oracles'. Bovet even, at one point, apologizes for his apparent digressions, asking that the reader pardon him for 'thus long exposing their Damnable Idolatry'. The point is that it is from this that, like a 'fountain . . . all other their Delusions, & wicked practises naturally flow'. Those who can be drawn, like Papists, to idolatry, the Devil 'may easily Impose upon to set up a Shrine' to himself, 'and enter into all the Mysteries of those Black and Diabolical Arts and Confederacies'.

Bovet held that the iniquities of the Restoration court, and the advance of Popery in the bosom of the English establishment, were, quite literally, diabolical. He uses witchcraft theory, to some extent at least, as the cover for an attack on Roman Catholicism. This is an argument for its continuing plausibility and appeal. It could hardly have been used as a way of

in *The Autobiography of the Hon. Roger North*, ed. A. Jessopp (1887), §§ 131–3. In this version of the Exeter story, the political anxiety again erupts, with force, if less specificity and no mention of the 'faction': 'A less zeal in a city or a kingdom hath been the overture of defection and revolution'. The last absolutely accredited execution for witchcraft took place under North and Raymond's aegis, at the Exeter Assizes, in 1684, at the start of James II's regime: see Ewen, *Witch Hunting and Witch Trials*, 43.

attacking Popery if it was without a semblance of credibility. Emphases might be modified, but the theory of witchcraft remained. 'Still', Bovet wrote in a phrase which might be a motto for the fate of ideas about witchcraft in following decades, 'the old Confederacy is kept up, tho under new Forms and Notions.'[17]

Francis North's association of witch-hunting with the 'faction' was a conscious reference back to the Civil War, typical of the political heat of the 1680s. Thomas Shadwell, at around the same time, felt professional anxieties as a playwright which paralleled North's as a lawyer and politician. Both were concerned with the prevalence and danger of political dissension. Factionalism was disrupting the operation of the law as well as the smooth-running of the theatre. Yet an interest in witchcraft was for Shadwell not so much a troubling throwback to the struggles of the 1640s as a useful distraction from the renewal of those troubles in the 1680s. Shadwell's problem as a writer had been that 'this unhappy division', the struggles between Whig and Tory, had meant that 'all run now into Politicks'. The bounds of comedy had been narrowed since, 'if you touch upon any humour of this time' you will necessarily 'offend one of the Parties'. '[T]herefore I resolved to make as good an entertainment as I could, without tying my self up to the strict rules of a Comedy; which was the reason of my introducing of Witches.' In other words, despite being himself 'somewhat costive of belief', despite recognizing the prevalence of the party of 'witch-mongers' like Glanvill and More, Shadwell hoped to use witchcraft as a non-contentious piece of theatrical entertainment, a spectacle which could not fail to grip his audience, of either party or none. The plot of *The Lancashire Witches*, despite the comedy, assumes the reality of witchcraft,[18] and in his preface to the published version Shadwell is disarmingly honest: 'the Actions, if I had not represented them as those of real Witches . . . the people had wanted diversion, and there had been another clamor against [him] . . . [he] would have been called Atheistical'. This is exactly the complaint North had made. If his colleague Raymond had not presented the actions of witches as real in his

---

[17] Bovet, *Pandaemonium*, 24, 35, 67, 97. Colonel Richard Bovet (not the author of *Pandaemonium*) was a radical in the 1650s, executed at Jeffrey's instigation in 1685, symbolically in front of Lord Stowell's house, whose lands he had sequestered in the Interregnum. I owe this information to Dr Jonathan Barry of Exeter University.

[18] Contrast Joseph Addison, *The Drummer; Or, the Haunted House. A Comedy* (1716), another play about witches and spirits: 'If e'er you smile, 'tis at some Party Stroaks | *Round-heads* and *Wooden-shooes* are standing Jokes; | The same Conceit gives Claps and Hisses Birth, | You're grown such Politicians in your Mirth! | For once we try (tho' 'tis, I own, unsafe) | To please you All, and make both Parties laugh', prologue.

courtroom, the people 'had wanted diversion, and there had been another clamor against [him] . . . [he] would have been called Atheistical'.[19]

In the courtroom and the playhouse witchcraft could still find an appreciative audience. North shows us how the topic of witchcraft might become politicized and open to use as part of a manœuvre by the 'faction' of Whigs and rabble-rousers. This was the absolute negation of what witchcraft theory had meant in the Restoration for Casaubon and his successors. Then it had been a negative symbol of the sacred unity of the community. North's suggestion that the faction might use witchcraft persecution to stir up trouble should not, however, be confused with the actual polarization of witchcraft as an issue, in itself. It is important to make this distinction, before going on, in the next chapter, to explore what happened when witchcraft did become definitively factionalized and associated with party labels, in the early eighteenth century. For, while North labelled witchcraft persecution as a manœuvre of democratical fanatics, he none the less recognized the need to avoid allowing the faction to turn it to political purposes, something from which the authority of the King's party could only suffer. Consensus on the issue had to be maintained, and that required the implementation of existing law, however embarrassing that might look to North's urbane colleagues back in the capital. Ironically, when witchcraft did become a party issue, decades later, it was the Whigs of the time who tried to pin this superstitious vulgarity onto Tories, rather than the other way round; and it was high-flyers and their associates who were concerned to use witch beliefs politically, to bolster the claims of a sanctified establishment.[20] Shadwell, incidentally, with his theatrical use of witchcraft, mimics the function of witchcraft theory for Restoration writers like Casaubon; he uses it to overcome the divisions within his audience, to create a unity of response in the playhouse, which the political divisions of the 1680s had denied to Shadwell's usual comic vehicles, fops and knaves, vanities and knaveries.

North was neither a secret believer in witchcraft, nor even a reluctant sceptic. It is quite clear from the tone of his letter to Jenkins that both he and his correspondent saw something ridiculous in the pursuit of old women and fantastical stories about saucer-eyed devils. Nevertheless, there is a current of confusion and moral ambiguity running through the letter—absent in Roger's later accounts—which suggest that witchcraft is still more than a joke. Whatever North believes in his heart of hearts, as

---

[19] Shadwell, *The Lancashire Witches*, preface, 99, 101.   [20] See Chs. 5–7 below.

a 'privat person' (Vilvain's phrase)—and it is difficult to know whether he rejects most accusations of witchcraft in practice, or the very existence of witchcraft in principle (his phrase about denying 'the very being of witches' suggests a distinction between degrees of scepticism about witches)— witchcraft is still part of the ideological landscape. It might be taken up and used as an instrument of policy by the 'faction'. Hence the equivocation of a politician trying to maintain a viable constituency and manage nascent public opinion. Witchcraft theory is not dead. It has a rationale, plausibility, and intelligibility. It is not, to adopt Dr Johnson's phrase, beyond the need for rational confutation. It has an audience. It has its uses. Hence North's irony and detachment—his 'real' beliefs, inasmuch as they are betrayed in that letter—are inconclusive. There had always been sceptics, more or less, from the very enactment of the Elizabethan legislation against witches. This sceptic was operating in a political environment in which witchcraft still made some sort of sense as a crime. How and when did this cease to be so?

If witchraft theory was embedded in the ideology of Restoration, in the work of Casaubon and his successors, how can it be understood in relation to the Revolution which succeeded it? Is it more than coincidental that after the Glorious Revolution there were no more executions for witchcraft in England?[21] Witchcraft theory, it has been suggested, was closely related to conceptions of the relationship between the secular and spiritual domains, and functioned as the negative image of a positive vision of a Christian polity. Surely, then, the change of priorities which the settlement of 1689 entailed must have altered witchcraft's position within prevailing ideological configurations. While the settlement achieved after the Revolution did not immediately establish a secular understanding of state and society, or even open an inexorable path towards such a development, it did weaken the ideal of a confessional political community which Reformation and Restoration theorists had lauded.

Some eighteenth-century commentators certainly saw things this way, binding together the issue of witchcraft with that of the confessional monopoly of the old regime. A 1750 charge to the Norfolk grand jury noted:

---

[21] John Trenchard and Thomas Gordon, *Cato's Letters*, 3rd edn. (4 vols.; London, 1733), iii. 90–118 (19 May–2 June 1722), 115: 'since the *Revolution* there has not, as I remember, been one Witch hanged, nor do I think that one Lawyer in *England* would condemn one, or any special Jury of Gentlemen find her guilty; though we are often told, and if we may judge by other Effects, have Reason to believe, that *Satan* is as busy now as he has been in the Memory of Man.'

It is at this Time no offence to be a Witch but to pretend to be so which is very penall by ye 9 Geo:2d so that it is now established as the indefeasible Right of every man that he may worship Almighty God in the Way he Judges most Worthy of him provided he does not disturb or Endanger ye Peace of the Society.

Seventeen years later another Norfolk charge told how the laws against witchcraft had been 'pleasantly got rid of . . . by this it is that our Religion wh always accompanys Civil Liberty & Freedom of thought is Establishd'.[22]

One way of examining the connection between the establishment of religious pluralism and the demise of witchcraft theory is by considering how witchcraft fitted into the world-view of a key Whig philosopher, John Locke.[23] If Locke was by no means a crucial figure in the pragmatic defence of revolution, nor the founder of a consensual tradition which sprang out of revolution and supplied the rationale for the Whig ascendancy of the eighteenth century, he was nevertheless a substantial figure within Whig mythology. It is Jonathan Clark who has encapsulated Locke's role in the eighteenth century most eloquently, as a philosopher 'revered, if at all, as a Whig household god, rather than deployed in real political battles'.[24]

Locke's epistemology, set out in *An Essay Concerning Human Understanding*, was extremely influential, if suspect, setting the terms for debate in succeeding decades. Locke presented his work as a modest part of the revolution in natural philosophy, posing as an 'Under-Labourer . . . clearing the Ground a little, and removing some of the Rubbish, that lies in the way to Knowledge'.[25] Nevertheless there was one piece of 'rubbish' he did not remove. Despite the bogey of materialism which attached itself to Locke, he retained as part of his world-view the spiritual ontology which underpinned, and was in turn underpinned by, witchcraft theory.[26]

If early eighteenth-century England was still a society poring over the Caroline divines, to adopt a phrase of J. C. D. Clark's, and if 1688 marked

---

[22] Lamoine, *Charges to the Grand Jury*, 365, 381.

[23] For the debate on Locke's relationship to the Revolution, see the introduction to John Locke, *Two Treatises of Government*, ed. P. Laslett (Cambridge, 1960); J. P. Kenyon, *Revolution Principles: The Politics of Party 1689–1720* (Cambridge, 1977), 2 and *passim*; John Dunn, *The Political Thought of John Locke* (1969), 8 and *passim*; Richard Ashcraft, *Revolutionary Politics and Locke's 'Two Treatises of Government'* (Princeton, 1986), *passim*.

[24] J. C. D. Clark, *English Society 1688–1832* (Cambridge, 1985), 50.

[25] John Locke, *An Essay Concerning Human Understanding* (1690), 'The Epistle to the Reader'.

[26] *Pace* John Yolton in his *Thinking Matter: Materialism in Eighteenth-Century Britain* (Oxford, 1984), 3 ff. and see below.

no definitive triumph for the tolerationism of Locke and his allies, Lockian arguments for a division between religion and civil society none the less came to acquire increasing plausibility. The *Letters on Toleration* which set out such ideas are at once prophetic and emblematic, both generally and, implicitly, for witchcraft theory. If theories of witchcraft, including those of Restoration England, were embedded in notions of the relationship between the secular and religious realms and jurisdictions, and the nature of a dedicatedly Christian polity, then the Revolution and its aftermath must have had some effect on the foundations of witchcraft theory, upon its functions and its plausibility. We have seen how, at the Restoration, witchcraft theory was rescued from the disrepute into which the Civil War and Interregnum had thrust it. The Revolution in itself did not signal an inexorable move away from the post-Reformation ideals of a Christian polity in which witchcraft theory was rooted, but it was an important step on the way to resolving the paradoxes and difficulties which the Restoration church had faced. The vision of a national church increasingly gave way to the fact of fragmentation, just as the eirenic fantasies of Erasmian divines on the European stage had been overtaken by political reality.[27] This is not to say that the vision disappeared altogether, only that in the battles fought between 1689 and 1715 a muted tolerationism was the victor, and witchcraft belief one of the victims.

WITCHCRAFT, GOVERNMENT AND HUMAN UNDERSTANDING

Richard Boulton, author of one of the last treatises to defend witchcraft theory, was very much a Lockian. A physician, he studied at Brasenose College, Oxford, in the 1690s. Early in his career, he sought John Locke's support in his application for a college scholarship.[28] He also wrote to Hans Sloane, secretary of the Royal Society and associate of Robert Boyle, seeking his patronage.[29] In an early publication, Boulton attacked

---

[27] See Hugh Trevor-Roper, 'Laudianism and Political Power', in *Catholics, Anglicans and Puritans: Seventeenth-Century Essays* (1987), esp. 51–60. The 'atmosphere of ecumenical hope', as Mark Goldie describes it ('John Locke, Jonas Proast and Religious Toleration 1688–1692', in John Walsh, Colin Haydon, and Stephen Taylor (eds.), *The Church of England c.1689–c.1833: From Toleration to Tractarianism* (Cambridge, 1993), 162), which attended Leibniz's conversations with Bossuet in 1684, demonstrates how persistent such ideals were; much the same is true with regard to national ecumenism in England well into the 18th c.

[28] The Mordaunt scholarship, which he did not win; Boulton later secured a Frankland scholarship; *Locke Correspondence*, vi. 375 f., 384 f.

[29] BL Sloane MS 4058 ff47–9.

Charles Leigh's views on the heat of the blood and action of the lungs. In 1698, he was employed by Charles Goodall, of the College of Physicians,[30] to attack, in print, some opponents of the college: John Colbatch, Johannes Groenvelt, and the pseudonymous Lysiponius Celer. Goodall promised, in return, to advance the young man's medical career in London. Things did not work out, and the unlucky Boulton, smarting at what he saw as his betrayal by Goodall, took his complaints before the public in the form of an open letter.[31] In 1713 and 1714 he published further medical treatises, less polemical in tone, on gout, scrofula, venereal disease, and fevers in general. These he dedicated to the very grand physician, Sir Richard Blackmore.[32] Whether a footnote in medical history, a no-hoper, or an intellectual nonentity, Boulton would have been of little interest to us had he not published, only a year after these serious efforts of 1713 and 1714, a book he no doubt intended as something of a potboiler, *A Compleat History of Magick, Sorcery, and Witchcraft*.

It was not just a potboiler, however, for Boulton's work became the germ of the last great witchcraft debate in England.[33] That Boulton's zealotry about witchcraft emerged from such a progressive natural philosophical milieu should not, by now, surprise us. Here was a physician who had written an epitome of Robert Boyle's philosophical writings;[34] who hoped to lay down 'the Rules of Mechanical Operations in a Human Body' and to supply a 'Rational Account of . . . Distempers';[35] a protégé of John Locke and Sir Richard Blackmore. Most tantalizing of all is the prominent citation of Locke on the title-page of the *Compleat History*, promising 'a Judgment concerning *Spirits*, by the late Learned Mr JOHN LOCKE'. An excerpt from the *Essay Concerning Human Understanding* is duly inserted in the preface.

Boulton's appropriation of Locke is intriguing. Could he, in good faith,

---

[30] A friend of Locke's, see Ashcraft, *Revolutionary Politics*, 591.

[31] Richard Boulton, *Treatise concerning the Heat of the Blood* (1698); [Charles Leigh], *Remarks on Mr Richard Bolton's piece concerning the Heat of the Blood* (Manchester, 1698); Richard Boulton, *A Letter to Dr Charles Goodall* (1698); Richard Boulton, *An Examination of Mr John Colbatch his Books* (1698). On this dispute see Harold J. Cook, *The Decline of the Old Medical Regime* (Ithaca, NY, 1986).

[32] Richard Boulton, *Physico-Chyrurgical Treatises* (1714, individual treatises with title-pages dated 1713); see Richard Blackmore's own *Discourses on the Gout, Rheumatism and King's Evil* (1726).

[33] A debate discussed at greater length in Ch. 6, below.

[34] Richard Boulton, *The Works of the Honourable Robert Boyle, Esq. Epitomiz'd* (4 vols.; 1699). See also his *The Theological Works of the Honourable Robert Boyle, Esq; Epitomiz'd in Three Volumes* (1715).

[35] *Physico-Chyrurgical Treatises*, preface.

have co-opted the philosopher of the new science *par excellence* to his defence of witchcraft belief? We can look at this question in two ways. Witchcraft has been seen as an effective focus for a comprehensive view of a Christian society which drew in all believers against an external, or externalized, enemy. How does this use of the notion of the witch relate to Locke's views on the relationship between the religious and the secular? Then again, Boulton evidently felt that his views on the reality of spiritual operations had some grounding in the doctrines of the new philosophy; he explicitly cites Locke's concept of spirit in support of his thesis. How did Locke's view on spirit relate to the witchcraft debate?

There was a long-standing association between witchcraft and toleration dating from the Civil War. If Puritans in the early seventeenth century had diabolized Popery, the sects were diabolized by their opponents in the 1640s. In the case of Thomas Edwards, author of the celebrated *Gangraena*, this meant more than simply accusing sectaries of being in league with the Devil. The very notion of toleration was a devilish invention, 'a meanes either to keep his [the Devil's] old possession, or being cast out to enter in again'. Edwards's position recalls that of authors of witchcraft tracts who placed rhetorical emphasis on scepticism as tantamount to witchcraft itself. Defining Christian society in opposition to a diabolical outsider, as the traditionalists did, one did not even require real witches; sceptics would do just as well, as we saw with Robert Wylie in Chapter 1. In what might be called a second-order phenomenon, sceptics are loaded with the attributes of witchery, defined as being outside society and as paradoxical evidence for the Devil's presence in the world, a presence they themselves deny or belittle.[36]

John Locke distanced himself from this sort of demonization. Over more than a year, he discussed with his Dutch remonstrant correspondent Philip van Limborch both the forthcoming publication of Limborch's *Historia Inquisitionis*,[37] and the well-known case of Balthasar Bekker. This Dutch Calvinist minister had been censured and prosecuted by his church for publishing a work, *De Betoverde Weereld*, in which he denied spiritual agency in the world, and the operations of witches and devils. The case was a particularly striking one, if only because the Dutch had been precocious in abandoning the actual prosecution of witches. Indeed, the

---

[36] Thomas Edwards, *Gangraena: or a Catalogue and Discovery of many of the Errours, Heresies, Blasphemies and pernicious Practices of the Sectaries of this time* (1646), 123; cf. William Prynne, *The Quakers Unmask'd, and clearly detected to be but the spawn of Romish frogs* (1655).

[37] (Amsterdam, 1692).

witch 'craze' never really reached the Protestant Netherlands. Bekker's treatment is therefore an apt and especially pure case of what we have called the second-order phenomenon, involving virulent attacks on those who deny the being of witches as well as or, in Bekker's case, rather than witches themselves.[38]

Bekker's book applied Cartesian reasoning to the notion of spirit. He assessed the credit of supernatural relations in the light of a careful epistemological framework which balanced reason and revelation. Spirits cannot act in the material world without having material bodies. As Limborch understood Bekker's argument, 'The one foundation for this opinion of his is a concept of spirit derived from Cartesian philosophy, which certainly identifies spirit with thought, but goes no further. As for thought, it cannot operate in any way outside itself; its operation is wholly immanent.' Limborch presents the case as one admirably suited to have applied to it the method outlined in Locke's *Essay*, which 'would be most profitable reading, especially for those people who build an entire system on some concept that is not sufficiently full and distinct'.

For Limborch, Bekker has an impoverished and 'inadequate concept of soul', which he is using as if it were adequate. He regrets the author's 'imprudence', which 'has provoked harsh judgments in the part of his fellows, some of whom do not hesitate to decry him as an atheist'. But, despite his disagreements with Bekker, the force of the letter is to declare the virtues of tolerance.[39] Bekker is not to be condemned out of hand, since 'not every error is associated with impiety'. Limborch finds the reaction of the Dutch church to Bekker's work 'a strange way of rooting out errors'.[40] His initial letter to Locke moves on from the Bekker case to Limborch's own 'account of the Holy Office', a tolerationist work which, in setting out the mechanism and horrors of the Inquisition, includes the persecution of supposed witches.[41] Locke was evidently sympathetic to Limborch's efforts against 'ecclesiastical tyranny'. His reply is full of wry touches, as he asks the fate of that man 'qui tam *mira* docuit de angelis in libro suo de Spirituum existentia', the use of the word *mira* gesturing

---

[38] *De betoverde weereld* (Amsterdam, 1691–3). See also, *Le Monde Enchanté, ou Examen des communs sentimens touchant les esprits* (Amsterdam, 1694); *The World Bewitched* (1695) (both include vol. i of Bekker's work and a synopsis of vols. ii–iv); and *The World Turn'd Upside Down* (1700; a translation of Bekker's own abridgement). On Bekker see, most recently, Jonathan Israel's discussion in his *The Dutch Republic: Its Rise, Greatness, and Fall 1477–1806* (Oxford, 1995), 925–33.

[39] *Locke Correspondence*, iv. 295–8, 17/27 and 21/31 July 1691. Translations by editor.

[40] Ibid. 301, 27 July 1691.

[41] Limborch, *Historia Inquisitionis*, bk. 3, ch. 21

ironically towards the *mira* and *miracula* of traditional demonology and pneumatology. Bekker himself has performed a wonder, having 'experienced his brethren's zeal . . . pro religione pro veritate pro Orthodoxia';[42] and, in another glance at wonders: 'Mirum si impune evadat', it would be a wonder if he escaped scot-free.[43]

Locke and Limborch shared an opposition to persecution as essentially unchristian wherever it occurred. For Locke, 'persecution is the same everywhere and plainly Popish; for any church whatsoever lays claim in words to orthodoxy and in practice to infallibility'.[44] Limborch's emphasis was a little different, as he detested persecution not 'because it is Popish, but because it is contrary to the spirit of the Christian religion; so, whether Rome or Geneva sets it up, for me it is alike condemned'.[45] Limborch and Locke's sarcasm at the expense of those who persecuted Bekker, their ridiculing of the Calvinists' zeal against those who denied witches and demons, indicates that witchcraft theory, even in the abstract, was not something they had any wish to defend. Moreover, Limborch, by including the persecution of witches in his *Historia Inquisitionis*, implicated it in the more general phenomenon of Popish persecution. Nevertheless, his assertion that not *all* errors are associated with impiety does imply that at least some are. Some theological errors *are* bound up with impiety. Limborch's is not some diffuse commitment to all-out toleration. Rather, the witch is being marginalized from the sort of discussion of toleration in which Locke and Limborch were engaged. The witches prosecuted in the past were innocent victims of persecution; and Locke and Limborch did not believe in the persecution of those who were sceptical about witchcraft either.

There is more to it, however. The existence, within Christian society, of individuals who engaged in the sort of impiety—diabolical contract— punished by the laws against witchcraft, was something that fitted very well, as we have seen, into the Restoration Christian discourse of men like Casaubon. The concept of the witch coupled the secular and the religious together in a way which contributed to his arguments. The witch was an inversion of godliness which could define acceptable society. The crime of witchcraft was a *religious* crime, an offence of impiety, prosecuted in a civil court. Witchcraft was an activity which commingled absolute hostility to both society and religion, government and divinity. For traditionalists like Casaubon, and even for Hobbes, the monarch was a similarly

---

[42] *Locke Correspondence*, iv. 329, 14 Nov. 1691.
[43] The same phrase recurs in a later letter: 'Si evasit mirum est', ibid. 400, 29 Feb. 1692.
[44] Ibid. 402, 29 Feb. 1692.   [45] Ibid. 695, 16 June 1693.

mixed conception, *persona mixta cum sacerdote*, a mortal god. The royal theorist of witchcraft, James I, had encountered witchcraft as a particular threat to divine monarchy.[46] Locke's vision of society, and of the relationship between the religious and the secular was utterly different. As Richard Ashcraft puts it, Locke's defence of 'liberty of conscience against the claims of all forms of political authority . . . necessitated an absolute separation between the sphere of religion (which was defined by its concernment for the eternal salvation of the individual's soul) and the sphere of politics (whose province extended only to men's estates and civil interests)'.[47] 'I regard it as necessary above all', Locke wrote, 'to distinguish between the business of civil government and that of religion, and to mark the true bounds between the church and the commonwealth.' These bounds are, on each side, fixed and immutable. The boundary which Locke established was very clear. 'The commonwealth', he wrote, 'seems to me to be a society of men constituted only for preserving and advancing their civil goods.' Or again, 'the whole jurisdiction of the magistrate is concerned only with these civil goods, and . . . all the right and dominion of the civil power is bounded and confined solely to the care and advancement of these goods.'

Locke takes, as Ashcraft underlines, the high road of toleration; but his scheme is hedged by exceptions. Those, for example, who deny God's existence, 'are not to be tolerated at all'. For an atheist, 'promises, covenants, and oaths, which are the bonds of human society, can have no . . . sanctity'. In Locke's view, 'the taking away of God, even only in thought, dissolves all'. In general, 'no doctrines, incompatible with human society, and contrary to the good morals which are necessary for the preservation of civil society are to be tolerated by the magistrate'.[48]

Neither of these exceptions, however, vitiates the division between the secular and the religious in Locke's radical treatise. The requirement for civility itself is fairly basic. Society is a matter of pacts between men; and pacts are only reliable if men hold to the belief in God. Only the God-fearing feel compelled to tell the truth. And God himself remains very firmly outside society. Contrast this with the mystical presence of God in the state advanced by James I, or the representative model canvassed by Hobbes. We make no sort of contract with God in Locke's system. This

---

[46] See Stuart Clark, 'King James's *Daemonologie*: Witchcraft and Kingship', in Sydney Anglo (ed.), *The Damned Art: Essays in the Literature of Witchcraft* (1977).

[47] Ashcraft, *Revolutionary Politics*, 496 f.

[48] John Locke, *Epistola de Tolerantia* (1689), ed. R. Klibansky (Oxford, 1968), 65, 67, 134, 130 (translations by editor).

in itself removes the rationale of inversion which lay behind so much witch theory, and even Hobbes's position on witchcraft relies on a witch who, despite delusions of power and deranged claims to real intercourse with the Devil, sets herself up against God and mortal god, the divinity and his representative.

Locke's point about doctrines which are contrary to the preservation of society relates to witchcraft much as does Limborch's belief in the possibility of impiety. It is self-evident that, if witches did exist, they would not be tolerable within civil society, since they actively spurn God and consort with the father of lies. Behaviour more likely to disrupt society could hardly be imagined.[49] Nevertheless, the symbolic appeal which the witch had, as amphibian denizen of the secular and sacred jurisdictions, was necessarily dissipated by the Lockian conception of society and toleration.

A measure of the difference between Locke and the apologists for witchcraft belief is his attitude towards Christian sects. 'The name of Christian', he wrote, 'may include different religions.'[50] One need only compare this with Casaubon's attempts to bring all religious parties together to see the different conceptions at work. To underline this contrast further, consider the work concerning toleration which Locke produced during the years before 1688, as a contribution to what Ashcraft calls 'Shaftesbury's revolutionary political movement'.[51] This was a manuscript written by Locke and his fellow radical James Tyrrell, replying to Edward Stillingfleet's notorious sermon of May 1680, 'The Mischief of Separation'. The emphasis on unity within an established church opened up the threat of Popish intrusion as far as Locke and Tyrrell were concerned: 'I see not where it can end . . . for by this way of reasoning [we must] . . . for unity sake . . . be brought under one universal monarchy'.[52]

The argument advanced here is that we can explain Locke and Limborch's relaxed attitude to Bekker, and the lack of interest in the pursuit of witches or witch-advocates it suggests, by looking at the social and religious theory of these proponents of toleration. If we were working from Locke's system outwards, we would not *expect* him to find the witch

---

[49] Cf. Pierre Bayle, 'Réponse aux questions d'un provincial' (1703–7), in *Œuvres Diverses*, iii., pt. 2 (The Hague, 1727), 562 f.: 'Les Tolérans les plus outrez ne peuvent rien dire en faveur d'un . . . sorcier' (the most extravagant tolerationists can say nothing in favour of . . . a witch).

[50] *Epistola*, 151. Cf. Richard Burthogge, *The Nature of Church-Government, Freely Discussed and set out* (1691), 31, 'the Churches of Christ . . . subsisted by themselves like so many little Republicks'.

[51] Ashcraft, *Revolutionary Politics*, 490.   [52] Cited ibid. 496.

an appealing concept. So the binding together of the issues of toleration and witchcraft belief—suggested not only by the conjunction in Locke's correspondence, but also literally by the original arrangement of Locke's papers now in the Lovelace collection—is not a matter of the humanitarian toleration of difference, but something more fundamental, a wholly other notion of the very differences which separate the sacred from the profane.[53]

If there is any area in which the tolerance of Locke can be said to have been stretched, it was in his treatment of Popery. However indulgent Locke or his contemporaries were, they were unable to tolerate, in any real sense, the admission of Roman Catholicism into the fabric of the state. This had, indeed, been one of the points of the revolution of 1688 and the subsequent settlement, just as it informed the political to-ing and fro-ing which ended in the Protestant Hanoverian succession of 1714. The interface between witchcraft and Popery within English religious and political discourse is well worth exploring; for it is precisely here that we find one of the keys to the fate of talk about witchcraft after the Revolution.

Popery and diabolism were, of course, inveterate partners in English Protestant apologetic. Both John Wagstaffe and his precursor, Thomas Ady, had defined witchcraft as idolatry, and hence equated Popery with witchcraft. Their intentions were sceptical, and witchcraft of the supernatural kind was left out in the cold. We have seen how Richard Bovet used his non-sceptical equation between witchcraft and Popery to condemn the political trends of the mid-1680s. Locke appropriates much of the rhetoric of the witchcraft discourse in his *civil* discourse of anti-popery. Roman Catholics are not objectionable as heretics, a religious and authoritarian category, but rather as 'subjects to a Prince that has declared enmity and war to us', owing their primary allegiance to 'another prince . . . of a foreign jurisdiction'.[54] As the *Epistola de Tolerantia* puts it, 'that church can have no right to be tolerated by the magistrate which is so constituted that all who enter it *ipso facto* pass into the allegiance and service of another prince'.[55] The notion of entering the allegiance of a spiritual enemy—the Devil—is replaced by that of allying with the Pope, a *religious* figurehead but, for Locke, an emphatically secular power. Catholicism is not to be tolerated, and on *political* grounds. Catholicism,

---

[53] Locke had materials about the Aikenhead blasphemy and Renfrew witch cases, originally in 'a bundle of MSS. on the subject of Toleration', Francis Horner, *Memoirs and Correspondence*, ed. L. Horner (1843), i. 487.

[54] Cited in Ashcraft, *Revolutionary Politics*, 503, 496.   [55] *Epistola*, 132.

with all its horrors (dominion by grace, absolutism, equivocation) re-places the witch as the defining outsider. This reflects a difference in conception of what society is. Moreover, it is striking that besides the transfer of rhetoric, and the conceptual substitution which this implies, the Pope is a figure defined by the same secular-cum-religious ambigui-ties which constitute the witch. Catholic allegiance to the Pope involves a dangerous elision of two categories, the civil and the religious. Drawing this out, we can identify Locke's use of Popery as a demonstration of the pernicious nature of such a confusion; and contrast it with the tradition-alists' use of witchcraft to yoke together the civil and the religious. Both concepts are vital focuses of the notion of difference, delimiting the boundary of the socially acceptable, the body of good citizens.

If the tolerationism of Locke and his associates, and the separation of the civil and religious spheres, removed the potency of the witch as symbol, much of the ontology of demonology remained unassailed by Locke's philosophy, as Richard Boulton realized.[56] There is a hint of this from Locke himself, in a letter to Nicolas Toinard, biblical scholar and a regular correspondent of Locke's, dated 14 October 1681. Locke asks Toinard to ask M. Bernier whether 'among the Eastern peoples, Turks as well as Pagans, there is any sorcery, ghosts, oracles and so on. Also, if the Devil appears to these people as he does in America, Lapland, and other pagan lands'.[57] Locke's conception of Christian society may have denied a role for witchcraft in a Lockian system; but he saw no objection to the *possibility* of diabolical intervention in the pagan world. He did not rule it out.[58] The *possibility* of spiritual operation was, as Boulton realized, left

---

[56] Though contemporaries worried about the possibility of Spinozism in Locke's work, see Yolton, *Thinking Matter*, 4.

[57] 'Je vous prie aussi de saluer de ma part Monsieur Bernier et de vous informer de lui si il y a parmi les Orientaux tant Turcs que Paiens, quelque Sorcelerie. Spectre, Oracles, ett et si le Diable se fait vaire a ces gens la comme en lAmarique, la Lapponie et autre part parmi les paiens.' My translation, *Locke Correspondence*, ii. 454. François Bernier was a traveller whose *Histoire de la revolution de l'empire du Mogol* (1670) is listed in Locke, *Works* (1823), x. 529, 'A Catalogue and Character of most Books of Voyages and Travels'.

[58] Cf. James Vernon, *Letters . . . to the Duke of Shrewsbury by James Vernon Esq., Secret-ary of State*, ed. G. P. R. James (3 vols.; 1841), ii. 302 f., 8 June 1699: 'I told the Bishop of Worcester [probably Stillingfleet] that his diocese is infected with notions about witches; he intends his clergy shall rectify their mistakes in that particular . . . He don't much contro-vert the power of devils in the Gentile world, and their extraordinary operations may still take place among the Pagans. He is inclinable enough to believe what some authors have writ of the strange effects in such places; but he thinks the Gospel, as far as it reaches, has destroyed the works of the devil . . . a man may be so profligate as to give himself to the devil, but he can have no assistance from him to hurt any body else in a supernatural way'. See also Richard Burthogge, *An Essay upon Reason, and the Nature of Spirits* (1694), 18 f.

intact by Locke's highly non-committal ontology.[59] Locke was at pains to
emphasize that we, as created beings unacquainted with the reality of
substance, have 'As clear an Idea of Spirit as Body': 'The Notion of Spirit
involves no more Difficulty in it than that of Body'.[60] Elsewhere he is
concerned lest the 'consideration of spirits' should come before 'the study
of matter and body'. Of neither will we be able to 'make a science'. The
study of spirits is rather 'an enlargement of our minds towards a truer
and fuller comprehension of the intellectual world, to which we are led
both by reason and revelation'.[61] In the *Essay* itself, Locke constructs a
traditional hierarchical chain of being which draws part of its rationale
from the differing levels of epistemological insight among created beings.
It is not 'to be doubted that spirits of a higher rank than those immersed
in flesh may have as clear ideas of the radical constitution of substances
as we have of a triangle'.[62] He makes the same point in his *Discourse of
Miracles*, that 'we know good and bad angels have abilities and excellen-
cies beyond all our poor performances or narrow comprehensions'.[63]
Following orthodox practice, Locke made sure to limit the power of all
created spirits, since 'wherever the Gospel comes, it prevails to the beating down the strong holds of Satan, and the dislodging the prince of the
power of darkness, driving him away with all his lying wonders'. For
surely 'it cannot be supposed God should suffer his prerogative to be so
far usurped by an inferior being, as to permit any creature, depending on
him, to set his seals, the marks of his divine authority, to a mission
coming from him'.[64]

Locke differs from the apologists for demonology not least because he
demotes it within the general run of religious discourse. Glanvill, More,

---

[59] Cf. John Beaumont, geologist and FRS, *An Historical, Physiological and Theological
Treatise of Spirits, Apparitions, Witchcrafts, and other Magical Practices* (1705), 337: 'our late
Mr *Lock*, in his Elaborate *Essay on Humane Understanding*, has fairly made out, that Men
have as clear a Notion of a Spiritual Substance, as they have of any Corporeal Substance,
Matter, or Body; and that there is as much Reason for admitting the Existence of the one,
as of the other; so that if they admit the latter, it is but Humour in them to deny the
former'. For similar Lockian arguments, see also *The Witch of Endor: Or, a Plea for the
Divine Administration By the Agency of Good and Evil Spirits. Written some Years ago, at
the Request of a Lady; and now Reprinted with a Prefatory Discourse, Humbly Addressed to the
Honourable Members of the House of C—s, who brought in their Bill (Jan. 27) for Repealing
the Statute of I Jac. Cap. 12. concerning WITCHCRAFT* (1736), 95 ff.

[60] John Locke, *An Essay Concerning Human Understanding* (1690), ed. P. Nidditch (Oxford,
1975), i. 297 f., § 5; 313, § 31.

[61] 'Some Thoughts Concerning Education' in *Works* (10 vols.; 1823), ix. 6, 205, 182 f.

[62] *Essay*, ii. 124, § 23, 'A Reflection on the Knowledge of Spirits'.

[63] 'A Discourse of Miracles' in *Works* (1823), ix. 264.

[64] Ibid. 261 f.

Boyle, Hale, and the rest had seen witchcraft as an eminently concrete instance of spiritual operation which could point us towards God. Locke, as pedagogue, disagreed. Having gently introduced the idea of God to a child, taught him to pray to him, to praise him and to recognize his good works, 'forbear any discourse of other spirits', Locke wrote. He is emphatic on this point, insisting that while 'what is to be known more of God and good spirits, is to be deferred', as for evil spirits, 'it will be well if you can keep him from wrong fancies about them, till he is ripe'.[65] It is dangerous to rely on stories of evil spirits to point towards God. This is more than a mere aversion to chapbook vulgarity. Children oppressed by the threat of evil will end up wishing 'to ease themselves of a load, which has sat so heavy on them'. They will 'throw away the thoughts of all spirits together, and so run into the other, but worse extreme'.[66]

All in all, Boulton's conscription of Locke to the cause of witchcraft belief seems misguided. Yet it should be clear that, as far as spiritual agency in the world was concerned, Locke was no devotee of Sadducistic modernism.[67] His scepticism was far more permissive in relation to demonic agency than that of Francis Hutchinson. This interpretation supports one of the major theses of this book, that the disappearance of witchcraft belief cannot be plausibly explained by the supposed triumph of a mechanistic world-view.

The absence of witchcraft theory in Locke's work indicates a different attitude towards the relation between the secular and divine realms in political theory; compare Hobbes—materialist in ontology, but possessed of a theory of witchcraft. Whatever the arguments about the pertinence or otherwise of Locke's theories to the Revolution settlement and perceptions of it, it cannot be denied that his vision of a separation between the civic and sacred realms, highly contested as it was, came to have increasing relevance, especially after the failure of the last assault on the citadels of Whiggery, between 1710 and 1714. Toleration proper may not have been achieved until the 1820s; but the ideal vision of a single great Christian society was moribund. Thus, in theory at least, 1689 was a date of great significance for the ideological fate of witchcraft; but what of the last years of Queen Anne, when the issues of 1689 were fought out in the centres of power for the last time? How did the 'rage of party' influence the history of witchcraft?

George Berkeley produced his *Treatise Concerning the Principles of Human*

---

[65] Ibid. 129, § 137; 131, § 138.   [66] Ibid. 184.

[67] Compare the remarks of his close associate and friend, Jean Le Clerc, in his review of Bekker's work in *Bibliothèque Universelle et Historique*, xxi. (Amsterdam, 1691), 149 ff.

Knowledge in 1710, as the rage of party was reaching its apogee. In this book, he effectively shifted the guarantee of spiritual substance from experimental evidence (as witch cases had been considered) to the surer ground of hard metaphysical necessity.[68] He sought to convince 'those who are tainted with scepticism, or want a demonstration of the existence and immateriality of *God*, or the natural immortality of the soul'. In this he was at one with Boyle, More, and Glanvill or, more recently, John Beaumont, geologist and FRS.[69] His methods, however, were very different, and that difference reflected the shift in intellectual assumptions which had occurred by 1710. Witchcraft no longer seemed a singularly effective argument for the activity or existence of spiritual substance in the world. This is not to say that Berkeley's shift of emphasis left no place for witchcraft in his world-view. 1712 saw a renewal of the debate about witchcraft in England; and when a similar occasion had occurred in Ireland in 1711, Berkeley appeared, cautious but firm, as a supporter of witch beliefs. He wrote a letter:

I shall at present trouble you only with the perusal of the enclosed relation the facts it contains are attested in several letters from very good hands that were present at the Tryal. Some of which I have seen. Particularly Dr. Coghil Judge of the Perogative [*sic*] Court has received an account of the whole sent him by Dr. Tisdal a very ingenious divine who was in Court while the evidence upon oath of several credible persons were given in. So that you may depend upon it this paper tho' but sorrily writ has nothing in it which was not sworn to and after the nicest examination thought true by the Court. The letters mention some other circumstances which still make the story more surprising, and are not to be accounted for without some preternatural power. This is certain that the eight women are condemned. The judges were Upton & Macartney, of whom the former is said to be greatly prejudiced against all belief of witches, and Dr. Tisdal (who had been a Fellow of our College) seems to me the most unlikely man in the world to be imposed on in an affair of that nature, into which he has strictly inquired. I know not what credit this is likely to meet with in London. For my own part as I do not believe one in a thousand of these stories to be true, so neither on the other hand do I see sufficient grounds to conclude peremtorily against plain matter of fact well attested.[70]

---

[68] Although that metaphysical necessity was, ultimately, based on an extreme version of empiricism, for which see the first sentence of part one, George Berkeley, *A Treatise Concerning the Principles of Human Knowledge* (Dublin, 1710). Later on Berkeley writes that 'it is plain we cannot know the existence of other spirits, otherwise than by their operations, or the ideas by them excited in us', George Berkeley, *A Treatise*, in *Works*, ed. A. A. Luce and T. E. Jessop (9 vols.; Edinburgh, 1948–57), ii. 107.

[69] Beaumont, *An Historical . . . Treatise of Spirits* (1705).

[70] Berkeley, *A Treatise Concerning the Principles of Human Knowledge*, preface. The letter is addressed to Percival and dated 14 Apr. 1711, printed in *Works*, viii. 46.

Berkeley's words show us how difficult it still was to jettison witch beliefs entirely, even as the philosopher was constructing a more reliable antidote to atheism. The particular story may be surprising; one in a thousand stories may be nonsense; yet if the evidence is compelling, if the prejudiced are convinced, the evidence nicely examined, Berkeley is still willing to entertain the credibility of the case. Witchcraft is not outside the pale of rational belief. As with Hugh Hare, the justice of the peace cited above, there is a profound sense of caution; but at the same time a recognition of the reality of the crime. In the case of Hare we have a general charge to a jury, something essentially theoretical; here, with Berkeley, we have something even more compelling. Men of wit and parts in the eighteenth century could accept the reality of the crime of witchcraft in an abstract way, but they were also prepared to follow their logic through to the the messy business of an actual trial. The difficulties involved in the crime of witchcraft necessitated caution, as had been recognized from the late sixteenth century,[71] but this did not vitiate the legal standing of the crime, nor, ultimately and no doubt rarely, the imperative for prosecution. Witchcraft was still a matter in which 'plain matter of fact well attested' might convince.

[71] As e.g. in France, see Ch. 9 below.

5

Party-Causes

These Doctrines have often been made Party-Causes both in our own and other Nations. One side lays hold of them as Arguments of greater Faith, and Orthodoxy, and closer Adherence to Scripture, and calls the other Atheists, Sadducees, and Infidels. The People easily fall in with such popular Pretences; and not only those that stand in the Prosecutor's way, and a few suspected Persons are sacrific'd, but sometimes Governments are shaken, if they oppose their Notions. Our present Freedom from these Evils are no security, that such a Time may not turn up in one Revolution or another.

Francis Hutchinson, *An Historical Essay Concerning Witchcraft* (1718)

INTRODUCTION

The ideological uses and appeal of witchcraft survived the Restoration despite the absence of anything which could be dubbed a witch 'craze' after the 1640s; and despite the discredit which the perceived affiliation between witchcraft persecution and both Puritan dogma and threatening disorder could draw down on witch beliefs. Witchcraft theory, in the hands of very different men like Thomas Hobbes, Meric Casaubon, and Joseph Glanvill, was remarkably resilient and adaptable to changing circumstance. It fitted in with broader, non-partisan conceptions of the nature of social order, and the relationship between the religious and secular realms. Witchcraft in English society, as in others before and since, was a negative representation and, arguably, a negative reinforcement of the ideal vision of society. Agreement as to the nature and identity of the paramount enemy of society—the witch—could reinforce consensus about the values which the community could agree to share. In particular, in English society and, indeed, in Christendom more generally, this meant that the witch's nature as a social *and* religious criminal was significant. The continuing relevance of witchcraft to a wide range of English intellectuals after the Civil War indicates a continuing commitment to a vision in which religious identity and civic identity merged, the product of a society scandalized by the idea of schism and still harking back to a vision of a unified Christendom—a unity to be achieved by sovereign fiat, intellectual tinkering, natural philosophical enquiry, sincerity of striving, somehow or other.

This consensual attachment to witchcraft disappeared, in a process which is best described on two interacting levels. First of all, the positive vision of society of which witchcraft was a negative representation became ever less compelling. Successive political settlements and debates (Royal indulgences, a stymied Toleration Act unaccompanied by the desired comprehension, the failure of the Harleyite ministry at the end of Anne's reign, and the triumph of Walpolean Whiggery) vitiated any serious design for the recreation of a Christian polity which might be defined by a shared set of religious fundamentals. The Reformation was coming home to roost, and the result was a half-hearted and stumbling pluralism.

Secondly, and in the very years of Robert Harley's crisis-torn ministry, particular events contrived to make witchcraft no longer a device of consensus, but rather an occasion for ideological dispute and, what is more, a symbol of it. So, at the same time as the positive vision of a Christian polity was having its last fling, the negative version was being rendered unattractive and self-defeating, a focus for dispute rather than a healing salve.

In subsequent chapters, an examination of the afterlife of witchcraft, and the ideological crannies in which witchcraft lurked up to the dissolution of the old regime around 1830—high-flying, Scottish, methodist, Hutchinsonian—serves to confirm and strengthen this interpretation of its demise.

WITCHCRAFT AND DISSENT

'Dissenting circles maintained a belief in witchcraft longer than others.' Barbara Shapiro's remark follows in a long tradition, one that dates back to commentators in the seventeenth century itself.[1] Francis North, as we have seen in the last chapter, made a political point about the association

---

[1] Barbara Shapiro, *Probability and Certainty in Seventeenth-Century England* (Princeton, 1983), 322. See also Thomas, *RDM* 581.

between witch-hunting and dissenters. He reinforced the connection between witch-hunters and dissent made in the Civil War by pointing to
the way in which, in the 1680s, history might, heaven forbid, repeat itself.
The 'faction' could use witch-hunting as a political tool. It was a commonplace from the late sixteenth century on that the hotter sort of Protestant was as apt to see witchcraft in misfortune, as Providence in good
tidings. Those who opposed both the persecution of witches and the self-
righteous separatism of the sects were happy to ridicule the two at once,
particularly relishing the equation between Popish superstition and Puritan excess which this established. If exorcism was a relic of Roman
darkness, for many churchmen the expulsion of devils from possessed
individuals by prayer and fasting did not seem much different.

Thus, the possession scandals of the 1580s and 1590s—centred on the
Puritan 'exorcist' John Darrell, deplored and manipulated by Samuel
Harsnet, future Archbishop of York[2]—were resurrected in a pamphlet
controversy of the 1690s concerning the 'Surey Demoniack'. Zachary
Taylor[3] complained that dissenters were pretending to cast out demons in
order to underline the superior spiritual efficacy of their ministry. The
case of the Surey Impostor, as Taylor called it, seems to have been almost
a blow-by-blow re-run of the possession cases of the late sixteenth century within a new context of what had become, since the Toleration Act
of 1689, quasi-legitimate sectarianism. In this body of 'Rhodomontado
Dialogues', this 'Rapsody of Fanaticism', this farrago of 'Romantic
Fancies', Taylor detected an attempt to promote fanaticism and, what is
more, a disturbing affinity between dissenting narratives and Popish leg-
end. The dissenters had 'Ambition enough to contend with the Papists
for the glorious Prerogative of casting out Devils', being just as superstitious in that regard. Dissenters, Taylor contended, 'mightily . . . admire
and imitate the Popish Politicks'.[4] This was the traditional churchman's

---

[2] On this episode see Thomas, *RDM* 576–80; Francis Hutchinson, *An Historical Essay Concerning Witchcraft* (1718), 193–209; and D. P. Walker, *Unclean Spirits: Possession and Exorcism
in France and England in the Late Sixteenth and Early Seventeenth Centuries* (1981), 61–73.

[3] A strong proponent of the legitimacy of the Orangist *coup d'état*; his anonymously
published tract, *Submission and Obedience to the Present Government* (1690), recommended
taking oaths of allegiance to William and Mary. He was eventually rewarded with the
rectory of Croston, Lancashire, in the gift of the Crown, in 1695. See also Zachary Taylor,
The Devil turn'd Casuist; or the Cheats of Rome (1696).

[4] Zachary Taylor, *The Surey Impostor: Being an Answer to a Late Fanatical Pamphlet,
Entituled The Surey Demoniack* (1697), 3, 6, 20, 58 f. Cf. Roger North, *Autobiography*, ed. A.
Jessopp (1887), 133: 'the popish impostures fill them [the common people] with legends of
their saints miracles, and the sectarian impostures cultivate the credulity as to witches, and
both triumph over Satan in their several ways of exorcitation'.

charge: conventiclers in league with Jesuits. These attacks were particularly wounding because it was precisely the point of the dissenting authors of the *The Surey Demoniack* to argue, as Richard Bovet had, that Popery was akin to diabolism. The ministers, as they themselves put it, suspected that their efforts to relieve the possessed were being hindered by (and the conjunction is notable) '*Romanists or Witches*'.[5]

While witchcraft belief as a whole was not a marginal, specifically sectarian affair by the 1680s and 1690s, dissenters certainly made a particularly active use of witchcraft and possession cases. Daniel Defoe, sometime candidate for the ministry, emerged from a very thorough grounding in dissenting culture; yet at the same time, his career as a publicist and propagandist placed him at the heart of political dilemmas, and involved him in engagement with a wide spectrum of political interests. Defoe is ideally placed to show us what significance, if any, witchcraft had in the early eighteenth century. Some of his best-known writings are suffused with supernaturalism. Even more importantly, his attitude to witchcraft theory shifted in ways which were unmistakeably conditioned by the course of political debate in the period from the Revolution to the Hanoverian succession.

DANIEL DEFOE AND THE LANGUAGE OF THE SUPERNATURAL

Daniel Defoe is best known for writing some of the earliest novels in English—*Robinson Crusoe*, *Moll Flanders*, and *Roxana, or The Fortunate Mistress*. After these books, which contain their own references to occult matters, Defoe wrote three works entirely about the supernatural. *The Political History of the Devil* (1726), *A System of Magick* (1727), and the *Essay on . . . Apparitions* (1727) are all, more or less, demonological treatises. Critics have noted this, but have disagreed on how to view Defoe's work. Maximillian Novak has identified Defoe's 'remarks on the treatment of witches' as being 'in the best spirit of rationalism'. Peter Earle contradicts Novak, writing that while 'the rational and modern Daniel Defoe accepted the reality of witches', this 'ran counter to the views of the educated men of his age who were becoming increasingly sceptical of the existence of witches'. Earle's claims present Defoe as a paradoxical figure on the frontiers of modernity. The prime exponent of the modern fictional genre was in the thrall of ancient superstition. Yet such a precise

---

[5] *The Surey Demoniack: or an account of Satan's strange and dreadful actings, in and about the Body of Richard Dugdale of Surey, near Whalley in Lancashire* (1697), 49, my emphasis.

paradox is difficult to credit if we recall the categorical imprecision, the generic uncertainty of Defoe's literary generation.[6] Things were not so clear.

Defoe was educated at Newington Green Academy, headed by Charles Morton, an ejected dissenting minister, who, upon its enforced closure, sailed for New England. Morton was a competent natural philosopher and went on to become vice-president of Harvard College, co-signatory to the preface of Cotton Mather's *Memorable providences relating to witch-craft* of 1689, and author of a set of lectures, *Compendium Physicae*, which Defoe possessed, and admired as signal proof of the virtues of a dissenting education.[7] It was, thought Morton, 'natural Theology that men should be industrious in Natural Phylosophy'. While his involvement with Mather showed a commitment to the dissemination of witchcraft beliefs, Morton was concerned to place the activity of the supernatural within due bounds. Chapter 23 of the *Compendium*, 'Of Seeing', casts doubt on the notion of the evil eye. Chapter 12, 'Of the Species of Mixt Bodyes, and of firey Meteors', uses the diabolical to define the limits of explanation; certain wondrous events, 'because no sufficient natural reason can be given them, . . . are ascribed to the power of the prince of the air, by divine permission'. Dreams are another area in which the diabolical has a place, as Morton explains in a piece of didactic doggerel: 'Men's dreams have reasons mixtures; Gods infusions | Or Satans tempting, troubling curst delusion'.[8]

Morton's natural philosophy taught Defoe much. It gave him one of his many styles: the plain, homely, often prolix style of Boyle himself. Defoe was fascinated with the making of credit-worthy testimony on the Boylean model.[9] We see this most clearly in his account of the apparition of Mrs Veal, where he 'emphasizes the social status of his witnesses, sifts clashing accounts, preserves the key circumstantial details which

[6] Maximillian Novak, *Defoe and the Nature of Man* (Oxford, 1963), 13; Peter Earle, *The World of Defoe* (1976), 42. On the evolution and instability of genres, see Michael McKeon, *The Origins of the English Novel, 1600–1740* (Baltimore, 1987), 25–64. On Defoe and the occult, see also Rodney Baine, *Daniel Defoe and the Supernatural* (Athens, Ga., 1968); Baine seems unable to accept the coexistence in Defoe of the serious and the meretricious, those colliding tones of mockery and earnestness, and consequently misjudges the political importance of his work in this area, see pp. 67, 131.

[7] Daniel Defoe, *More Short Ways with the Dissenters* (1704), 5 f.; Charles Morton, *Compendium Physicae*, ed. S. E. Morison (Boston, 1940); Cotton Mather, *Memorable providences relating to witchcraft* (1689), preface.

[8] Morton, *Compendium Physicae*, 4, 161, 87, 195.

[9] On the Boylean style and the literary technology of experiment, see S. Shapin and S. Schaffer, *Leviathan and the Air-Pump* (Princeton, 1985).

guarantee assent, and omits those which would deprive his witnesses of credit'.[10] From the experimentalists Defoe also derived his model of collective advance, which permeates his writings on trade and technology, and makes Crusoe's isolated, slow and painful recovery on his island a study in the contrast between individual limitations and the achievements of social solidarity.

Defoe's attitude to supernaturalism and to providences doubtless had its origin at Newington Green too. A relatively early work, *The Storm*, echoes Morton and the dissenting tradition, with its collection of 'Remarkable Providences and Deliverances'. It also applies natural philosophy and the issue of its limits as an explanatory framework, to natural theology. Talking of the natural causes and origins of winds, ''Tis apparent, that God Almighty seems to have reserved this, as one of those secrets in Nature which should more directly guide them [natural philosophers] to himself.'[11]

The proper role of particular providences and of specific divine interventions is later discussed in *Robinson Crusoe* and *A Journal of the Plague Year*.[12] Crusoe remembers 'a strange Concurrence of Days, in the various Providences which befel me'.[13] The *Journal* shows the complex balance between its protagonist H.F.'s pursuit of providential signs—including 'the strong impressions which I had on my mind for staying' in London during the Plague—and Turkish 'predestinating notions', which meant that 'every man's end' was 'unalterably beforehand decreed'. Defoe was fascinated by the question of the Plague's own providential operation. He seems to advocate what one might call a mitigated supernaturalism: 'we must consider it as it was really propagated by natural means; nor is it at all the less a judgment for its being under the conduct of human causes and effects'. Defoe keeps the way clear for miracles, while allowing himself discussion of the disease itself as a natural phenomenon.[14]

Defoe found the supernatural to be a stubbornly problematic field, in which simple judgements cannot be made. The scope which traditional theology allowed to divine intervention, and natural wonders, 'by Divine

[10] Simon Schaffer, 'Defoe's Natural Philosophy and the Worlds of Credit', in J. Christie and S. Shuttleworth (eds.), *Nature Transfigured* (Manchester, 1989), 21. See also M. Schonhorn (ed.), *Accounts of the Apparition of Mrs Veal* (Los Angeles, 1965).

[11] *The Storm: or a Collection of the Most Remarkable Casualties and Disasters which Happened in the Late Dreadful Tempest, Both by Sea and Land* (1704), in L. A. Curtis (ed.), *The Versatile Defoe* (1979), 280.

[12] On providences in the early modern period, see Thomas, *RDM* 90–132.

[13] *Robinson Crusoe* (Oxford, 1981), 133.

[14] *A Journal of the Plague Year* (Harmondsworth, 1966), 33, 205.

permission', opened up a space for the Devil, under licence from God. The providential and the diabolical were, moreover, seen to exist in close and confusing proximity. As with dreams—'God's infusion' or 'curst delusion'—they were difficult to disentangle.

Early on in *Robinson Crusoe*, Defoe's hero makes a symbolic journey from blind superstition to a properly grounded faith. Shipwrecked, he notices an unexpected and providential growth of barley, a few months after his arrival on his desert island. He initially concludes in astonishment 'that God had miraculously caus'd this Grain to grow without any Help of Seed sown'. When, however, he comes to recall that some time earlier he had shaken out a bag of apparently ruined chicken-meal in that very place, he 'must confess, my religious Thankfulness to God's Providence began to abate'. Further consideration, recorded in his journal, leads him towards the same sort of mitigated supernaturalism adopted in the *Journal of the Plague Year*, with a recognition of providential action within the natural sphere: 'it was really the Work of Providence as to me, that should order or appoint, that 10 or 12 Grains of Corn should remain unspoil'd . . . as if it had been dropt from Heaven'.[15]

Much later, however, Crusoe's confidence, built on the trust in Providence which follows this conversion, is shaken by the appearance of a single human footprint on the shore, some way from his habitation. Accustomed to the security of his solitude, 'I stood like one Thunderstruck, or as if I had seen an Apparition'. The singularity of the occurrence—'for how should any other Thing in human Shape come into the Place? Where was the Vessel that brought them? What Marks was there of any other Footsteps? And how was it possible a Man should come there?'—leads him to conjecture it as an inverted providence, in other words, a diabolical intervention. 'Sometimes', he writes, 'I fancy'd it must be the Devil; and Reason joyn'd in with me upon this Supposition.' The Devil's purpose would be to terrify; a licensed attack on the sovereignty of Divine providence, undermining Crusoe's confidence in his protection under God. In the end this interpretation is rejected by Crusoe, not because the Devil could not so act, but largely by reasoning from probability. The Devil 'could not be sure' that Crusoe would see the footprint: ''twas Ten Thousand to one whether I should ever see it or not'. All this 'seem'd inconsistent with the Thing it self, and with all the Notions we usually entertain of the Subtilty of the Devil'.[16]

The Devil offers a destabilizing alternative to divine providence. He

[15] *Robinson Crusoe*, 78 f.   [16] Ibid. 153–5.

can intervene in the world as a real presence—he can take on human shape—but reason, having generated the fear of him, can deal with him. In *Robinson Crusoe*, the most consistently moralistic of Defoe's great fictions, the author lays out and highlights the hypothetical operation of the Devil in the world. He shows us the possible insinuation of the Devil into this fictional, but realistic, space as an inversion of the operation of divine providence, which itself forms the central theme of the book. He also raises some classic demonological issues—notably that of whether the Devil can work miracles—and the more general theological problem of how the operation of the Devil can be reconciled with the goodness of God ('*if God much strong,*' asks Friday, '*much might as the Devil, why God no kill the Devil, so make him no more do wicked?*'). The Devil was a real inhabitant, if a problematic one, of Defoe's world. There is an overlap between the possibility of this real presence, and a more metaphorical understanding of the Devil, as 'God's Enemy in the Hearts of Men'. In itself, this suggests the potency of the notion of the Devil; it is only in our confident modern-day dismissal of the Devil, after all, that we can make a clear distinction between real and metaphorical uses.

The natural and the supernatural coexist in Defoe's account of providence and the diabolical. God operates both naturally and supernaturally; the Devil is both real and metaphorical, a moral and a physical threat. There is the same confusion in *Moll Flanders* when the Devil 'appears' to Moll; and in *The Fortunate Mistress*, the tale of Roxana. The boundaries between metaphor and reality are never absolutely defined. When the Quaker woman finds Roxana's Dutch lover for her, her response is difficult to place: 'Then THOU hast dealt with the Evil One, Friend, *said I very gravely*: No, no, *says she*, I have no Familiar; but I tell Thee, I have found him for Thee.' Similarly, when worrying that her daughter has discovered her true identity, Roxana decides that she 'durst not ask her what was *Roxana*'s real Name, lest she had really dealt with the Devil, and had boldly given my own Name in for Answer'.[17] Sexual infatuation is frequently referred to as 'Possession' by a '*Spirit*', and, in the realm of unmistakable metaphor, Roxana's daughter 'haunted . . . [her] like an Evil Spirit'.[18]

The language of witchcraft was always being used in a metaphorical sense, as a figurative embellishment.[19] But Defoe was prepared to give the word 'devil' figurative and literal uses which are not sharply distinguished;

---

[17] *Roxana* (Oxford, 1981), 220, 289. [18] See ibid. 234, 310.
[19] Cf. Defoe, *Review*, 3/131, 2 Nov. 1706, facsimile bk. 8, 523.

in the same way as sinning itself formed a seamless continuum, from omission to commission, from idolatry and disobedience to witchcraft itself.

'OUR CONVERSE WITH THE WORLD OF SPIRITS . . .'

Well before writing his fictional histories or his occult treatises, Defoe had discussed communication with spirits, in his government-sponsored paper, the *Review*. His concern was typically Boylean, as we might expect from a student of Charles Morton.[20] It was Boyle who was sure that 'to grant . . . that there are intelligent beings that are not ordinarily visible does much conduce to the reclaiming . . . of atheists'.[21] In a supplement to the *Review*, in November 1704, for instance,[22] Defoe discusses evidence for the immortality of the human soul: 'Our Converse with the World of Spirits is a thing in our Opinion very certain, and if farther search'd into, might serve very much to illuminate this Affair; it demonstrates much of a future Existence, and perhaps might discover a great many Niceties we are not yet Masters of.' Mr Review, as he styled himself, went on to place supernatural events within the context of an empirical natural philosophy,[23] one which eschewed the dangers of Cartesian rationalism, and attempted to convince doubters without any initial reference to revelation. Putting aside 'reveal'd Knowledge', and recognizing the impossibility of an 'absolute Demonstration', he asked how one could, without some resort to the 'Influence of Spirit unembodied', explain 'Visions, Foresight, Forebodings of Evil or Good, and whence such things come'.[24] Defoe knows that 'to bring the Scripture in as any proof here, would be to no purpose, because these Gentlemen are too fond of exploding all Matters of Faith, and flye to the Wilderness of Philosophy',[25] a wilderness which he illustrates with a series of sub-scholastic queries on

[20] Morton was a fellow of Wadham College, Oxford, in the 1650s, at the same time as Boyle, Wren, Sprat, and Petty were in Oxford; see Paula Backscheider, *Daniel Defoe: His Life* (Baltimore, 1989), 14.

[21] Boyle to Glanvill, 18 Sept. 1677 in his *Works*, ed. T. Birch (6 vols.; 1772), vi. 57 f. See also 10 Feb. 1678, ibid. 59 f.

[22] 'A Supplement to the Advice from the Scandal Club', no. 3, Nov. 1704, Defoe, *Review*, facsimile bk. 3, 6.

[23] As Defoe put it in 1708, 'SEEING is in the Sence of our Speech a full Demonstration', the senses 'capable of sufficient Demonstration in Fact', *Review*, no. 4/155, 7 Feb. 1708, facsimile bk. 11, 620.

[24] *Roxana*, 222: 'I was a little surprised even before I knew anything of who it was, my mind foreboding the thing as it happened (whence that arises, let the naturalists explain to us).'

[25] Cf. Daniel Defoe, *A Political History of the Devil* (1726), 72.

being, substantiality, spirit, and matter. His response is essentially within a Lockian framework. The problem is the whole notion of matter which we 'ought to have defin'd' more rigorously. The essay goes on to discuss the nature of fire, paradigm and first order of spirit according to Richard Baxter, an author whose works would have been familiar at Newington Green.[26]

On the other hand, Defoe was as keen as his mentor Morton to avoid credulity. The reply to a letter of July 1705 moves from subject to subject: from fairies, to spells, to the apparent inability of apes to speak; from the spurious supernatural, to the diabolical supernatural, to the operation of providence in the world:

To the *first*, Certainly there never were such Beings in any Place, but the empty Heads of old Women, and in Penny Story-Books . . . To the *second*, 'Tis allow'd, that in Ancient Times, the Devil had frequent Communication with Men, and as a subtile Spirit, has Power of doing things invisibly, which therefore seems to Spectators to be done by the Man himself, with whom such Correspondence was held.[27]

Here diabolical intercourse acquires an ambiguity which rather diminishes its credibility. Though Defoe never quite makes a fairy-story of it, his equivocation is apparent. We are talking about '*Ancient Times*': the Devil *had* frequent communication. But then we move into the present tense: he '*has* Power of doing things invisibly'. This '*seems* to Spectators to be done by the *Man* himself': it is a matter of seeming, and the male malefactor recalls distant tales of necromancy rather than modern witchcraft as practised by old women in villages. And so back to the past tense: 'with whom such correspondence *was* held'. From the past to the present and back again, but Defoe never arrives at a definitive conclusion. The present day is not addressed.

We notice the same sort of tone, with its avoidance of the serious issue, in the occult works of the 1720s. 'As to the Real Black Art,' wrote Defoe, 'or Dealing with the *Devil* by way of Compact, Intercourse, Witchcraft, and such like, we find so little of it left, that we have some reason to say 'tis quite out of Use'.[28] In neither of these periods of Defoe's career did

---

[26] For Baxter and also Matthew Hale on fire and spirit, see e.g. *Additional Notes of the Life and Death of Sir Matthew Hale* (1682).

[27] 'The Little Review; or, an Inquisition of Scandal', no. 14, 20 July 1705, in Defoe, *Review*, facsimile bk. 5, 55. On belief in fairies compare *Spectator*, no. 604, 8 Oct. 1714, and see Thomas, *RDM* 724–34. Reginald Scot thought the fear of fairies had been replaced by fear of witches; while in the later 17th *c*. Sir William Temple and John Aubrey suggested that fairy beliefs had only recently died out.

[28] Daniel Defoe, *A System of Magick* (1727), 378.

witchcraft seem to be a particularly pressing issue. The same is true more generally. The urgency of the debate in the years of Restoration right up to the mid-1680s was absent. If belief in witchcraft within a public arena is ideologically conditioned, then as a subject for dispute it may go into hibernation from time to time. The debate about witchcraft does not, in this sense, have a seamless history to be charted. Instead we see a series of longer or shorter engagements during which the belief seemed relevant, threatened, or threatening; and periods of silence which do not, in themselves, mean that the belief is dead. It is simply not being aired. It is liable to be revived. It lingers in the back of the public mind. 'Pamphleteering attention to controversial topics in early-eighteenth-century England', writes one historian, 'usually came in bursts, not in a steady stream.'[29]

Hence it was that, in the year 1711, Daniel Defoe in the pages of his *Review* explicitly demanded the acceptance of traditional witchcraft beliefs.[30]

THE RAGE OF PARTY

To understand why Defoe should have moved witchcraft centre-stage, one needs first to understand his position within the political world in 1711. Much maligned in his lifetime—and subsequently—as a political harlot, a pen for hire, a turncoat, and a hack, a 'Hot-brain'd Scribler', Defoe was contemned as the tool of party; his nickname, the Devil, was a byword for faction.[31] At first sight he might seem to be an unlikely soulmate for the master whom he served, on and off, for ten or so years, Robert Harley. Although Harley had started his political career as a Whig, and ended up as something like a Tory, he consistently sought moderation and was resolutely against the dominance of party.[32] 'If care had been taken,' at the Restoration, he declared in the 1690s, 'Parties might have been prevented, and we should have had but one, and that for the good of England.'[33] This was an attitude reflected throughout a career which saw him fall from his position within the ruling triumvirate (with Godolphin and the great captain, Marlborough) into opposition, and again from effective premiership into retirement and disgrace.[34]

---

[29] J. C. D. Clark, *English Society 1688–1832* (Cambridge, 1985), 144 n. 112.

[30] Defoe, *Review*, 8/90, 20 Oct. 1711, facsimile bk. 20, 363.

[31] See Backscheider, *Daniel Defoe*, 81 f.

[32] He was from a dissenting family who counted Richard Baxter among their friends, see Angus McInnes, *Robert Harley: Puritan Politician* (1970), 189.

[33] Speech, 26 Jan. 1694, to the House of Commons: W. Cobbett, J. Wright *et al.* (eds.), *The Parliamentary History of England . . . to . . . 1803* (36 vols.; 1806–20), v. 830.

[34] On Harley, see McInnes, *Robert Harley*; and Brian W. Hill, *Robert Harley: Speaker, Secretary of State and Premier Minister* (New Haven, 1988).

Despite Defoe's reputation as a turncoat, or (as more recent critical views have suggested) a Protean genius,[35] he was very much Harley's man. He came into Harley's employment when he was at the nadir of his fortunes, recently pilloried for seditious libel, in debtor's prison. He retained for his rescuer a gratitude which survived the Lord Treasurer's fall from grace in 1714, and expressed what seems to have been unalloyed joy when Harley returned to power in 1710. They were subsequently in almost daily contact. Each undoubtedly influenced the other, and there was a distinct analogy between their political instincts and ideological preferences. This transcended the fact that one, Harley, was a gentleman occasional conformist with Tory affiliations, while the other, Defoe, was a merchant dissenter whose political leanings were primarily Whig. Two pieces of a jigsaw, their prejudices fitted them together, while their oppositions constituted a sort of elective affinity. As Harley well knew, and one historian has observed, there was no better way for a quasi-Tory like Harley to appeal across party lines than to use as his propagandist a quondam Whig like Defoe. It was for this sort of behaviour precisely that Harley and Defoe were excoriated.

This was an age in which government came to be dominated by the politics of party, as distinct from the mere play of faction at court. Government by party came to be a structural feature of the British polity. Disunity and schism came to be embedded in the political system itself. Yet, somewhat paradoxically, both parties eschewed party. It was the Tory North who, in the previous century, had called the Whigs 'the Faction'. One's opponent indulges in party politics. One never does so oneself. Those who sought to play parties off against each other, to stand above party, were accused of the worst sort of ill-principled politicking and partisanship. They suffered insults from both sides. As party, in retrospect, was coming to be a means of government and the substance of politics, it remained something shameful and illegitimate. The Revolution settlement, as it developed, tended to entrench this development of parties, in religion and in government. The Harleyite ideal resisted this, but that very resistance was liable to be misunderstood in the midst of the inexorable 'rage' of party.

At the very outset of their partnership, in 1704, Defoe, in a letter, recommended to Harley what seems in retrospect an eminently Harleyite programme, founded on moderation and the desire for unity: ''Tis Plain

---

[35] For a warning against accepting such a view of Defoe on the basis of the misattribution of conflicting pamphlets, see P. N. Furbank and W. R. Owens, *The Canonisation of Daniel Defoe* (New Haven, 1988).

Those Gentlemen who Propose This Union by Establishing One Party and Suppressing Another . . . Offer That which has been often Essay'd, and has as often Miscarryed.' Despite, or perhaps because of, his own and Harley's dissenting background, Defoe offered 'Methods of Mannagement of the Dissenters' which asserted that "'Tis Not Necessary in the present Conjuncture to Restore The Dissenters to Offices and Preferments', supporting only a toleration operated to the benefit of the ministry, a bare 'Liberty of Conscience'. Such management 'by Fathfull Agents' might help 'to Settle The Generall Temper of The Party'. Defoe speaks of a 'Generall Union of Affection' in the nation as opposed to a union 'in principle' which could not be expected. Nevertheless he does glance at a more ambitious and comprehensive long-term aim: 'I Premise Also by the Way That I am Persuaded Freedom and favour to The Dissenters is The Directest Method to Lessen Their Numbers and bring Them at last into the Church.'[36]

Defoe had come to work for Harley in the aftermath of the furore surrounding the former's *Shortest Way with the Dissenters*. This pamphlet, satirically adopting the voice of the high-church bigot, demanded that dissenters be not affectionately persuaded but thoroughly stamped on. In his 1704 letter to Harley, Defoe complained of the likes of such hot Tories who claimed 'that whoever was a True Son of the Church or Wisht well to it, Was Oblig'd to hang Out the Bloody Flag of Defiance Against the Dissenters'.[37] Yet when, after a period writing in the Whig interest, and after Harley's removal from the governing triumvirate in February 1708, Defoe returned to Harley's stable in 1709/10, it was largely thanks to the advent of high-flying fever. The high-flying clergyman Dr Henry Sacheverell had been prosecuted by a Whig-dominated ministry for seditious libel, convicted, but only lightly punished, the occasion for much celebration in street and pulpit. Dissenting chapels were wrecked, and the bloody flag was well in evidence. The Queen felt able to reconstruct the ministry, and brought Harley in at its head both to exploit and to control the high-flying tide. The balance of political discourse had shifted. Extremism of the sort which both Harley and Defoe despised had brought them back into the arena of power; but both were intent on moderating that extremism and standing above party.

One of Harley's major problems was the pursuit of his balanced policy, to 'maintain the ancient government of England in Church & State', within

[36] Daniel Defoe, *Letters of Daniel Defoe*, ed. G. H. Healey (Oxford, 1955), no. 15, Aug.–Sept. 1704?, 50–6.
[37] Ibid. 52.

the context of what he saw as an irreligious clique of a Whig opposition on one side, and the clamourings of the hotter Tories on the other. His view of the Whig 'junto' whom he succeeded in power had long been negative. The Whigs, he was already suggesting in 1701, have 'not only discharged themselves from all obligations of religion, but also have for many years been promoting, first Socinianism then Arianism and now Deism in the State'. He had written to Defoe in Scotland in 1707, vowing that 'if God spares me life' he will 'pull off the mask from the real atheists and pretended patriots'. In 1709, on the threshold of being able to fulfil that promise on the back of the high-flying tide, he declared that 'what used to skulk in corners and shelter itself under the names of latitude and freethinking' the Whigs now 'publicly own; and Deism is the bond of their Society'.[38]

This is what Harley came to power to rescue the kingdom from. He did not want to effect that rescue by in turn surrendering to the wave of high-flying which had swept the country, with an influx of impatient Tory members after the 1710 elections. Throughout his ministry he retained some Whigs in office and in the Privy Council, much to high Tory disgust. He spoke to the Whiggish journalist Richard Steele of comprehending Whigs and Tories within the government. Perhaps the best summary of his policy is to be found in a crisp memorandum of 1710: 'Graft the Whigs on the bulk of the Church party'.[39] The aim was to transcend the party labels, to draw erstwhile Whigs and erstwhile Tories, waverers and moderate men of varying persuasions, towards the centre, isolating the extremes. The very idea of party was anathema: 'As for Parties in generall,' he had written, ' it hath long been my opinion, that Parties in the State is knavery and Parties in Religion is hypocrisy.'[40]

Less a political manœuvre designed to secure the passage of other policies than a central aspect of policy in itself, Harley's bridge-building involved the refurbishment of a party-afflicted body politic, 'healing the breaches on both sides which have thus wounded the nation'.[41] As those words of Harley's indicate, party fever was as much a religious as a political problem. These two spheres were interpenetrating, and to heal

---

[38] Hill, *Robert Harley*, 35, 106. See also Robert Greene, *Principles of natural philosophy* (1712), dedicated to Robert Harley as the protector 'of our most Holy Faith, against the Insults of the several *Atheists, Deists, Socinians*, and I may now say, *Arrians* [Whiston and Clarke?] of our Age'.

[39] Clayton Roberts, 'The Fall of the Godolphin Ministry', *JBS* 22/1 (1982), 79.

[40] Manuel Schonhorn, *Defoe's Politics: Parliament, Power, Kingship and 'Robinson Crusoe'* (Cambridge, 1991), 102.

[41] Defoe, *Letters*, 271.

the wounds of the body politic was ultimately something of a sacred pursuit. All of Harley's policies have, ultimately, to be seen within the context of what his biographer McInnes calls the 'translation of ideas from the sphere of theology to the sphere of politics', an imperative which has been somewhat obscured by the dominance of diplomatic issues and the peace with France in most writing about Harley's regime.[42] The desire to escape from party government is a desire to return to some sort of Christian union within the polity, as Defoe had suggested in his 1704 letter. More specifically, Defoe's task as Harley's journalistic agent was, to borrow a piece of Harleyite propaganda, to counter 'the many blasphemous, heretical, Jesuitical, atheistical, schismatical and republican books and pamphlets that have been industriously dispersed and encouraged (even in these remote parts of your majesty's dominions) in order to foment divisions among your majesty's dutiful subjects, disturb their peace, and alter, if not subvert, the establishment in Church and State'.[43] All the key notions of Harley's programme are here: the concern about irreligion; the danger of factions within the state; and the subversion of the establishment.

Defoe's personal ideological concerns were always much closer to this programme of Harley's than some have suggested. They shared, as Downie puts it, 'an anachronistic ideology stemming from the political world of . . . earlier and much younger days'.[44] While we have come to accept a Defoe 'strangely purged of all but Whig philosophising',[45] the picture of a progressive, secular-minded Whig is not entirely plausible; and not only because of the occult interests sketched above. Defoe's supernaturalism was not some quirk or a cobwebby vestigial corner of his imagination, but part of a conservative and religious cast of mind, embedded as much as Harley's in visions of a polity free from party, and a Protestant nation at one. 'Government in general', as Defoe says, 'is of Divine and Natural Right', and in numerous of his works he elaborates a picture of an elect nation under a strong king, with a version of contract theory owing more to Old Testament narrative than Lockian theorizing, and an early faith in the mystic nature of the constitution which could lead him to refer to 'a

---

[42] McInnes, *Robert Harley*, 190.

[43] Address of the county of Radnorshire presented to the Queen after the Sacheverell trial. Its sentiments, as Alan Downie points out, were 'typically Harleian', and it was attributed to Harley: J. Alan Downie, *Robert Harley and the Press* (Cambridge, 1979), 118.

[44] Ibid. 23.

[45] For this phrase, see Schonhorn, *Defoe's Politics*, 45 f. Contrast Backscheider's Lockian Defoe (*Daniel Defoe*, esp. 168–72) with Schonhorn's much more complex figure.

kind of *Trinity* in our Government, as well as in our Faith'.[46] Defoe was, as one commentator suggests, unable 'to conceive of a vision of society and government that was silent on the intercession of God's voice in the nomination of the right ruler'.[47] The streak of conservatism, with a dissenting twist, is thoroughgoing. Defoe's immersion, as a dissenter, in the seventeenth-century contractarian tradition outlined in Chapter 1 is well worth remembering when considering his stance on witchcraft,[48] as is his advocacy of a Sauline narrative of political leadership, taken from the Old Testament. Taking witchcraft seriously is something at one with an Old Testament approach to politics; and the story of the witch of Endor, whose ministrations had confirmed Saul's fall from God's favour, confirms the real perils of witchcraft.

Defoe was just as hostile to party as Harley. This meant both standing above party and drawing upon the common concerns of both parties. Anti-Whig and anti-Tory, he espoused doctrines that were both Whig and Tory shibboleths. In the *Review*, the paper which he started at Harley's instigation, and continued through his Whig employment and again through Harley's ministry until 1713, Defoe consistently complained about party; and after the demise of the *Review*, anti-party rhetoric remained a feature of his writing, and in particular of some of the occult writing of the 1720s.[49] The function of the *Review* under Harleyite patronage was to harness the likes of Defoe, dissenting and other Whigs, to the Harleyite programme; to construct a coalition which could avoid excess. What he had written to Harley in 1704 remained true, and was particularly apt, in the circumstances of 1711. It was 'the Moderate Men of both Partyes' who were 'the Substantiall part of the Nation'. Defoe considered such men to be the country's 'Refuge when the Men of Heat Carry Things too far'. In them alone can 'the Govornment . . . be Safely Lodg'd'.[50] In seeking to appeal to men of both parties and neither in 1711, to appropriate the middle ground, Defoe faced a different task from that he had in 1707. The years around 1707 were a period of increasing Whig ascendancy, culminating in the elections of 1708 which gave the party its

---

[46] Daniel Defoe, *The Advantages of the Present Settlement* (1689), 19 f. and id., *Reflections upon the Late Great Revolution* (1689), 37, cited in Schonhorn *Defoe's Politics*, 19 f. and 108 f.

[47] Ibid. Schonhorn, *Defoe's Politics*, 41 f.   [48] Ibid. 28.

[49] On the demise of the *Review*, see Backscheider, *Daniel Defoe*, 341: 'he had tried to write impartially but had inadvertently embroiled himself in destructive party politics again.' The Harleyite programme was no longer sustainable by 1713, neither, therefore, was the Harleyite *Review* Defoe had been publishing since 1710.

[50] Defoe, *Letters*, 53.

largest majority since the 1688 revolution. Writing in 1711 Defoe saw a new equilibrium established by the Sacheverell trial, the reconstruction of the ministry, and the Tory landslide in 1710. He plied a stern fundamentalism calculated to bridge the gap between Dissenter and traditionalist and cast out the free-thinkers of modish Whiggery. This is the best way to understand Defoe's sudden espousal of witchcraft belief in a public arena.

Defoe, in fact, fits well into the pattern of Restoration witchcraft theorizing laid out above. Downie has called Defoe and Harley's ideology anachronistic, and there is a sense in which we are dealing with ideological disputes which still involve poring over the Caroline divines, despite the intervention of the Revolution. Harley certainly felt that it was in the latter part of Charles II's reign that politics and religion had taken a turn for the worse. The element of anachronism is only apparent in retrospect. Many features of the Revolution settlement, its very meaning included, were contested. Neither the division between the sacred and secular realms which opened up, nor the emergence of party government, was predetermined. Hence, in Defoe and Harley's world-view, witchcraft was still able to fulfil the function it had for Meric Casaubon. The content of witchcraft belief, with its emphasis upon real spiritual action in the world, and its role in the combating of atheism, was important. It could have an appeal to both dissenters and churchmen, with their rejection of Whiggish irreligion. All decent, pious men are to draw together against the sceptics and against witches; and here it is that we see the overlap with the symbolic role of witchcraft as a marker for the boundaries of a unified Christian society.[51]

The chronology of the witchcraft piece in the *Review* is vital to this reading. It appeared after the Sacheverell trial, in the midst of the rage of party, but before Harley's schemes of moderation had evaporated, and before witchcraft itself became embroiled in party controversy in the notorious Jane Wenham witch trial of 1712. In October 1711 the witchcraft issue, such as it was, might be considered safe, a means of constructing a community of opinion. The appeal was both to traditionalism and to a particular form of dissent, the tradition in which Defoe had been educated. Witchcraft could help establish the *Review* as a paper of a distinct character, buttressing its pro-government line. The *Review* could

---

[51] Defoe's eirenicism was extended to Catholics in Crusoe's *Farther Adventures*; the possible function of opposition to the Devil as a guarantee of Christian unity was given an explicit airing. See *The Life and Adventures of Robinson Crusoe* (2 vols.; 1840), ii. ch. 6, 138, and also 136.

be seen as a plain dealer which happened to back the ministry; the constellation of interests to which it appealed with such a stance is important. Belief in the ministry is compatible with Christian fundamentals.

Remarks in opposition newspapers make it clear that this defence of the ministry against suspicions of heterodoxy or irreligion was an urgent task: 'How long will ye be of Opinion that they can possibly intend to preserve your Religion, who have themselves none at all? Is not one half of their Hearts in the *Conventicle*, and the other over the Water, whilst the *Poor Church of England* has only what remains after *this Dividend*?' So said the *Medley* in April 1712. A month or so later, the *Flying Post* made a parallel point:

one Thing the Examiner should not have forgot, which is, that no sooner a Tory dies than Abel [Roper] marks him down with all his good Qualities in his High-Church Calendar of Saints, as a Genuin Son of the Church; tho', perhaps, every Body else might think him as great an Atheist, as *the Author of a Tale of a Tub*.[52]

The Tories obviously had no monopoly on the theme of a church in danger, and the presence of someone like St John in the ministry could feed suspicion of irreligion at the heart of government. The *Medley*'s remarks confirm a public perception of Harley's policy, with half its heart in the conventicle, and half with the Jacobitical Tories, a plausible enough picture of a policy which sought to graft the Whigs onto the body of the church party.

Desire for moral renewal, and political considerations, coalesced in 1711. In an open letter to the Archbishop of Canterbury in August 1711, the Queen herself complained of the growth of heresy and profanity. There is a sense in which the mood recalls those Scottish campaigns of moral renewal, anti-deism, and concern about witchcraft, from the 1690s on, discussed in Chapter 1. Defoe had been in Scotland just before the publication of the *Review* piece on witchcraft. Two months after the Queen's complaint, Defoe focused on a doctrine, witchcraft, which could attain broader support than the often divisive calls for the defence of the Church made by Atterbury and the hotter Tories gathered together as the October Club.

Defoe's article was preceded by a letter published in the *Review* in the autumn of 1711. 'This Question of Witchcraft is much Controverted,' his 'Importun[ate]' correspondent concludes, having cited Glanvill, Webster, Scot, and More, 'and so intricate and abstruse, as perhaps you will think it no despicable Subject for the Exercise of your Pen in some of your

---

[52] *Medley*, no. 14, 14–18 Apr. 1712; *Flying Post*, no. 3213, 1–3 May 1712.

Reviews, after you have done with the *South-Seas*, and the *Stock Jobbers*.'
This correspondent—whether a real member of the public, or one of
Defoe's impersonations—wrote in to complain about the imprimatur
granted in 1676 to John Webster, for a work attacking the witchcraft
beliefs of Joseph Glanvill 'one of the same [Royal] Society': 'to what
purpose is the *Imprimatur* of a Society to a Book, if it be not that such
Books being approv'd by those Societies, as the best Judges of Matters
relating to their own Professions, the Vulgar Readers may the better
believe them?'[53]

Defoe starts the article proper, a few weeks later, with two paragraphs
strenuously denying the political relevance or, indeed, the importance of
the subject he intends to deal with.[54] A discussion of witchcraft is proposed as a 'little Interval . . . a Digression' from treatment 'of the publick
News, Treaties of Peace, Proposals, and Preliminaries' which have done
and 'are like to take me up a great deal of Time'. No doubt a pause from
the peace issue was welcome both to readers and to an author taxed with
the complexities of changing course while trying to keep up the illusion
of consistency. But Defoe rather overplays his nonchalant tone—'it is not
so much for any Weight in the Question before me, that I enter upon a
Decision of this kind of Doubt'—and effectively contradicts it when he
complains of 'the Atheistical Use which many People make of this Difficulty, and which it is evident, they wish should be a Difficulty, by the
Pains they take to make it so', a remark which places the article in the
centre-ground of Harley's concerns.

To the question then, utterly direct and in the present tense: 'whether
there is any such Thing as a Witch?' Defoe goes on to make a series of
standard answers. First, the argument from legal custom, in which he
echoes Matthew Hale and countless others. 'It would', he writes, 'be a
very odd Thing that our Laws should Empower the Judges to Condemn,
and the Civil Magistrates to put People to Death for *Witchcraft*, if there
were no such Thing in the World.' Before continuing, he asks us to cut
to the core of the debate. He rejects the interminable arguments, the
sallies and counter-sallies of '*Glanvil, Webster, La Hontan,*[55] and others'.

---

[53] Defoe, *Review*, 8/83, 4 Oct. 1711, facsimile bk. 20, 335. The juxtaposition of witchcraft and stockjobbery in one sentence might remind us of Defoe's *The Villainy of stock-
jobbers detected* (1701), 6, where those shady operators are referred to as 'this new *Corporation
of Hell*'.

[54] Defoe, *Review*, 8/90, 20 Oct. 1711, facsimile bk. 20, 361–4.

[55] See e.g. *Dialogues de monsieur le baron de Lahontan et d'un sauvage de l'Amerique*
(Amsterdam, 1704), 46 f. 'Seroit-il possible que tu croïes ces bagatelles?' asks Adario, a
Huron, meaning tales of witchcraft.

He does not want to get immersed in an over-sophisticated debate, 'Reasoning against Foundations and Principles, confuting Demonstrations, *and the like*, which is a part of Logick I never was taught'. He will escape the impasse by concentrating on definition, on Holy Writ, and on prescription. He asks three questions:

1. What is understood by a WITCH?
2. What has the Scripture in it, towards the Proof of *Witchcraft*?
3. What Demonstrations are there of the Thing, in common Experience?

Defoe then cites the familiar texts from the Pentateuch and another from Chronicles. Even to ask if there is any such thing as a witch, Defoe says, is to be irreligious, to 'set aside all Scripture Testimony; and this tends to abundant Atheism'. Moving on from scriptural testimony, which can, sadly, have no influence on those who 'Ridicul[e] . . . all the Accounts of Things in the Holy Bible', the *Review* cites 'Testimony, from the Mouths of those who have been Convicted of Witchcraft in all Ages, and have confess'd'. The crimes of witches are the traditional ones. They have 'a Familiar, or Personal Converse with the Devil, with whom they have enter'd into Hellish Compacts, Covenants, and Combinations, for the Hurt and Delusion of themselves and their Fellow-Creatures'. All the essential features are here: Devil, compact, and *maleficium*. Evidence is particularly abundant in the histories of England, New England, and Scotland. Add to this confessions from witches accused by witches in the course of legal process, and the belief of those who have heard the evidence, and one has demonstration accommodate to the fact. No absolute demonstration is possible in 'so dark a Matter'.

Defoe's approach is utterly different here from that he was to pursue in the occult works of the 1720s, where he often allows a general argument to pass merely in order to tell a good story. 'I am', he writes in the *Review*, 'only enquiring into the General,' and therefore, will not 'fill this Paper full of a vast Variety of Stories to amuse and amaze the Reader'. Writing on witchcraft in the *Review*, Defoe has a sober and serious purpose. The final paragraph is absolutely firm, and thoroughly unambiguous:

there are, and ever have been such People in the World, who converse Familiarly with the Devil, enter into Compact with him, and receive Power from him, both to hurt and deceive, and these have been in all Ages call'd *Witches*, and it is these, that our Law and God's Law Condemn'd as such; and I think there can be no more Debate of the Matter.

The two poles of the argument, the two repositories of testimony, are Scripture and 'the Records of Justice', a pairing redolent enough of some sort of confessional society, but far from the invocation of the sacerdotal which was to occur the following year in defences of the condemnation of Jane Wenham as a witch. The central portion of the article focuses on scripture; this is vital to its appeal and purpose. Its citation of 'common experience' is a broad reworking of the sort of empiricism we see elsewhere in Defoe, an empiricism which draws both on the evidence of the senses and on the common wisdom of mankind accumulated through the ages. If this cumulative process leads in some cases to technological and commercial advance, should we reject what it has to say about witchcraft? In conclusion, one can see very easily how the legitimation of witchcraft belief could fit into the Harleyite programme which Defoe was trying to sell; and recognize that here, in 1711, a skilled journalist and propagandist saw the endorsement of the belief in witchcraft as something which could, however obliquely, serve the interests of the ministry. The belief in witchcraft was obviously a live issue which was open to manipulation. It was, however one construed it, a political fact.

THE *SPECTATOR*

Three months previously Joseph Addison had published an article on witchcraft in the *Spectator*. This was a piece of which Defoe would have been aware and to which he was, if indirectly, responding. Defoe's *Review* and the *Spectator* of Steele and Addison vied for the attention of and influence over 'honest Men of both Parties'.[56] While the *Review* spoke moderation in order to construct a coalition around Harley's ministry, the *Spectator* had an opposition, Whig agenda which informed all its efforts to transcend party allegiances.[57] Both papers complained about the reign of party, both chose an avowedly neutral figure as mouthpiece, both pitched themselves on the ground of moderation. But whereas Defoe's tendencies were, in a broad sense, conservative, nostalgic, even reactionary, Mr Spectator generally advanced the cause of those whiggish shibboleths, politeness and urbanity.

[56] Joseph Addison *et al.*, *The Spectator*, ed. D. F. Bond (5 vols., Oxford, 1965), ii. 1, no. 126, 25 July 1711. The phrase in which this occurs shows how close Defoe's and Addison's rhetoric could move, without any real similarity in aim: 'the honest Men of all Parties should enter into a Kind of Association for the Defence of one another and the Confusion of their common Enemies'.

[57] The *Spectator* promised from the outset 'to observe an exact Neutrality between the Whigs and Tories, unless I shall be forc'd to declare my self by the Hostilities of Either side', i. 5, no. 1, 1 Mar. 1711.

The *Spectator* for 14 July 1711 (no. 117) set off with a familiar caveat:

There are some Opinions in which a Man should stand Neuter, without engaging his Assent to one side or the other. Such a hovering Faith as this, which refuses to settle upon any Determination, is absolutely necessary in a Mind that is carefull to avoid Errors and Prepossessions. When the Arguments press equally on both sides in matters that are indifferent to us, the safest Method is to give up ourselves to neither.[58]

This is a classic piece of *Spectator* advice, with its espousal of moderation, urbanity and even 'a hovering Faith'. Avoid at all costs the social vices of fanaticism, prejudice, and partisanship. Although Addison's stance is against party in the strict sense it is, as one might expect, Whiggish in its ideology of politeness. 'It is with this Temper of Mind', Addison continues, 'that I consider the Subject of Witch-Craft.' So, in the succeeding essay he maintains a balance in argument which verges on self-contradiction. The radically sceptical motto out of Virgil—*ipsi sibi somnia fingunt*, 'they create their own dreams'—already conflicts with the prescription for the rational suspension of belief or disbelief, that 'when the Arguments press equally on both sides in matters that are indifferent to us, the safest Method is to give up our selves to neither'. Hearing 'Relations that are made from all parts of the World', Mr Spectator 'cannot forbear thinking that there is such an Intercourse and Commerce with Evil Spirits, as that which we express by the name of Witchcraft'. Yet it is the 'ignorant and credulous' who all too often believe such stories. It is 'People of a weak Understanding and crazed Imagination' who are usually accused of witch-craft. It is striking how 'many Impostures and Delusions of this Nature . . . have been detected in all Ages'. The conclusion is paradoxical, teasingly perverse: 'I believe in general that there is and has been such a thing as Witch-Craft; but at the same time can give no Credit to any Particular Instance of it.' How can one legitimately assent to a general proposition, to none of whose constituent instances one is prepared to give credence? Empiricism seems to have been abandoned, the inductive and deductive processes severed by Addison's reasoning.

The rest of the essay approaches the English case via the tale of the old crone Moll White's encounters with Sir Roger de Coverley, and a warning against overheated imaginings of the operations of witches. Sir Roger, we are told, 'would frequently have bound her over to the County Sessions, had not his Chaplain with much ado persuaded him to the contrary', a nice demonstration of Addison's temperate brand of Whiggery with its

---

[58] Ibid., i. 479–82.

image of the rational clergyman.[59] The article ends with an appeal to the humane instincts of its audience, and an almost sociological account of the origins of witchcraft accusations and confessions:

I have been the more particular in this Account, because I hear there is scarce a Village in *England* that has not a *Moll White* in it. When an old Woman begins to doat, and grow chargeable to the Parish, she is generally turned into a Witch, and fills the whole Country with extravagant Fancies, imaginary Distempers, and terrifying Dreams. In the mean time, the poor Wretch that is the innocent Occasion of so many Evils begins to be frighted at her self, and sometimes confesses secret Commerces and Familiarities that her Imagination forms in a delirious old Age. This frequently cuts off Charity from the greatest Objects of Compassion, and inspires People with a Malevolence towards those poor decrepid Parts of our Species, in whom Human Nature is defaced by Infirmity and Dotage.

The *Spectator* piece on witchcraft is a subtle affair because Addison is trying to speak above party.[60] He will not offend those of his readers who regard witchcraft belief as an index of orthodoxy; he will even endorse some such belief in very general terms. But he will at the same time point to the actual squalid consequences of witch belief, out in the countryside; and rub it in with a little fable touched with gentle satire. Sir Roger is, after all, not some monstrous being of prejudice and superstition, but an appealing if misguided Tory country gentleman, 'rather beloved than esteemed'. He teaches us a lesson, but only because he shares in our own failings and virtues. Addison's piece is immensely persuasive because it plays so carefully to its audience. None but the fiercest free-thinking sceptic is going to be offended by the moderate adherence to witch belief; and many a believer will be pulled towards scepticism by the force of Moll White's story. The *Spectator* is attempting to address not a Whig clique, but a broad range of opinion, 'Honest Men of all Parties', at a time when the centre of gravity of political discourse has shifted away from Whiggish rational piety towards something more muscular. If taking that audience with you on a subject like witchcraft required politic concession, so be it.

In itself Addison's article demonstrates how plausible witchcraft belief

---

[59] On the rationality of clergymen see Richard Steele *et al.*, *The Tatler*, ed. D. F. Bond (3 vols., Oxford, 1987), 1, 170, no. 21, 26–8 May 1709 [possibly by Swift]; [Richard Bentley] (Phileleutherus Lipsiensis), *Remarks upon a late Discourse of Free-Thinking* (1713), 32 f.

[60] Contrast this with Addison's straightforwardly disdainful comments on Swiss witch beliefs in *Remarks on . . . Italy &c.*, repr. in *Miscellaneous Works*, ed. A. C. Guthkelch (2 vols.; 1914), ii. 225.

was in 1711. Witchcraft is not dismissed out of hand,[61] however much its consequences may be deplored. If the range of opinion on witchcraft runs from Addison's *Spectator* piece to Defoe's in the *Review*, it is clear that witchcraft belief was not, in 1711, a *mere* matter of ridicule, beyond the need for rational confutation. Beyond this, however, one can detect in the *Spectator* an attempt to construct an alternative consensus around the witchcraft theme, an inversion of the Restoration writings on witchcraft and something to which Defoe, in the *Review*, a few months later, was replying. For, if Defoe was appealing to a tradition within which witchcraft belief negatively defined a Christian community—against witches and against sceptics—Addison's stance turns the tradition inside-out. He makes us accomplices in a very different sort of witchcraft belief, one drained of any worldly implications and so etiolated as to be unreal. His article starts off very generally by recommending that we give up 'prepossessions'; the abandonment of the supernatural discourse of *possession* is just one result of adopting such an attitude, an attitude which informs all the *Spectator*'s injunctions.[62] We are offered an alternative to a union formed by traditional belief. Instead of witchcraft belief defining a community of orthodox Christians opposed to the Devil and his works— both witchcraft and atheism—it is Addisonian indifference itself which will constitute Mr Spectator's community of politeness.

This essay, riven with contradiction as it is, is bound together by such reappropriations and refashionings of the matters of witchcraft. We are told to shun possession by such beliefs, not believe in possession; we must gather together in indifference to witch beliefs, not commitment to them; and we must see that it is credulity itself which must be, however gently, demonized, rather than witches themselves. Thus the idea of diabolical transformation, a stock-in-trade of demonographers, is given a new twist as we see the doting old woman becoming chargeable to the parish and being thus '*turned into* a Witch'. She is passively acted upon by credulity and public opinion which generate the ensuing wonders, 'extravagant Fancies, imaginary Distempers, and terrifying Dreams'. This is the Whig demonology of ignorant rusticity; or, as Addison was to put it in his 1715 comedy *The Drummer*, 'idle Stories to amuse the Country People'. As

---

[61] Cf. the similar balanced attitude in his essay on ghosts, *Spectator*, i. 455, no. 110, 6 July 1711; 'ridiculous Horrours' are dismissed, but the 'general Testimony of Mankind' and 'Relations of particular Persons' in favour of the reality of ghosts treated with respect.

[62] Although the erstwhile Whig Swift, having been captivated by Harley in 1710, said of his friend Addison that 'party had so *possess'd* him, that he talked as if he suspected me'; cited in Peter Smithers, *The Life of Joseph Addison*, 2nd edn. (Oxford, 1968), 200, my emphasis.

with so much else in the *Spectator*, Addison's approach to witchcraft is to open up a divide between polite urbanity and the charming but ultimately dangerous foibles of the countryman.[63] As a piece of imaginative journalism, the tale of Moll White shows the London *Spectator* reader what the consequences of witchcraft belief can be.

Defoe sought to appeal above party by making witchcraft a common belief; Addison sought to do so by first calming passions, and then applying gentle ridicule, with his story of Moll White and Sir Roger. Addisonian moderation and ridicule ultimately won. A notorious witch trial in 1712 showed how partisan witchcraft belief could be made—thus vitiating any use it had for Defoe—and how it could become the stuff of dangerous fanatical passions. By 1715, Addison could use a comedy about witchcraft and ghosts to 'please you All, and make both Parties laugh'.[64] Sensible men of any political persuasion would want to discard these vulgar, dangerous beliefs.

THE WENHAM TRIAL

Defoe's *Review* article and Addison's in the *Spectator* were followed, in 1712, by furious disputes over the trial of Jane Wenham, the 'witch of Walkern'. This controversy spawned at least eight pamphlets and a broadsheet,[65] some going into two editions, the major account into six. The trial itself was a subject for debate in London,[66] as well as a popular attraction. 'Thousands of People . . . from all Parts of the Country' flocked to see her in gaol; as for the trial itself, 'so vast a Number of People . . . [had] not been together at the Assizes in the memory of Man'.[67]

Wenham's case was in many ways typical.[68] Reputed to be a wise-woman, she was refused charity and then accused of cursing those who had refused her. When persuaded to drop her defamation case against her accusers, she submitted to private arbitration before the local minister,

---

[63] Cf. *Censor*, no. 11, 4 May 1715, bemoaning the belief in '*Fairies, Daemons, Spectres*, the Powers of *natural Magick*, and the Terrors of *Witchcraft*' which has spread 'from the *Cottage* to the *Farm*, from the *Farm* to the *Squire's Hall*'.

[64] Joseph Addison, *The Drummer* (1716), prologue.

[65] Including thoroughly sceptical pieces in issues 92 to 96 of the *Protestant Post-Boy* between 3 and 12 April 1712. These were then published in book form as *The Impossibility of Witchcraft* (1712).

[66] *The Impossibility of Witchcraft*, 1: 'The Discourse of the Town having been very much taken up, for some Days past, with a Trifling Pamphlet'.

[67] *An Account of the Tryal, Examination and Condemnation of Jane Wenham* (1712), BL 515.1.6 (28).

[68] On the trial and subsequent controversy see P. J. Guskin, 'The Context of Witchcraft', *Eighteenth Century Studies*, 15 (1981).

Gardiner, a believer in witchcraft. She was dissatisfied with the outcome, and more cursing and village tension culminated in her committal, imprisonment, and appearance at the assizes, after having confessed to witchcraft under pressure from Mr Gardiner. She implicated thirteen other women, all later released; and at her trial sixteen witnesses, including three clergymen, testified to her witchcraft. Strange objects were brought in evidence, magic ointment and cakes of feathers. She was brought in guilty by the jury, but the judge, Justice Powell, secured a reprieve.

The most prolific writer in the ensuing debate, Francis Bragge, wrote three pamphlets in favour of Wenham's conviction,[69] mounting a vigorous attack on Sadducism and what he saw as Whiggish scepticism.[70] From his high-church perspective he berated his opponents for their 'Prejudices' and lambasted them for their failure to be genuinely empirical, since they had 'beforehand resolved to believe nothing at all of it, let the Proof be what it would'.[71] Bragge was eager to associate the Church of England and its priesthood with certain forms of miracle-working, attacking 'some People' who

have thought fit, in a Public Manner, to express their Wonder, that Two Divines should concern themselves in a Thing of this Nature, as if detecting the most Abstruse, and Hidden Works of the Devil, and his Spiteful and Malicious Vassals, were a Business wholly Foreign to, and inconsistent with, the Duty of a *Minister of Christ.*

Bragge was 'not at all ashamed to own . . . such Holy Charms or *Amulets* against *Satan* . . . let the World call 'em *Exorcisms,* or by what other Invidious Names they shall think fit'. He hoped that some of the events of the Wenham affair might create 'a due Reverence and Respect to Prayers in general, and those of our Holy Church in particular'. The tone is, throughout, an intensely high-flying one, and Bragge is the first to complain of accusations of 'priestcraft', his aim to draw clear lessons from so 'many and so strange *Mysteries of Iniquity*'.[72]

---

[69] His was not the only credulous contribution to the debate: see also, G.R., *The Belief of Witchcraft Vindicated* (1712).

[70] The preface to his *A Defense of the Proceedings against Jane Wenham, wherein the Possibility and Reality of Witchcraft are Demonstrated from Scripture, and the concurrent Testimonies of all Ages* (1712) attacks '*Scepticks* and *Freethinkers*' and complains of their 'ridicule'.

[71] [Francis Bragge jun.], *A Full and Impartial Account of the Discovery of Sorcery and Witchcraft, Practis'd by Jane Wenham* (1712), preface.

[72] Ibid., preface and 34. Cf. [Thomas Gordon], *A Seasonable Apology for Father Dominick, Chaplain to Prince Prettyman the Catholick, But now lying in Durance under the Suspicion of secret Iniquity. In which are occasionally inserted some weighty Arguments for calling a General*

Bragge used the Wenham trial not only to advance high-flying principles, but also to damn the Whigs: the politicization of the trial is striking.
'As for Mother *Wenham*,' Bragge wrote:

I hear she has found out a Way to get plenty of Money while she is in Prison. She
says she was prosecuted out of Spite, only because she went to the *Dissenting
Meetings*: And by this Means, she gets Contributions from the Party: And of a
wicked old Witch, is on a sudden become a *precious Saint*.[73]

Wenham's charge might have been true; the association between the
practice of witchcraft and one particular sect, Quakerism, was often made
in the seventeenth century. George Fox, the mid-seventeenth-century
Quaker leader, was accused of enchantment. The choice of language,
notably the word *Saint*, is inflammatory; Puritan sects are invoked in the
same breath as diabolism. Bragge continues with pointed irony: 'This
Story put me upon enquiring of Mr *Gardiner*, whether she had ever been
counted a Dissenter, and he declares that he never before heard that she
us'd to go to any Place of Divine Worship, and that he never took her to
be of any Religion at all.'[74] Bragge wants to have it both ways. He will not
grant Wenham any religion, but will not be denied his opportunity to
diabolize the dissenters, wishing 'the Fanaticks much Joy of their new
Convert'.[75] In the matter of a few lines, the young clergyman manages to
place Dissent, 'the Party', fanaticism, and witchcraft in a disturbing complicity. Yet he never allows his rhetoric to settle too much. It remains
dishonestly flexible. Jane Wenham is not religious, therefore she is a
witch; and at the same time, she is a witch and a dissenter, and therefore
dissent is tantamount to apostasy.

One of the replies to Bragge, *A Full Confutation of Witchcraft*, has a
subtitle which is in itself revealing. It claims that in its pages 'the Modern
Notions of Witches are overthrown, and the Ill Conseqences of such
Doctrines are exposed by Arguments; proving that, Witchcraft is
Priestcraft'. Priestcraft is Toryism. How different this is from Addison's
approach in the *Spectator* the previous year, as much as Defoe's differs

---

*Council of the Nonjuring Doctors, for the further Propagation of Ceremonies, Unity, Dissention,
and Anathemas; and for the better Improvement of Exorcism and March-Beer* (1723) (discussed
in Ch. 7 below), 30: 'he braggs [!] of his great Power over the Devil; yet he is eternally
frighting you with the Devil's great and invincible Power'; and *A Full Confutation of
Witchcraft: More particularly of the Depositions against Jane Wenham Lately Condemned*
(1712), 5, condemning the 'stale Artifice of Exorcisms'.

[73] [Francis Bragge jun.], *Witchcraft farther displayed* (1712), introduction.
[74] Ibid. See Thomas, *RDM* 580 f.
[75] Bragge, *Witchcraft farther displayed*, introduction.

from Bragge's. The tone here is Whiggishly urbane, but at the same time resolutely and dismissively sceptical:

I am fully aware what Hazards a Man of a Publick Character, exposes his Reputation to, in talking freely, much more in writing on such a Topick, especially in the Country, where to make the least Doubt, is a Badge of Infidelity; and not to be superstitious, passes for a dull Neutrality in Religion, if not a direct Atheism. And here, *Sir*, I cannot but envy one Privilege you enjoy in Town, which is, a Freedom of Thought and Talk.[76]

Country beliefs are disparaged, rationally disdained as those of the ill-educated rustic, but with more violence than Addison ever mustered. The author 'never yet came under the slavish Ties of popular Compliances, or ever suffer'd my Judgment to mingle with the Crowd'. These beliefs are brutally rubbished as 'the wild Testimonies of a parcel of Brain-sick People, who often stand in need of Dieting and Shaving themselves'.[77]

The tendency towards anticlericalism is strong, as when the author asks why Jane's curse upon the clergyman who had failed to give justice in the matter of her defamation had not fallen on the head of the cursed Mr Gardiner himself, but rather upon his hapless servant: 'That Question, upon second Thoughts, may be too free: What! Thunder-strike Oaks? What! a Clergy-man lie exposed to the Fury of the Devil? No, no, they are all of the holy Seed, and cannot be reach'd by any infernal Power.'[78] Claims like this betrayed the Lockian sentiments of the writer, at least in his division of secular government from religious concerns: 'without Question, under this side of Heaven, there is nothing so sacred as the Life of Man, for the Preservation whereof, all Policies or Forms of Government, all Laws and Magistrates are most especially ordain'd.'[79]

After her pardon, Jane Wenham was given refuge on the estate of a Whig landowner, where Francis Hutchinson visited her a few years later.[80] She had become part of the Whig mythology of Tory superstition, and her trial marked the definitive end to the possibility of witchcraft prosecution in England; and an end to any idea that witchcraft belief could inhabit some sort of politically neutral and abstract realm, as a marker for the sacralized state in its Harleyite conception, or any other. The language of the Wenham dispute had been highly charged, Bragge pitting 'frothy Libertines' against 'the *Grave*, the *Wise*, and the *Learned* in all Ages'.[81]

---

[76] *A Full Confutation of Witchcraft*, 3 f. [77] Ibid. 4 f.
[78] Ibid. 8. [79] *The Impossibility of Witchcraft*, 30 f.
[80] Hutchinson, *An Historical Essay Concerning Witchcraft*, 130.
[81] Bragge, *A Defense of the Proceedings against Jane Wenham*, preface.

Ultimately, gravity, wisdom, and learning when brought to support serious and engaged witchcraft belief came to be seen as froth in the highest degree. It was no longer respectable to believe in witchcraft except, perhaps, in the hovering, indifferent manner of Mr Spectator. An active belief had become, as we shall see, the property of fanatics and the prerogative of the fringe.

Witchcraft theory had been useful both as a symbolic marker of boundaries of the sacral state, and in its provision of a common enemy to unite orthodox Christians. Walls were placed around Christian society to defend and define it against witches and sceptics alike, the enemies of God and man. Now, in the course of the Wenham trial, witchcraft theory had become a source of the very factionalism which it was meant to deny. The process of desacralization implicit in certain interpretations of the Glorious Revolution, I argued in the last chapter, sapped the rationale of the Restoration version of witchcraft theory. This was the very theory, I have argued in this chapter, which Defoe was using in 1711. The Wenham controversy demonstrated that witchcraft as ideology was dead.

THE POLITICAL HISTORY OF THE DEVIL

In his fictions of the 1720s, Defoe maintained a highly nuanced and essentially ambiguous view of the supernatural, weaving the literal and the metaphorical together. Defoe is the focus for an exploration of the disappearance of committed, mainstream witchcraft belief in this chapter. Concentrating on an individual reflects the partly individualistic aspect of belief. The progress and development of each person's set of beliefs is necessarily an idiosyncratic matter. Yet at the same time, language and discourse together impose constraints upon what it is possible to believe at any particular time. This is true in any case, but particularly important with Defoe. His stance changed in public and, since he was a skilled and engaged polemicist, reflected his view of public belief, of what might be acceptable, of what could be embraced or would be inevitably dismissed. We have discovered a moment in Defoe's career at which it seemed to him plausible and useful directly to address and endorse witchcraft belief. Witchcraft belief at this point had an aim, for Defoe, for his milieu, and for his intended audience. The novels represent the unravelling of that clarity into a tangle of literal and metaphorical threads leading nowhere in particular; this can be seen even more clearly in the occult works of the 1720s, where the embarrassed, half-hearted, disorganized nature of the retreat from belief is exhibited. It is impossible to extract anything like a *line* from the miscellaneous jumble of ironies which go to make up *the Political History of the Devil* and the anything but systematic *System of Magick*.

There may not be a line to follow, but there is a discernible tone, and one which relates to the picture of Defoe we have drawn. The *Political History* includes a vignette of the Devil, looking back upon his failures in anger, seeing 'what a Fool he had been to expect to crush Religion by Persecution'. He has since discovered that the 'utmost Liberty in Religion' is far more effective, 'sowing Error and Variety of Opinion'. In this passage, Defoe reflects his jaundiced feelings about the victory of toleration and the failure of the projected 'union of affection' he had envisaged in his letter of 1704 to Robert Harley. 'Liberty and Dominion' are, in Defoe's eyes, a work of devilish politics to effect the 'Ruin of Religion, as we shall have room to shew in many Examples, besides that of the Dissenters in *England*, who are evidently weaken'd by the late Toleration'.[82]

After the Wenham controversy, and after the triumph of party represented by the failure of Harley's programme (how neatly the two coincide), Defoe essentially withdrew from hardline witchcraft belief, leaving behind fictional and satirical uses. These had always been there, as in the 'Miscellanea' appended to the witchcraft issue of the *Review*, which mocks some of Defoe's bugbears—mostly extreme high-flyers—as 'no witches', that is, fools. Now, such satire was in the foreground. Witchcraft was a joke, stripped both of its danger (as an occasion of faction) and of its function (as a salve for faction). As for 'the Real Black Art, or Dealing with the *Devil* by way of Compact, Intercourse, Witchcraft, and such like, we find so little of it left, that we have some reason to say 'tis quite out of Use'.[83] In the occult works themselves Defoe offers an interpretation of this process. The Devil has no need for witches now—he sits in councils of state themselves, courtesy of the reign of party which followed the Hanoverian triumph and Walpole's rise. Party strife had demonstrated, in the Wenham controversy, the ideological redundancy of witchcraft theory. Now party rule triumphed in Defoe's eyes. The idea of witchcraft lost much of its usefulness in his scheme of things. It re-emerged, parodically inverted, as a metaphor for party conflict and party rule themselves. As Henry Fielding's Jonathan Wild 'would often . . . say . . . party men often made a bad bargain with the devil, and did his work for nothing'.[84] In Defoe's history of the Devil, witches properly speaking

---

[82] *Political History*, 198. [83] *A System of Magick*, 378.
[84] Henry Fielding, *Jonathan Wild* (1743; Harmondsworth, 1982), 67.

were no longer needed because diabolism (factional rule incarnate) reigned at the very seat of power.

The Political History of the Devil was advertised as a survey of 'the influence *the Devil* has in the Politicks of mankind': 't'would be hard to prove that there is or has been one Council of State . . . down to the year 1713 (we don't pretend to come nearer home) where the *Devil* by himself, or his Agents in one Shape or another, has not sat as a Member, if not taken the Chair.' Defoe's satires are often 'to be rung backward like the Bells when the Town's on fire'; and the point here is that it is precisely *since* 1713, and the defeat of the Harleyite scheme of union, that the Devil has been entrenched, first in the high-flying domination up to the Hanoverian accession, and then in the Whig party rule of Walpole and his cronies. If we 'don't find our Houses disturb'd as they used to be . . . that Children don't vomit crooked Pins and rusty stub nails', it is because the Devil now acts 'immediately . . . by a magnificent Transformation'. This method 'is really very modern'.[85] *A System of Magick*, in offering us some consolation, reminds us where the deceiver has gone:

It is impossible to close this Article of the *Magicians* Power being limited, without an agreeable Reflection upon the modern Furies of our Age, your Party Leaders and Politick Scheme-Makers; what merry work they would make in the World, if the *Devil*, their Head Engineer, was not limited, and not in Condition to trust them with the Power of doing Mischief as they desire it.[86]

Under the party regime, the Devil had no need for witchcraft. He was already esconced in power; embodied within the State, he had no need to threaten it from without. The brief respite from a party-dominated ministry between 1710 and 1713—for this is how Defoe interpreted those years[87]—had provided the last opportunity for witchcraft belief as an ideological expression of the sacral State and its aspirations.[88]

---

[85] *Political History*, 9, 260, 227, 388, 389.   [86] *A System of Magick*, 216.

[87] See Defoe's *The Secret History of the October Club*, 2nd edn. (1711), for Defoe's own account of this period, especially 14, 32, 42, 50. The October Club is, significantly, 'this black Divan'.

[88] For the association between factionalism and witchcraft in the early eighteenth century see also e.g. R. Skerret, MA, *Peace and Loyalty, Recommended in a Sermon Preach'd at the Lent-Assizes Holden at Brentwood in Essex* (1720), who complains of 'such Variety of Sects and Parties . . . *What Peace so long as the Whoredoms of thy Mother* Jezebel, *and her Witchcrafts are so many?*', 29; and James Smith, BD, *An Examination of the Signs of the Times: Or, Seasonable Remarks on Mr Massey's Sermon. Proving That 'tis an Unscriptural, Prevaricating and Seditious Libel* (1722): 'Such is the Spirit of Faction, such the Desire of being distinguish'd as a Party-Man . . . that the Devotion which ought to be paid to the great Creator of all things, is turn'd into the Service of the Devil', 6.

6

The Last Debate?

No evidence can *prove* witchcraft; since there *can never be* any evidence of it, good or bad, trustworthy or the reverse.

> J. S. Mill in Jeremy Bentham, *Rationale of Judicial Evidence*, ed. J. S. Mill (1827)[1]

RICHARD BOULTON

In 1715 Richard Boulton published his first book on witchcraft, *A Compleat History of Magick, Sorcery, and Witchcraft.*[2] With its 'Judgment concerning Spirits, by the Late Learned Mr JOHN LOCKE', Boulton's work is nevertheless little more than the familiar collection of narratives in the spirit of Joseph Glanvill and Robert Boyle. It was only after the publication, in 1718, of Francis Hutchinson's *Historical Essay Concerning Witchcraft*, with its attack on Boulton, that the wounded author felt moved to issue a more analytical work, his *Vindication*, published in 1722.

Boulton was no Francis Bragge, and high-flying political rhetoric does not enter into his work. Indeed, it seems more than likely that he was a Whig, and not only because of the association with Locke. Boulton's *Physico-Chyrurgical Treatise of . . . the Kings-Evil* was significantly timed to appear during the succession crisis of 1714/15. Boulton's attack on the theory of the royal touch, and his rational account of the king's evil, reads like an attack on divine-right monarchy and Stuart pretensions:

several have pretended to mighty Secrets, and have boasted so much of their *Arcana*, that one should wonder how they should find out such Secrets; since they give so little Reason could be likely to discover, what they *pretend* [my emphasis]

---

[1] J. S. Mill, *Miscellaneous Writings*, vol. xxi of *Collected Works of John Stuart Mill* (1989), 30.

[2] For Boulton, see Ch. 4 above.

to; And I am apt to think, that their design is to amuse and impos upon the World, rather than propose any advantage to the *Publick*; when they *pretend* [my emphasis] to do that which they are not willing to make *Publick*, and think it unable to stand the Test and Judgment of the Learned.

The hints are irresistible: Boulton wants 'to avoid the Censure and Scandal of Pretenders'. It was, indeed, the Stuart kings who, maintaining the claim to thaumaturgic efficacy, 'boasted so much of their *Arcana*'. By publishing, at this delicate time, a work which sought a rational account of the origin, increase, progress, symptoms, and 'Methods of Cure, different from what hath been hitherto proposed' of the king's evil, Boulton was making a political statement. Queen Anne had renewed touching for scrofula—the infant Samuel Johnson was one of her last 'patients'—and Boulton's failure directly to mention touching, even as a discredited cure, is notable.[3]

If Boulton was no Tory, neither was he a devotee of irrationalism or mysticism. He had earlier attacked the medical writer John Colbatch's precipitate resort to supernaturalism in diagnosis: 'But the wonderful Discoveries of this Mr *Colbatch* are not a little to be Admired! For he is the first Man that ever perceived the Devil to appear in the shape of the Gout'.[4] Part of the aim of Boulton's later writing about witchcraft was to defend and define the competence of the physician, who can distinguish quite well enough 'betwixt the Symptoms of real and natural Distempers, and Accidents that proceed . . . from supernatural Causes'.[5]

Boulton was hardly in the vanguard as a medical man, if his numerous publications are anything to judge by. He was, nevertheless, a partisan of modernity in natural philosophy, and presented much of his witchcraft theory in the language of the moderns.[6] There is the citation from Locke

---

[3] *Physico-Chyrurgical Treatises* (1714), preface. On touching, see Raymond Crawfurd, *The King's Evil* (Oxford, 1911), esp. 138–61. For Whiggish opposition, and the association with high-sacral, Stuart monarchy, see e.g. Richard Blackmore, *Treatise on the King's Evil* (1735), preface. Crawfurd records, 144, that it was at Harley's instance that 'the Privy Council determined to issue proclamations, stating when the Queen would perform the miracle'. It had been in William's reign, with the king 'showing open disdain', that medical men had begun to publish their 'reasoned scepticism'; Crawfurd, *King's Evil*, 140. *OED* cites Gilbert Burnet as authority for pre-1715 usage of the word *pretender* in this context.

[4] Richard Boulton, *An Examination of Mr John Colbatch his Books* (1698), 159.

[5] Richard Boulton, *The Possibility and Reality of Magick, Sorcery, and Witchcraft, demonstrated. OR A Vindication of a Compleat History of Magick, Sorcery, and Witchcraft. In Answer to Dr Hutchinson's Historical Essay* (1722), 89.

[6] See e.g. *A Treatise of the Reason of Muscular Motion* (1697); *A System of Rational and Practical Chirurgy* (1713); *An Essay on the Plague* (Dublin, 1721); *Some Thoughts concerning the Unusual Qualities of the Air* (1724); and the works cited in Ch. 4 above.

in the *Compleat History*, which we have already considered in Chapter 4: that intriguing 'Judgment concerning *Spirits*'. This is filled out in part 2 of his *Vindication of a Compleat History*, where Boulton discusses 'the Nature of Material and Immaterial Substances'. At the beginning of creation, the first matter was homogeneous but, through the effects of motion, broke up into 'parts of different Sizes, Shapes and Magnitude'. This process of fragmentation created different qualities in the world, or, rather, in our perception of it. Boulton embraces the key hypothesis of the mechanical philosophy.[7]

Ever the medical man, Boulton goes on to apply these insights to physiology. 'Material Substances' are 'always liable to these Alterations, are not only said to be corruptible . . . but as they compose human Bodies . . . these Bodies are liable to Decay, and to be put out of their Natural State'. This is especially so in the case of the liquid parts of bodies. These alterations, or corruptions, are effected not only by external causes, but also by 'strong Impressions of Passions of the Mind'. 'The Temperature of the Body', he avers, 'is to be discovered by the Influence of the Soul', while 'if the Body be afflicted the Soul suffers, and the Spirits are depressed, and consequently the whole languishes and decays'. By introducing this composite mechanical and psychosomatic model, Boulton finds an up-to-the-minute rationale for witchcraft beliefs. Since our own souls can damage our bodies, how much more so can the 'Superior Orders', that is, spirits, good and evil. They can 'move violently the small Minute Parts of Fluid Humours'. The immaterial must act on the material, since 'when Matter was first created if immaterial Substance could not affect Matter, the Parts of Matter had never been put in Motion'. It does so according to the limitations of the mechanical stucture of matter. In this way, Boulton defines the action of spirit via physiology and mechanism, establishing a distinct realm of the preternatural lying between the miraculous, prerogative of God, and nature in her ordinary course.[8]

The reception of Boulton's work indicates the way in which witchcraft theory, after the rage of party, became an anachronism. By publishing the *Compleat History* in 1715, he was seeking to participate in a tradition which had been denied its ideological rationale, eviscerated by the trauma of the Wenham controversy. This was to be made clear in the course of the ensuing debate between Boulton and Francis Hutchinson. Boulton's

[7] For which see John Locke, 'Elements of Natural Philosophy' in *Works*, ed. St John (1854), ii; Robert Boyle, 'The Origin of Forms and Qualities', in *Works*, ed. T. Birch (6 vols.; 1722), iii. 1–137; René Descartes, *Les Principes de la Philosophie* (Paris, 1647), pt. ii.

[8] Boulton, *Vindication*, 159 ff., 166, 177, 179.

Compleat History of 1715 elicited a reply from Hutchinson in 1718, a
reply which has gone down in history as the last word in the witchcraft
debate, a masterpiece of humane rationalism. Boulton's own reply to
Hutchinson, his *Vindication* of 1722—a discursive treatise rather than a
collection of narratives—was ignored by its target and dismissed by contemporaries. Jacques Daillon, in his *Daimonologia* of 1723, viewed Boulton's
efforts as beneath contempt. Boulton's arguments are 'so weak', that 'he
will find himself disappointed, if he expects an Answer. I shall only
transcribe his Title Page, and I take that to be Answer enough.'[9]

The difference between the responses to Boulton's works of 1715 and
1722 is a measure of how quickly the new consensus settled. The *Compleat
History* was answered by as substantial a work as the *Historical Essay*; the
Vindication met with Daillon's condescension and virtual silence. Later
historians have been just as curt. Richard Boulton has been consistently
marginalized, ignored altogether, or dismissed as an eccentric. Hutchinson's
work has had the intellectual, if not the actual, priority. Wallace Notestein,
for instance, elides Boulton's two books on witchcraft to give Hutchinson
the last real say: 'Hutchinson's work was the last chapter in the witch
controversy. There was nothing more to say.'[10] Keith Thomas points to
the Wenham controversy as the occasion for Hutchinson's *Historical Essay
Concerning Witchcraft*, leaving Boulton, again, out in the cold.[11] Hutchinson
himself, on the contrary, supposed that his essay would not have been
published if Boulton's book, which might 'very likely do some Mischief,
had not lately come forth'. By 1722, the *Vindication* needed no rational
confutation from Daillon.[12]

Boulton may have been an anachronism, but he should not be ignored.
The broad trajectory of his work on witchcraft, and of the responses to it,
traces, as we have seen, an outline of the fate of witchcraft discourse after
1715, in the early years of the new Hanoverian regime. Hutchinson was
on the winning side, and Boulton's reply to him was out of place by the
1720s, when his *Vindication* was published. Hutchinson, however, was
not the all-conquering sceptic, confident in his powers. The history of the
emergence of his book was a complicated one.

---

[9] Comte du Lude, *Daimonologia or, a treatise of spirits . . . [with] reflections on Mr Boulton's
answer to Dr Hutchinson's 'Historical Essay'* (1723), 158.

[10] Wallace Notestein, *A History of Witchcraft in England from 1558 to 1718* (Washington,
1911), 343, his very last sentence. Notestein calls Boulton's work 'haphazard' (340), but
takes the *Vindication* as a mere supplement to a second edition of the 1715 work, rather than
a substantial treatise in its own right. See also R. H. Robbins, *Encyclopaedia of Witchcraft
and Demonology* (New York, 1959), 254.

[11] Thomas, *RDM* 689.   [12] *Historical Essay*, preface.

THE *HISTORICAL ESSAY*

It was in 1706 that Hutchinson had inadvertently passed his chapters on witchcraft via the Bishop of Norwich to the Archbishop of Canterbury.[13] Discouraged from publishing a work which, in its attack on witch beliefs, might offend the Scottish godly prior to the ensuing Union, his attitude was not the outrage of the fearless rationalist, but anxious submission. He asked his friend Hans Sloane for advice as to 'what must be done to prepare its way . . . For till that restraint be taken off I must by no means venture it, neither dare I do anything towards the removing of it.'[14]

Hutchinson went back to Sloane in 1712, the year of the Wenham trial, probably sensing the opportunity to publish something topical. Sloane 'had some time since the trouble of perusing some historical Collections & Observations I had made upon this Subject, & I have them by me with some little improvement since you last saw them'. Despite the improvements, Hutchinson remained cautious. While he 'would not be unwilling to venture any such censures as I should meet with from some', he will submit everything to the 'prudence & judgment' of Sloane, that luminary of the Royal Society, '& will either send my papers up or forbear according as you advise'. While he disclaimed any knowledge of the ins and outs of urbane discussion of the topic, Hutchinson's previous musings about witchcraft encourage him to offer some dispassionate advice to assist the authorities in avoiding the 'Folly & imprudence' which all too often attended the 'management' of witch trials. Hutchinson's overwhelming concern is the 'great trouble & disturbance' caused by witch trials 'not only to the poor old Creatures, but to all timerous [*sic*] Persons, & the whole Neighbourhoods where they are . . . which if it once gets head, our learned Judges will find hard to suppress, till its own Mischief hath convinced the World of the Guilt & Folly'. There is a hint here not of a society long removed from the idiocies of witch belief, but of a community teetering on the edge of hysteria.

Now, six years after Canterbury's restraint on publication, Hutchinson was still concerned to secure 'official' approval for his work. He defers to authority, both Sloane's and that of the judge who had presided over the trial: 'The Judge who tryed her & hath the Life of the poor Woman upon him, & hath heard most of ye Arguments about it, is the likeliest Person

---

[13] See Ch. 1 above.
[14] BL Sloane MS 4040, f 302, 4 Feb. 1706. Hutchinson was enthusiastic about the union, see his *Sermon preached . . . May 1st 1707, being the Day of thanksgiving for the Union of England and Scotland* (1708).

to know what is proper in this Case.' Hutchinson does not wish to overreach himself or to cause offence: 'I am a perfect stranger to him, it would be a piece of Presumtion for an obscure Country Parson to trouble him with his Papers.' He therefore seeks access to the judge, Sir John Powell, via Sloane. If Powell 'will give himself the trouble of reading' Hutchinson's papers, '& shall afterward approve of them so far as to give leave to have them dedicated to him it will encourage the Reader to venture more freely in making his judgment of the case'. What is more, such a dedication would protect Hutchinson, acting as 'a security to me from such insulting Treatment as may chance otherwise to meet with'. Hutchinson believed that his book would be intensely controversial in 1712, as would have seemed likely from the frayed tempers of the Wenham controversy.[15]

Hutchinson's failure subsequently to publish in 1712—which must have been, in terms of publicity and sales, a missed opportunity—indicates how contentious the subject was, within the élite circles in which Hutchinson moved. Damage to his career may well have been a consideration. Witchcraft in 1712 was a dangerous subject, because views about it had become so highly polarized; it was not something for an ambitious clergyman to dabble in. 'Open contests', to cite words from another controversy over witchcraft, could 'mean an inextinguishable flame'.[16] For Hutchinson and his advisers in 1712, witchcraft proved, yet again, too risky a subject for publication. Only the subsequent and abrupt descent of witchcraft into the domain of reflex ridicule made his undertaking a respectable one, one which might end in a bishopric, something Hutchinson no doubt wanted and which he did, at Down and Connor in Ireland, ultimately secure.

NATURAL ORDER; SOCIAL ORDER

Francis Hutchinson was a Whig on his way up: a graduate of Catharine Hall, Cambridge; doctor of divinity; from 1692, the year of the Salem witch trials, vicar of St James's, Bury St Edmunds, site of the Hale witch trial; chaplain to the King from 1715; and Bishop of Down and Connor from 1721. Like any Whig prelate worth his salt, Hutchinson promoted the reasonableness of religion, but he did not go so far as to replace revelation with reason. Boulton accused him of a dangerous surfeit of

---

[15] BL Sloane MS 4043 f 38, 3 Apr. 1712.
[16] The Salem trials: *Calendar of State Papers, America and West Indies, 1689–1692*, § 2551. Sir William Phips to William Blathwayt, 12 Oct. 1692, Boston.

rationalism, asking if everything '*monstrous*' must needs 'be absurd in respect of Belief, that is so in regard to the common Rule of Reason'.[17] In fact, Hutchinson maintained the same sort of balance between reason and revelation that we find in Boulton's own work. 'No piercing Eye', Hutchinson writes 'cou'd read those [Christ's] Doctrines in the face of the Sky.'[18] He does not want to deny that spirits are present and active in the world, averring that 'the sober Belief of good and bad Spirits is an essential Part of every good Christian's Faith'.[19] Eager to preserve the ontology of spirit, he preaches the 'certain Existence of Spirits', of angels 'of great Force and Power', of a 'nobler, active Substance, superiour to passive insensible dead Matter' which is 'the Substance of the Angelick Natures and the Souls of Men'.[20] This did not preclude a thorough commitment to natural philosophy. Hutchinson and Boulton were not divided by natural philosophy; they vied for its imprimatur. In the case of the swimming of witches, their disputes over the hydrostatics of the phenomenon read like a parody of the Boylean debates of the 1670s.[21] While Boulton wants to appeal to the new science to bolster witchcraft theory, Hutchinson is convinced that the progress of natural philosophy has been an effective agent in the decline of witchcraft beliefs among educated people. Too many historians have taken Hutchinson's views on the matter at face value.

The *Historical Essay* is fulsome in its praise for the Royal Society, and for English rationalism. Britain was 'the very first in modern Improvements of natural and experimental Philosophy', and, 'so I believe . . . one of the first in gaining and spreading true Judgment' in the matter of witchcraft.[22] The two are connected. At the very outset of the book, the new science is called in as a model:

Rational Arguments without Facts, can never decide this Case. A Man may as well compose a true System of Natural Philosophy, without Experiments, as state the Case of Witchcraft, without a careful Enquiry into those Appearances of it, that have made so many Wise Men believe it.[23]

[17] Boulton, *Vindication*, 82.

[18] Hutchinson, *Historical Essay*, sermon 1, 'The Christian Religion Demonstrated', 233.

[19] Ibid., dedication, p. vi.   [20] Ibid., sermon 2, 'Concerning Angels', 260.

[21] While Hutchinson points out that variations in the specific gravity of the victims may suffice to explain their differential buoyancy, Boulton asserts that body density does not, as Hutchinson would have it, vary according to age. Hutchinson, *Historical Essay*, 138 f.; Boulton, *Vindication*, 122 f.

[22] Hutchinson, *Historical Essay*, 133. Cf. [Richard Bentley] (Phileleutherus Lipsiensis), *Remarks upon a late Discourse of Free-Thinking* (1713), 32–4.

[23] Hutchinson, *Historical Essay*, 12.

Hutchinson is concerned for a balance between reason and experience, between system and fact. He implicitly appeals to the dominant natural philosophical text of the period, Newton's *Principia*, in which mathematical, or rational, principles are seen to be mirrored in experience. An 'Enquiry into Appearances' which have, in the case of witchcraft, misled 'so many Wise Men', no doubt through attempts to save the appearances, will reveal the true basis of the phenomena in question. Just as Ptolemaic astronomy and Aristotelian dynamics have been superseded by Newton's system, so too will the old witchcraft theory be overtaken by a new interpretation of the facts.

Later on, Hutchinson fills in this vision by opposing two sets of rules to reason by, one profitable, one pernicious. One scheme operates in 'those Times and Places that have been troubled with few Witches'; the other is 'a Catalogue of the Principles of those Times and Men that have been troubled with and have hang'd great Numbers'. The former, 'some few, safe, negative Rules' can be profitably compared with some of Newton's rules of reasoning set out in book 3 of the *Principia*: '1. Do not intrude into Things that you have not seen, *Col.* 2. 18', writes Hutchinson. Is this not the very substance of Newton's objections to Cartesian mechanism, which demand that we should 'not . . . relinquish the evidence of experiments for the sake of dreams and vain fictions of our own devising'? Other passages might be compared to Newton's avowal, '*hypotheses non fingo*', that he frames no hypotheses. 'Things odd and unaccountable are to be respited', Hutchinson writes, 'till we understand them.' And, again, 'where there is no known Rule to decide by, make no Judgment'. Newton and Hutchinson agreed on the vitality of God's active providence in the world since, according to the latter, 'it becomes us to shew our Faith in God, by leaving doubtful Cases to his Providence, which is powerfully present and active in the World'.

It is notorious that Newton's work was all things to all manner of men, a piece of established knowledge to be fought over by opposing philosophical sects. Both sides in the debate over active principles, for instance, sought the sanction of a Newtonian genealogy. The Newtonian style of reasoning, the rational–cum–empirical method, was appropriated in a similar way. Like so many others, Hutchinson was some sort of Newtonian. He wanted an active, interventionist God, a strong current in Newton's work; his rules of reasoning can be construed as Newtonian; and compare the Hutchinsonian requirement that 'all real Truths' be 'and ever must be, uniform, and of a piece with one another', with Newton's famous injunction: 'the analogy of nature . . . is wont to be simple, and always consonant to itself.' All this is just what we would expect from a Whiggish divine of the early eighteenth century.[24]

There is a political edge to Hutchinson's commitment to natural philosophy. The *Essay* is very much a product of the aspiring Whig hegemony which expressed itself in both the Riot Act and the propagation of Newtonian mechanics. Hutchinson, a sympathetic biographer of Archbishop Tillotson,[25] is almost a textbook example of Margaret Jacob's ideal type of Newtonian Latitudinarian, a propagandist for the Whig order of things. The title-page of the *Essay* promises 'Observation upon Matters of Fact', in the manner of the experimental philosophy; and cites the first epistle of Timothy, with its 'Warning against Fanatical Men': 'But refuse profane and old Wives Fables, and exercise thy self rather with Godliness.'

Hutchinson earnestly distanced himself from any hint of fanaticism. He was a determined opponent of enthusiasm, of which witchcraft belief was, in his eyes, a particularly disreputable branch. In 1708, he intervened in the controversy over the French prophets, the enthusiastic Protestant refugees known as the Camisards, with his book, *A Short View of the Pretended Spirit of Prophecy Taken from its First Rise in the Year 1688, to its Present State among us. Together with some Observations upon their Doctrines and pretended Miracles. And Examples of such like Delusions in the World.*[26] The Camisards' claims, Hutchinson declared in this trial run for his book about witchcraft, 'want . . . *good proof* '. There are no 'Credible Witnesses', only 'very bad Men'. Hutchinson is, as had been the case with the Wenham trial, concerned about public order. He bemoans 'disorderly behaviour', and asserts that the Camisards' 'way of Life and Worship' demonstrated that 'they were fallen into a religious Frenzy', that their 'Imagination' was 'as plain a touch of Madness as any of the Follies of *Bedlam*'. Against such spiritual disorder Hutchinson offers the ideal of an authorized priesthood, 'a settled Order of Teachers',

---

[24] Ibid. 54 f., 230; Isaac Newton, *Philosophiae Naturalis Principia Mathematica*, 2nd edn. (1713), 'Regulae Philosophandae III'. See also John Henry, 'Occult Qualities and the Experimental Philosophy: Active Principles in Pre-Newtonian Matter Theory', *HS* 24 (1986); P. M. Heimann, 'Voluntarism and Immanence', *JHI* 39 (1978); Margaret Jacob, *The Newtonians and the English Revolution* (Ithaca, NY, 1976). For another sort of Newtonian, see Anita Guerrini, 'The Tory Newtonians: Gregory, Pitcairne and their Circle', *JBS* 25 (1986).

[25] 'With soft Words and strong Arguments he reasoned away the Superstitions of the Idolaters of *Rome*, and with the Warmth of his Charity melted the stubborn Hearts of several *Non-Conformists* of his own Country'; F. H[utchinson], *The Life of the Most Reverend Father in GOD, John Tillotson* (1717), 9.

[26] On the Camisards, see Hillel Schwartz, *The French Prophets* (Berkeley, 1981), esp. 88 and n.

who are to teach 'Piety, Virtue, and humble Submission to Government'. They are to be 'furnished with Learning and such degrees of Knowledge as we can attain to': 'Philosophical Learning' which is the 'Knowledge of God's Works of Nature'; and 'Historical' learning, which is the 'Knowledge of his Works of Providence'.[27]

Hutchinson's story-telling in the *Historical Essay* is coloured by similar current concerns. He paints John Darrell, the Elizabethan Puritan 'exorcist', as a man full of 'Enthusiastical ill-grounded Notions', stirring up no end of trouble in Nottingham where 'People flock'd to hear him . . . [and] he entertained them with Sermons of Devils, and Possessions . . . till the Maids were afraid to fetch Beer out of the Cellars, without Company with them'. This tone of superiority, binding together idle amusements, beer, serving wenches, and brute stupidity into a picture of vulgar superstition, is characteristic not only of Hutchinson but of much writing about 'popular superstition' in the eighteenth century. Here it is made all the more dangerous by the 'Violence and Anger' apparent at Darrell's public meetings, such that the cowed local political authorities 'would not meddle' in the business.

Elsewhere, in his *Compassionate Address to . . . Papists*, Hutchinson underlined the political dangers of such behaviour. 'Those Counterfeits in *Casting out Devils*', for instance, 'were contriv'd here at Home by the Managers of *Babington's* Conspiracy and the *Spanish* Invasion.' This had been a scheme intended 'to put the Minds of the People into such a Temper, that they might be fit to venture upon the hazardous Actions they had prepar'd for them'. In general, a 'furious sermon', a 'lying miracle', or a '*French* Prophet', any of these, might 'have often great effect upon Mens Minds, and disturb them in their honest Labours, and dispose them to vent'rous Actions'. The relevance of such dangers, six years after the Wenham trial and three years after the Jacobite rebellion, would have been obvious.[28]

For Hutchinson, the unreliability of the populace is reflected in their adoption of false beliefs. Boulton and Hutchinson showed their very different attitudes to popular belief in a discussion of one particular piece of natural history. In witch-lore, witches' familiars are supposed to steal butter

---

[27] 16, 3, 45, 13 f., 39, 36. Cf. Hutchinson's letter of 12 Oct. 1723 to Sloane, from Ireland, requesting data on eclipses. 'If one coud open their Minds [those of his flock] a little in Civil [i.e. natural] things it might perhaps help them to judg better in Religious'. BL Sloane MS 4047, f67.

[28] Hutchinson, *Historical Essay*, 195, 201, 205; Francis Hutchinson, *A Compassionate Address to those Papists, Who will be prevail'd with to examine the CAUSE for which they Suffer* (1716), 15.

and leave traces of it in their tracks. This substance is popularly identified with a milky residue commonly seen on plants. Hutchinson 'cannot but stand amazed' when he sees '*Swedish* Judges, and Dr *Horneck* after them, learn from the Rabble' to call this stuff '*Witches Butter*'. He offers a fanciful natural explanation: grasshoppers are the carriers rather than possessed cats or diabolical ravens.[29] Warming to Hutchinson's literalism, Boulton points out that the amount of 'butter' carried by a cat or raven would be much greater than that manageable by any conceivable grasshopper:

tho' the latter might be called *Witches Butter*, from some Likeness with the former . . . this which comes from Grasshoppers, is called so by the Rabble; the other *Witches Butter*, by those the Doctor is too timorous in ridiculing with a suppositious Oversight, which appears to be none.[30]

At first sight, we are back to the squabbling over science. Both writers want to condemn the views of their opponents as vulgar and unscientific. The disagreement does, however, reveal a fundamental difference in attitude. Whereas Hutchinson equates popular superstition and demonology, and rejects a whole system of belief, Boulton has a different conception of vulgar error. It is not the adoption of a false system of belief but a category mistake within a system. It is a failure to make proper identification—and here we return to Boulton's *esprit de corps* as a physician—or to draw the line between natural and supernatural in the right place. Boulton's response to Hutchinson's attempts to taint witchcraft theory with dangerous vulgarity are robust, and he firmly corrects his opponent's distorted priorities, which place social status before truth. 'I shall be glad', Boulton boasts, 'to be one of those People always, that fall in with such popular Pretences.'[31] His antagonist is just as forthright:

as our common People are of themselves too forward in receiving such superstitious Notions tho' they tend directly to the shedding Blood, I hope all good Men will agree with me, in thinking, that the more Infection is scatter'd abroad amongst the People by ill Authors and covetous Booksellers, the more need is there of proper Assistances to help weak Minds, in judging of such dark, yet strong and bloody Delusions.

The metaphor is one of public hygiene. These notions are an 'infection'. What is needed are 'proper Assistances to help weak Minds'—persuasion or perhaps even confinement? Men like Boulton are, punningly, 'ill'; their agents, plain greedy.[32]

---

[29] Hutchinson, *Historical Essay*, 99.   [30] Boulton, *Vindication*, 85 f.
[31] Ibid. 155.   [32] Hutchinson, *Historical Essay*, 108.

Hutchinson's major preoccupations were civility, authority, and order. In the context of Scottish union, this had involved postponing a direct attack on witchcraft prosecution. Hutchinson appreciated the stabilization of British politics that the union offered, while hoping in the long run to insulate English society from destabilizing Scottish superstition.[33] At the time of the Wenham trial, in the heat of party disturbances, Hutchinson was confirmed in his view of how dangerously factious witchcraft persecution could be. By the time the book actually appeared, Hutchinson embodied the nervous stability of the early Hanoverian regime, anxious to distance itself from factionalism, and threatened by proscribed Tories and the surly mob alike.

As far as Hutchinson was concerned, Boulton was pandering to the prejudices of the mob. There is indeed something almost provocative, verging on the politically dangerous, in Boulton's gladness 'to be one of those People always that fall in with . . . popular Pretences'. That is not to say that Boulton rejects authority *per se*. He refuses to construct vulgar beliefs in the way Hutchinson would like to. Like Methodists later in the century, he stands four-square with plebeian beliefs, as long as they are doctrinally sound; and, as for John Wesley, the 'Rule and Standard' of his belief is scripture, 'as it is translated and published by the consent of the Church, and with their Approbation, who are the Heads of the Church, and have most Right and Probability of leading me in the right Way'. Boulton is not against authority; he simply views Hutchinson's authority as usurped. 'If we disbelieve Sacred Writings,' Boulton writes, anticipating Wesley, 'must not all Religion be slighted?' Hutchinson is condemned both as an authoritarian with 'as much Infallibility as the Pope' and, ironically given Hutchinson's anti-fanaticism, as a fanatic 'opposing moral Proof and the Testimony of Scripture, with his bare *ipse dixit*.' Hutchinson's line on witchcraft is no more than 'the Opinion of Two or Three private Men'.[34]

Boulton's *Vindication* encapsulates the feelings of those who felt excluded from the political nation in 1722. No Tory, he may nevertheless have been the sort of Whig Defoe had been appealing to in 1711, desirous of Christian unity, worried by the rising tide of irreligion. By no means a Jacobite, indeed, a Hanoverian loyalist in 1715, Boulton was sufficiently dissatisfied by 1722 to play with the sort of populism which put him

---

[33] For Hutchinson's attitude towards the union of 1707, see his *Sermon preached . . . [on] the Day of thanksgiving for the Union of England and Scotland.*

[34] *Vindication*, pp. v f., 155 f., ix, 99, 135; Henry Moore, *The Life of the Reverend John Wesley* (Leeds, 1825), 323: 'The giving up witchcraft, is in effect giving up the Bible.'

alongside Tories, Jacobites, and their disaffected Whig allies. Witchcraft belief might have provided, to adopt Nicholas Rogers' analysis of the appeal of Stuart claims, a 'language of political blasphemy . . . designed to draw Whig anger, to tease and unsettle the Court'.[35]

If Hutchinson exhibits all the anxieties of the Whig grandee, Boulton's reflexes are grounded in political and religious nostalgia, with a desire for what a Jacobite of the 1690s called the 'Catholick good' of 'Unity', and a recognition that 'all diabolical Art tends to violat Unity'.[36] Boulton's Christian community is defined against the Devil, and on the basis of a core of necessary beliefs, including the belief in witchcraft. Boulton's religion, like that of Defoe's Mr Review before, or that of Wesley after him, is altogether a stern business. He wants to 'make People afraid of the Devil and his works, and shew the Necessity of imploring Divine Assistance'.[37] Severity in the service of unity is coupled with eirenicism, however. Roman beliefs about witchcraft are not to be rejected, but welcomed as 'rather an additional Confirmation of what we believe, since both we and they consent jointly to the same Sense of the Scriptures which confirms both our Beliefs'.[38] The key to Boulton's attitude is his redeployment of Christ's own words, '*they that are not against us, are on our part*'. This is a formula with which he means to defend dissenting exorcists but which, in its almost Manichaean tendency, shows that Boulton's Christian community is one defined against outsiders.[39]

The rationale of acceptable religion for Hutchinson is politeness and social order, hence his rejection of what he sees as enthusiastic beliefs, springing out of Popery and fanaticism. In one sense, Hutchinson's is, like Boulton's, a broad church. He wants to 'open the Door for Communion . . . as wide' as possible, offering 'an honest Latitude, or True Catholick Christian Largeness of Heart'. But, as ever, the aim is a Whig style of Christian civility, Addisonian in flavour. The good parson must imitate St Paul, in being all things to all men, the aims being 'Obedience to the Laws, and . . . Christian Communion', in that order. 'The great End of Religion', Hutchinson opined in a phrase that could have come straight out of the *Spectator*, 'is to calm and soften the Roughness of Men's passions.'[40]

[35] Nicholas Rogers, 'Riot and Popular Jacobitism in Early Hanoverian England', in E. Cruickshanks (ed.), *Ideology and Conspiracy: Aspects of Jacobitism, 1689–1759* (Edinburgh, 1982), 83, 85.

[36] 'Grounds of a true Catholick', a list made by Lord Nairne, Bodleian Carte MS 208, f 224a.

[37] Boulton, *Vindication*, 35 f. [38] Ibid. 149.

[39] Ibid. 117. [40] Hutchinson, *A Compassionate Address*, 19–22.

Unlike Defoe, Boulton did not refashion his witch beliefs to suit a new era. Where Defoe transformed witchcraft into a symbol for faction, Boulton straightforwardly denied the relevance of faction to witchcraft. He would, in a significant turn of phrase, 'never blame any Party for their close Adherence to Scripture'.[41] Hutchinson means precisely the opposite. His writing explicitly confirms the account of the witchcraft debate set out in the last chapter, and I quote at length Hutchinson's summary of the risks of witchcraft belief, past and present:

These Doctrines have often been made Party-Causes both in our own and other Nations. One side lays hold of them as Arguments of greater *Faith*, and *Orthodoxy*, and closer Adherence to Scripture, and calls the other *Atheists*, *Sadducees*, and *Infidels*. The People easily fall in with such popular Pretences; and not only those that stand in the Prosecutor's way, and a few suspected Persons are sacrific'd, but sometimes Governments are shaken, if they oppose their Notions. Our present Freedom from these Evils are no Security, that such a Time may not turn up in one Revolution or another.[42]

The sense of current anxiety in this passage, and elsewhere in Hutchinson's essay, should not be overlooked. From our own perspective, the 'witch-craze' came to an end around 1700. Executions had stopped some years before, belief was on the wane. Hutchinson's perspective is different. He starts out by listing the substantial number of works supporting witch beliefs which had been published in the decades before his book. He warns that it could all too easily happen again. Waves of panic had been preceded and followed by isolated prosecutions. The last big scare in England had been in the revolutionary 1640s. Isolated prosecutions trickled on through the remainder of the century. From the viewpoint of the nervous Whig insider in 1718, it might seem that another wave could only too easily arrive. The Pittenweem witch-scare had preceded the Scottish union by only three years, and 1712 had seen the Wenham trial, stoked by political partisanship. Perhaps only a precarious end to instability had been achieved. Witch-lore continued to infect the minds of the populace. Books about witchcraft are 'read with great Eagerness', in 'Tradesmen's Shops, and Farmer's Houses'. Such vulgar narratives are 'continually levening the Minds of the Youth'. Given the 'sore Evils these Notions bring where they prevail', Hutchinson is clear that they must be 'combated, oppos'd, and *kept down*'.[43]

The irony here is that Hutchinson's book was, in any serious sense, the

---

[41] Boulton, *Vindication*, p. xii.   [42] Hutchinson, *Historical Essay*, 181 f.
[43] Ibid., p. xiv, my emphasis.

last word on the subject. A new wave of witch persecution never arrived. Despite Boulton's *Vindication*, Hutchinson's work represented the effective closure of debate. Subsequent commentators, including Daillon, as we have seen, dismissed Boulton out of hand. Witchcraft, as we shall see, occasionally returned to a dimmer political limelight. Nevertheless, the factionalization of witchcraft in 1712, and the comparative, precarious stabilization of political life which followed the Hanoverian accession, can be said successively to have initiated and completed the demise of witchcraft theory as a system of belief in England. This is something Hutchinson's work confirms; but the *Historical Essay* remains Janusfaced, looking anxiously back to an unruly past, but using that image of unruliness to construct the prospect of an untroubled and polite (in the Addisonian sense) future.[44]

It was only in retrospect that the demise of witchcraft theory among the educated seemed an obvious and inevitable development, a dawning of reason. For all his polemic, Hutchinson trod carefully, as in this letter to Arthur Charlett, master of University College:

I hope . . . [my] principles are thus v. right as well as safe & prudential, I am apt to think that time will confirm them. If ever experience(s) doth shew the contrary, I have no Interest to tempt me to shut my eyes against it, & I hope in such a case I shoud have virtue enough to make me . . . change notions.

'At present', Hutchinson wrote in a curiously dissociating phrase, 'I am of the same mind with my Book.'[45] His stance in the letter to Charlett reflects his constant concern, throughout the whole process of writing and publishing a book about witchcraft, to be 'safe and prudential'. In a period of transition and uncertainty, he treads carefully. This is the testimony of his *personal* experience, from 1706 to 1712 and beyond: writing about witchcraft is a tricky business.

Hutchinson's words underline his commitment to an empirical stance; they do not adequately describe the debate in which he was participating, however. We may question whether he was really prepared to change his mind. More than that, the testimony of experience(s) alone is not enough to explain the demise of witchcraft theory as public belief. Witchcraft theory was not straightforwardly tested in the realm of experience, found wanting, and consequently discarded. When John Stuart Mill wrote, a century later, that 'no evidence can *prove* witchcraft; since there *can never*

---

[44] Bruno Latour, *Science in Action* (Milton Keynes, 1987), 7–13.
[45] Bodleian Library, Ballard MS 38 f27, dated 17 July 1718, from Bury. Cf. Hutchinson, *Historical Essay*, 229: 'I doubt not, but Time and Experience will confirm farther.'

be any evidence of it, good or bad, trustworthy or the reverse', he meant to affirm the victory of rationality; at the same time, however, his remark implies that victory was not achieved by empirical argument in the abstract, or an appeal to the facts. If there can be no evidence to prove witchcraft, it is because the decision to believe in or dismiss witchcraft theory is not, ultimately, about evidence. It is about a way of seeing.[46]

---

[46] 'Jeremy Bentham's Rationale of Judicial Evidence' (1827), in John Stuart Mill, *Miscellaneous Writings*, vol. xxi of *Collected Works of John Stuart Mill* (1989), 30.

7

Afterlife

[The] Antient System . . . [is] broken up, the Vessel of Sorcery shipwreckt and only some shattered planks and pieces disjoyned floating
and scattered on the Ocean of the human Activity and Bustle.

  Ezra Stiles, pastor at Newport, Rhode Island, later president of
  Yale College, diary entry, June 1773[1]

WITCHCRAFT AND HIGH-FLYING

The association between high-flying and witchcraft belief established by
the Wenham trial was compelling. It was being used to warn against
priestcraft and praise freethinking only a year later in 1713:

since the *Reign* of Dr SACHEVERELL, when the Clamours against *Free-Thinking*
began to be loudest, the Devil has again resum'd his Empire, and appears in the
shape of Cats, and enters into confederacy with old Women; and several have
been try'd, and many are accus'd, thro all parts of the Kingdom for being Witches.[2]

By 1715, this notion of a brief renascence of witch-hunting under
high-flying influence had become part of a Whig interpretation of recent
history. White Kennett blamed the revival of witchcraft persecution on
the rage of party. In his sermon, 'The Witchcraft of the present Rebellion', Kennett confirmed the significance of the Wenham controversy:

Nay *Witchcraft* in the Letter, with Prosecutions and Trials upon it, did begin to
revive amidst the late Party-Zeal, and if the Judges would have countenanc'd the
Superstition, GOD knows how far those feats of *Popery* might have grown upon us.[3]

---

[1] Franklin Dexter (ed.), *The Literary Diary of Ezra Stiles* (3 vols.; New York, 1910), i.
385 f., cited in Richard Godbeer, *The Devil's Dominion: Magic and Religion in Early New
England* (Cambridge, 1992), 228.
  [2] Anthony Collins, *A Discourse of Free-Thinking* (1713), 30.
  [3] White Kennett, *The Witchcraft of the present Rebellion, A Sermon preach'd . . . On Sunday 25th of September, 1715* (1715).

Kennett was determined that this was to be the last blast of these party-driven, superstitious, Popish feats. The rhetoric of witchcraft was to be refocused. It may be inadvisable to pursue '*Witchcraft* in the Letter'; but rebellion is as the sin of witchcraft, and deserves to be rooted out in the same way.[4]

A Seasonable Apology for Father Dominick (otherwise known as Francis Atterbury, at that time imprisoned for his supposed role in the Jacobite 'Atterbury Plot') appeared a decade after Collins's *Discourse of Free-Thinking*.[5] The author, probably the satirist Thomas Gordon, tells us of 'Some grave Divines and deep Casuists' who 'maintain, that the Father of Lies endeavours to ape the Father of Light in many things . . . *lo*, cry they, *the Devil has his Deputies and Ministers too*!'

> They likewise hold, and bring Proofs for it; that he has numerous female Deputies in every Corner of the Universe: For what are Witches but the Devils Embassadresses, the zealous Pastoresses, who feed his Familiars and his daily Negotiatrixes to win People to him, and bring in his Harvest?

The voice moves on to be more specific:

> For this end, he has an old wither'd Journey-woman or two in every District. The learned *Jane Wenham* was one of them; she was tried some Years ago at *Hertford*, for holding a Schismatical Conventicle of Cats and Gossips, who were great Hereticks, and went a caterwauling from the Church.

The author makes a clear connection between sacerdotalism and witch belief. His high-flying 'Client' has 'the Keys of both Worlds at his Girdle' and his 'greatest Wonder is' that he cannot 'with this Master-key of his, open the sublunary Lock that holds him fast in Durance, especially when they say, even Witches and Necromancers can do it'. The way to rise is to be 'a furious Broker of Ceremonies' and 'a zealous Maintainer of *occult Qualities*'. The very title of the book binds together all the notions of the Wenham era: 'Nonjuring Doctors . . . Ceremonies, Unity, Dissension . . . Anathemas . . . Exorcism and March-Beer'.[6]

---

[4] Cf. 'A Panegyrick' (1696/7) cited by Paul Monod, *Jacobitism and the English People, 1688–1788* (Cambridge, 1989), 56 f., who attributes it either to Henry Hall or to John Grubham Howe: 'Rebels, like witches, having signed the rolls | Must serve their masters, though they damn their souls.' As Monod puts it: 'As in witchcraft, rebellion reversed the natural order of things, subverted the meaning of words and set the world upside down.'

[5] See G. V. Bennett, *The Tory Crisis in Church and State* (Oxford, 1975), chs. 12–14.

[6] [Thomas Gordon], *A Seasonable Apology for Father Dominick, Chaplain to Prince Prettyman the Catholick, But now lying in Durance under the Suspicion of secret Iniquity. In which are occasionally inserted some weighty Arguments for calling a General Council of the Nonjuring Doctors, for the further Propagation of Ceremonies, Unity, Dissention, and Anathemas; and for the better Improvement of Exorcism and March-Beer* (1723), 7 ff., 14, 28.

A year or so later, Gordon's *Humourist*, a journal directed against 'the *ardent Zeal* of her [the Church's] orthodox Sons . . . full of *Lunacy* and *Zeal*', devoted two essays to the topic of witchcraft, whose 'wretched gaping Spirit still haunts Mankind, and still subjects them to endless Impositions and shameful Delusions, of which *one Party of Men* have made a plentiful Harvest'.[7] It is the Tory party that is meant.

So it was to continue, for decades. Tobias Smollett's picaresque hero Peregrine Pickle has a tutor, one Mr Jolter, a man of 'zeal . . . so exceedingly fervent . . . an high-churchman, and of consequence a malecontent'. When Peregrine talks of the 'idle notions' of sorcery and witchcraft, 'now justly exploded by all sensible men', it is Jolter who 'could not help signifying his dissent'. He opposes Peregrine's scepticism with 'the authority of scripture, quotations from the fathers, and the confession of many wretches who suffered death for having carried on correspondence with evil spirits'. He also cites 'the evidence of Satan's Invisible World, and Moreton's', that is, Defoe's, 'history of witchcraft'.[8]

The polarization of the Wenham trial did not necessitate that, in reality, all believers in witchcraft were Tories, or all Tories believers in witchcraft. Witchcraft was a marginal belief, with Tory resonances, not an article of faith. Beliefs among Tories ranged from the scepticism offered by Henry Stebbing in his pamphlet on the Wenham trial,[9] via the honest doubt of the antiquary Thomas Hearne or of Samuel Johnson, to the outraged credulity of John Wesley, who attacked Smollett's manner of speaking about witchcraft as 'extremely offensive to every sensible man who cannot give up his Bible'.[10]

Hearne couched his support for Jane Wenham's innocence in a context which suggests he did not reject the possibility of witchcraft outright. 'Notwithstanding Wenham's Condemnation,' he wrote, 'the Judge got her repriev'd. And justly too. For I am fully satisfy'd since that the poor Woman was abus'd, & that she was far from being a Witch.' The case deserved very careful consideration, 'all the Circumstances' being 'very strange and surprizing'.[11]

---

[7] Thomas Gordon, *The Humourist: being essays upon several subjects* (2 vols.; 1724–5), 74.

[8] Tobias Smollett, *The Adventures of Peregrine Pickle* (1751; Oxford, 1983), 78, 182. Moreton's history is Defoe's *Political History of the Devil*. Talk about witchcraft and the devil figures prominently in *Peregrine Pickle*, as does a scene of fraudulent conjuring, 551–75.

[9] *The Case of the Hertfordshire Witchcraft Considered* (1712), but for doubts on this possible attribution see Wallace Notestein, *A History of Witchcraft* (Washington, 1911), 374.

[10] *The Journal of Rev. John Wesley* (4 vols.; 1906), iii. 412, entry for 4 July 1770.

[11] Thomas Hearne, *Remarks and Collections*, iii, ed. C. E. Doble (Oxford, 1889), 327, entry for 30 Mar. 1712.

Samuel Johnson was a sentimental Tory, even a Jacobite fellow-traveller. His remarks on witchcraft, as recorded by James Boswell, issued from his Tory outlook, tempered by the characteristic Johnsonian common sense. In the Hebrides journal we find the following exchange:

Crosbie 'But it is not credible, that witches should have effected what they are said in stories to have done.'—*Johnson* 'Sir, I am not defending their credibility. I am only saying, that your arguments are not good, and will not overturn the belief of witchcraft—(Dr Ferguson said to me, aside, 'He is right')—And then, sir, you have all mankind, rude and civilized, agreeing in the belief of the agency of preternatural powers. You must take evidence: you must consider, that wise and great men have condemned witches to die.'[12]

Boswell's *Life of Johnson* records a similarly measured opinion—'you have not only the general report and belief, but you have many voluntary solemn confessions'—which suggests that Johnson was doing more than scoring debating points. Boswell's gloss confirms this:

He did not affirm anything positively upon a subject which it is the fashion of the times to laugh at as a matter of absurd credulity. He only seemed willing, as a candid enquirer after truth, however strange and inexplicable, to shew that he understood what might be urged for it.[13]

John Wesley's commitment to witchcraft belief has to be seen in the context of his Tory upbringing and nonjuring affections, as well as his biblical fundamentalism. 'The giving up witchcraft', Wesley declared in 1768, 'is in effect giving up the Bible.' He knew 'no reason . . . why we should suffer even this weapon to be wrested out of our hands', a weapon against 'Deism, Atheism, and Materialism'. In his journal, he wrote:

the infidels have hooted witchcraft out of the world; and the complaisant Christians, in large numbers, have joined with them in the cry. I do not so much wonder at this, that many of these should herein talk like infidels; but I have sometimes been inclined to wonder at the pert, saucy, indecent manner wherein some of those trample upon men far wiser than themselves; at their speaking so dogmatically against what not only the world, Heathen and Christian, believed in all past ages, but thousands, learned as well as unlearned, firmly believe at this day.

Wesley's belief in witchcraft was in many senses a microcosm of his career. Coming out of an élite high-church tradition, he ended up appealing

---

[12] *Boswell's Life of Johnson. Together with Boswell's Journal of a Tour to the Hebrides and Johnson's Diary of A Journey into North Wales*, ed. G. B. Hill and L. F. Powell (6 vols.; Oxford, 1934), v. 45 f., Monday 16 Aug. 1773.
[13] Ibid. 178 f.

to a very different sort of audience: much larger and socially diverse but politically excluded. The same might be said of witch beliefs.[14]

The attitude of the polite classes towards Wesley's brand of supernaturalism is encapsulated in William Hogarth's print of 1762, *Credulity, Superstition and Fanaticism* (illustration 2). From the pulpit a priest-cum-harlequin-cum-Methodist preaches, manipulating two puppets for the edification of his congregation: a witch and cat on a broomstick; and the Devil with a gridiron. His text is indicative: 'I Speak as a Fool.' The meeting-house is filled with a crowd of enthusiasts, praying wildly, cradling and kissing idolatrous images, one figure drowsily listening to the ministrations of a whispering demon. In the foreground Mary Tofts, a well-known impostor, is busy giving birth to rabbits. The boy of Bilson spits nails. A sort of thermometer measures the enthusiasm from lukewarm to raving: it is topped by the drummer of Tedworth, and stands on volumes of Wesley's sermons and 'Glanvil on Witches'. Elsewhere we can see 'Whitfield's Journal' and James I's 'Demonology'. Outside the window, a pipe-smoking Turk watches, bemused. The caption to the print is from St John's gospel: 'Believe not every Spirit, but try the Spirits whether they are of God: because many false Prophets are gone out into the World.'

An earlier unpublished version of this print, *c*.1761, had been entitled *Enthusiasm Delineated*, its intention 'to give a lineal representation of the strange Effects of the litteral and low conceptions of Sacred Beings as also of the Idolatrous Tendency of Pictures in Churches and prints in Religious books &c.' It thus represents a low-church reaction against high-flying, crypto-Catholic excess, as well as an artist's professional satire on fashionable Continental painting. The later version retains its equation of Methodism and Romanism, a new twist on the notions of the 1640s which bound Jesuits and sectaries together. The particular context of *Credulity, Superstition and Fanaticism*, according to Ronald Paulson, was the case of the Cock Lane Ghost,[15] an episode of supernaturalism in which Wesley and his Methodists had become heavily involved. Both

---

[14] Henry Moore, *The Life of the Reverend John Wesley* (Leeds, 1825), 323; Wesley, *Journal*, iii. 412, entry for 4 July 1770. On Wesley's high-flying roots, see J. B. Green, *John Wesley and William Law* (1945), and Henry D. Rack, *Reasonable Enthusiast: John Wesley and the Rise of Methodism* (1990), 48 ff.

[15] In Jan. 1762, knocking and scratching in the London house of the methodist Richard Parsons led to the interrogation of a supposed ghost; by late Feb. the incident had been revealed as a sham. 'The methodists', wrote Horace Walpole, 'had endeavoured to establish in Warwickshire, not only the belief, but the actual existence of ghosts. Being detected, they struck a bold stroke, and attempted to erect their system in the metropolis itself.' The affair had echoes of the Tedworth drummer, reported in Glanvill's *Saducismus Triumphatus*. See Ronald Paulson, *Hogarth: Art and Politics* (3 vols.; Cambridge, 1993), iii. 362–6.

2. *Credulity, Superstition and Fanaticism*, by William Hogarth (1762)

prints, however, link Methodism with high-flying, and the prominent place of witchcraft in the second is yet another confirmation of the high-flying image of witchcraft. The importance here of Hogarth's print is in its construction of witchcraft and fanaticism: the alliance we found in Defoe, between the church party and dissenters, has become the politically marginalized, if threateningly popular, phenomenon of Methodism. The belief in the necessity of witchcraft belief had migrated from one to the other.[16]

Credulity, Superstition and Fanaticism finds its polar opposite in an earlier print of Hogarth's, *The Sleeping Congregation* (illustration 3), published in the year of the repeal of the Jacobean witchcraft laws, 1736. Lechery is present in the face of clerical neglect. The women in the congregation, with their hooked noses, steeple hats,[17] and sinister air, are distinctly unsettling, even threatening. As compared to their dopey male companions, they seem alert and secretly watchful. The biblical text inscribed on the pulpit is from Paul's letter to the Galatians, chapter 4, verse 11: 'I am afraid of you, lest I have bestowed upon you labour in vain.' The preceding verses, which give that anxiety its context, point towards the worship of other gods, to apostasy, idolatry, and witchcraft:

Howbeit then, when ye knew not God, ye did service unto them which by nature are no gods. But now, after that ye have known God, or rather are known of God, how turn ye again to the weak and beggarly elements, whereunto ye desire again to be in bondage?

These two prints, nearly thirty years apart, make a pair, with their contrasting views of congregation and churchmanship, highlighting as they do two diametrically opposed dangers for the church, enthusiasm and torpor.[18]

Other hints can be picked up from Hogarth. John Hutchinson, author of *Moses's Principia* (1724), was a notorious anti-Newtonian philosopher of the eighteenth century, claiming to have derived his own system of natural philosophy from the Bible by reading it in the original Hebrew without points. Hutchinson's work was resolutely Trinitarian and conceived of itself as a blow struck against rampant deism. Hogarth's execrably punning *Frontispiss* (see frontispiece) was designed for an anti-Hutchinsonian work of the 1760s. It shows a witch, steeple-hatted, with a broomstick, sitting on a crescent moon, pissing onto the rocks below. Amidst the rocks we see rats or mice nibbling and exploring a volume of Hutchinson, of Newton, and a telescope. It is unclear whether the pissing witch is engendering the vermin, or flushing them away. The mouse which has fed on the philosophy of Hutchinson lies dead on the book. Paulson reminds us that the Hutchinsonians argued for glory over gravity, complaining

---

[16] See *Hogarth's Graphic Works*, ed. R. Paulson, 3rd rev. edn. (1989), 175–8.

[17] Customary wear for witches in prints by the 1730s, see below, p. 170.

[18] Hogarth produced a new version of *Sleeping Congregation* two weeks after the publication of *Credulity, Superstition and Fanaticism*; see Ronald Paulson, *Hogarth*, ii. 354–7.

3. *The Sleeping Congregation*, by William Hogarth (1736)

that 'gravity had got the better of revelation'.[19] In the Hutchinsonian
scheme of things, a thin circulating fluid accounted for celestial phenomena. The sun was its grand source. It emanated through the universe as
light, returning as air or spirits, and was in turn melted down by the sun

[19] *Hogarth's Graphic Works*, 197.

into light again. Hogarth takes this idea literally, and applies gravity to a stream of urine.

No commentator has convincingly explained why there should be a witch at the centre of this anti-Hutchinsonian image. It is the high-flying nature of Hutchinsonian philosophy that supplies the answer, and makes Hogarth's design another example of the association between high-flying and witch beliefs after the Wenham trial. Newtonianism was at the centre of the new establishment, confirmed in 1715. 'In retrospect', writes the historian John Gascoigne,

the Glorious Revolution came to be viewed as the victory of reason over the mystifications of the nonjurors and jacobites; England's governing classes expected, then, that the Church of England—the nation in its religious guise—should also emphasize its conformity with reason and embrace such masterpieces of rational analysis as Newton's *Principia*; to place too much emphasis on the gulf between human reason and revelation in the manner of the nonjurors called into question the ideology of the system of government with which the Church was intimately involved.[20]

Newtonian philosophy was reviled by many nonjurors and high-flyers. 'It is their Newtonian philosophy', wrote George Hickes to Roger North in 1713, 'wch hath Made Not onely so many Arians but Theists, and that Not onely among ye laity but I fear among our devines.'[21] Hutchinson's metaphysic provided high-flyers with an apparently systematic means of rebutting Newtonian rationalism. Its emphasis on the profound separation between the material and spiritual realms and upon biblical fundamentals placed it in opposition to the received version of Newton's philosophy, and, indeed, the temper of the times. It was a deft satirical move to graft witchcraft onto Hutchinsonianism. Hogarth's audience would be reminded of the affinity between high-flying and superstition; and recall the healthy role of Newtonianism in purging the world of such nonsense.[22]

The *Frontispiss* is pure satire. Christopher Smart's poem *Jubilate Agno*, written between 1758/9 and 1763, tells the same story, in a more serious,

---

[20] John Gascoigne, 'Politics, Patronage and Newtonianism: the Cambridge example', *HJ* 27/1 (1984), 23 f.

[21] Ibid. 22.

[22] See the following chapter on the role of Newton's nephew, biographer, and successor at the Mint, John Conduitt, in the repeal of the Jacobean witchcraft legislation. On Hutchinsonianism, see C. B. Wilde, 'Hutchinsonianism, Natural Philosophy and Religious Controversy in Eighteenth Century Britain', *HS* 18 (1980); id., 'Matter and Spirit as Natural Symbols in Eighteenth-Century British Natural Philosophy', *BJHS* 15 (1982).

if bizarre, vein. The broken nature of this long poem, and the circumstances of its composition—poor Kit Smart in the hospital for the insane—gives much of its rarefied subject matter and learned references the appearance of fragments from a shattered system of thought. The physicotheology of *Jubilate Agno* has been identified as Hutchinsonian, and it is resolutely anti-Newtonian and anti-mechanistic.[23] A high-flying tone is often to be heard.[24] This is the voice of a profound traditionalist modulated by alienation. 'The Lord illuminate us against the powers of darkness', he writes. A curious poetic literalism is at work—'For there are still serpents that can speak—God bless my head, my heart and my heel'—with a sense of a world alive with occult influences: 'For the AIR is contaminated by curses and evil language.'[25] It is with all this in mind that one confronts Smart's sequence of lines about witchcraft:

For the devil hath most power in winter, because darkness prevails.
For the Longing of Women is the operation of the Devil upon their conceptions.
For the marking of their children is from the same cause both of which are to be parried by prayer.
For the laws of King James the first against Witchcraft were wise, had it been of man to make laws.
For there are witches and wizards even now who are spoken to by their familiars.
For the visitation of their familiars is prevented by the Lord's incarnation.
For to conceive with intense diligence against one's neighbour is a branch of witchcraft.
For to use pollution, exact and cross things, and at the same time to think against a man is the crime direct.
For prayer with musick is good for persons so exacted upon.[26]

Smart had at one time explicitly condemned witch-hunting.[27] Here, in his madness, the scavenging intellect transcends that rejection. These are not the ravings of a lunatic, but the treasured arcana of the reactionary obsessive. They are given meaning by their participation in a Hutchinsonian

---

[23] e.g. 'For Newton nevertheless is more of error than of the truth, but I am of the WORD of GOD'; 'For I have shown the Vis Inertiae to be false, and such is all nonsense'; 'For the rising in the BAROMETER is not effected by pressure but by sympathy'; 'For the Centre is the hold of the Spirit upon the matter in hand'; 'For QUICK-SILVER is spiritual and so is the AIR to all intents and purposes'. Fragment B, §§ 195, 183, 213, 184 in *The Poetical Works of Christopher Smart i: 'Jubilate Agno'*, ed. Karina Williamson (Oxford, 1980), 42–9.

[24] e.g. 'For I pray God be gracious to the house of Stuart and consider their afflictions'; 'For I bless God that the CHURCH of ENGLAND is one of the SEVEN ev'n the candlestick of the Lord', § 71, 126, ibid. 24, 32.

[25] Ibid. § 90, 26; § 18, 15; § 221, 49.　　　[26] §§ 296–304, ibid. 60 f.

[27] In *The Midwife; Or Old Woman's Magazine* (3 vols.; 1751–3), ii. (1751), 61–9.

schema, but to the eighteenth-century mainstream they could only appear, in William Mason's words, 'mad as ever'.

Smart's earlier opposition to witch belief had been voiced in a 1751 article deploring the mob lynching of an old couple, Ruth Osborne and her husband, at Tring in Hertfordshire. This case conformed in many ways to the classic pattern, starting with the refusal of charity, but had ended with the hysterical beating and murder of the two Osbornes, and the execution of the ringleader of the assault, a chimney sweep called Thomas Colley. This *cause célèbre*, reported in the *Gentleman's Magazine*, was an indication that within a rural milieu witchcraft belief continued in its traditional form, though discountenanced by the representatives of the law, and by workhouse officials who had sheltered the Osbornes.[28]

Among the less humble too, such beliefs could arouse concern. Edward Moore, writing as Adam Fitz-Adam in his journal the *World*, adopted the persona of a believer in witchcraft who objected to the 1736 repeal of the witchcraft legislation. His main concern is not, as it was for John Wesley, how the repeal had affected 'our religious belief, according to the Scotch proverb, "Tauk awaw the deel, and good bwee to the Lord"'. He maintains, instead, a satirical tack, thinking of repeal 'only in a moral light, as it has given such encouragement to WITCHCRAFT in this kingdom, that one hardly meets with a grown person either in public or private, who is not more or less under its influence'.

Fitz-Adam goes on to ascribe to witchcraft all the wickedness of the age, which, he notes, so many perceive: 'that universal and uncontroulable rage of PLAY'; 'that spirit of pride and passion for expence'; all the 'folly and absurdity' which 'must be obvious to the common sense of all mankind'; 'the spirit of Jacobitism, which is so well known to possess many of his Majesty's protestant subjects in this kingdom'.[29] Now, 'FROM all these considerations

it is much to be wished that a new WITCH ACT may take place next session of parliament. *Vox populi est vox dei*, is a wise and a true saying; and that the *vox populi* is in favour of such an act, let the late proceedings at Tring, and some similar occurrences in other parts of England bear testimony.

This satire is directed against the riotous plebeians at Tring, and also, no doubt, against the eighteenth-century moral majority who saw plays

---

[28] See *The Tryal of Thomas Colley* (1751); *The Remarkable Confession, and Last Dying Words of Thomas Colley* (1751); *Gentleman's Magazine*, 21 (1751).
[29] The Osbornes had been Jacobite sympathizers in 1745, one of the reasons for their unpopularity.

and expense and folly as works of the Devil. Fitz-Adam does, however, suggest the existence of a more substantial agenda. Witchcraft belief is part of a particular high-flying ideology rather than mere idiot rusticity. He links the Tring lynching with opposition to the government's bill for Jewish naturalization, half-seriously suggesting that the passing of a new witch act might help to silence 'the clamours which have gone forth so grievously against the jew bill'. 'It is', he writes, 'shrewdly suspected that the same people who imagined their religion to be at stake by the repeal of the one, are at present under the most terrible consternation at the passing of the other.'[30]

The 'Jew Bill' controversy had resurrected the rhetoric of the rage of party, provoking a multiplicity of pamphlets and a number of prints.[31] The measure itself was slight, permitting but not enacting the naturalization of Jewish denizens by Act of Parliament, but the ensuing furore brought together anti-Semitism, xenophobia, and high-church extremism, leading to the repeal of the Act. The whole matter was the occasion for vigorous propaganda in the elections of 1754. It was the perceived attack on what remained of the sacramental test which formed a major objection to what was, practically speaking, an almost inconsequential bill. This debate was an explicit revival of the 'rage of party' in the context of the definition of the confessional state. Fitz-Adam's perception of a connection between the 'Jew Bill' controversy and witchcraft belief makes sense in such a context. Of thirteen prints I have examined on the subject, seven have diabolical associations, while four include figures of devils or witches.[32]

At the same time, widespread hysteria was being generated over another set of archetypical outsiders, the gypsies. A young woman, Elizabeth Canning, claimed to have been abducted by an old gypsy woman, Mary Squires. Squires had then taken her to be tortured in an Enfield bawdy-house. Henry Fielding, in his capacity as a justice of the peace in London, was gullible enough to fall for Canning's story. It subsequently emerged that Squires, who had won the confidence of the Lord Mayor, Sir Crisp Gascoyne (a supporter of the 'Jew Bill'), had an unimpeachable alibi. Elizabeth Canning was transported for perjury. Nevertheless Mary Squires remained the focus of much hostility. She and her associates were

---

[30] *The World* [Adam Fitz-Adam i.e. Edward Moore], 34, 23 Aug. 1753, 202–7. This article was later adapted by Oliver Goldsmith, *The Bee*, viii, 24 Nov. 1759, 'On Deceit and Falshood' in *Works*, ed. A. Friedman (5 vols.; Oxford, 1966), i. 494–7.

[31] See T. W. Perry, *Public Opinion, Propaganda and Politics in Eighteenth Century England* (Cambridge, Mass., 1962).

[32] BM, *Sat.* 3202–10, 3265–6, 3268, 3270.

described, in a revealing phrase, as 'Street-Robbers and Gypsies, who have scarce even the Appearance of Humanity'.[33]

A print published in 1754 brought the two sets of outcasts together, gypsies and Jews, in a commentary on the parliamentary elections in London and Oxford. London and Oxford are represented in the background of the print; towards the two cities the respective candidates and their friends make their way along two roads. In the London procession, Crisp Gascoyne is prominent, inquiring for Mary Squires: 'Why where are you Mother Sq—r—s wth your infernal Troop?' A friend directs his gaze upwards to the lady in question, accompanied by three witches on broomsticks: 'Infernal! Sr C—pe why they are up in the Air yonder.' The witches themselves are in conversation:

'I am afraid we are too late Sisters.'
'Where have you been Sister Canidia?'
'I have been in N—rf—lk making a Parson's wife miscarry.'
'I live in N—rf—lk too sometimes, did you never Hear of the Old Woman at Saul?'

Gascoyne's party is then followed by a party of Jews, including the leading financier, Sir Sampson Gideon (actually a pragmatic opponent of the 'Jew Bill'.)[34]

The Gypsy's Triumph, of 1753 (illustration 4)[35] is another commentary on Gascoyne's activities. The man trusted Jews. He trusted gypsies. Can we trust him not to join with all the enemies of society? This is the high-flying knot of beliefs which the print and its caption satirize:

> Behold the Man who thought it no Disgrace,
> To save the Sovereign of the Lapland Race.
> His power by Magic joind may still the Rage
> Of Lyes, But who can Envious Wrath Asuage.

This tag accompanies a picture which shows Gascoyne and Squires supported by gypsy witches, and is supplemented by extracts from *Macbeth*.

Yet another print, *A True Draught of Eliz: Canning* (illustration 5)[36] shows a heroic picture of the martyred Canning and views of her Enfield

---

[33] *A Full and Authentic Account of the Strange and Mysterious Affair Between Mary Squires a Gypsy, and Elizabeth Canning*, 2nd edn. (1754), 74.

[34] *All the World in a Hurry, or the Road from London to Oxford* (1754), BM, *Sat.* 3270. Canidia was a woman of Neapolis, against whom Horace inveighed as a sorceress; Saul is both a Norfolk village and a reference to the tale of Saul and the Witch of Endor.

[35] BM, *Sat.* 3214.

[36] (1753), BM, *Sat.* 3211. See also BM, *Sat.* 3210, *The Commite[e] of Ald—m—n* in which Gascoyne declares 'The Prince of Darkness gave me pelf | to serve the Gipsey and my self.'

4. *The Gypsy's Triumph* (1753)

prison—both previously published to win sympathy for her case. It adds
to these images a picture of Squires in conversation with Sir John Hill
(one of her supporters); and the satirical key which makes the whole
ensemble a 'true draught'. This picture belies the heroic portrait of
Canning, and pours scorn on the popular credulity which would rather
believe that Mary Squires was a witch who could fly, than that her alibi

5. *A True Draught of Eliz: Canning* (1753)

might be true. It is subtitled 'E. Canning vindicated, or M. S—s ye Gypsies Flight to Enfield Wash'. It shows the gypsy on a broomstick, the top of her steeple hat buried in the clouds, declaring: 'I can be at Abbotsbury and Enfield Wash, both at one Time.' Beneath her, a spectator cries out: 'There she goes'. Another declares that 'The Witches Act must be put in force again'.

IMAGES OF WITCHCRAFT

In these prints the witch is identified by her steeple hat, point-apron, broomstick, and cat: a fossilized image of the plebeian countrywoman of the late seventeenth century, and a stereotype which has persisted into the children's books of the late twentieth century. As an eighteenth-century chapbook puts it:

A Witch, according to my Nurses account, must be a hagged old Woman, living in a little rotten Cottage, under a Hill, by a Woodside, and must be frequently Spinning at the Door; she must have a black Cat, two or three Broomsticks, an Imp or two, and two or three Diabolical Teats to suckle her Imps.[37]

This immediately identifiable stereotype was a development of the eighteenth century. For the two centuries of active, legitimate witch persecution, the witch was generally portrayed as a woman of plebeian origin, with no particular attributes beyond the occasional animal familiar. This was not an image which could be read if it was standing on its own, without accompanying text. Only in the course of the eighteenth century, after the supply of real victims had dried up, did the image of the witch become fixed as its last incarnation: as the plebeian woman of the late seventeenth century, in an appropriate and easily identifiable costume. This was the costume that was popular at masquerades through much of the eighteenth century: and it might be said that it was at the masquerade that the image of the witch was first really fixed. A drawing at Windsor, attributed to Egbert van Heemskerk, depicts a masquerade in the Long Room of the Opera House in 1724. A number of men wear tall harlequin hats, but one figure is clearly distinguished as a witch, with steeple hat and apron. A painting at Helmingham shows a masquerade scene at the Haymarket theatre. In the left foreground a figure is dressed in steeple hat, black dress, and cape. The disguise was still current in 1773, in C. White's print in the Guildhall library, *A Masquerade Scene in the Pantheon*. In the centre foreground, a witch with crone-like features wears steeple hat, cape, and buckled shoes, and carries a stick, as she dances with a horned animal grotesque.[38] In the masquerade procession mounted for Garrick's Shakespeare Jubilee at Stratford-upon-Avon in 1769, the

---

[37] *Round about our Coal Fire: or Christmas entertainments . . . Adorn'd with many curious cuts* (*c*.1730), BL 12354.d.4. (1), 14 f.

[38] These three pictures reproduced in Aileen Ribeiro, 'The Dress Worn at Masquerades in England 1730–90', dissertation, Courtauld Institute, University of London (1975).

three witches are in masquerade witch costume with steeple hats, brooms, and aprons (illustration 6).[39]

The presence of witches at the masquerade is all the more interesting because of the explicit links made between diabolism and the masquerade by a number of eighteenth-century moralists.[40] To many, masquerade represented more than merely, in Hogarth's phrase, 'the Bad Taste of the Town'. The opportunities for sexual licence and social charade seemed threatening to traditional mores and to hierarchy. Bishop Gibson of London portrayed the danger in stark terms in his sermon to the Societies for Reformation of Manners in 1723. Masquerades were 'Loose and Atheistical Assemblies', to be seen within a wider diabolical context in which 'the Empire of Sin and Satan upon earth is enlarged, and the Cause of God and Religion loses ground'.[41] The essay *Of Plays and Masquerades* (1719) spoke suggestively of masqueraders 'entring into a League with the World, the Flesh and the Devil . . . against Reason and Religion'.[42] John Gay, in an unpublished ballad, rebuked the Swiss impresario Heidegger, who promoted masquerades, for being 'so wicked | to let in the Devil without e'er a Ticket', an ambiguous play on another popular masquerade costume used to similar effect in Hogarth's print *Masquerades and Operas*.[43] Fielding's poem of 1728, 'The Masquerade', is obviously playful:

> So for his uglines more fell,
> Was H—d—g—r toss'd out of hell,
> And in return by Satan made,
> First Minister of Masquerade.

A play by Penelope Aubin, *The Humours of the Masqueraders*, published in 1733, presents us with an extended metaphor of devilry and masquerading. Archpole and his friend Sprightly pose as spirits in order to frighten the husband of Archpole's lover, the justice, Mr Megrim. Mrs Megrim complains that her husband was 'very naughty to leave me so, to be haunted by the Devil or one of his Emissaries, as you fancied'. The

[39] Reported, with illustration in the *Oxford Magazine* (1769).

[40] The devil in masquerade is a popular title and theme in English satirical prints, e.g. BM, *Sat.* 1567, a fold-up devil in skirts.

[41] Edmund Gibson, *A Sermon Preached to the Societies for the Reformation of Manners* (1723), 19, 5.

[42] *Of Plays and Masquerades* (1719), 28.

[43] 'A Strange and Wonderfull Relation how the Devill Appeared last night At the Masquerade in the Hay-Market' (?1718) in P. J. Croft, *Autograph Poetry in the English Language* (1973), i. 64–7.

6. *The procession at the Jubilee at Strafford-upon-Avon* (1769)

cuckold's retort is that 'Women seldom fear the Devil, or his Works.'
This is hardly true of his puritanical hypocrite of a housekeeper, Mrs
Frible, who swallows the deception whole: 'Oh! Sir, the Devil has surely
set his foot in the Chamber . . . every Thing is bewitch'd . . . the Evil one
has surely took Possession of this Place.' Slender, the cook, is similarly
credulous, sensing a satanic presence since 'the Fires burn blue', a well-
recognized symptom. Megrim, even when he has seen through the
charade, continues to speak of it in diabolical terms. Cuckoldom is 'the
worst of devils'; 'There's Magick in her Lips; she's all Delusion'. At
the dénouement, he addresses his wife as a witch: 'You Sorceres, Syren,
Crocodile, tell me who is that Devil that makes me and you Monsters.'
Throughout the play there is satirical use of the perception, dating from
the 1720s and earlier, that the masquerade is somehow diabolical. This
notion informs the central conceit of the work, the impersonation of
devils by masqueraders, and their virtual equation. Megrim's view of
events is, in the course of the comedy, transformed from a supernatural
to a naturalistic or secular one, retaining nevertheless the diabolical connotations surrounding women and their supposed sexual misdemean-
ours.[44] The plot of *The Humours of the Masqueraders* reveals better than
any mere analysis the ill-defined but undeniable transformation from the
literal to the metaphorical which witchcraft underwent in this period.

Hogarth's counterfeit *Masquerade Ticket* of 1727 (illustration 7) shows
a confused crowd of masked and costumed revellers, their inclinations
measured by a pair of 'lecherometers', some of them clustering about a
sacrifice to Priapus.[45] The best-defined, most easily read figure, in the
foreground, slightly left of centre, is a witch, in steeple hat and apron.
Within the whole structure of the picture she is more than an incidental
detail, one charade among others. For, above the door at the end of the
chamber depicted in the print, hangs a painting of a diabolical Sabbath.
Horned figures on the periphery, a goat being mounted in the centre, a
vomiting figure on the far left, and a figure in ecstasy with arms uplifted;
these are all forms associated with the witches' Sabbath as shown in
paintings and prints of the sixteenth and seventeenth centuries. Thomas
Gordon, in his essay 'Of Masquerades', outlines the relationship between sabbath, masquerade, and bacchanal. Having cited Livy's account
of 'some Nocturnal Assemblies lately set up at Rome; I think he calls
'em *Bacchanals*', he ascribes to this relation 'all our dreadful Accounts of

---

[44] The play is subtitled *The Merry MASQUERADERS: OR THE Humorous CUCK-
OLD*, 10, 14–17, 60.
[45] *Hogarth's Graphic Works*, pl. 113, cat. 109.

7. *Masquerade Ticket*, by William Hogarth (1727)

Witches'. He then gestures towards the diabolical associations of the masque, which 'originally denotes an old Hag, a Witch'.[46]

Witchcraft or devilry had always been used, more or less seriously, as ways of condemning or satirizing. We have seen how the satirical could coexist with the serious in Defoe's work. There is certainly no shortage of devils and witches at work in eighteenth-century satire, whether in commentary on sexual mores, financial peculation, or political corruption. The South Sea Bubble generated a plethora of prints, including Hogarth's *Emblematical Print on the South Sea Scheme* of 1719 (illustration 8).[47] Here Defoe's notion of a devilish scheme-maker is given full reign. The presiding genius of the picture, standing central and apart, is the goat, symbol of both Devil and lechery, surmounting the merry-go-round. Other figures on this contraption include a crone-like figure very like Hogarth's image of a witch in his illustrations to Charles Gildon's *New Metamorphosis*.[48] The meaning of the picture in all its detail is irrecoverable in its complexity; the motto points to this fact, and to an overarching theme of the piece: 'So much for Monys magick power | Guess at the rest you find out more'.

Other prints on the South Sea scandal used a similar repertoire. One portrayed the Devil as chief bubbler, seated on a cloud; another had the Devil as the voice of suicidal despair, whispering into the ears of the ruined. Even a secular interpretation, *The Bubblers Bubbl'd or the Devil take the Hindmost*, had verses referring to the diabolical roots of the scandal: 'Here Fortune does her smiles dispense, | Like other jilting witches'.[49]

Robert Walpole, the 'Skreenmaster general' who had cleared up the South Sea scandal, was pursued by diabolical imagery for much of his career. *Bob the Political Ballance Master* addresses the Devil. In *The Treasury or his Honour Bit*, a devil flies off with Walpole, declaring 'He's D——d Weighty'. A political stink comes from Walpole, 'a Lapland witch . . . [who] has a great support by ye sale of wind'. In *The Night Visit, Or the Relapse*, the Devil peeps in while Bob makes off on a broomstick.[50] Scotsmen were, predictably, teased with witchcraft.[51] Witchcraft went hand in hand with sexual peccadilloes, as in the bawdy ballad *The Black Joke*, depicted in, for instance, Hogarth's *Rake's Progress*, plate

---

[46] Thomas Gordon, *The Humourist*, ii (1725), 187 ff. Cf. Meric Casaubon, *A Treatise Concerning Enthusiasme* (1656), 8 f.

[47] *Hogarth's Graphic Works*, pl. 12, cat. 10.   [48] Ibid., pl. 41, cat. 38, 1723/4.

[49] See BM, *Sat.* 1629, 1621, 1625.   [50] BM, *Sat.* 2576, 2560, 2495, 2559.

[51] e.g. BM, *Sat.* 3896, 3859, 3852.

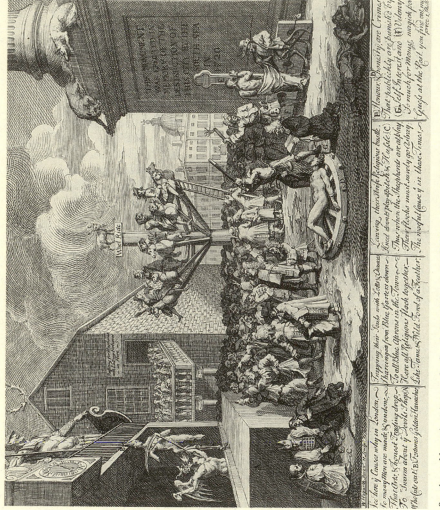

8. *An emblematic print on the South Sea Scheme, by William Hogarth (1719)*

3;[52] or in plate 3 of the *Harlot's Progress*, in which Moll Hackabout, *aficionado* of the masquerade, has a witch's hat and a birch-cum-broomstick prominent on her wall.[53]

Much of this use of witchcraft has the same sort of ambiguous status as in Defoe. In a period when the status of witch beliefs was shifting from the intellectually tenable to the downright disreputable, the metaphorical intensity of talk about witchcraft was never quite clear. The temptation is to assimilate these pieces of satire to our own use of images of witchcraft and diabolism in metaphor; and there is, necessarily, some continuity, and no clear break between eighteenth-century uses and our own. Nevertheless, these fragments cannot be casually dismissed as pieces of decorative frippery, the embellishment of a point rather than part of the point itself. Consider Arthur Bedford's 1719 contribution to the religious campaign against the early eighteenth-century English stage, *A Serious Remonstrance In Behalf of the Christian Religion, Against The Horrid Blasphemies and Impieties which are still used in the English Play-Houses, to the great Dishonour of Almighty God, and in Contempt of the Statutes of this Realm. Shewing their plain Tendency to overthrow all Piety, and advance the Interest and Honour of the Devil in the World.* The tone is set from the title-page, with its epigraph, that 'to compliment Vice, is but one Remove from Worshipping the Devil'. Chapter 3 shows 'Witchcraft and Magick encouraged by the Stage':

Another Method, made use of at the *Play-Houses*, is to entertain their Followers with *magical Representations, conjuring*, or *consulting* the *Devil*. This surely can be no great Diversion, at least no proper one for *Christians*, and may be apt to fill the Heads of raw and ignorant Persons with false and dangerous Notions, as if the *Devil's* Power and Knowledge was much greater than it is; insomuch that they may come in time to think it their Interest to be upon good Terms with him; as we hear of many in our own Country, who have been so wicked, as to make Compacts with him, and as some of the *Indians* are said to *worship* him for fear lest he should hurt them: and thus the *Worship* of *God* is of course laid aside, and all hope of his Favour and Blessing is renounced and forfeited.

---

[52] *Hogarth's Graphic Works*, pl. 142, cat. 134 (1735). The composition of this print, in particular the gesture of the 'posture woman' in the foreground, reflects that of the witch in Frans Francken's *Hexenkuche* (*c.*1610) and its derivatives: see U. A. Härting, *Studien zu Kabinettmalerei des Frans Francken*, ii (Holz, 1983), Inv. 1074; Victoria and Albert Museum, *Catalogue of Foreign Paintings before 1800* (1973), no. 128; and the print version by Jaspar Isac, Bodleian Douce Collection 13/W1.1 (88) and in Bibliothèque Nationale, *Les Sorcières* (Paris, 1973), cat. no. 247. For the *Black Joke*, see also BM, *Sat.* 3745 (1760).

[53] *Hogarth's Graphic Works*, pl. 129, cat. 123 (1732).

This is more than metaphor. It reflects back on the 'metaphorical' expressions in White Kennett (rebellion is as the sin of witchcraft) or Gibson (masquerades enlarge the empire of sin and Satan) and confirms their earnest intent. Bedford's construction of play-acting as witchcraft is set in a context of orthodox Anglicanism. 'When you are tempted to go to the *Play-house*,' he writes, 'consider your *Baptismal Vow*.' These sorts of entertainments are 'a disservice to our *King*, our *Church*, and our *Constitution*'.[54]

Having migrated from the village hovel and the assizes to the playhouse, Bedford's idea of witchcraft echoes Restoration theory, defining the united Christian community against the unacceptable in its midst. But times have changed. Witchcraft in the letter has receded; the Devil's power is hemmed in, not puffed up; these are representations rather than bald actualities. This is a general feature of the period after 1715. The 'Antient System', as the American diarist Ezra Stiles, pastor at Newport Rhode Island, and later president of Yale College, put it in 1773, is 'broken up, the Vessel of Sorcery shipwreckt and only some shattered planks and pieces disjoyned floating and scattered on the Ocean of the human Activity and Bustle'.[55] Stiles was referring to magical practice; but his words apply just as much to perceptions of witchcraft. Gypsies, Jews, poetasters, politicians, fraudsters, masqueraders of all sorts: these are what remains of the accusation of witchcraft. The Devil seemed to be everywhere, just as the idea that he might be nowhere was being canvassed. He bribed electors; urged foreign powers to evil schemes; encouraged the Pretender.[56] As for witchcraft itself, suspicions of conjuring abounded. Benjamin Martin, lecturing on electrical miracles at Bath, was 'taken . . . for a magician'.[57] The 'Jacobin fox', John Thelwall, in retreat in Wales, had such 'fits of abstraction . . . solitary rambles, among the woods and dingles' that he was taken for an adept walking in the woods 'to talk with his evil spirits'.[58] The boundary between figurative and literal over the eighteenth century is broad and undulating, reflecting a system of belief in transformation rather than the easy determination that witchcraft had never existed.

[54] Title-page, 9, 377 f. Cf. Smart, *Jubilate Agno*, § 345, 64: 'For all STAGE-Playing is Hypocrisy and the Devil is the master of their Revels.'

[55] See n. 1 above.

[56] BM, *Sat.* 2498, 2449, 2636. See also BM, *Sat.* 2661, *Briton's Association against the Pope's Bulls*, in which the Devil, booted and spurred, rides like a witch upon a broom.

[57] Benjamin Martin, *Supplement containing remarks on a rhapsody of adventures of a modern knight-errant* (Bath, 1746), 28 f.

[58] Thelwall's own words, cited by E. P. Thompson in 'Hunting the Jacobin Fox', *P & P* 142 (1994), 118.

Ezra Stiles's remark also reflects the understanding that witchcraft and demonology had lost their systematic quality, leaving only fragments, those 'shattered planks and pieces disjoyned'. One stray plank was the newly polite art of conjuring. Conjuring manuals might offer miracles to the assiduous student which ranged over the practical, the biblical, the philosophical, the alchemical, and the nonsensical:

to seem to turn water into wine; Palingenesy . . . or the Art of reviving the Dead . . . an artificial volcano . . . cement for mending broken China . . . Secret Writing . . . a sure way to catch a Pickpocket . . . an artificial Spider which moves by Electricity . . . a philosophical Mushroom . . . a curious method of restoring a fly to life, in two minutes, that has been drowned twenty-four hours . . . a curious experiment to prove that two and two do not make four . . . fulminating Gold . . . to seem to swallow a long Pudding made of Tin.[59]

Demonology itself, denied its ideological roots, came to seem bizarre and arbitrary, easy prey for the novelist Wilkie Collins who, in the person of his sexually frustrated evangelist, Miss Clack, ridicules a shattered system of thought:

I instantly opened my bag, and took out the top publication. It proved to be an early edition—only the twenty-fifth—of the famous anonymous work (believed to be by precious Miss Bellows), entitled The Serpent at Home. The design of the book—with which the worldly reader may not be acquainted—is to show how the Evil One lies in wait for us in all the most apparently innocent actions of our daily lives. The chapters best adapted to female perusal are 'Satan in the Hair Brush;' 'Satan behind the Looking Glass;' 'Satan under the Tea Table;' 'Satan out of the Window'—and many others.
    'Give your attention, dear aunt, to this precious book—and you will give me all I ask.' With those words, I handed it to her open, at a marked passage—one continuous burst of burning eloquence! Subject: Satan among the Sofa Cushions.[60]

This, however, is to move forward into the 1860s, where we started with George Eliot: a generation after the final dissolution of the Old Regime in the period 1828–32; at the very moment of the second Reform Act; and long after the repeal of the witchcraft Act. Witchcraft, in the seventeenth-century sense, remained a crime until 1736; the next chapter will consider how the Jacobean legislation came to be repealed.

---

[59] *The Second Edition of the Conjuror's Repository; or, the whole art and mystery of magic displayed* (1809), 14, 19, 24, 26, 35, 50, 55, 125, 108, 125, 30, 16.
[60] Wilkie Collins, *The Moonstone* (1868; Harmondsworth, 1986), 267–8.

8

Repeal

Crosbie 'But an act of parliament put an end to witchcraft.'—
Johnson 'No, sir; witchcraft had ceased; and therefore an act of
parliament was passed to prevent persecution for what was not witchcraft. Why it ceased, we cannot tell, as we cannot tell the reason of
many other things.'

James Boswell, *Journal of a Tour to the Hebrides*,
Monday 16 August 1773[1]

CHURCH MATTERS

Religious controversy broke out with renewed vigour in the 1730s after a
decade of relative stability presided over by Walpole's 'Pope', Edmund
Gibson, Bishop of London.[2] Gibson himself sensed in Parliament 'an evil
spirit . . . working against Churchmen and Church matters'. He had wished
to revive the jurisdiction of ecclesiastical courts, and commit the execution of laws against vice and irreligion to the ecclesiastical hierarchy. He
spoke in a letter to Walpole of being 'tossed about and insulted by people
of almost all denominations, many of whom were known to stand very
well with the Court'. As Hervey noted in his memoirs, the 1735–6
session of the new Parliament devoted its chief discussions to 'Church
matters'. An attempt to repeal the Test and Corporation Acts was followed, most disastrously for Edmund Gibson, by the furore over the
Mortmain and Quakers' Tithe Bills, which led to his final break with
Robert Walpole. As in the years preceding the Hanoverian succession,

---

[1] *Boswell's Life of Johnson. Together with Boswell's Journal of a Tour to the Hebrides and
Johnson's Diary of a Journey into North Wales*, ed. G. B. Hill (6 vols., Oxford, 1964), v. 45 f.

[2] The Archbishop of Canterbury, William Wake, was senile.

accusations of priestcraft and irreligion were bandied and anathemas hurled.[3]

This anticlerical temper was not a mere whim of elements within the House of Commons. It extended throughout the élite, with the hubbub surrounding the nomination of the supposedly deistical Dr Rundle to the see of Gloucester; the abuse and criticism newly directed at Bishop Gibson's own magnum opus, the *Codex Juris Ecclesiae Anglicanae* of 1713, which had given theoretical form to attacks on ecclesiastical jurisdiction; and the controversy on the nature of heresy between James Foster, a dissenting lecturer, and Henry Stebbing, a high-church divine. All this added to the sense of religious ferment. The uproar ended in the political arena with Gibson's withdrawal from the charmed circle of power, and in the contemplative realm with William Warburton's *Alliance between Church and State* of 1736 which set out new rules of engagement.[4]

Witchcraft disappeared from serious discourse in the period following the extinction of the rage of party; but a period of parallel and intense religious controversy two decades later revived the issue, in attenuated form. The relevant context for the repeal of the witchcraft statutes in 1736 was not a putative spirit of legislative reform, but rather half a decade or more of ecclesiastical upset.[5] The religious controversies just outlined were exactly the sort of thing which Walpole had sought to avoid through Gibson's management of the Church. Having wanted to move away from the sectarianism of the last years of Anne, Walpole had ended up with a prelate whom some saw as being bent upon imitating William

[3] Norman Sykes, *Edmund Gibson* (Oxford, 1926), 123–82 and esp. 148–9; John Hervey, *Memoirs of the Reign of George II* (2 vols.; 1849), ii. 87. See also Stephen Taylor, 'Sir Robert Walpole, the Church of England, and the Quakers' Tithe Bill of 1736', *HJ* 28 (1985).

[4] M. Foster, *Examination of the Scheme of Church Power laid down in the Codex* (1735). See e.g. H. Stebbing, *A letter to mr Foster on the subject of heresy* (1735); J. Foster, *An answer to dr Stebbing's Letter on the subject of heresy, a letter* (1735). Stebbing possibly contributed *The Case of the Hertfordshire Witchcraft Considered* (1712) to the Wenham debate, but see Wallace Notestein, *A History of Witchcraft in England from 1558 to 1718* (Washington, 1911), 374. J. C. D. Clark, *English Society 1688–1832* (Cambridge, 1985), 137–41. Paul Langford, *A Polite and Commercial Society* (Oxford, 1989), 38–44. For a caveat as to Warburton's significance, see Stephen Taylor, 'William Warburton and the Alliance of Church and State', *JEH* 43 (1992).

[5] Although the House of Lords, agreeing on 24 Feb. 1735/6 to meet in committee on 26 Feb. to discuss the bill for the repeal of the Witchcraft Act, did suggest 'that the Judges do then attend', *Journal of the House of Lords*, 9 Geo II, 1735/6. On motives and means for 18th-c. legislation, see Joanna Innes, 'Parliament and the Shaping of Eighteenth-Century English Social Policy', *TRHS*, 5th ser. 40 (1990), esp. 77 f. (on the role of judges and law officers); 82 (on anti-Walpolean moves for law reform); 89 (on the role of the executive in generating or directing legislation).

Laud. The repeal of the Witchcraft Act in early 1736 might have been
seen as an indication that such high-church pretensions were being expelled from the body politic in their most absurd form. But can we get
any further than this in relating the measure to the to and fro of political
manœuvre?

The problem with the 1736 repeal is that it seems to emerge from
nowhere. Witchcraft theory had lost credibility and usefulness in the
wake of its adoption by Tory factionalism, and the ensuing Whig ascendancy; but the process by which this ideological transformation became a
root-and-branch change in mentality is more difficult to judge. By the
time of the 'Jew Bill', in 1753, when images of witchcraft were deployed
in the satirical print (whether as an implicit condemnation of the absurd
high-flying fanaticism of those who opposed Jewish naturalization, or as
a reminder of the diabolical motivation of the Jewish lobby, we cannot be
sure), we know that belief in witchcraft was eccentric, its use in propaganda a reworking of the rhetorical deposits of the generations. The year
1736 is a different matter. What is more, the precise purpose of the bill
is unclear because of the paucity of surviving parliamentary evidence.
There are no official records of any parliamentary debate beyond the bare
outline provided by the journals of the houses. Government involvement
in the initiation of the bill is, as so often, difficult to fathom.[6] Any account
must be tentative and rely on the accumulation of anecdote or the extra-
polation of motive. Despite all these problems, it certainly seems worth
asking why the Witchcraft Act was repealed in 1736, whether there was
opposition, and from whom.

The bill's sponsors included John Crosse, described by Horace Walpole
as 'a very good friend to my brother', Robert, and a fairly representative
Old Whig; and John Conduitt, who served as master of the Mint from
1727 until his death ten years later. A frequent speaker for the government in the House, he opposed the repeal of the septennial act, that
coping stone of Whig stability, in the 1735/6 session. What makes
Conduitt's sponsorship of repeal more interesting is that he was Sir Isaac
Newton's nephew by marriage, his chosen successor at the Mint, and the
guardian of the Newtonian tradition. Conduitt's involvement in the repeal of the Witchcraft Act may well have enhanced the identification of
Newtonianism as the ideology of a sound and rational Whig settlement
which purged the nation of antique superstition. The bill was presented

---

[6] See Innes, 'Parliament and the Shaping of Eighteenth-Century English Social Policy',
85 (on paucity of records); 89 (on obscurity of motive).

to the Commons and delivered to the Lords by Conduitt; Crosse chaired the committee of the whole House which considered the bill before third reading.

The third and final sponsor, Alderman George Heathcote, was 'one of the most frequent and violent speakers for the opposition'. Heathcote was, according to Lord Egmont, 'a republican Whig', who in March 1731 participated in the anticlerical assault by moving the motion to prevent the translation of bishops. Even more significantly, in the year of the repeal of the Witchcraft Act, he spoke in favour of the repeal of the Test Act. He did not oppose the government out of sheer spite, and on several occasions voted with the ministry.[7]

These are a mixed lot, but if we are looking for a common thread, the sponsors of repeal might be seen as representative of an emerging 'coalition' between some ministerial and opposition Whigs in reaction to the revived high-flying favoured by Gibson, and his attempts to advance ecclesiastical influence. The same groups formulated and supported the schemes concerning Quaker tithes and mortmain which drove Gibson from power. The Quaker tithes bill was read for the first time in the Commons a week before the new Witchcraft Act received royal assent; and the day after the third reading of the witch bill, a motion for the repeal of the test laws was lost in the Commons. According to Stephen Taylor, at this stage in his career, 'Walpole probably hoped that debate on religious issues, by appealing to ideology, would emphasize the differences between opposition whigs [who supported some measure of relief for the Quakers] and Tories [who did not]'.[8] Repeal of the witchcraft legislation may have played a symbolic role in indicating the increasingly, though not definitively, secular nature of the state, legislation less liable to offend or inconvenience than the repeal of the Test and Corporation Acts. It is striking that when those latter measures were under threat again, in the 1820s, witchcraft emerged once more as an issue, however faintly.[9] But while repeal of the witchcraft legislation may have formed a fairly uncontentious part of the response to feelings that the state was in danger (no one was suggesting, after all, that Gibson was a proselytizing

[7] Romney Sedgwick, *The House of Commons 1715–1754* (2 vols.; 1970), under name of member; *Journal of the House of Commons*, 9 Geo II, 1735/6.

[8] Taylor, 'Sir Robert Walpole, the Church of England, and the Quakers' Tithe Bill of 1736', 58.

[9] Within the framework of the *ancien régime*, the test and laws against witchcraft continued to be somehow perceived as bound together: see discussion below of *Antipas: a solemn appeal to the Archbishops and Bishops with reference to several Bills . . . especially that concerning Witchcraft and Sorcery* (1821), opposing the repeal of the Irish witchcraft legislation.

believer in witchcraft) there was some opposition, and it is important to analyse its motivation.

A GREAT PLOTTER

A historian chancing upon a stray parliamentary opponent of the witch-craft repeal in 1736 might be forgiven for labelling the individual concerned as a mere eccentric. If repeal was the progressive and inevitable result of a communal 'loss of belief' in the late seventeenth century, this is self-evidently so. Any opposition was, in the event, wide of the mark. The contemporary mood suggests the same: two parliamentary journals, Edward Harley's and Thomas Wilson's, allude to repeal with no hint of controversy.[10] Yet the loner could, instead, be a key to unlock yet more of the ideological secret history of the expulsion of witchcraft from public affairs. Unusual certainly, in his willingness to raise the issue in Parliament, he is a man with a history and with interests which, however marginalized, might be profitably analysed rather than rejected out of hand as straightforward lunacy. The eccentric in question was the brother of the Earl of Mar, rebel leader of 1715: James Erskine, Lord Grange.

The received account of Erskine's stand on sorcery is utterly contemptuous and dismissive. It derives from a liberal cleric, Alexander Carlyle, who abhorred Erskine, a friend of the family, as 'a Real Enthusiast . . . at the same time Licentious in his Morals'. Erskine

contracted such a violent aversion at Sir Robert Walpole, That having, by Intrigue and Hypocrisy, secur'd a Majority of the District of Burghs of which Stirling is the chief, he threw up his Seat as a Judge in the Court of Session, was Elected Member for that District, and went to London to attend Parliament, and to overturn Sir Robt W, not merely in his own opinion, but in the opinion of many who were Dupes to his Cunning, and his Pretensions to Abilities that he had not. But his first appearance in the House of Commons, undeceiv'd his Sanguine Friends and silenc'd him for ever.

He chose to make his Maiden Speech on the Witches Bill, as it was call'd; and Being learn'd in Demonologia, with Books on which Subject his Library was fill'd, he made a Long Canting Speech, that set the House in a Titter of Laughter, and convinc'd Sir Robert That he had no Need of any extraordinary Armour against This Champion of the House of Mar. The Truth was that the Man neither had Learning nor Talents nor Ability. He was no Lawyer, He was a Bad

---

[10] *The Diaries of Thomas Wilson, DD, 1731–1737 and 1750, son of Bishop Wilson of Sodor and Man*, ed. C. L. S. Linnell (1964), entry for Thursday 26 Feb. 1735/6; Edward Harley, CUL MS Add. 6851 [Parliamentary Journal for 1734–51], entry for 22 Jan. 1735/6, f30.

Speaker. He had been rais'd on the Shoulders of his Brother the Earl of Mar in the End of the Reign, but had never Distinguish'd himself. In the Genl Assembly itself, which many Gentlemen afterwards made a School of Popular Eloquence, and where he took the High Flying Side that he might annoy Government, his appearances were but rare, and unimpressive. But as he was understood to be a Great Plotter, he was suppos'd to Reserve himself for some Greater Occasions.[11]

This anecdote is alluded to in Keith Thomas's *Religion and the Decline of Magic*, setting a seal on the accepted model of the decline of witchcraft; but by unpicking it in detail we can build up a very different picture of Erskine.[12] To view the 1736 repeal as a piece of legislative tidying-away evades the need for explanation; in the same way, to label Erskine's opposition as mere eccentricity is to dismiss his actions as inexplicably bizarre. They may have been, but they deserve an attempt at a rational examination first. We need to explore the motivation of his stand in this particular instance, to relate it to his other political actions, unwinding the tangled mess of his political career to understand why Erskine, undoubtedly capable of shrewd behaviour, could have been so spectacularly off course.

We can start by reconstructing Erskine's intellectual formation and milieu. Only thus can his opposition to the 'Witches Bill' be understood. His desire to 'overturn Sir Robert Walpole' and 'annoy Government', his relationship to the Earl of Mar and his reputation as a 'great plotter' will all have their part to play. For the purposes of this chapter, however, the vital recognition is that Erskine's ideological affiliations in the years between 1715 and 1745 are a link between two important features of the discourse of witchcraft up to 1715 as outlined in the chapters above. It will emerge that Erskine, as a Scot and a 'high flyer', indeed opposed the repeal as part of a more general attack on Walpole; but his opposition drew its consistency from a concern for Scottish rights and Scottish religion, and a related anxiety about the spiritual standing of the 'Robinocracy'.

Erskine's diary reveals that in his youth he was far from being the sort of convinced Presbyterian we have earlier implicated in the defence of witchcraft belief and prosecution in Scotland. In the late 1690s he had condemned Scots Calvinists as 'narrow spirited and prejudiced creatures' and affected 'a great esteem for John le Clerc at Amsterdam', reckoning him

---

[11] *The Autobiography of Dr Alexander Carlyle of Inveresk, 1722–1805*, ed. James Kinsley (Oxford, 1973), 7 f. Carlyle was a liberal minister of the Kirk, associate of Hume, Robertson, and Adam Smith. On Erskine's demonological library, which Carlyle saw, see ibid. 32.

[12] Thomas, *RDM* 694.

'one who had shook off these prejudices and thought freely'.[13] By 1708 Erskine might have been over such youthful free-thinking, but remained ironically dismissive of the supposed virtues of clerical government:

It is a good thing that now both Church and high Kirk join in their principles as to screwing up the power of the clergy; which I hope will teach people that Church and Kirk are at the bottom of the same kidney, and that neither ought to be too much indulged or trusted to.[14]

By this time Erskine was a successful lawyer, well on the way to influence. Snug in the bosom of the Stuart establishment, he was successively member of the faculty of advocates (1705), Lord of Session (1707), and finally Lord Justice Clerk (1710). In the years around 1707 he was as keen on the union as any Scotsman on the make, despite the caveats:

I'm much affraid that there may still be a great deall of uneasyness about it. [But] I'm sure it is in the power of the Government and Parliament of Brittain to make the Union not only durable, but most acceptable and advantagious to this country, as I expect it shall.

An ardent pragmatist, he was full of scorn for the 'fury and impertinence of biggots on either side'.[15]

The death of Queen Anne and the ensuing rebellion were turning-points in Erskine's career. In 1714 he was dismissed from his post. In 1715 his brother Mar led the Jacobite uprising, and the family estates were, in turn, sequestered. In subsequent decades Erskine did his best, in his own words, 'to preserve from ruine the forfeited famillys of my friends and relations'. Having been a student companion of Walpole's Scottish agent, Islay, Erskine thought he had a sure route back into the confidence of the government. He had been disappointed, and his family slighted, as he made clear in a letter of 1733:

Such has long been their way, to profess great friendship to me and the familly . . . and much readyness to do us good, and seemingly to propose better for us than we do for ourselves; but when it came to the execution, to prevent the doing of it by shifts, tricks, and lies . . . Why should we sit still and let them trick us into poverty, contempt, and insignificancy?[16]

---

[13] James Erskine, Lord Grange, *Extracts from the Diary of a Senator of the College of Justice* (Edinburgh, 1843), 83. These are extracts from the MS listed in HMC, *Report on the Manuscripts of the Earl of Mar and Kellie* (1904), marked 'Memoirs VI'. Most of it relates to Erskine's religious experiences.

[14] Letter to his brother Mar, 29 Jan. 1708 in HMC, *Mar and Kellie*, 426.

[15] Ibid.

[16] 'Letters of Lord Grange' in *The Miscellany of the Spalding Club*, iii. (Aberdeen, 1846), 27, 37.

In the same period, after 1715, Erskine's religious leanings were transformed. By the 1720s he was the very model of a Kirk man, active in the affairs of the General Assembly, well-known for 'strengthening the hands of the zealous orthodox ministers'. 'It verie much refreshes me', wrote one correspondent, 'to find any, especially of your high station, that often live at the greatest distance from God, fill'd with just and clear apprehensions of true religion, and the decayed and languishing state thereof in this dead and withered time.' Indeed, the decayed and languishing state of religion, in its broad and narrow senses, became a theme of Erskine's opposition to Walpole's regime. He complained of the great man's 'openly rediculing all vertue and uprightness'; of the 'geddyness and corruption of our age'; and an addiction to 'lewd and idle Diversions'. He gave his friend Robert Wodrow a picture of an irreligious court, with Queen Caroline continually 'bantering and scolding the narrou principles of the Church of Scotland'.[17]

This last remark alerts us to the framework within which this spleen and religious anxiety were exercised. From 1715 on Erskine was moving towards a thoroughgoing defence of Scots rights and Scots particularity, in both politics and religion. We need not, as so many of Erskine's enemies did, stoop to accusations of hypocrisy.[18] To start with, family and personal honour were legitimately bound up with national honour in the case of a family as prominent as Erskine's; 'poverty, contempt, and insignificancy' threatened not only the Erskine clan, but the whole kingdom under the new dispensation. Walpole and his crew were 'these oppressors of the familly we belong to, and enemys of Britain'. Religion and politics were bound up together, too, as Erskine's attitude to the Simson affair acutely demonstrates.[19]

John Simson was a notorious Scottish theologian, prosecuted in the General Assembly of the Kirk for teaching unsound doctrine. The case created uproar and became one of the *causes célèbres* of eighteenth-century Scottish ecclesiastical politics. Erskine, deeply involved in the prosecution of the deistical Simson, was convinced that the affair was being used by the Walpole administration as part of an attack on Scottish rights and integrity:

ther seems to be a designe, at some Assembly, to throu up him [Simson], or some other bone of contention, to break and divide us: That when our Assemblys break

---

[17] John Wylie to Erskine, 8 May 1721, HMC, *Mar and Kellie*, 521; Andrew Darling, minister at Kintoul, to Erskine, 3 Feb. 1724, HMC, *Mar and Kellie*, 525; 'Letters of Lord Grange', 56, 57; *The History and Proceedings of the House of Commons* (1742), ix, 93, 5 Mar. 1735; Robert Wodrow, *Analecta*, ed. M. Leishman (4 vols.; Glasgow, 1842), iv. 146.
[18] See Wodrow *Analecta*, iii. 510, 306.   [19] 'Letters of Lord Grange', 47.

upon this or other points, they will be prohibited by the King, and either Com-
missions, or some other select meetings, called by the King's writt, will have the
managment of Church affairs.[20]

For Erskine, as for so many others before the '45 rebellion, the religious
and state affairs of Scotland were of a piece, and seemed increasingly
under threat from English interference. The unionist careerist, sceptical
of temperament, came to believe, under the pressure of a variety of
events, that the balance of the 1707 settlement was being overturned by
the actions of a corrupt and irreligious ministry. It is within this context
that we have to locate Erskine's opposition to the witch bill, taking him
as seriously as his friend Robert Wodrow did. Erskine, Wodrow wrote,

hath made a bold appearance for the truth; and if any suspect him as forming a
designe to manage a party among the Ministry, and to affect leading and dictating
to them, such, in my opinion, have acted a very imprudent part at this time in
supporting Mr Simson so much, since by this method they have given that
eminent person a handle (wer he seeking one) to recommend himself to the
affections of all in Scotland, who have a concern for the purity of doctrine, and
preventing error in this Church.[21]

Before outlining the sequence of events which may have led to Erskine's
speech of 1736, Erskine's relation to the understanding of witchcraft
outlined in earlier chapters of this book needs to be charted. First of all,
while his personal beliefs, his inner and inaccessible convictions, are
debatable, it is worth noting that from the 1720s to his death he was
unambiguously supernaturalist in religion, both in matters of the operation of divine grace and the ministrations of the Devil and his agents.[22]
Secondly, Erskine's early if temperate enthusiasm for the Anglo-Scottish
union does place him initially outside the orbit of the Presbyterian knot
who saw true witchcraft belief as a mark of Scottish rectitude as against
English infidelity; but his increasing suspicion of the English government
and concern for Scottish identity and honour make his visible support for
the Jacobean witchcraft legislation an ideological manœuvre within an
identifiable tradition.[23] Finally, Erskine was, as our opening anecdote has
it, a 'high-flyer': hot for the rights of the Kirk; for the power of the

---

[20] For Simson, see *DNB*; *Analecta*, iv. 144.

[21] *Analecta*, iii. 511.

[22] See e.g. *Analecta*, iii. 207, 410; ii. 47, 86 f., 171, 255, 323, 379.

[23] For the distance between the pre-1715 Erskine and e.g. Robert Wylie, an opponent of
union and proponent of legislation against witches, see HMC, *Mar and Kellie*, 273, Erskine
to Mar, 20 Aug. 1706.

General Assembly; for the restriction of lay intrusion into clerical privileges. His refusal to distinguish between the religious and political well-being of his nation has been noted. Despite the doctrinal chasm which separated such Calvinist high-flyers north of the border from high-flyers and nonjurors in England, there is an affinity in their common attitude to the proper relationship between the sacred and secular domains, an affinity which was reflected in the resilience of witchcraft theory within both groups. This makes it all the more striking that Erskine was, in his later years, an associate of John Wesley, whose condemnation of the repeal of the Witchcraft Act reflected his own high-flying roots as well as his scriptural fundamentalism.[24]

The attack on Scottish rights reached its apogee in 1734 during the election of peers to represent Scotland at Westminster, under the terms of the Union. Troops were used to overawe the electors. Members of the Whig opposition—Chesterfield and Carteret—approached the dismissed peers in the wake of the election, and proposed that steps should be taken to force the ministry to account for the apparent malpractice. The peers engaged two men as their chief advisers, Dundas and a lawyer, James Erskine of Grange. Erskine was heavily involved in opposition manœuvres, and the government started to move against him, introducing a bill to prevent Scottish lords of session like himself from being elected to the House of Commons. He quit his employment to secure his seat.[25]

Having been alienated from the mainstream of Westminster politics, 'represented as a hypocrite, and pretender to religion . . . as divisive and factious', angry at 'lossing his friends at London', Erskine was now pushed back into the centre of affairs by political crisis.[26] The period which followed the failure of Walpole's Excise scheme was one of threatening instability for the ministry, in its relations with Scotland as elsewhere. In 1735 Dundas, Erskine's colleague, gave his son an apocalyptic vision of a 'struggle for the sinking liberty of our country [Scotland] till God in his providence interpose to save us'. Erskine himself declared that 'the opposition to Sir Robert Walpole and Ilay is stronger and more rooted than, perhaps, it was to any ministry since the Revolution . . . high church, whig and dissenter, closely united in it, and all their own disputes buryed

---

[24] HMC, *Report on the Laing Manuscripts* (2 vols.; 1914, 1925), ii. 348.

[25] See G. W. T. Omond (ed.), *Arniston Memoirs: Three Centuries of a Scottish House 1571–1838* (Edinburgh, 1887), 82 f.; Erskine's speech against the manipulated election in *The History and Proceedings of the House of Commons*, ix. 69–71; Pulteney to Erskine, 24 Feb. and 22 Mar. 1734, and Earl of Stair to Erskine, 20 Mar. 1734, all in HMC, *Mar and Kellie*, 531–4.

[26] *Analecta*, iii. 306, 511.

in this common pressure'.[27] It was in the midst of this turmoil that Erskine chose to speak against the new witchcraft legislation.

We have seen how in 1711 the Harleyite Daniel Defoe sought to bury disputes and appeal to 'high church, whig and dissenter' by writing in support of an orthodox belief in witchcraft. Whatever Erskine's hopes as to the likely appeal of witchcraft belief to disaffected Tories, his speech against repeal must be seen primarily as that of a Scottish member, concerned for Scottish particularity in government and religion, and for the maintenance of orthodoxy in the island as a whole (a favourite Scottish theme since the 1630s).[28] In the 1730s Erskine was still a supporter of the union between England and 'North Britain', joining with the Whig opposition to espouse the complaints of England as well as his own nation. He used English grievances as a lever to effect common relief: '[Walpole] makes bold schemes against our libertys, as was most certainly his excyse scheme which he pushed like a mad man after England.' But he had a particular concern for English invasion of Scottish prerogatives, complaining that 'in England, nothing is made of our Act of Settlment, and all pouer is undoubtedly in the hands of the Supream Court [sc. Parliament]'. True religion was the target of an irreligious, scheming, Anglicizing ministry, with Walpole and Islay seeking 'our breaking in peices' and making 'Mr S[imson] an instrument to tear and rent us'.[29] In the year following repeal, Erskine was still pursuing Scottish interests, speaking in the debate on the Porteous riots, and opposing the bill of pains and penalties against the city of Edinburgh.

Erskine's behaviour seems altogether less eccentric in such a context. It shows us a specifically Scottish tradition trying to operate in an English arena. What is more, Erskine was no dolt. The worthy Wodrow eulogized him; Pulteney and other members of the opposition wooed him; Walpole feared him enough to frame legislation to exclude him from the House of Commons. What remains to be explained is the chasm between the sponsors of repeal, with their negative manœuvre to paper over the cracks in the Whig coalition; and Erskine, with his positive gesture, via witchcraft, to the ranks of outraged Scottish and, perhaps, English orthodoxy. The chronology is unfortunately lost to us. We cannot know precisely when

---

[27] *Arniston Memoirs*, 81, Dundas to his son at Utrecht, 6 Feb. 1735; 'Letters of Lord Grange', 44. By late 1736 Thomas Wilson was convinced that 'Scotland and England are ripe for Rebellion', see his *Journal*, 178, entry for 24 Oct. 1736.

[28] See Conrad Russell, *The Causes of the English Civil War* (Oxford, 1990), 118–22 on 'Scottish Imperial' policy in the 1630s and 1640s.

[29] *Analecta*, iv. 144.

Erskine spoke, in response to what, or whether his intervention elicited or followed the amendment which extended the new legislation to Scotland. But Erskine's decision to speak against the 'Witches Bill' was a miscalculation. He mistook the complexion of the House of Commons, and the shift in the status of English discourse about witchcraft which had followed 1712/14. He was playing by Scottish rules. That anecdotal 'titter of laughter' in the House may indeed have ended Erskine's career as a serious politician, but it did not silence him, nor can it be denied that Erskine had his reasons for responding to the repeal. The development of his religious and political stance pushed him closer to a position which earlier Scots had adopted, where belief in witchcraft became for Erskine, as it had been for them, a matter of national pride, a symbol of independence, and an act of resistance to a deistical and irreligious English ministry. It may well be that repeal, calculated from one angle to define a common Whiggish rationalism, was also intended to split the opposition, or at least to expose the likes of Erskine to a salutary dose of ridicule. It may be that Erskine hoped to carry disaffected Tories and dissenters with him.[30] We can be sure that 'his sanguine friends', the anti-Walpolean Whigs with whom he had joined forces, were disappointed. The paucity of opposition to repeal within the House of Commons does not tell us much about the private beliefs of individual members, the residual prejudices and sentiments of Tory or Scottish members. But the fact that only Erskine was bold enough, or misguided enough, to brave the giggling and scorn of the House tells us something about the triumph of polite and 'rational' discourse, and the rising blushes which must have stifled any budding expressions of a private belief in the power of witches. Nursing for so long his Scottish resentments, smarting from English abuse, Erskine confused the English and Scottish contexts of opposition and his attacks were brushed aside as uncouth nonsense.

MORE OPPOSITION

James Erskine evidently saw the repeal of the witchcraft act as part of a more general assault upon the citadels of fidelity. He worried about the credentials of English bishops, 'none of them being firm to any set of doctrinall principles, they are much dispised'. One of his particular *bêtes noires* was Benjamin Hoadly: 'Bangor, nou Sarum, is sunk into a hackney

---

[30] Cf. Taylor, 'Sir Robert Walpole, the Church of England, and the Quakers' Tithe Bill of 1736', n. 25.

writer', he declared to Wodrow around 1730.[31] Hoadly's reputedly deistical *Plain Account of the Nature and End of the Sacrament of the Lord's Supper* appeared in 1735. The issue of Hoadly's free-thinking in the *Plain Account* was the starting-point for the only extant pamphlet straightforwardly opposing the repeal of the Witchcraft Act, written in the form of an address to the sponsoring members, and attached to a reissue of an earlier eighteenth-century text, *The Witch of Endor: Or a Plea for the Divine Administration By the Agency of Good and Evil Spirits*. It manifested many of the same concerns as Erskine and may help us to understand latent prejudices which remained, for the most part, unexpressed.

This address recapitulates many of the old arguments about witchcraft, but it focuses primarily on the threat of free-thinking which the repeal of the witchcraft legislation represented, 'the design being to secure some of the Outworks of Religion, and to regain a Parcel of Ground, which bold Infidelity hath invaded'. The author is sarcastic and addresses the House of Commons with heavy irony: 'I dare not entertain the least Thought, Gentlemen, that you have any of the Freethinking Qualities, that are so prevalent, at this Time of Day'. While implying that the arguments against a proper belief in witchcraft are irredeemably vulgar, the product of ignorance and raillery, the author wryly exempts his distinguished audience: 'It would be inexcusable to trouble you any longer, Gentlemen, with this Way and Manner of decrying Witchcraft; and I'll venture to Prophesy [!], such sort of Arguing will not be made use of in your own Learned Debates upon the same subject.'[32]

It is Francis Hutchinson, now Bishop of Down and Connor, whom the pamphleteer wants to discredit. He paints him as a vulgarian, free and easy with fantastical stories about the contortions and wonders which may be achieved (implausibly) by nature alone, without the intrusion of the supernatural. Hutchinson's book is full of tales about showmen and charlatans, so many indeed that his opponent, with a nod and a wink, can 'profess . . . [that] I am perfectly Ignorant whence our Right Reverend, got all this KNOWLEDGE, or where his SOBER AUTHORS are to be met with'. The pamphleteer shows his opponent playing with dangerous vulgarity and outrageous free-thinking. He poses a disturbingly plebeian, if episcopal, threat to traditional orthodoxy.

The author of the address mixes an urbane and witty tone—punning and cracking jokes about the Gin Act, the other 'spiritual' crisis of 1736[33]

---

[31] *Analecta*, iv. 146.   [32] *The Witch of Endor* (1736), pp. xlv, xliii.
[33] Ibid., pp. xxv–xxvi, xxxiii. Cf. *The Hyp-Doctor*, no. 285, 23 Mar. 1736.

—with intellectual and theological argument. He wants to unmask the central contradiction in Hutchinson's discourse, between the denial of the reality of witchcraft on the one hand and the assertion on the other that, as Hutchinson put it, 'the sober belief of good and bad Spirits is an Essential Part of every good Christian's Faith'. How can this assertion and this denial be squared? For, as the author has it, it is 'inconsistent with such a Belief, that all Communications should be reckoned Imaginary, and that the Intellectual World should not serve the Purposes of an Almighty Being, in rewarding or punishing according to the Divine Appointment'.

The author is keen in associating the 'Fundamental Part of the Statute' with the 'Protestant Religion and Interest', which 'as 'tis grounded on the Holy Scriptures, so it stands, and I hope, will ever stand, supported by the Legislature'. His definition of witchcraft is a broad one—'any sort of Communication with, or Operations upon the Intellectual, and Corporeal World'—and, having cited the Bible, and Hutchinson himself, on the necessity of spiritual ministration and depredation, he asks how the legislature can possibly be considering what he calls an 'absolute Repeal'. This last phrase suggests the possibility that the witchcraft legislation could have been revised so as to minimize prosecution, while retaining its ideological and defining function, in both religion and statecraft; a contemporary nod to the conceptual distinction between ideology and persecution. But then, the author is adamant that, as 'an Offence capital immediately against the Divine Majesty', witchcraft deserves to be punished. The association between orthodox belief in witchcraft and the maintenance of true religion culminates in this passage:

[I] must believe, that, in the Preamble of your Bill (which I have not seen) you have taken all possible Care to guard against the Suggestions of a censorious Age; by supporting the Christian Doctrine, and declaring to the World (as Bishop Hutchinson does) That the sober Belief of Good and Bad Spirits is an essential Part of every good Christian's Faith.[34]

There is also a social threat lurking behind this legislation, which points back to the condemnation of Hutchinson as a dangerous truckler with plebeians and free-thinkers: 'However, it must be said, the contrary Temper [i.e. free-thinking] is too obvious amongst us without Doors; and this has induc'd me to trouble you in such a Manner . . .' The author poses as a hard-nosed realist who can tell the honourable members about

---

[34] *The Witch of Endor*, pp. viii, xxviii, v.

affairs in the outside world, 'however merry you may have made your-
selves about SPIRITS in St Stephen's Chapel'. Witchcraft belief is an important buttress of orthodox religion, which Parliament neglects at its
peril.

The postscript alludes to a very different sort of pressure from without
doors, 'your Electors . . . [and] Thousands besides' who require an answer to these objections. His assessment of the balance of clerical opinion
is straightforward: witchcraft can be considered as 'an Affair purely of a
Religious Nature, abstracted from the Civil Punishment; and, if I might
ask; what, if the Concurrence of an English Convocation had been had, in
making such a General Repeal?' Witchcraft is evidently a Tory issue, and
the cherished belief of a silent majority of the English clergy. The author
manages to bind up witchcraft with another recognizably Tory grievance,
the disappearance of a sitting Convocation. This involved the entrusting
of the nation's spiritual interest to Parliament. In the pamphlet as a
whole, the author asks the legislators to exercise their spiritual respons-
ibilities with care. In this particular passage, he asserts that were the clergy
to have a say, as would be proper in a consideration 'abstracted from the
Civil Punishment', the matter would stand very differently.

So we can identify this address as thoroughly Tory in ideology. It sides
with the ordinary clergy, as against two bishops, and condemns free-
thinking and plebeian vulgarity (the author even worries that his 'unknown' printer may have been 'procrastinating' the appearance of his
book, siding 'with the Majority'). This reading of the text allows us to
define the sense in which those who supported the old witchcraft legislation felt embattled; and to catch the authentic but silent meaning of the
constituency—marginalized, embarrassed, ridiculed—from which its author emerged. It was a constituency which Erskine's 'long canting speech'
in the Commons failed either to reach or arouse.[35]

LATER REPEALS

It is misleading to represent the repeal of the Jacobean legislation against
witchcraft as a mere footnote to the history of rationalism. Repeal did not
emerge from nowhere as an afterthought, part a process of mopping-up

---

[35] Ibid., pp. xliii, xlix–l, xxvii. Compare the pamphleteer's concern for Convocation,
with that of Erskine and his predecessors—like Robert Wylie—for the continued existence
and dignity of the General Assembly of the Scottish church. High-flying, in Scotland and
England, was being bound up with the issue of witchcraft.

in a struggle against superstition that had been won some time 'between the Restoration and the Revolution'.[36] It had a context and a meaning. Both are, to some extent, recoverable. Erskine and the anonymous author of the 'Address' represent an identifiable collection of concerns which can be seen at work long before 1736.

Nor was repeal an undifferentiated and simple, or a solely English, process. The Parliamentary procedure of discussion and amendment resulted not in a simple repeal as had been envisaged by the bill's sponsors, but in a new Witchcraft Act which punished imposture, that is, the pretended 'use or exercise [of] any kind of Witchcraft, Sorcery, Inchantment, or Conjuration'. The Lords' consideration of the bill also ensured the extension of the new legislation to Scotland; an afterthought which is a neat example of the insensitivity to the affairs of North Britain about which Erskine complained. The late measures against imposture may have had an ideological function, serving to underline the new reading of the Old Testament injunctions against witchcraft which those who wished to ditch the prosecution of witches had long favoured.[37]

The contingencies of British constitutional arrangements allowed for a brief, but revealing, recrudescence of the witchcraft debate at the very moment when the more general political and religious inheritance of the 1689 settlement came to be seriously debated for the last time. The years following the French Revolution had seen a substantial easing of pressure for measures of religious and constitutional reform. In 1787, Beaufoy's motion for the repeal of the Test and Corporation Acts was defeated in the Commons; in 1790, a similar motion was withdrawn from Parliament without a division. Nevertheless, the principle of religious toleration—though not full emancipation—continued to be extended. In 1780 the Gordon riots had failed to wreck the Catholic Relief Act of 1778; in 1777, dissenting ministers and schoolmasters had been relieved from the necessity of subscribing to the Thirty-Nine Articles. This cautious retreat from the legacy of the Glorious Revolution and its 1715 confirmation continued after 1789. Considerations of national security led to the proposals which in 1793 extended the franchise to Irish Catholics, within an unreformed Parliament. In 1812, the Unitarian Relief Act was passed,

---

[36] H. T. Buckle, *The History of Civilisation in England* (new edn., 1871), iii. 363.

[37] For amendments, see *Journal of the House of Lords*, 26 Feb. 1735/6, and *Journal of the House of Commons*, 4 Mar. 1735/6. On the proper reading of the scriptural injunctions against witchcraft, see *The Witchcraft of the Scriptures: A sermon preach'd on a Special Occasion. By Ph[ilip] S[tubbs] LL.D* (1736), esp. 19, 22, 24; and Joseph Juxon, *A Sermon upon Witchcraft* (1736).

and the Conventicle and Five-Mile Acts, legacies of the Restoration settlement, were repealed.

The years from 1815 to 1829 were to see the death throes of the old ecclesiastical and constitutional order. As Twiss put it in his biography of a leading reactionary, Lord Eldon, 'the dangerous dispositions which had for a time been absorbed or overlaid by foreign hostility, were again let loose upon the constitution of England.'[38] In 1816, a motion for Catholic relief was defeated in the House of Lords. The watershed came in the 1820s, and one opponent of change, in the religious or the political sphere (if he even admitted such a distinction) was quite clear about the diabolical inspiration behind the soon-to-be-effected repeals of the Test and Corporation Acts, amounting to 'nothing less than a satanic impatience of godly discipline—a hatred of, and rebellion against, constituted authorities'.[39]

Another author, writing some years earlier in that heated decade, agreed with this refusal of 'any Concession to Dissenters or Papists' alike. He was writing ostensibly against further repeal of the witchcraft legislation; not the English legislation, dispatched in 1736, but the Irish statute which had stood outside Westminster's jurisdiction until 1801 and the Act of Union. In 1821, the witchcraft issue came again to Westminster.

The young member for Limerick, Thomas Spring-Rice, elected in the Whig interest in 1820, a man who won an early reputation as an expert on Irish affairs, suggested some reforms to the criminal law in Ireland, some tidying-up:

[He] moved for leave to bring in a bill for the repeal of the capital punishments attached to the commission of certain offences in Ireland. The crimes from which he proposed to remove capital punishment were, stealing privately in a shop; the forcible abduction of women; and the concealment of effects by bankrupts. He also proposed to repeal certain laws against witchcraft. It was right, he observed, that the punishment of crimes should, in every instance, be as conformable as possible to public opinion; and in Ireland this was particularly necessary, where there existed such a disposition to prosecute for many capital offences, and such a horror of informers.[40]

Leave was given for a bill to be brought in, and what resulted as far as witchcraft was concerned was '1 & 2 Geo IV c. 18 (6 April). An Act to Repeal an Act, made in the Parliament of *Ireland* in the Twenty eighth Year of the Reign of Queen *Elizabeth*, against Witchcraft and Sorcery'.

---

[38] Cited in Clark, *English Society*, 384.

[39] S. Hyde Cassan, *Considerations on the Danger of any Legislative Alteration Respecting the Corporation and Test Acts; and of any Concession to Dissenters or Papists* (1828), 28.

[40] *The Parliamentary Debates* [Hansard], iv (1821), col. 1167 for 7 Mar. 1821.

This repeal was, without doubt, a measure of administrative reform pure and simple, undertaken without any reference to the ideological history of witchcraft theory. The same cannot be said of the pamphlet that opposed repeal, entitled *Antipas*.

Who was Antipas? The author himself was anonymous, but his chosen model can be found in the book of Revelation: 'I know thy works, and where thou dwellest, *even* where Satan's seat *is*: and thou holdest fast my name, and hast not denied my faith, even in those days wherein Antipas *was* my faithful martyr, who was slain among you, where Satan dwelleth.'[41] The writer sees himself as a lone defender of the faith against the depredations of the Devil.

The work sets out as an attack on the dilution of the Revolution settlement, with complaints against anti-trinitarianism at large and, more topically, against the new Roman Catholic Disability Removal Bill. This received its third reading on 2 April and was subsequently lost in the Lords. All Antipas's complaints are couched in the form of 'an earnest and solemn appeal' to the Lords ecclesiastical of the upper house:

Had such an appeal been made to your Lordships in a respectful but forcible manner, before the fatal removal of those outworks which the piety and wisdom of our ancestors had raised against the most daring enemies of Religion, the torrent of infidelity would have been stemmed, or diverted from its course; it could not have inundated, as it has done, every street in our cities, and every village in our land.[42]

The author is one against the crowd, and perhaps one of the 'meanest' of the Church 'establishment'. The 'outworks' referred to are the measures against dissenters and unbelievers which had been repealed or moderated in recent times. A link is made between Popery and radical dissent:

The revival of Popery was for centuries the dread of England: to prevent this our reformers laboured—our patriots bled. The progress of infidelity has, of late, formed a new and equally just ground of apprehension for her safety: the learned have fought against its abettors with the pen, the brave with the sword.

At the very moment when the Papacy is falling from influence, and when the scourge of atheistical Jacobinism has been driven from the face of Europe, 'on a sudden this warfare ceases—an armistice is demanded and allowed to both—restrictions are done away—laws are repealed—

---

[41] Revelation 2: 13.
[42] *Antipas* (1st edn., 1821), 7. There was a 2nd edn. in 1821.

concessions are granted—every avenue is to be cleared—and every door, even that of the "bottomless pit!" is to be opened at once.'[43]

These developments are seen in prophetic terms ('come, let him that standeth on the watch-tower, report what he seeth'[44]); and in terms of social hygiene. The author is an Elijah standing against the infatuation of the people, against emancipation, against the repeal of the test, against democracy, against reform: 'The nature of a cause will never be changed by the number of its advocates. A disease would not assume the character of health by becoming epidemic; nor does a confederacy cease to be formidable in proportion to the increase of its partisans.'[45]

Diabolism is brought in as a further sign of the times, and as an overarching category embracing the twin threats of Popery and infidelity, 'another and a more desperate enemy still, the parent and instigator of the other two'. The 'Ruler of the darkness of this World' has 'another instrument of assault'. In these days of supposed enlightenment, this weapon is all the more dangerous 'because the least expected'; its reality is asserted in spite of all the efforts of 'modern philosophy, or modern policy'. Denial and scepticism are not the proper means of resistance; rather one should resist 'by putting on the whole armour of God'. The instrument in question is 'SORCERY or WITCHCRAFT'.[46]

Antipas offers a wide definition of this diabolical crime, partly, no doubt, to confirm the association between sorcery, Popery, and infidelity which is the pamphlet's primary concern. Under the term is comprehended 'all kind of influence produced by collusion with Satan; all persons who have dealings with Satan, if not actually entered into formal compact with him'.[47]

The emphasis throughout the rest of the tract is firmly upon the explication of passages from Scripture. The usual injunctions against witchcraft are cited in support of legislation against witchcraft. *Antipas* also fulfils its role as a prophetic work by citing extensive passages from Bishop Horsley on the meaning of passages from Isaiah, and by adopting a vigorously eschatological tone; 'INDIFFERENCE TO THE SIGNS OF THE TIMES IS CRIMINAL', Horsley had declared, and *Antipas* views the prophecies of Isaiah, as explicated by the Bishop, as 'remarkable' anticipations of the

---

[43] Ibid. 16 f.

[44] The epigraph on the title-page, Isaiah 21: 6.

[45] *Antipas*, 13. For another image of morbidity, see 39: 'what Chiron can arrest the process of dissolution in that BODY POLITIC, which should exhibit the morbid anatomy of a Protestant king and a Papal council?'

[46] Ibid. 17.   [47] Ibid.

crisis of the 1820s. Here, for example, is Isaiah on the Egyptians: 'I will destroy the counsel thereof; and they shall seek to the idols, and to the charmers, and *to them that have familiar spirits*, and to the wizards.' Horsley interprets:

> The rulers of the Egyptians misled the people by erroneous politics. Ignorant of the designs of Providence, they formed false conjectures of the effect of their alliances, and of the event of their wars, and their treaties; and misinterpreted what Providence brought to pass, at every step. This is a declaration of the dulness of the Egyptians to perceive the hand of God in their affairs, and foresee the impending judgment.[48]

Antipas is sure of the conclusion to be drawn from scriptural exegesis: that the crime of sorcery is a sin which 'has ever been marked by the most signal vengeance of Almighty God in the case of individuals; and the permission or encouragement thereof, on the part of governments, has been uniformly followed by national judgments'. The practice of witchcraft 'is the certain mark of a people abandoned to confusion, and popular tumult; and *the permission of it in a government, the positive mark of infatuation*'. The onset of the millennium is clearly at hand, for 'this abominable delusion of Satan, practised in the first age of the Christian era, will be prevalent in the last'.[49]

The author has an acute sense that his views are marginal. We have already noted his aversion to accepting sheer weight of numbers as an argument for emancipation and reform. He evidently feels embattled, as both the choice of a Christian martyr for pseudonym, and numerous passages in the text testify. 'I am aware', he writes, 'that these opinions or any others concerning Antichrist, are become very unfashionable'. He feels the power of urbane ridicule at work as he cites a report from the *New Times* concerning parliamentary debate on the Irish Witchcraft Act's repeal. The bill having been passed, 'Lord——observed, that midnight was a most appropriate time to pass such a measure.—(*laughter*)'. With inexhaustible indignation, Antipas fumes that such a solemn measure should be 'no matter of MIDNIGHT MERRIMENT in a Christian Senate'.[50]

What strikes us now is how well *Antipas* fits into the stream of reactionary literature produced in the final years of the old dispensation. Revd. Stephen Hyde Cassan is matched by works like Edmund Greenfield's *The Glorious Exaltation of the Holy Lamb of God, Our Lord and Saviour Jesus Christ, over all the Powers of Darkness* of 1820; or, from a Catholic

---

[48] Ibid. 22 f., 28, citing Horsley's *Biblical Criticism*, ii. 189.
[49] *Antipas*, 18, 21, 25.   [50] Ibid. 31, 35, 36.

writer, *The Confessed Intimacy of Luther with Satan, at whose suggestion he abolished the Mass . . . [with an] introduction by Rev John Lingard,* 1821.[51]

The last flowering of the old politico-religious debate was thus accompanied by a revival of the witchcraft issue. It has already been seen how the discourse of witchcraft could return to the political arena even after the repeal of the relevant statutes, as during the Jew Bill crisis of 1753. The issues that had accompanied its last major manifestation, 1710–14, and assisted in the process of its marginalization, were themselves being revived. This late incarnation in 1821 had its own very distinct features. Around 1700, the apologetic for witchcraft belief was still associated with a desire and longing for Christian unity; while sceptics such as Francis Hutchinson seem to have expanded on Lockian hints in order to replace one diabolical enemy, the witch, by another, the Pope. In *Antipas* these distinctions disappear: witch, Pope, infidel, and dissenter are all part of the same diabolical continuum. As the author puts it, 'conciliation of Dissenters has opened the mouth of blasphemers—concession to Catholics may yet "give place to the devil" '; or, more tersely, 'A Papal relapse may terminate in a Pagan crisis'. The author cites Bishop Jewel for historical confirmation that the power of Popery and the incidence of witchcraft go hand in hand.[52]

At the same time, however, *Antipas* exhibits all the nostalgic marks of the witchcraft theory of the years around 1700. It has already been suggested in this book that witchcraft theory was an intellectual entity with a particular affinity for sacralized versions of the state. The witch was a focal point for a quasi-religious conception of political authority, a mixture of the anti-sacerdotal and anti-regal qualities analogous to and a diabolical inversion of that paramount exemplum of the mixed person, the king himself.[53] The author of *Antipas* certainly held the state to be a mystical body, as we may see in his final call to the legislature: 'Your Lordships are called, as Christians, and called as legislators, to "wrestle not against flesh and blood, but against principalities and powers, against the rulers of the darkness of this world, against spiritual wickedness in

---

[51] For a survey of this sort of literature, see Robert Hole, *Pulpits, Politics and Public Order in England 1760–1832* (Cambridge, 1989).

[52] *Antipas*, 39 f. and also see 43, citing Jewel's sermon before Elizabeth in 1559: '[he was] not indifferent as to the subject of Witchcraft and Sorcery.—He could discern its connexion with Popery . . . he lamented the increase of the evil at the time when England was emerging from the darkness and emancipated from the bondage of the Papal See.'

[53] 'Rex Angliae est persona mixta cum sacerdote.' See Clark, *English Society*, 135. See also Stuart Clark, 'King James's *Daemonologie*', in Sydney Anglo, *The Damned Art: Essays in the Literature of Witchcraft* (1977).

high places".[54] Witchcraft and Jacobinism were akin in their efforts 'to throw off the restraints of religion, morality and custom, and undo the bands of civil society'.[55]

The author of *Antipas* viewed the settlement of 1689 as a creature continuous even to his own day; the 'long eighteenth century' from the Glorious Revolution to his own day was a seamless whole as far as religious legitimacy was concerned. Thus, in his final lines, he repeated William Jane's traditionalist cry of 1689, itself an echo from the thirteenth century: 'NOLUMUS LEGES ANGLIAE MUTARI'.[56]

The 1736 legislation was itself repealed in the 1950/1 session of Parliament with the intention of preventing possible prosecutions of well-meaning spiritualists. Chuter Ede, Home Secretary, was Whiggish in every sense, asserting that 'this Measure is a considerable advance in the direction of religious Toleration'. Another member, Lieutenant-Commander Thompson, saw the measure in a more engagingly eccentric light, making a speech which encapsulates many of the false conceptions besetting the historian of witchcraft:

If, as I hope, the House gives a Second Reading to this Bill today we shall be doing rather a remarkable thing. I do not speak as a Spiritualist, but in my view we shall be reaffirming an outlook and a point of view very necessary in an increasingly material age. In 1735 [*sic*] the Witchcraft Act brought to an end officially what had, in fact, been at an end for some years—the belief in the reality of witchcraft. Witchcraft had been practised from the very beginning of time; during the 16th and 17th centuries there was tremendous activity in England and on the Continent, but with the dawn of the 'age of reason', so called, belief in the reality of witchcraft faded . . . By 1735 the official view was that these powers no longer existed, whether they were good or evil, and we have been committed to a sort of official scepticism ever since that day . . . [this bill will] reaffirm that we honestly admit that there are powers given to some people in the community which enable them to do things which, for 215 years, we have not believed were physically possible.

This passage sums up many historical misconceptions, unwittingly hints at a truer perspective, and suggests unexpected continuities in the history of witchcraft legislation.[57]

This book set out by questioning the cogency of notions according to

---

[54] *Antipas*, 42.   [55] Ibid. 28.   [56] Ibid. 43.
[57] Hansard, Vth ser. vol. 481, session 1950–1, cols. 1486, 1467 [1 Dec. 1950]. On 20 June 1950 Charles Botham had been convicted on three counts of false pretences. He had also been charged with two counts of conjuration under the 1735/6 Act, but these were not considered by the court.

which belief in the reality of witchcraft 'faded' in the wake of a nebulous 'age of reason', some time around 1700. As an intellectual assumption about the genealogy of our own beliefs, this position runs very deep, as Lieutenant-Commander Thompson's remarks show. Once the assumption has been questioned, and we ask whether witchcraft might not have been a serious issue in 1700 and beyond, our whole perspective on this issue shifts radically.

As we have seen, the 1735/6 Act did not commit everyone to scepticism as regards the existence of these powers, 'good or evil'. Even after 1736, apologists for the old attitudes continued to speak out; but their fate was increasingly to be marginalized and ridiculed. The repeal of the Jacobean legislation set the seal on a polite consensus that convictions of witches for real sorcery were unsafe. This was, then, a confirmation of an 'official view' in force since the end of the 'rage of party'. It is here that Thompson's remarks point towards the perspective canvassed in this book: the history of the fate of witchcraft theory is largely the history of an official point of view and its transformations, transformations effected both by specific, and contingent, political events, and by longer-term shifts in the structure of ideology.

Finally, of course, 215 years on, witchcraft legislation was once more being used to fight bigger battles to defend spiritual values 'in an increasingly material age'. The witchcraft issue in England has had its various uses, in the seventeenth, the eighteenth, the nineteenth, and even the twentieth centuries.[58]

---

[58] 14 and 15 Geo. 6. Ch. 33. Fraudulent Mediums Act, 1951 (an Act to repeal the Witchcraft Act 1735, and to make in substitution for certain provisions of section four of the Vagrancy Act 1824, express provision for the punishment of persons who fraudulently purport to act as spiritualistic mediums or to exercise powers of telepathy, clairvoyance, or other similar powers. 22 June 1951). For recent, non-historical, debate about witchcraft, see 'Propaganda, fantasy and lies blur reports of ritual abuse', *Guardian*, 10 Sept. 1990; 'Save Poor Little Witch Girl; Drugged child rape victim's nightmare in lair of Satan', *News of the World*, 6 May 1990; 'I sacrificed my babies to Satan', *Sunday Mirror*, 25 Mar. 1990; 'Witch Story to Believe?', *Spectator*, 24 Mar. 1990; 'Root Out Satanists . . . Mrs Thatcher last night vowed to rid Britain of devil worship orgies involving the sexual abuse of children', *Sun*, 14 Mar. 1990. For early reports of the end of the affair, see *Independent on Sunday*, no. 221, 24 Apr. 1994, 'Government inquiry decides satanic abuse does not exist'. For a recent discussion of the connections between modern theories of satanic child abuse and early-modern theories of witchcraft, see Leslie Wilson, 'Salem's Lot', in *London Review of Books*, 17/6, 23 Mar. 1995.

9

Witchcraft Abroad

INTRODUCTION

This book has set out to explain an undeniable change in English intellectual life. The existence of witchcraft, with a diabolical pact at its core, was held to be plausible by credit-worthy members of the English educated classes in 1660. By the time of the repeal of legislation against witchcraft in 1736, this belief had become a matter for ridicule, seriously entertained only by the marginalized, the eccentric, or the vulgar. Within this very broad and uncontentious chronology, discriminations have been made. Concentrating on the issue of witchcraft theory's status in public discourse, rather than the number of its adherents or the frequency of prosecution, conviction, or execution for witchcraft, I have suggested that witchcraft theory retained its credibility beyond 1700; and that the final crisis of the rage of party in England was a key moment in the dissolution of that credibility, as the theory was overtaken by rational disdain. Persecuting witches had been 'declared', as Byron's narrator puts it in *Don Juan*, 'an act of inurbanity'.[1]

To explain the demise of a reasoned theory of witchcraft involves elaborating how such a body of doctrine made itself acceptable in its heyday. Which features of witchcraft theory made it compatible with the intellectual outlook of so many apparently credible seventeenth-century philosophers and men of affairs? The early chapters of this book have shown how a conservative and supernaturalist Restoration ideology embraced witchcraft theory, despite its earlier affiliations with both a discredited theology of contract and the dislocations of the Civil War. Witchcraft theory was nothing if not adaptable. If even as radical a thinker

---

[1] *Don Juan*, canto 17 (1824), in George Gordon, Lord Byron, *The Complete Poetical Works*, ed. J. J. McGann (7 vols.; Oxford, 1986–), v. 658 f.

as Thomas Hobbes retained witchcraft as part of his system, then its resilience as a concept is clear. An outright rejection of witchcraft was difficult to achieve because it fitted so well the assumptions of a Restoration consensus in which even Hobbes participated. A discussion of another philosopher much influenced by Hobbes, John Locke, demonstrates that a change in ideological assumptions could make witchcraft irrelevant in a way that Hobbes's radical, anti-supernaturalist ontology (from which Locke distanced himself) did not.

One possible objection to my approach is its apparent parochialism. The demise of witchcraft theory certainly did not happen in England alone. Over the period 1600 to 1800 witchcraft made the same journey from plausibility to ridicule throughout Europe. How can so nuanced an explanation in England cope with what appears to be a European phenomenon? How could English party politics, for instance, explain such a universal, apparently inexorable process of decline?

From a theoretical point of view, such an objection mistakes the nature of my argument for England. In particular, it misunderstands the relationship between the particular and general in my, and perhaps any, historical argument. I am not attempting a knock-down, reductionist, causal explanation in which the decline of witchcraft belief is attributed solely to the occurrence and outcome of a single trial in Hertfordshire, or the course of party politics over a narrow period. The relationship between the Wenham trial and the fate of witchcraft theory is not a matter of cause and effect in this simplistic way. The Wenham case expressed and focused the course of debate as it stood in 1712. While the way in which it unfolded undoubtedly contributed to a loss of credibility for witchcraft theory in the public arena, it forms only part of a story in which witchcraft theory lost its ideological rationale. The demise of witchcraft theory and the resolution of the rage of party were common expressions of the retreat of the sacral conception of the state. They move in a parallel, only intermittently causal relation.

My explanatory model is bipartite. Having exposed the grounding of witchcraft, both before and after the Restoration, in conceptions of the sacral, confessional state, I associate the demise of witchcraft with the retreat of those conceptions (see Chapter 4). The events of 1710–14 were the instantiation of the legacy of the Glorious Revolution, both for witchcraft, and for the religious and political constitution of the state. The foundations of witchcraft theory were sapped in the late seventeenth century, along with the foundations of the sacral state, but only in the early eighteenth century was this process confirmed, and the edifice dismantled.

An apparently parochial English argument can, therefore, be closely bound into a much larger tale of secularization and desacralization. This, in turn, gives it a European point of reference; and just as the history of secularization and desacralization in different European states has distinct contours, varying chronologies, and wholly different patterns of events associated with it, so does the history of witchcraft belief. As a way of demonstrating the viability of my English explanatory model, I now present a case study of witchcraft theory in France. This will be undertaken in some detail, to try and match the approach to the English case. The aim is not to produce a point-by-point comparison, with a list of similarities and differences; but rather, a parallel narrative which is both compatible and illuminating.

THE CASE OF FRANCE

The formal decriminalization of witchcraft in England took place relatively late, in 1736, a full fifty years after the last witch was executed. Historians have therefore tended to view it as an afterthought. France, on the other hand, had a legal declaration against the prosecution of witches at exactly the time the optimistic student of progress might hope, as the great witch-hunts were winding down and the Enlightenment was getting under way.

In July 1682 Louis XIV issued an edict, 'for the punishment of various crimes, notably those of poisoners, those who call themselves *devins*, magicians, and enchanters; and for the regulation of grocers and apothecaries'.[2] This measure was promptly registered at the *Parlement* of Paris on 31 August in the same year.[3] It has been widely interpreted as having put a final seal on the demise of witchcraft in France.[4]

By the early seventeenth century, the *Parlement* of Paris, the foremost

[2] 'Pour la punition de différens crimes, notamment des Empoisonneurs, ceux qui se disent Devins, Magiciens & Enchanteurs; & portant reglement pour les Epiciers & Apothicaires'. This is only the title given in certain editions of the text, as noted in Robert Mandrou, *Magistrats et sorciers en France au XVIIe siècle* (Paris, 1968), 479.

[3] Repr. in François André Isambert *et al.* (eds.), *Recueil général des anciennes lois françaises* (Paris, 1821–33), xix. 393 f.

[4] Starting, in England, with William Blackstone, *Commentaries on the Laws of England* (4 vols.; Oxford, 1769), iv. 60 f.: 'But all executions for this dubious crime are now at an end; our legislature having at length followed the wise example of Louis XIV in France, who thought proper by an edict to restrain the tribunals of justice from receiving informations of witchcraft.' More recently see Robin Briggs, 'Witchcraft and the Community in France and French-speaking Europe', in his *Communities of Belief: Cultural and Social Tensions in Early Modern France* (Oxford, 1989), 7; Arlette Farge, *Subversive Words: Public Opinion in Eighteenth-Century France* (Cambridge, 1994), 85.

sovereign court of France, was already highly cautious about the crime of witchcraft. Within its jurisdiction its centralized appellate system had made efforts to suppress major outbreaks of witch-hunting. In 1601, the swimming test had been prohibited; while in 1624 automatic appeals in cases of witchcraft were imposed, perhaps with governmental connivance.[5] According to Alfred Soman, who has done painstaking work in the archives of the *Parlement*, between 1626 and 1639 only three capital sentences were carried out (in 1626, 1632, and 1635). Such caution was undoubtedly a reflection of juristic worries about the erosion of standards of proof when suspicions of witchcraft were allied to panic. The three capital sentences in question were the result of trials in which documentary proof (a written pact with the Devil) had been supplied; this confirms that the *Parlement*'s caution was about proof, and did not concern the actual existence of witchcraft. Parisian caution may also have reflected fears about disorder.[6] These developments do not necessarily reflect a precocious and thoroughgoing scepticism; or even the sort of scepticism common at the end of the seventeenth century and later, which admitted the reality of the crime while denying entirely the possibility of its equitable detection and punishment. The crime remained; punishment was, if infrequently, meted out; appeals did not dry up in the face of Parisian indifference but continued to be generated for the *Parlement* to process.[7] As one might argue for witchcraft in England, the effective cessation of capital sentences was not necessarily equivalent to the abolition of the crime.

Soman revises the chronology of decline set out in Robert Mandrou's *Magistrats et sorciers en France au XVIIᵉ siècle*. He pushes back the Parisian disengagement from witch-hunting to the beginning of the seventeenth century and denies the singular impact of the great possession scandals which play such an important role in Mandrou's book. This allows us, in turn, to disengage belief from prosecution, in parallel with the English example. For, if the *Parlement* of Paris was developing arguments restraining witch persecution as early as the 1580s, as Soman suggests—arguments

---

[5] See Alfred Soman, 'La Décriminalisation de la sorcellerie en France', repr. in his *Sorcellerie et Justice Criminelle: Le Parlement de Paris* (Aldershot, 1992), 197. Cf. Thomas *RDM* 551, on the swimming test. Soman also notes, between 1600 and 1604, a series of parliamentary decisions which, he maintains, established obligatory appeal in practice.

[6] Soman: 'Les groupes dirigeants en France semblent avoir moins peur de la sorcellerie que des désordres nés de la chasse', 'Décriminalisation', 187.

[7] Soman speaks, 'Décriminalisation', 197, of 'le dernier arrêt de mort, le 14 juillet 1625, pour fait de sorcellerie'; he then mentions the three executions in 1626, 1632, and 1635, implying at the same time that late executions, in general, were related to blasphemy or 'des escroqueries de charlatans'. See also Soman, 'Decriminalizing Witchcraft: Does the French Experience Furnish a European Model?', in Soman, *Sorcellerie et Justice*, 1.

which came to fruition around 1600, and led to the effective restraint of prosecution from 1624 on (with the implicit approval of Richelieu)—then a direct link between loss of belief and the end of persecution is less convincing. The slowing of persecution in the 1620s, continuous as it was with long-term jurisprudential trends dating from the 1580s, did not occur because of a transformation in belief or the rise of scepticism. Control, not abolition, was the immediate and avowed aim.

Soman also indicates the politicization of the witchcraft issue before these developments, during the wars of religion. The witch panics of 1587 in north-eastern France are bracketed with the sort of 'eschatological anguish' which characterized the *processions blanches* in the province of Champagne in the 1580s, something of which the Crown disapproved. 'There is an evil at large in Champagne,' declared Jacques de la Guesle, *procureur général du roi*, in 1588: 'which is that most of the people there are held to be witches.'[8] Fervour against witches was, as ever, part of a more general fervour against irreligion and heresy. While Paris was under siege, up to 1594, the *Ligueurs*, Catholic extremists in rebellion against the Crown, had a grip on the *Parlement* which prevented the moderate party, those who were cautious about witchcraft, from exercising their views. With devout extremists in control, the kingdom was to be cleansed. The *Ligue* accused Henry III himself of sorcery, in a 'violent tract'.[9] On the basis of all this, one can go some way with Soman's assertion that 'the triumph of Crown and *Parlement* over the *Ligue* necessitated a rejection of the mental world of witch hunters'.[10] Political conditions had changed, but this did not necessitate the rejection of witch beliefs all together. These, in familiar vein, continued to have their uses—for Richelieu and his agent Laubardement at Loudun in 1633–4, for instance,[11] and elsewhere. Moreover, whatever our conclusions about the Parisian *ressort*— and Soman perhaps too easily assimilates *Parlement* to Crown—large and influential as it was (encompassing the Île de France, Picardy, Orléanais, Touraine, Maine, Anjou, Poitou, Angoumois, Champagne, Bourbonnais, Berry, Lyonnais, Forez, Beauplais, and Auvergne), it was not all France, and if the prosecution of witches was on a tight rein within the Parisian orbit, elsewhere witch-hunting did continue after the 1620s.

---

[8] 'Y a ung mal en la Champaigne', s'est [*sic*] qu'on estime la plupart des habitans sorciers.' Cited in Soman, 'Décriminalisation', 189.

[9] H. C. Lea, *Materials towards a History of Witchcraft*, ed. A. C. Howland (Philadelphia, 1939), iii. 1291 f.

[10] 'Decriminalizing Witchcraft', 21 n. 20.

[11] Mandrou, *Magistrats et sorciers*, 265–9. For the Loudun story, see a collection of texts with commentary edited by Michel de Certeau, *La Possession de Loudun* (Paris, 1990).

Parts of the state apparatus, then, were still committed to the rooting out of witchcraft, on a variety of levels: in the centre, the political dangers of witchcraft persecution, apparent during the wars of religion, and the fear of disorder or the perversion of the judicial order, led the *Parlement* to restrict the persecution of witches around 1600. At the same time the laws against witchcraft remained in force. As Jacques d'Autun put it as late as 1671, in his *L'Incrédulité savante et la crédulité ignorante au sujet des Magiciens et sorciers*, largely devoted to decrying the persecution of witches: 'It is a a calumny against the most august *Parlement* of France to say that this tribunal treats the crimes of witches as no more than chimeras.'[12] He recalls that the magistrates of Paris have indeed condemned sorcerers, that they are not excessively indulgent, indeed not indulgent at all. At the peripheries, meanwhile, actual persecution of witches could remain an instrument of local policy.

Problems for the Crown emerged under the reforming rhetoric of Louis XIV. The contradictions between Parisian caution and the possibility of provincial zeal became apparent. Mandrou suggests that the decisive moment of clarification came with the Normandy affair of the 1670s. The procedural misgivings of late sixteenth-century Parisian *parlementaires* may well have caught on in most of the other provincial sovereign courts by the 1660s. The *Parlement* at Rouen was, however, packed with *dévots*, and had a traditional antipathy to Parisian claims of superiority, especially in the realm of witchcraft. When a bout of witch-hunting came before the *Parlement*, opinions were divided and the *premier Président*, Claude Pellot, decided to refer the matter to Colbert, Louis XIV's chief minister and his patron.

Pellot, reiterating Colbertian principles, reproved the disorder represented by a contradictory set of jurisprudences. 'The matter', he wrote, 'is important enough for His Majesty to make some regulation about it, and for the judges to say what proofs are necessary to condemn such people.'[13] The Rouen *Parlement* remained unconvinced by the arguments

---

[12] 'C'est une calomnie que l'on impose au plus auguste Parlement de France quand l'on dit que tous les crimes des sorciers ne sont que des chimères et pures illusions devant son Tribunal, qu'ils ont mis un bandeau sur les yeux à la Justice pour ne les voir pas.' R. P. Jacques d'Autun [Jacques Chevanes], *L'Incrédulité savante et la crédulité ignorante au sujet des Magiciens et sorciers. Avecque la response à un livre intitulé Apologie pour tous les grands personnages qui ont esté faussement soupçonnés de Magie* (Lyons, 1671), cited in Mandrou, *Magistrats et sorciers*, 436.

[13] 'La matière . . . est assez importante, afin que Sa M. fist quelque réglement là-dessus, et que les juges seussent quelles preuves il faut pour condamner pareilles gens.' For the Colbertian rhetoric of reform see *Mémoires de Louis XIV*, ed. C. Dreyss (2 vols.; Paris, 1860), quoted in R. Mettam, *Government and Society in Louis XIV's France* (1977), 1 f.

which Pellot offered. They were also, no doubt, offended by his air of rational superiority, and solemnly reaffirmed their desire to advance 'the glory of God and the relief of your peoples who are oppressed by fear'.[14] Nothing could be more indicative of their attachment to a programme of 'acculturation', of their conception of their proper role as defenders of a Christian order, under royal supervision. They insisted, against the Colbertian Pellot, that Norman jurisprudence was all of a piece with that of other regions of France: 'The *Parlement* of your province of Normandy has not found, up to now, that her jurisprudence is different from that of your other *Parlements*.'[15] They catalogued judgements and declared 'in an unequivocal statement . . . [that] all these Acts show that the accusation of witchcraft is entertained, and punished with death, in all the *parlements* of your kingdom, and demonstrate the uniformity of their jurisprudence'.[16] In line with the late medieval tradition of a provincial loyalism dedicated to royal authority, but jealous of its capacity to mediate it, Rouen, insulated from the fashionable nostrums of the Parisian judicial milieu, was implacable.

The consequence was the imposition of Pellot's, and Colbert's, will by royal fiat. An *arrêt* was accompanied by a promise to introduce a truly unified jurisprudence, along Parisian lines, in this area. This 'general declaration for courts, jurisdictions, and justices' would lay down the procedures which judges would have to follow in witch trials, and 'establish the quality of proofs and evidences which can be received and upon which the judges will be able to base the condemnation of the guilty'.[17] As Mandrou points out, it took ten years for anything resembling this ordinance to be produced. The reformed criminal code of Saint-Germain-en-Laye had been published in August 1670, without a word about witchcraft. On the surface, this is surprising, given the royal intervention in a possession case at Auxonne not long before, which had seemed to imply new rules of procedure. The Norman controversy followed hard upon the 1670 criminal ordinance, and yet the Crown took no decisive action to

[14] 'de la gloire de Dieu et du soulagement de [vos] peuples qui gémissent sous la crainte'.

[15] 'Celui de votre province de Normandie n'a point trouvé jusques ici que sa jurisprudence fût différente de celle de vos autres Parlemens.'

[16] 'en un formule sans équivoque . . . [que] tous ces arrêts font foi . . . que l'accusation du sortilège est reçue et punie de mort dans tous les Parlemens de votre Royaume, et justifient l'uniformité de leur Jurisprudence': Mandrou, *Magistrats et sorciers*, 451.

[17] 'les procédures qui doivent estre faites par les juges dans l'instruction des procès pour crime de sortilège, estably la qualité des preuves et des témoins qui pourront estre reçues et sur lesquelles les juges pourront fonder la condamnation des coupables', ibid. 457 and cf. declaration in the Pau case, 458–62.

eliminate contradiction in the field of witchcraft.[18] It did nevertheless commission the development of some of the concepts which were to feature in the 1682 ordinance.

Scrupulous to a point, and anxious to cajole his parliamentary colleagues, Pellot had asked Pierre Lalemant, theologian and chancellor of the University of Paris, to prepare a memorandum on the subject. Lalemant's conclusions prefigured the 1682 ordinance in their division of the real crime in two: witchcraft is either poisoning or sacrilege. The main difference was Lalemant's clerical emphasis on the role of the Church and the imposition of penance. The arguments by which Lalemant reaches these measured conclusions are, however, a mass of contradiction and reflect, in turn, upon the intellectual genesis of the 1682 measure.[19]

Lalemant's concern seems to have been to appeal to every instinct and every possible argument to counter the case against witches; but in doing so he piles so many considerations promiscuously one on top of another, that intellectual disorder results. Rather than arguing for the implausibility of the witch's actions, he takes it for granted; yet, at the same time, he is prepared to leave unassailed those 'amazing' stories of magicians, 'of which we have had examples even in our own century'. He is unable to be radically sceptical and shifts ground disconcertingly. *'Even if'* witches have committed crimes in co-operation with the Devil, the latter's complicity ensures the mitigation of the crime, since the witch's consent can hardly be said to have been freely given. Having admitted the possibility of magic, Lalemant now lets down the barrier one notch further, to admit that some of these deluded witches may indeed have committed the crimes of which they are accused, but may enter a plea of diminished responsibility. This argument echoes Sir Robert Filmer's in the 1650s; and no more than Thomas Hobbes or John Webster was Lalemant able to dismiss the crime of witchcraft entirely. If Lalemant's document lacks

---

[18] Mandrou, *Magistrats et sorciers*, 425.

[19] 'Consultation du Père Lalemant, Chancelier de l'université pour Sainte-Geneviève, à la demande de Claude Pellot, Premier Président du Parlement de Rouen' [Bibliothèque Sainte-Geneviève, MSS 487], printed in Robert Mandrou (ed.), *Possession et sorcellerie au XVIIe siècle: textes inédits* (Paris, 1979), 223–30: 's'ils sont bien convaincus d'être empoisonneurs, il faut les punir comme les loix l'ordonnent . . . s'ils n'ont fait tort à personne, et . . . ils ne soient coupables d'autre crime que d'avoir renoncé à leur baptême et d'avoir voulu se donner au Démon: ou ils veulent bien se corriger et alors il faut les remettre entre les mains de l'Église qui les instruira mieux qu'ils n'estoient, et qui leur fera faire pénitence de leurs péchés; ou ils demeurent obstinés dans leurs opinions extravagantes, alors on les devra punir comme on punit les frénétiques obstinés, les sacrilèges, les impies et les blasphémateurs; en quoi il faut apporter beaucoup de prudence.' See Mandrou's comments in his *Magistrats et sorciers*, 453–6.

intellectual rigour, it may be because its essential aims were those of a civil servant's memorandum, offering a variety of arguments to support a conclusion already arrived at, that is, that the persecution of witches should be discouraged for all the reasons the Paris *Parlement* had been recognizing since the 1580s. It certainly did not offer its arguments in a spirit of thoroughgoing scepticism; and, moreover, it was not absorbed into French law until another crisis had intervened, one which also conditioned and reflected the Crown's attitude towards the crime of witchcraft.

THE POISONS AFFAIR

Even if the Norman case (and a contemporary, if less contentious case before the *Parlement* of Pau) cleared the minds of the King's counsellors, as Mandrou has it, it still did not result in swift action to deal with the problem in a definitive fashion. It was a series of events within the circle of the court, that primary institution within Louis's political understanding, which finally compelled the imposition of order in the business of sorcery.[20] That scandal is crucial in understanding the meaning of Louis's 1682 ordinance on witchcraft.

The notorious '*affaire des poisons*', in which the King's mistress, the mother of his legitimized children, was implicated in sorcery, sacrilege, and poisoning, was at its height around 1680. Its genesis was protracted.[21] In November 1677 Nicholas-Gabriel de La Reynie, lieutenant-general of police in Paris, had started to uncover a network of alchemists and counterfeiters. From 1678 on, Louvois, Louis XIV's minister of war, and La Reynie corresponded regularly on the matter. Poison started to figure within the alchemical milieu. In January 1679 La Reynie had one Marie Bosse arrested on suspicion of poisoning, along with La Vigoureux, '*dévineresse*'. Bosse was the wife of a counterfeiter who had been condemned to the galleys, and was herself a fortune-teller. She practised

---

[20] On the primacy of the court, see *Mémoires de Louis XIV* in Mettam, *Government and Society*, 1 f.

[21] The most recent and full history of the affair is Jean-Christian Petitfils, *L'Affaire des poisons: alchimistes et sorciers sous Louis XIV* (Paris, 1977). There is no modern academic study of the poisons affair. See the following: François Bluche, *Louis XIV* (Oxford, 1990), 273–81; Ines Murat, *Colbert* (Paris, 1980), 395–414; Frantz Funck-Brentano, *Princes and Poisoners* (London, 1901); Frances Mossiker, *The Affair of the Poisons: Louis XIV, Madame de Montespan and One of History's Great Unsolved Mysteries* (London, 1970). Many of the original documents are printed in F. N. N. Ravaisson (ed.), *Archives de la Bastille* (Paris, 1866–1904), v–vii; and Pierre Clément (ed.), *Lettres, instructions et mémoires de Colbert* (6 vols.; Paris, 1861–9), vi. 'Affaires Religieuses—Affaires Diverses'.

chiromancy, had masses said for successful marriages, and was interested
in alchemy and in handling stolen goods.

In the month of La Bosse's arrest, Louvois wrote to Robert, *procureur
du roi* at the Châtelet, and demanded that he bring the matter to a conclusion. With the need for a discreet and swift form of judicial procedure
—to avoid scandal—an extraordinary jurisdiction was called for. On 7
April 1679 letters patent were issued for the famous '*Chambre Ardente*', so
named in reference to medieval courts which had judged similar crimes,
courts draped in black and lit by torches. Judges were handpicked for
their devout disposition, and care was taken to have medical and toxological
experts, doctors and apothecaries, at hand. The process was outside nor-
mal legal process, via *lettre de cachet*, jail, interrogation, reports to the
court, and sentence without appeal, which could be followed by further
questioning and torture. The creation of this special jurisdiction outraged
established magistrates like the *premier président* of the *Parlement* of Paris,
Guillaume de Lamoignan, who defended his '*justice immaculée*' and pro-
tested against the very existence of a separate court for poisoning and
sorcery.[22]

Poison and sorcery had always been bound together. Potions had been
a vital part of magical practice since time immemorial, used in association
with charms and verbal formulas to prevent conception, to induce fertil-
ity, to awaken love, or to kill.[23] Keith Thomas speaks of the 'deep-rooted
association of poison with sorcery', citing Joseph Blagrave's definition of
sorcery as the use of poison, as against witchcraft, which he associated
with image-magic.[24] The familiar interpretation of the 1682 ordinance,
and its relationship to the poisons scandal, is that poisoners partly replaced sorcerers in the league of infamy. A causal relation is implied
between the development of a (modern) naturalistic account of poisons,
and the demise of belief in sorcery. Yet the modern attitude towards
poison was not an *aperçu* won through the exercise of unfettered reason;
it was mediated by crises like the poisons scandal, and a matter for
disagreement and debate, for ambiguity and confused boundaries.[25]

At a time when the operation of physic was little understood, the boundary between the natural and the supernatural effects of administered

[22] Petitfils, *L'Affaire*, 54 f.

[23] See Valerie I. J. Flint, *The Rise of Magic in Early Mediaeval Europe* (Oxford, 1991),
esp. 235–7.

[24] Thomas, *RDM* 191, 438, citing *Blagrave's Astrological Practice of Physick* (1671), 135.

[25] One member of the Chambre de l'Arsenal clearly made the distinction, disagreeing
with La Reynie on the competence of the court, according to Madame de Sévigné, letter of
14 Feb. 1680 to Madame de Grignan, in *Correspondance* (3 vols.; Paris, 1974), ii. 835 f.

substances was ill-defined. Outbreaks of witch-hunting in France (in particular the last significant outbreak in the 1690s, in Brie) were sometimes associated with the nefarious activities of shepherds who poisoned animals.[26] From the beginning, too, the poisoning mania at Louis XIV's court was bound up with sorcery. Well before the *Chambre Ardente* affair, in 1668, Le Sage, a notorious sorcerer, and his assistant Abbé Mariette—as so often, a renegade priest—were arrested and charged before Paris's Châtelet Court. Their practices included the manufacture of love potions and the performance of sinister rites including 'black masses', all intended to wean the King off his mistress of the moment, Madame de La Vallière. This scandal in miniature—in which some prestigious names had been mentioned, including those of the Comtesse de Soissons, the Duchesse de Vivonne, and Madame de Montespan—was hushed up. What emerged much later in the *Chambre Ardente* affair was of very much the same nature, and even more embarrassing.

La Bosse and La Vigoureux were involved in poisoning and chiromancy, and had an extensive and high-born client list. Even more damaging material, however, emerged in the case of another fortune-teller, arrested on the evidence of the first two. This was Catherine Deshayes, 'La Voisin', who was well known to the authorities. As La Voisin and her accomplices awaited trial, more details of the extent of poisoning, and of sorcery, within the highest court circles, began to emerge. Ominously, attendants of the King's mistress, Madame de Montespan, appeared in the testimony. Louis was immediately cautious. He wrote to his lieutenant of police, La Reynie, to ensure that records of interrogation were kept on separate sheets, easy to abstract from the official account; the records of interrogation implicating the high-born and highly placed were to be ruled out of court.[27]

By October it had emerged from the interrogations that the Duchesses of Vivonne, Angoulême, and Vitry and the Princess de la Tingry had wanted to retrieve a document in the possession of a sorceress associated with La Voisin called La Filastre. This paper was a pact with the Devil in which 'there might be something against the King'. As witchcraft

---

[26] See *Factums et arrest du parlement de Paris, contre des bergers sorciers, executez dans la province de Brie* (Paris, 1695), copy in the Douce collection, Bodleian Library; and Richard Simon [M. de Sainjore], *Bibliothèque Critique* (Amsterdam, 1708), ii. 120: 'Il est constant, que les Paysans, sur tout dans les pays gras & de patûrage, sont extremement envieux, & qu'ils ne sçauroient pas souffrir la prosperité de leurs Voisins'. These people poison animals and 'on nomme communément Sorciers'.

[27] For the air of secrecy, see also Madame de Sévigné's letter to Madame de Grignan, cited at n. 25 above.

mingled with treason or *lèse-majesté*, the net spread still wider.[28] Once La
Voisin had been executed, further details emerged from her daughter, 'la
fille Voisin', concerning the involvement of the King's mistress, the mother
of his much-favoured legitimized children, in magical efforts to regain
the King's affection, to gain political influence over him, or even to harm
him. 'This resolution against the King had only been taken because the
lady had not succeeded with other schemes', the mother had told the
daughter, recounting tales of ceremonies undertaken. There was the burning of faggots for the said lady, accompanied by the reading of the lady's
name and that of the King, with the accompanying formula: 'Faggot, I
burn you; it is not you that I burn, but rather the body, the soul, the
spirit, and the reason of Louis of Bourbon.' Other stories were more
grotesque: miscarried babies, throats cut, and blood consecrated to cele-
brate a black mass; the appearance of 'a lady of quality', later said by two
witnesses to have been Madame de Montespan, at one of these masses,
'upon whose belly' the ceremony was performed, 'the lady being totally
naked'.[29]

The point at issue here is not the truth or falsity of these salacious
accusations. The complexity of the interests at work and the evidential
problems are immense. On the one hand, it is not clear whether the
motivation of the accused in telling these tales could have been simply the
implication of the great in order to delay and complicate the legal process;
on the other hand, could these corroborating witnesses, closely incarcer-
ated as they were, have none the less communicated with each other? The
archetypal nature of the stories, with their blend of sexual irregularity,
infanticide, and sacrilege is clear; but they could relate just as plausibly
to the actions of depraved aristocrats, under professional instruction, as
to the defensive invention of those same professional charlatans under the
threat of capital condemnation. The poisons scandal shows us what has
been called the 'élite' version of witchcraft, with its diabolism, black
masses, and covens, operating in some sort of marshland between élite
and popular culture, in an arena which straddles the urban and the court
milieu. This should certainly give pause to any historian who wants to
see a clear separation between polite and popular culture in this period,

---

[28] 'Il pouvait y avoir quelque chose contre le roi.' Petitfils, *L'Affaire*, 73.
[29] 'Cette résolution contre le Roi n'avait été prise que parce que la dame n'avait pu
réussir à d'autres desseins qu'elle avait'; 'fagot, je te brûle; ce n'est pas toi que je brûle, c'est
le corps, l'âme, l'esprit, le cœur et l'entendement de Louis de Bourbon'; 'une femme de
condition . . . sur la ventre de laquelle . . . la dame étant toute nue'. Ravaisson, *Archives*, vi.
243, 256.

or any simple élite retreat from superstitious beliefs caricatured as the preserve of the vulgar. The sorcery aspects of the poisons affair cannot be interpreted as some sort of seventeenth-century Gallic Hell-Fire Club. The element of comedy was absent; ambiguity was rife. While La Reynie was encouraging the performance of a play about *false* enchantments,[30] trying to play down the reality of demonic agency, he was simultaneously reading the demonological work of Jean Bodin to assist him in his investigation. It may indeed be that the poisons scandal initiated some sort of retreat from superstition on the part of the French nobility; but if so, the political causes and implications of the affair are central. Despite a plethora of breathless accounts, this remains, as one of the more breathless puts it, 'one of history's great unsolved mysteries'.[31]

The poisons affair was *the* scandal of its epoch, and should not be dismissed as no more than tittle-tattle. Madame de Sévigné spoke of 'Chaos . . . there's great agitation, people send out for news, and go looking for it in other people's houses'. Père de Rosel remarked on the general agitation outside the charmed circle of the court, telling the Prince de Condé: 'It's the subject of every conversation in Paris; no one speaks about anything else.' Abroad the scandal was a reproach to French honour. 'In every foreign country', wrote Madame de Sévigné, '"Frenchman" means poisoner; there's never been such a scandal at a Christian court.' The poisons scandal had a potential for seriously destabilizing French political life: his mistress, the 'second queen', accused of sorcery and *lèse-majesté*; aristocrats imprisoned and subject to extraordinary legal process; distrust abounding; scandal rife.[32]

Louis XIV was a king immersed daily in the business of dominating and manipulating a court. 'Court "rationality",' writes Norbert Elias in his classic study, involved 'the calculated planning of strategy in face of the possible gain or loss of status'.[33] Elias is describing the behaviour of a nobility which had been drawn to and was held at court. His work analyses court rationality as a means of controlling the powerful; but it also throws light on the strategies of the King. Court life had a mutuality

---

[30] Thomas Corneille and Donneau de Vizé, *La Devineresse ou les faux enchantements* (1680).

[31] Mossiker, *The Affair of the Poisons*, title-page.

[32] Petitfils, *L'Affaire*, 76, 80; Murat, *Colbert*, 401. 'Le chaos . . . On est dans une agitation, on envoie aux nouvelles, on va dans les maisons pour apprendre'; 'C'est la matière de tous les entretiens de Paris; on ne parle d'autre chose'; 'Dans tous les pays étrangers un Français voudra dire un empoisonneur . . . il n'y a guère d'exemple d'un pareil scandale dans une cour chrétienne.'

[33] Norbert Elias, *The Court Society* (Oxford, 1983), 93.

about it, with a ritual aspect which bound both monarch and subject. The poisons affair put this under threat. Louis XIV was incessantly concerned with the gain or loss of status, and the maintenance of his royal dignity. As Peter Burke has argued in a recent study, Louis was profoundly involved in the manufacture, ornamentation, and circulation of images of himself.[34] These representations were being played out in a variety of ways before a variety of audiences: his court; his subjects; the courts and peoples of Europe; those further abroad; and posterity too.

In the light of all this, the poisons affair must surely be seen as a profound disturbance to the Bourbon regime. The ultimate form of *lèse-majesté* was being alleged to have occurred at the very heart of the court: an attack had been made on the body or soul of this most Christian king, *Rex Christianissimus*, in supposed alliance with the Devil. Moreover, this scandal was being transmitted through all the arenas in which the King attempted to maintain the integrity of his regal image. The possibilities for ridicule were manifest. More significantly, here was a sense of the King losing control of his spiritual monopoly; a king at the mercy of his courtiers, besieged by diabolical powers.

1682

It was a scandal at the hub of the French kingdom—a highly contingent and political affair—which forced the elaboration of the 1682 ordinance. As an edict this was undoubtedly an expression of royal will and of royal policy. It was meant to be executed. But we should not see it in the cold light of modern conceptions of legislative action, as a measured response to an administrative and judicial problem in the kingdom at large. There is an air of unreality about the edict. So highly restrictive were its provisions relating to the business of apothecaries and shopkeepers that it seems unlikely that those particular paragraphs were much attended to or even capable of enforcement (paragraphs 7 to 11). It was a response to fears about sorcery and about poisoning, but fears generated more within the court than in the wider community. Those fears need to be anatomized as much as the reality of problem and executive response. The edict should be analysed in its ideological formation as much as its practical embodiment. The starting-point, as we have seen, was the place of production, the court.

The edict was, first of all, an act of royal reassertion. In focusing on Chancellor Lalemant's definition of sorcery as either poisoning or sacrilege, the Crown ensured that it maintained its pre-eminent control of access to

---

[34] Peter Burke, *The Fabrication of Louis XIV* (New Haven, 1992).

the spiritual domain. Thus the preamble to the measure, surprising to anyone expecting the straightforward rejection of superstitious beliefs:

The execution of the ordinances of our predecessor kings against those who call themselves '*devins*', magicians, and enchanters, *having been neglected for a long time*, and this *relaxation* having attracted from foreign countries many of these impostors . . . these practices having come to our knowledge, we would have all possible cares taken to bring to an end, and to stop, by appropriate means, the progress of these detestable abominations.[35]

The rhetoric of this passage is unexpected, with its talk of power hitherto unexercised, and a threat from outside. The ordinance is not presented as a piece of rational humanism cleansing the law of cruelty, but as a measure reinvigorating the law. This preamble is a response to the poisons scandal, but one which seeks to reassert royal control over an 'abomination' and to redefine the threat as coming from outside the kingdom, or from foreigners at least (whereas the '*devins*' of the poisons affair seem to have emerged from the very heart of the kingdom), the better to mobilize against it and separate from it. The crime of witchcraft is being refocused. The measure is presented in the trappings of Louis's reform programme, as a return to law and order after a period of anarchy and neglect. The good king restores the laws to their pristine excellence. It does not deny the force of the old laws against witchcraft; it seeks to renew them and to add new precautions to them. This reading of the preamble allows another context to be identified. In narrative terms, the edict can be seen as the end-point both of a jurisprudential concern for an ordered procedure in witchcraft trials dating from at least 1670; and as the specific product of the poisoning and sorcery scandal at court. One can also, however, look sideways at other legislation being issued at the same time, to gauge the preoccupations of the King's government.

The 1680s were the years in which the King's concern to present himself as *Rex Christianissimus*, and as a source of religious authority, manifested itself in restraints upon French Protestantism, the '*Religion Prétendu Réformée*', culminating in the Revocation of the Edict of Nantes in 1685 and the enforcement of religious conformity. The summer of the sorcery edict, 1682, saw ambiguous moves in this direction, a concern for conversion but a desire to preserve due form and the proper execution of

---

[35] 'L'exécution des ordonnances des rois nos prédécesseurs contre ceux qui se disent devins, magiciens et enchanteurs, *ayant été négligée* depuis long-temps, et ce *relâchement* ayant attiré des pays étrangers dans notre royaume plusieurs de ces imposteurs . . . Ces pratiques étant venues à notre connoisance, nous aurions employé tous les soins possibles pour faire cesser, et pour arrêter, par des moyens convenables, les progrès de ces détestables abominations' (my emphases). Isambert *et al.*, *Recueil général*, xix. 393.

existing edicts. Louis wrote a letter to his bishops and archbishops in July 1682, touching the conversion of Protestants to the orthodox faith. 'I hope that your zeal,' he wrote, 'backed up by my authority, may bring the affair to a satisfactory conclusion.'[36] The year 1682 saw a succession of edicts and declarations relating to the Reformed church.[37]

The revocation of the Edict of Nantes had been long prepared. Since the mid-1670s and before government had increasingly pressurised the Huguenots, eroding their remaining privileges.[38] The revocation put the seal on a decline which was already evident. A recent biographer has seen this as the key to Louis's error in revoking the edict, with a failure 'to comprehend that Protestantism was slowly disintegrating and that it would be enough to ignore it'.[39] This may well be true, but it is vital to understand what an actual revocation could do over and above the piecemeal restriction of toleration. If the revocation was a 'bolt from the blue' for foreign princes, with a negative symbolic value in foreign policy which quiet retrenchment would have avoided, it also had a positive symbolic value for Louis in the face of the community which he headed, a secular and spiritual simulacrum.

'*Une foi, une loi, un roi*' was the slogan of the conversion; the 'federalism', spiritual and secular, which Henry IV's Edict of Nantes had seemed to represent was to be expunged from the kingdom. The sorcery edict was issued, therefore, at a time when the Crown's monopoly of spiritual access, and its paramount power within the body politic, was being reasserted. The emphasis on sacrilege within the 1682 edict also seems an inevitable product of the atmosphere in which it was produced. The accelerating concern to make the kingdom into a single community was reflected in concerns about sacrilege, among both Jews and Protestants. As the latter were put under increasing pressure to conform, responding to a mixture of Catholic zeal, royal authority, and downright force, stories emerged of the new converts spitting out the Eucharist and trampling upon it.[40]

---

[36] Ibid. 'J'espère que votre zèle, appuyé de mon autorité, pourra le conduire à une fin heureuse'. Note that until 1682 there was 'no specific statute against witchcraft', Brian Levack, *The Witch-Hunt in Early Modern Europe* (1993), 87.

[37] Isambert *et al.*, *Recueil général*, xix. 387.

[38] See e.g. Elisabeth Labrousse, '*Une foi, une loi, un roi: essai sur la révocation de l'Édit de Nantes* (Paris, 1985); and Geoffrey Adams, *The Huguenots and French Opinion, 1685–1787: The Enlightenment Debate on Toleration* (Waterloo, Ontario, 1991), 7–13.

[39] Bluche, *Louis XIV*, 632.

[40] On the Jews, see Roland Mousnier, *The Institutions of France under the Absolute Monarchy 1598–1789* (Chicago, 1979), 415 f. Some Huguenots *convertis* became convinced that by swallowing the host they had committed the sin against the Holy Ghost and fell into despair: ibid. 402. Forced conversions were abandoned in 1687.

Another relevant measure of mid-1682 was the *Déclaration contre les Bohémiens ou Égyptiens*, dated, from Versailles, 11 July. An order for the arrest and enslavement of gypsies, it represents the same sort of mentality as the preamble to the sorcery ordinance, with the desire to enforce laws that had fallen into desuetude and to clamp down on the enemies of the community.[41] At the same time as the laws against one enemy of society, the witch, were being defined, other enemies were receiving renewed attention.

In the period of the edict against sorcery and poisoning, the Crown seems to have been concerned to define the Christian and national community around itself and against threatening foreign forces, religious or Bohemian; to elevate the status of the Crown; and to deny alternative sources of power.[42] That, in such a period, and faced by the sorcery allegations of the poisons affair, the Crown should have concerned itself with the crime of witchcraft is unsurprising. This concern involved reinventing witchcraft rather than abandoning it. The traditional interpretation of Louis's 1682 ordinance is as a measure putting an end to the recognition of witchcraft as a crime. In fact, witchcraft continued to be recognized as a crime, and even the text of the ordinance itself does not support the notion of a straightforward abolition.

This process of reinvention largely ignored the difficult issue of the demonic efficacy of witches, preferring to concentrate on those who

under the pretext of horoscope and divination, and by means of the *prestiges* of the operations of pretended magical actions and other similar illusions, which this sort of people are wont to make use of . . . have caught out divers ignorant or credulous people, who have themselves insensibly engaged with them, passing from vain curiosities to superstitions and from superstitions to impieties and acts of sacrilege.[43]

The text avoids engaging with the existence of an alternative real source of threatening spiritual power, a black cult which could threaten Louis's

---

[41] Isambert *et al.*, *Recueil général*, xix. 393 f.

[42] See the declaration on the extension of regal rights relating to episcopal and archepiscopal vacancies, Jan. 1682; the edict relating to ecclesiastical power, Mar. 1682, which starts by declaring 'l'indépendance de notre couronne de *toute autre puissance que de Dieu*' (my emphasis); the approval of the 'Article of the Third Estate' denying deposition by ecclesiastical authority or any papal power to annul oaths of allegiance. Isambert *et al.*, *Recueil général*, xix. 374, 379.

[43] 'sous prétexte d'horoscope et de devination, et par le moyen des prestiges des opérations des prétendues magies et autres illusions semblables, dont cette sorte de gens ont accoutumé de se servir . . . auroient surpris diverses personnes ignorantes ou crédules qui s'étoient insensiblement engagées avec eux, en passant des vaines curiosités aux superstitions, et des superstitions aux impiétés et aux sacrilèges'.

authority. The avowed aim was to exercise a strict control over the crime against which the 'ordinances of our predecessor kings' had supposedly been directed:

we have judged it necessary to renew the old ordinances and, what is more, to add to them new precautions, as much in regard to all those who use malefices and poisons, as those who, under the vain profession of *devins*, magicians, sorcerers, and other similar names, condemned by divine and human laws, infect and corrupt the spirit of the people by their discourse and practices, and by the profanation of that which religion holds most holy.[44]

There is no interruption here of the laws; no sense that witchcraft has ceased to be an offence, or was ill-conceived as a crime in the past. Instead, the reader finds continuity and a subtle shift of emphasis towards a new conception of the crime of witchcraft.

Ambiguities are embedded in the text. New precautions are added to old ordinances, which are thus renewed in passing, without being too closely specified. The word '*maléfice*' equivocates between magic and mere mischief. This lack of absolute clarity might have been intentional, arising from a need to finesse the political difficulties of precision in a touchy area. It could, more likely, have been the product of unclear thinking, or unresolved issues. Which reading we choose is in some ways beside the point, in the face of the text (ambiguous) and its context (highly political). The lack of clarity, perhaps also of the possibility of enforcement, was reflected in the occasional provincial prosecution of maleficent, diabolical witchcraft after 1682, which Mandrou notes. 'The declaration of 1682', he writes, 'did not illuminate scrupulous consciences in the instant it was read.'[45]

Seventy years later, the Habsburg declarations against witches and magic were modelled on Louis's edict of 1682, and they exhibit similar ambiguities. In July 1753 came a decree forbidding the casting of spells; in March 1755, one against vampires and 'posthumous magic'; finally, in August 1756, a decree against superstition and magic. This has a sceptical element—'superstitions should be prohibited, punished, and eventually

---

[44] 'nous avons jugé nécessaire de renouveler les anciennes ordonnances, et de prendre encore, en y ajoutant de nouvelles précautions, tant à l'égard de tous ceux qui usent de maléfices et des poisons, que de ceux qui, sous la vaine profession de devins, magiciens, sorciers, et autres noms semblables, condamnés par les lois divines et humaines, infectent et corrompent l'esprit des peuples par leurs discours et pratiques, et par la profanation de ce que la religion a de plus saint'.

[45] e.g. July 1683, Alsace, appeal—one execution, plus imprisonment, others set free; Tournai, 3 Apr. 1685—condemned witch released by the *Conseil*. Mandrou, *Magistrats et sorciers*, 491, my translation.

removed altogether'—but retains a significant iota of credulity joined to
the same sort of encroachment of central power that Louis XIV's measure had involved: 'if there were some occurrence not readily explainable
in natural terms . . . no one in the future should interfere without first
informing Her Majesty . . . she will . . . order what she considers most
fitting and expedient.' This, as Franco Venturi has suggested, was the
crux, removing 'from the parish priests, inquisitors and local authorities
all power to deal with the world of magic, while the state, at the centre,
assumed all responsibility for the struggle against it'.[46]

AFTER THE EDICT

French attitudes to beliefs about witchcraft retained a perplexed quality
until well after the effective end of prosecution, to a much greater degree
than in England. Pierre Bayle dealt with the witchcraft issue in a number
of chapters of his *Réponse aux questions d'un provincial* (1703–7), a work
'hark[ing] back to the days when Bayle himself was a provincial filled
with curiosity about the rich intellectual life of far-off centres of learning'.[47] Yet Bayle's remarks about witchcraft are not an uncomplicated
metropolitan put-down to provincial backwardness. He does not confirm
or deny the existence or possibility of real witchcraft. His remarks are
conditional. If there really are people who 'make a pact with the Devil,
giving themselves to him, and stipulating that he will use his power to
satisfy their passions, then they are *ipso facto* worthy of execution'.[48]

Bayle is nevertheless clear that much supposed sorcery is the effect of
imagination, a real effect proceeding from a process whose aetiology is too
often misunderstood. He is just as clear, however, that such sorcery can
merit punishment as deservedly as the real witchcraft he has gone out of
his way not to deny. *Imaginary* witches are just as culpable because they
think they have dealt with the Devil, attended solemn assemblies or

---

[46] Franco Venturi, 'Enlightenment versus the Powers of Darkness', in *Italy and the
Enlightenment: Studies in a Cosmopolitan Century* (1972), 125 f. See also G. Klaniczay, 'The
Decline of Witches and the Rise of Vampires under the 18th-century Habsburg Monarchy',
in *The Uses of Supernatural Power* (Cambridge, 1990). Compare also Philip Kuhn's account
of the Chinese sorcery scare in the 18th c.: sorcery was 'seen as the "black" counterpart of
the imperial cult'. Out of control it could 'convey an image of instability and imminent
crisis'. The state required the monopoly of spiritual access. Philip A. Kuhn, *Soulstealers: the
Chinese Sorcery Scare of 1768* (Cambridge, Mass., 1990), 89 f.

[47] Elisabeth Labrousse, *Bayle* (Oxford, 1983), 45.

[48] 'S'ils sont de véritables sorciers, c'est-à-dire, s'ils ont fait réellement un pacte avec le
Démon pour se donner à lui, & pour stipuler qu'il emploiera sa puissance à satisfaire leurs
passions, ils sont dignes *ipso facto* du dernier suplice . . .'.

diabolical chapters, and extended Satan's empire: 'it is immaterial for the quality of an act of will whether its object really exists, or only exists as an idea.' Spinoza himself could not neglect to punish witchcraft, since in a witchcraft trial 'he ought not to have consulted his own system of thought, but that of the accused'. Bayle pointedly refuses to take the humane line of Webster or Weyer; his position is more akin to Hobbes's, though without the expression of any opinion as to whether witchcraft exists as a 'real power'. These witches are not mad; they show 'no mark of an imbecilic mind'. Just as criminal is the behaviour of those who exploit, even unwittingly, public credulity: 'pretended enchanters are worthy of a corporal penalty, in proportion to the ill they had a mind to cause.'[49]

Bayle goes on to make a distinction between two questions: is punishment merited, and is punishment necessary or prudent? This is a matter 'more charged with complication, and more confused with labyrinths'. Should judges be allowed or encouraged to prosecute witchcraft, or should the custom of the *Parlement* of Paris be followed; 'dismissing the charges against witches who are only found guilty of imagining going to the Sabbat'?[50] Bayle compares the situation with political apostasy: rebellious subjects are, indeed, deserving of punishment, but sometimes it is prudent to leave them unpunished. 'Would one not avoid a great evil,' he asks, 'if one prevented judges from entertaining such accusations [of witchcraft]?' This is all very well, says Bayle, but he finds himself, as he says again, embarrassed. Ought one to recommend the abandonment of a criminal category founded, however tenuously, in reality?[51]

Certainly, to reduce incidence of witchcraft to its minimum, prudence is required. Bayle quotes Malebranche's familiar opinion, that 'in the places where witches are burnt, you see nothing but witches'.[52] Paradoxically, the prosecution of witches, regardless of whether they are real or supposititious, only increases the number of criminals. Having ventilated

---

[49] Pierre Bayle, *Œuvres Diverses*, iii, pt. 2 (The Hague, 1727), 562–4. 'il est indifférent pour la qualité d'un acte de l'ame que son objet existe réellement, ou qu'il n'existe qu'en idée . . . il n'auroit point dû consulter son propre systême, mais celui des accusez . . . aucune marque d'imbécillité d'esprit . . . les enchanteurs non persuadez sont dignes d'une peine corporelle, à proportion du mal qu'ils ont en dessein de causer'.

[50] 'plus chargée d'embaras, & plus embrouïllée de labyrinths . . . de renvoïer les sorciers, qui ne se trouvent coupables, que de l'imagination d'aller au Sabat'.

[51] 'Que des sujets qui se révoltent soient punissables, cela ne soufre point de difficulté parmi les Docteurs en politique . . . mais il y a des conjonctures, ou il est de la prudence de les laisser impunis . . . N'éviteroit-on pas un plus grand mal si l'on défendoit aux Juges de connoître de cette sorte de crimes?'

[52] 'dans les lieux où l'on brûle les Sorciers, on ne voit autre chose'.

this theory, which we first saw used in the Lalemant memorandum, Bayle ends by recommending not the suspension of the crime of witchcraft, or even the effective cessation of witchcraft prosecution,[53] but rather the application of caution: 'if the sovereign powers do not want to prevent magistrates from recognizing the crime, it is necessary at least that they have a new code made on the subject, and that they only appoint for the purpose enlightened judges of integrity, free from all prejudice.' Free, let it be noted, from *every* prejudice, on either side, since 'to believe nothing and to believe everything are extreme positions, neither of which is valid'.[54]

Bayle's case is interesting not because he was committed to the prosecution of witchcraft (he was not), but because he was unable honestly and straightforwardly to reject the concept of witchcraft. One can say that this was so because Bayle was pragmatically avoiding danger, concealing his own more thoroughgoing scepticism (the self-censorship–cum–irony argument often deployed in modern discussions of late seventeenth-century religious beliefs); or because his own views were as cautious and anxious as his writing. In the end it hardly matters, since either interpretation places witchcraft belief more firmly within the bounds of Francophone orthodoxy around 1705 than anyone has previously recognized. Perhaps we can at least consider the idea that men like Bayle may have meant what they said, and that modern scepticism about such ideas as witchcraft did not emerge in one fell swoop.

With that supposed *nonpareil* of Enlightenment, Diderot and d'Alembert's *Encyclopédie*, published in the 1760s, one might have expected to find a little shameless scepticism. Initially, one is not disappointed, if the entry on 'sorcellerie (magie)' is anything to go by: 'magical operation, shameful or ridiculous, stupidly attributed by superstition, to the invocation and power of demons'.[55] This succinct dismissal is followed by historical analysis which, in making the traditional moves, associates the disappearance of witchcraft with the triumph of reason and interprets Louis XIV's famous ordinance in misleadingly robust terms:

In the end it was only due to the birth of reason towards the end of the last century, that we have the declaration of Louis XIV which in 1672 [*sic*] prohibited

---

[53] That death is the punishment for witchcraft 'c'est là le sentiment le plus ordinaire des Jurisconsultes, & des Casuistes, soit Catholiques, soit Protestans', ibid. 578.

[54] Ibid. 577–9. 'si les Souverains ne veulent pas interdire aux Magistrats la conoissance de ce crime, il faudroit pour le moins qu'ils fissent faire un nouveau code là–dessus, & qu'ils ne la commissent qu'à des juges éclairez, integres, & vuides de toute préoccupation . . . ne croire rien & croire tout sont des qualitez extrêmes, qui ne valent rien ni l'une ni l'autre'.

[55] 'opération magique, honteuse ou ridicule, attribuée stupidement par la superstition, à l'invocation & au pouvoir des démons'.

all the courts of his kingdom from entertaining simple accusations of *witchcraft*: and if since then there have been, from time to time, some accusations of *maleficium*, the judges have only condemned the accused as profane, or if they used poison.[56]

This trenchant piece of enlightenment mythography is followed by a far less confident entry on *sorciers* and *sorcières*, '(Hist. anc. & mod.)'. It presents a very different version of intellectual history in which 'the most celebrated Englishmen of the past century', namely Barrow, Tillotson, Stillingfleet, Clarke, and, above all, Locke, 'remark that those who urge that spirits engage in no communication with men, have either read the holy scriptures very negligently, or, though they pretend not to, in fact despise authority'.[57] The article ends by endorsing the position which Malebranche and Pierre Bayle had adopted in the previous century, one by no means as advanced even as Addison's tentative and fractured scepticism:[58] 'to give credence too lightly to all accounts of this sort, or to reject them absolutely, these are two equally dangerous extremes.' In the final reckoning, reason is seen to be identifiable by methods and procedure rather than content: 'To examine and weigh up the facts, before giving your assent, this is the middle way, the pursuit of which indicates rationality.'[59] In the matter of witchcraft, the phenomenon *cannot* be dismissed out of hand:

as soon as one admits the events set out in the scriptures, one also admits other similar events which occur from time to time: extraordinary events, supernatural, but in which the supernatural is associated with characteristics which denote that God is not the author of them, and that they happen through diabolical intervention.[60]

---

[56] 'Enfin ce ne fut qu'à la raison naissante vers la fin du dernier siecle, qu'on dut la déclaration de Louis XIV qui défendit en 1672 [*sic*], à tous les tribunaux de son royaume d'admettre les simples accusations de *sorcellerie*: & si depuis il y a eu de tems-en-tems quelques accusations de maléfices, les juges n'ont condamné les accusés que comme des prophanateurs, ou quand il est arrivé que ces gens-là avoient employé le poison.'

[57] 'les hommes les plus célebres que l'Angleterre ait produits depuis un siecle remarquent que ceux qui ne sauroient persuader que les esprits entretiennent aucun commerce avec les hommes, ou n'ont lu les saintes Ecritures que fort négligement, ou, quoiqu'ils se déguisent, en méprisent l'autorité.'

[58] For which, see above pp. 128–32.

[59] 'Ajouter foi trop légèrement à tout ce qu'on raconte en ce genre, & rejetter absolument tout ce qu'on en dit, sont deux extrêmes également dangereux . . . Examiner & peser les faits, avant que d'y accorder sa confiance, c'est le milieu qu'indique la raison.' Cf. Bayle, 'Réponse', 579: 'Ne croire rien & croire tout sont des qualitez extrêmes, qui ne valent rien ni l'une ni l'autre' ['To believe nothing and to believe everything are extreme positions, neither of which is valid'].

[60] 'dèsqu'on admet les faits énoncés dans les Ecritures, on admet aussi d'autres faits semblables qui arrivent de tems en tems: faits extraordinaires, surnaturels, mais dans [*sic*] le surnaturel est accompagné de caracteres qui dénotent que Dieu n'en est pas l'auteur, & qu'ils arrivent par l'intervention du démon'.

It is tempting to try and save the phenomenon, to rescue the *Encyclopédie* and the old model of the disappearance of witch beliefs, by reading this whole passage as ironic. The invocation of the rational pantheon—and especially John Locke—is, however, unlikely to be tongue in cheek. The whole tendency of the piece forbids such an interpretation. It is measured, balanced, and rational. Irony or satire signals its presence with a good deal more gesticulation.[61]

If Bayle and his encyclopedic successors were so riven, it is nevertheless surprising and instructive to find more robust assertions of the orthodoxy of witchcraft belief centre-stage in eighteenth-century French culture. Nine years before the dissolution of the *ancien régime*, in 1780, M. Muyart de Vouglans, *conseiller au grand conseil*, published, 'avec approbation et privilege du roi', his consideration of the criminal laws of France, in their natural order.[62] Book 3 considers the different types of crime and their penalties, and the first part 'dans . . . [l']ordre naturel' is devoted to 'Des Crimes contre la Religion, ou Crimes de Lese-Majesté Divine'. Chapter 1 is on blasphemy. Chapter 2 looks at atheism, deism, polytheism and 'tolérantisme', that is, 'celui qui admet indifféremment toutes sortes de Religions', that which admits indifferently all sorts of religion. Chapter 3 moves on, logically enough, to 'Magie & Sortilege'. Here Muyart de Vouglans is concerned with witchcraft in all its forms—*maleficium*, superstition, mountebankery. Rather than replacing it with the second or third, or both, he maintains all three in equilibrium. Magic is the crime of those 'who use diabolical illusions, either to deceive with false predictions, or to cause harm to some person'.[63] After quoting the Sun King's ordinance on witchcraft, he elaborates the distinction between

---

[61] *Encyclopédie* (Neufchâtel, 1765), xv, under topic. The articles are by d[e] J[aucourt] (sorcellerie) and either de Jaucourt, again, or, more plausibly, Diderot (sorciers et sorcières). For Locke on witchcraft see Ch. 4 above. Cf. also the moderation of the Rovereto scholar, Girolamo Tartarotti, *Del Congresso Notturno Delle Lamie Libri Tre . . . S'aggiungono due dissertazione epistolari sopra l'arte magica* (Rovereto, 1749), who sought only 'quel vero mezzo, in cui la Verità come in suo seggio risiede' (dedication). See Franco Venturi, 'Enlightenment versus the Powers of Darkness'. Tartarotti was opposed by more fearless sceptics, e.g. Gianrinaldo Carli, Scipione Maffei in his *Arte Magica dileguata; lettera del Signor Marchese Maffei al Padre I. Ansaldi* (Verona, 1749), and Paolo Frisi. Venturi cites other credulous writers including Giovanni Sebastiano De Vespignanis and Father Daniele Concina (p. 118), Father Tommaso Maria Mamachi, Costantino Grimaldi (p. 120). The debate continued.

[62] Muyart de Vouglans, *Les Loix Criminelles de France, dans leur ordre naturel* (Paris, 1780), 101–3. Compare him with e.g. J. B. Denisart, *Collection de décisions* (Paris, 1756), who recommends 'la voie moyenne' and Parisian jurisprudence; or P. Guyot, *Le Répertoire universel* (Paris, 1784–5), who denies the existence of real sorcerers. These are both cited by Mandrou, who notes that 'certains milieux dévôts' continued to denounce sorcerers.

[63] 'qui emploient des illusions diaboliques, soit pour tromper par de fausses prédictions, soit pour causer du dommage à autrui'.

false prediction and harmful magic. The former is less heinous than the
latter, though its simple element of fraud[64] is compounded by 'a sort of
blasphemy, attributing to the Devil knowledge which is reserved to God
alone'.[65] This does not, however, mean that Vouglans sees the 1682 ordinance as a simple replacement of *maleficium* witchcraft by sacrilegious
witchcraft. 'Witchcraft properly speaking' remains a recognizable offence
at law, which cannot be 'punished by anything less than execution'.
Indeed, 'this penalty ought even to extend to burning, since it often
happens, that these acts of witchcraft are accompanied by poison and
sacrilege'.[66]

The chapter ends with the author's general observations on the topic,
which clarify even further his commitment to the legal cognizance of
witchcraft as a crime. While he recognizes the problems of 'pretended
diabolical illusions', he is

very far from applauding the outrageous declarations of these pretended free-
thinkers, who fall into the opposite extreme, wanting to use the frequency of such
events in ancient times, and above all in the so-called *century of ignorance*, to deny
the pertinency of belief today, rejecting absolutely the actual existence of magic.

The animus directed against free-thinkers is quite pronounced, the necessity of the reality of magic unmistakable: 'such an assertion is condemned by the decisions of the church, which makes it a particular point
of belief for us, through the anathemas which she pronounces against
magicians, witches, etc. as is seen in the rituals which are read in parish
sermons.'[67] And it is striking that the legitimation of the notion of the real
crime of witchcraft is rooted in ecclesiastical practice, but expressed in

---

[64] On the prevalence of fraudulent witchcraft in the early 18th c., 'un grand désordre qui
augmente de jour en jour et qui ne se borne pas à la corruption des mœurs, mais qui tend
à destruire la religion dans tous ses principes', see the memoir of René Voyer, comte
d'Argenson, lieutenant de police, reprinted in Mandrou, *Possession et sorcellerie*, 279 and
275–328.

[65] 'une espece de blasphême, en attribuant au Démon une connoissance qui n'est réservée
qu'à Dieu seul'.

[66] 'Des sortileges proprement dit . . . moins punis que du dernier supplice . . . cette peine
doit même aller jusqu'à du *feu* lorsque, comme il arrive le plus souvent, ces sortileges sont
accompagnés de poison & de sacrilege'.

[67] 'ces prétendues illusions diaboliques . . . bien eloigné d'applaudir aux déclamations
outrées de ces prétendus Esprits-forts, qui tombent dans un excès tout opposé, en voulant
se faire un prétexte de ce que ces exemples étoient beaucoup plus fréquens anciennement,
& sur-tout dans ces temps qu'on appelle *siecle d'ignorance*, qu'ils ne le sont aujourd'hui pour
se croire en droit, de nier absolument l'existence actuelle de la Magie . . . une pareille
assertion se trouve condamnée par les décisions de l'Eglise, qui nous en fait un point
particulier de croyance, par les anathêmes qu'elle prononce contre les Magiciens, Sorciers,
&c. comme on le voit par les *Rituels* qui se lisent aux Prônes des Paroisses'.

civil law. We note again the way in which witchcraft blends the secular and religious domains, negatively representing, even reinforcing, a sacralized conception of the state.

From the bosom of legal orthodoxy to the pinnacles of Enlightenment and proto-Enlightenment practice, there was an inability absolutely to deny the continued relevance, however attenuated, of the crime of witchcraft.[68] As an interpretation of the 1682 ordinance of Louis XIV within the whole context of French law, Vouglans (who cites the ordinance in the company of more ancient laws) seems to confirm the picture we derived from the circumstances of the production of that edict: the crime of witchcraft was being realigned, not abolished.

Eleven years after the publication of Vouglans' commentary, as the *ancien régime* itself was in dissolution, witchcraft did finally disappear from the framework of French law. In 1791 the Constituent promulgated a penal code which was, in part, a repudiation of 'crimes imaginaires', in other words, heresy, *lèse-majesté* against the divinity, *sortilegium*, and magic, 'the truly sacrilegious pursuit of which has for such a long time offended the divinity, and for which, in the name of the heavens, so much blood has stained the earth'.[69]

The longevity of witchcraft as a crime was not merely theoretical, although the legal position does seem to have been somewhat confused, despite Vouglans's certainties. For instance, in 1743 Bertrand Guillaudot, a renegade priest, was burnt alive at Dijon, convicted of illicit involvement in treasure-seeking, a practice which often involved the invocation of demons. Twenty-nine others were arraigned at Lyons. Five were condemned to death, including three more priests who had celebrated sacrilegious masses. One was burnt alive. Five went to the galleys, three into exile, four were fined.[70] The first striking fact is that these treasure-seekers were not ignorant illiterates. Guillaudot himself was, earlier in his career, singled out as the protégé first of Jean-Joseph Languet, sometime Bishop of Soissons and Archbishop of Sens; and then of his brother Jean-Baptiste Languet, co-seigneur of Gergy. His accomplices included a range of artisans, but also a canon of Saint-Paul de Lyon and a doctor turned

---

[68] See also Montesquieu, 'L'Esprit des Lois' in *Œuvres complètes* , ed. R. Caillois (2 vols.; Paris, 1949–51), ii. 435 f.: 'Maxime importante: il faut être très circonspect dans la poursuite de la magie et de l'hérésie.'

[69] 'dont la poursuite vraiment sacrilège a si longtemps offensé la divinité, et pour lesquels, au nom du ciel, tant de sang a souillé la terre'. Jacques Godechot, *Les Institutions de la France sous la Révolution et l'Empire*, 3rd edn. (Paris, 1985), 152, citing report of Lepelletier de Saint-Fargeau.

[70] Lea, *Materials*, 1305.

merchant. This was magic in an urban and relatively educated milieu, not the mere stuff of desperate peasant superstition.

How was this crime considered by those who prosecuted it? The charge, John McManners contends, was sacrilege 'as, since the Edict of 1682, "magic" did not exist as a crime in its own right'.[71] The legal position was, as we have seen, less straightforward. Guillaudot's sentence accuses him 'of having stolen a chasuble, a stole, and a maniple from the church at Gergy, of having written several impious and abominable little books full of magical figures and invocations to evil spirits'. How these *malins esprits* or evil spirits were regarded by the authorities we do not know. The *Parlement* of Burgundy, in re-emphasizing Guillaudot's faults, noted 'all the scandals, acts of sacrilege, of impiety and superstitious practices mentioned in the proceedings'. The nineteenth-century historian of these events, Henri Beaune, opined on this basis that the edict did not punish either simple magic, or *sortilegium*, or *maleficium*, unless they were accompanied by impieties, sacrilege, or superstitious practices. This implies, at least, that witchcraft was an issue, but only recognized at law when compounded by other offences. The scope for legal confusion, given the jurisdictional complexities and the ambiguity of the 1682 text, is manifest. The important point is that witchcraft, somehow or other, was still an issue.[72]

Mandrou noted a few cases of witchcraft prosecuted clearly *as* witchcraft after 1682; but perhaps the most fascinating case is that of Catherine Cadière and her confessor, Père Girard, a scandal which generated an extensive pamphlet literature at home and abroad. Voltaire, writing in his 'Prix de la Justice' in the 1770s, asked: 'Are we in the century of the Montesquieus and Beccarias, . . . [given that] magic is still discussed'? As recently as 1750, he notes, the papers reported the burning of a nun as a witch in Würzburg. Whether or not this is true—Voltaire, with heavy sarcasm, refuses to believe that the bishop could have allowed (as, in fact, he had), 'such an idiotic piece of barbarism'—one need only go back another twenty years to find the same sort of thing going on in France: 'in 1730 half of the *Parlement* of Provence condemned to be burnt, as a

---

[71] John McManners, *Death and the Enlightenment* (Oxford, 1985), 549 n. 28. See also H. Beaune, 'Les Sorciers de Lyon: épisode judiciaire du xviiie siècle', *Mémoires de l'Académie impériale . . . de Dijon*, 2nd ser. 4 (Dijon, 1868).

[72] 'd'avoir volé une chasuble, une étole et un manipule dans l'église de Gergy, d'avoir écrit plusieurs livrets impies et abominables remplis de figures magiques et invocations aux malins esprits . . . tous les scandales, sacrilèges, impiétés et pratiques superstitieuses mentionnées dans la procédure'. Beaune, 'Sorciers de Lyon', 79.

witch, the imbecilic and indiscreet Jesuit Girard, while the other half pronounced in his favour, with costs.'[73]

Father Girard was Catherine Cadière's spiritual director. She had joined an informal group of female devotees, the Third Order of St Theresa, and sought Girard's particular attention, feeling herself called to sainthood. Failing in her endeavours, and distanced from Girard in her subsequent retirement to the convent of Sainte-Claire-d'Ollioules, she started having fits, convulsions, and hallucinations. She then accused her patron of having bewitched and seduced her. The *Parlement* of Aix heard the case, which became a European *cause célèbre*, as much for its steamier elements of sex and sadism, as for the accusation of sorcery which it involved. A verdict was reached on 11 October 1731, with, in the first instance, a divided court, as Voltaire had pointed out. The casting vote of the president of the court, Lebret, ensured that the substantive charges were dropped. Cadière was returned to her mother, and Girard handed over to the ecclesiastical authorities, thence to account for his irregular conduct as a priest. The decision was unpopular with the Aix populace,[74] but Girard was cleared by the church and died in retirement at Dôle in 1733.

Cadière's accusations against Girard were a mélange of sorcery and sacrilege, and, what is more, they were directed against a priest—precisely the sort of witchcraft upon which the 1682 edict, in its second and third articles, had focused.[75] The outraged sceptical author of the *Dénonciation des factums de M. Chaudon avocat de la demoiselle Cadière* pointed to the credulity of the judges who could condemn Girard. How could one believe that this hitherto virtuous man could become 'all at once the most wicked of all men, make a pact with the Devil, and give himself to him'?[76] Girard's lawyer was adamant that, whatever the legal charge, the accusation of sorcery stood at the centre of the whole business

---

[73] Voltaire, 'Prix de la Justice et de l'Humanité' [1777] in *Œuvres* (Garnier, Paris, 1883), xxx. 549. 'Sommes-nous dans le siècle des Montesquieu et des Beccaria . . . on parle encore de magie . . . une barbarie si idiote . . . en 1730 la moitié du parlement de Provence condamna au feu, comme sorcier, l'imbécile et indiscret jésuite Girard, tandis que l'autre moitié lui donnait gain de cause avec dépens.'

[74] See the final section of the collection of documents concerning the Cadière case, *Recueil général des pièces concernant le procez entre la demoiselle Cadière . . . et le père Girard, Jésuite* (2 vols.; Marseilles, 1731).

[75] See *Mémoire Instructif pour Demoiselle Catherine Cadière*, in ibid., i.

[76] *Dénonciation des factums de M. Chaudon avocat de la demoiselle Cadière; à messieurs les avocats du parlement de Provence* (n.p., 1731), ii. 8. 'Tout à coup le plus scelerat de tous les hommes, pactise avec le Diable, & se donne à lui'.

—which also involved 'Quietism, Spiritual Incest, Procurement of Abortion, and Subornation of Perjury'. 'It was by the means of this diabolical Art', he declared, 'as *La Cadiere* asserts, that he accomplished his incestuous Purpose, [and therefore] it seems reasonable that we should chiefly labour to overthrow that, seeing if Father *Girard* be not a Sorceror, it follows of necessary Consequence that he is not Incestuous.'[77] If this tactic was in any sense machiavellian, in trying to draw attention away from a host of plausible charges, to a single, less plausible one, it barely worked. Half the court were actually prepared to accept Girard's trial as a sorcery trial, and convict accordingly. This is what astonished Voltaire. The English publisher of Cadière's case was sceptical in the face of all these Continental, papistical goings-on—'the superstitious will attribute . . . [these things] to the operation of the Devil; but I cannot persuade my self they are any thing more than the tricks of Legerdemain.'[78]

'In the end', writes Voltaire, echoing Malebranche and Bayle, 'witches ceased to be burnt, and they disappeared off the face of the earth.'[79] But he saw that victory for reason as precarious and all too recently won. The Girard–Cadière case showed this, as did that burning, all too true, in mid-century Würzburg. So too did intellectual life, with publications, in this century of reason, of works like a credulous account of the devils of Loudun in 1749, written, of course, by a priest.[80]

This story of the fate of witch beliefs in France does not conflict with that which I have drawn for England. Once again, witchcraft theory is being taken seriously much later than previous accounts have suggested; once again its currency is a matter of ideological concern, its modulations in its heyday bound up with political events. The élites of eighteenth-century France seem to have been able to take witchcraft seriously even longer than their English counterparts; but then, the ideal of the sacralized state persisted stronger and longer in France than in England. The Edict of Nantes was revoked in the same period as the Act of Toleration was enacted in England; witchcraft theory, ridiculed and marginalized in

---

[77] *The Defence of F. John Baptist Girard*, 4th edn. (1732), 1. 6 f. discusses the diabolical pact; 13 discusses natural causes.

[78] *The Case of Mrs Mary Catherine Cadiere, Against the Jesuit Father John Baptist Girard*, 10th edn. (1732), publisher's preface.

[79] 'Enfin, on a cessé de brûler les sorciers, et ils ont disparu de la terre'. Voltaire, 'Prix de la Justice'.

[80] 'Ce qui peut encore être plus étrange, c'est que, dans notre siècle, où la raison semble avoir fait quelques progrès, on a imprimé, en 1749, un *Examen des diables de Loudun*, par M. Ménardie, prêtre. Et dans cet examen on prouve, par plusieurs passages des *Cas* de Pontas, que Grandier avait en effet mis quatorze diables dans le corps de ces quatorze nonnes, et qu'il mourut possédé du quinzième. M. de Ménardie, prêtre, n'était pas sorcier.' Ibid.

England by 1736, was seriously canvassed by a French royal counsellor in the 1780s. It is certainly not the case that the 1682 ordinance represented a precocious triumph of French rationality, a first blast on the enlightenment trumpet. It was the act of a state apparatus concerned to assert its own religious and political primacy. The chronologies in England and France were different, but the forces at work were of much the same sort: political intrigue, religious ferment, social change at a variety of levels. The evidence so far gathered suggests that any more extensive account of the demise of witchcraft theory in France will be rooted in just the same principles of explanation as, and will bear a family resemblance to, the English case history offered in the first part of this book.

9. Man surrounded by demons, untitled drawing by Francisco Goya (1824–8)

Conclusion

Truth is *eternal*; and what is once true will be true for ever. *Veritas non accipit Magis et Minus.*

Francis Hutchinson, *A defence of the Antient Historians* (1734)

This has been a history of the disavowal of witchcraft theory. Its examination of the expulsion of witchcraft from the set of rational beliefs in England does have an air of particularity about it. In fact, it is a specifically English history of witchcraft that has been written, deliberately focused upon contingencies, and upon the peculiarities of English political and religious life. The foregoing analysis of French witchcraft theory was not an attempt to draw general principles out of an exercise in comparative history, but rather a riposte to any suggestion that national histories of 'disenchantment' make no sense; two case studies, then, the second much contracted, and constructed with the first very much in mind. Ideally, one would at this juncture offer yet more such case studies; the patience of the reader might well, however, be exhausted. Further comparisons with other European states or nations might amount to little more than a banal exercise in list-making. Nevertheless, a handful of further juxtapositions reinforces the notion of compatible yet distinct narratives with a family resemblance.

Erik Midelfort, towards the end of his study of *Witch Hunting in Southwestern Germany*, describes how witch persecution waned. 'Enlightenment' did not come from books, but from the realization that witch-hunts destroyed 'all sense of community, and all inhabitants as well'. The lesson was slow in being learnt and small trials 'persisted well into the eighteenth century'. The attitude towards the Devil 'had not changed fundamentally' and 'skepticism was not yet in the air'. Small trials were 'viable', because they did not depend on the unwieldy mechanism of mass denunciation; 'but the large panic trial, the severe social purgation, was dead by its own hand.' How different German witch-hunting was from what went on in England: more ferocious, more bound up with notions of night-flying and the sabbath. Yet at the same time parallels emerge. Large-scale persecution was much more a German than an English phenomenon, yet its dynamic in both nations was much the same. It was self-consuming; but at the same time, did not in turn make witch beliefs impossible. A crisis of confidence in the judicial procedures for dealing with witches 'may have forced men to search their traditions for a new understanding of the interrelations of God, the devil, and the world'. But such a process rarely involved 'a genuine disbelief in the devil or a denial of witchcraft'. Midelfort finds no such denials in the German Southwest, and writes that 'men had lost instead the ability accurately to detect witches'.[1]

Persecution in German-speaking lands reached heights never attained in England or the French kingdom; political authority was more fragmented, local action more intense. Nevertheless, there was a similar range of activity, from persecution in times of disorder through state-inspired campaigns to the steady trickle of what Lyndal Roper calls, in the context of Augsburg, 'witchcraft of an everyday, unremarkable kind'.

As in France or England, witchcraft theory did not have to be radically rejected in order to secure an end to the trials. The most effective panacea was caution. It was Spee's aptly named *Cautio Criminalis*, published early on, in the 1630s, 'qui a fait un grand fruit', in Leibniz's words, converting German princes to a new view of witch trials.[2] Serious academic work on witchcraft nevertheless continued in German universities well into the eighteenth century. At the University of Halle (nicknamed *Hölle* or hell), a moderately sceptical inaugural dissertation in October 1701[3] was swiftly followed by Christian Thomasius's notorious and thoroughly sceptical *De Crimine Magiae*, which opened the floodgates to furious controversy, drawing in university officials, theologians, lawyers, judges, and pastors.[4] It

---

[1] H. C. Erik Midelfort, *Witch Hunting in Southwestern Germany, 1562–1684* (Stanford, Calif., 1972), 191, 195 f.

[2] *Die Philosophischen Schriften von Gottfried Wilhelm Leibniz* (Berlin, 1885), vi. 'Essais de Theodicée', 157, § 97. Friedrich von Spee, *Cautio Criminalis* (Rinteln, 1631); the Jesuit Spee was Canon of Würzburg, had assisted at executions, and advised the Prince-Elector of Mainz, who took his caution on board.

[3] Felix Braehm, 'De Fallacibus Iudiciis Magiae', 22 Oct. 1701.

[4] Christian Thomasius, *Dissertatione de Crimine Magiae* (Halle, 1701) and also his *De Origine ac progressu Processus inquisitorii contra Sagas* (Halle, 1712). Johann Reich defended Thomasius in his *Kurtze Lehr-Sätze von dem Laster der Zauberey* (Halle, 1702; translated from the Latin) and two further books in 1703 and 1704. A *Programma* issued at Halle in 1701 by Johann Franz Buddäus argued against Thomasius. Other works included Jacob Brunneman, *Discours von betrüglichen Kennzeichen der Zauberey* (1st edn. 1708; 2nd edn. Halle, 1727); and the moderately sceptical Justus Henning Böhmer, senior professor of law at the Academia Fridericiana, in his *Jus Ecclesiasticum Protestantium* (Halle, 1714).

was here that the work of John Webster was first published in German, as late as 1719; and an apparently acceptable thesis for the doctorate in law in 1700 catalogued the different species of apparitions sent by Satan to buffet and injure mankind. In his recent study of early seventeenth-century witch-hunting in Bavaria, Wolfgang Behringer notes the persistence of debate into the late eighteenth century, with an ideological component which to some extent mirrors the situation in England, Anthony Collins on one side, John Wesley on the other: 'Enlightened thinkers lumped multifaceted religious traditions together with witch beliefs in their attacks; conservative theologians did the same in their counter-attacks.'[5]

Except in the borderlands of the Basque country, where notorious witch-hunts did occur, witchcraft, while an orthodox belief in sixteenth- and seventeenth-century Spain, was not an occasion for mass persecution, even on the English scale.[6] In his work on the outbreak of witch-hunting in the Basque region, Gustav Henningsen provides a clear summary of the Spanish case. Largely because of the unprecedented outbreak of 1614, new instructions were issued which, as 'the expression of a skepticism felt by only a minority of Spanish bureaucrats', reduced the probability of further such crazes. Even among the inquisitors many felt that burnings should continue, well into the seventeenth century. Yet it was largely due to 'the centralized method of government of the Inquisition and the authority of *la Suprema*' that an unpopular decision involving the end of witch-burning could be implemented 'about a century before the remainder of Europe changed its policy'.

This is a familiar phenomenon, the restriction of witch-hunting in areas with strong administrative control—the Île-de-France, the kingdom of England.[7] Henningsen goes on to point out, however, that the restriction of the witch-craze—politically desirable from many points of view—did

---

[5] Andreas Becker, *Disputatio Judica de Jure Spectrorum* (Halle, 1700); Wolfgang Behringer, *Hexenverfolgung in Bayern: Volksmagie, Glaubenseifer und Staatsräson in der Frühen Neuzeit* (Munich, 1988), 412 f., my translation.

[6] For instance, only one out of 2,000 at Saragossa's public *autos-da-fé*, 1550–1600, was a witch. On the Spanish Inquisition see, most recently: William Monter, *Frontiers of Heresy: The Spanish Inquisition from the Basque Lands to Sicily* (Cambridge, 1990), esp. 3–26 (conversos), pt. 3 (moriscos and protestants), and ch. 12 (the 'forgotten offense', witchcraft). See also Stephen Haliczer, 'The Jew as Witch: Displaced Aggression and the Myth of Santo Nino de La Guardia' in M. E. Perry and A. J. Cruz (eds.), *Cultural Encounters: The Impact of the Inquisition in Spain and the New World* (Berkeley, 1991).

[7] See Robin Briggs's *Communities of Belief: Cultural and Social Tension in Early Modern France* (Oxford, 1989), ch. 1, 'Witchcraft and the Community in France and French-Speaking Europe'.

not imply or necessitate the extinction of witchcraft as a legitimate piece of élite belief, or as a criminal offence: 'Spain was to continue holding witch trials long after this type of case had been abandoned by all other European courts.'[8]

Recent work on New Spain suggests that across the Atlantic, too, witchcraft belief remained a feature of Spanish culture, and a political tool. At the same time, the active pursuit of witchcraft was discouraged. According to Fernando Cervantes, in a recent book, the Franciscan approach to diabolism in Mexico could be explained 'in terms of a local and primarily circumstantial political preoccupation'. His analysis centres on a possession case of 1691–2, in which a woman was exorcized, having been afflicted by spirits allegedly sent by a group of witches. Despite Franciscan attempts to use the case for the aggrandizement of their own religious order, the result was disorder. The Carmelite Manuel de Jesús María wrote to the Inquisitors: 'The holy religious orders are nearing a very grave confrontation which is emerging from the disunity and the differences of opinion over the recent happenings. Already there are signs of disturbances and controversies from which harmful scandals can ensue.' In the end, and as so often within the Spanish milieu, it was the Inquisition which brought the scandal to an end by the exercise of its customary, cautious authority. Yet 'there is', Cervantes writes, 'no convincing evidence to suggest that inquisitorial scepticism was the result of the influence of mechanical philosophy.' In the end,

diabolism was played down or ignored not because it was too credulous but, on the contrary, because it might lead to incredulity . . . As far as the inquisitors were concerned, the danger of the demoniacs' remarks did not lie in the power that they gave to Satan over their bodies, but in the way in which they threatened to turn the traditional concept of the devil into an incredible and ridiculous idea, and it is in this defensive spirit, rather than in a climate of precocious intellectual scepticism, that the best sense can be made of the new inquisitorial contempt for popular diabolism.

Moreover, for those who hold that the process of progressive disenchantment never went into reverse, the hiccough in New Spain is instructive. The last decades of the eighteenth century 'witnessed a reversal of the dwindling inquisitorial interest in cases of superstition and a marked increase in long and meticulous cases involving demonic pacts and invocations'.[9]

---

[8] Gustav Henningsen, *The Witches' Advocate: Basque Witchcraft and the Spanish Inquisition, 1609–1614* (Reno, Nev., 1980), 389.

[9] Fernando Cervantes, 'The Devils of Querétaro: Scepticism and Credulity in Late Seventeenth-Century Mexico', *P & P* 130 (1991); id., *The Devil in the New World: The Impact of Diabolism in New Spain* (New Haven and London, 1994), 146, 148.

What is so suggestive about the Spanish case is the way in which witchcraft remained of ideological importance into the eighteenth century. It was part of the image of the *ancien régime* for both its opponents and its advocates. Inasmuch as the *ancien régime* was a serious political entity in eighteenth- and even early nineteenth-century Spain, witchcraft theory remained a usable ideological resource, even more so than in England, where it had been swiftly pushed into the distant margins occupied, at the last gasp, by the author of *Antipas*.

In one of a sequence of satirical dialogues, written in 1816, Francisco Sanchez Barbero presents us with one character who stands for conservative ideals and, significantly, advocates the reality of witchcraft:

In the presence of the world, I challenge you, most reverend Feijóo, with all your host of devotees, past, present, and future, who, with insolent tongues and without shame, deny, have denied, and will deny the real existence of witches. They exist —I say so. If it's not enough for me to say it, I'll prove it with reasons, with arms, just as you wish, in the street, in the square, from the pulpit, and out in the fields.[10]

Benito Feijóo was a major Spanish sceptical writer, whose multi-volume *Teatro Critical* appeared from 1720 to 1759. By 1780 it had run into fifteen editions, winning the approval of an enlightened court and leading one admirer to proclaim that 'thanks to the immortal Feijóo spirits no longer trouble our houses, witches have fled our towns, the evil eye does not plague the tender child, and the eclipse does not dismay us.'[11] The versified rant above is not simple fantasy or implausible satire either. In 1791 the Inquisition in Barcelona mounted a case against a woman who confessed to having pledged herself to the Devil and taken part in witches' sabbaths.[12] In his enforced retirement in 1798, the reforming minister Gaspar Melchor de Jovellanos chose to read and note some books on the subject of witchcraft, remarking on some 'excellent ideas for banishing pointless belief in witches, spells, spirits, divines, etc.'[13] In 1813 belief in witchcraft was advocated in the parliament of Cádiz by a deputy, the learned Fray Maestro Alvarado.[14] In Spain, as Gwyn Williams writes,

[10] My own (free) translation, of *Poetas líricos del siglo XVIII*, ii, in *Biblioteca de Autores Espanoles*, lxiii. 593, cited in Julio Caro Baroja, *The World of the Witches* (1964), 214. 'During the political struggles of the early nineteenth century', Baroja writes, 'belief in witchcraft came to be identified with ultra-conservatism. Those who supported absolutism and despotic forms of government could legitimately be accused of it.'
[11] *Diccionario Feyjoniano*, cited in Gwyn A. Williams, *Goya and the Impossible Revolution* (1976), 25.
[12] Henningsen, *The Witches' Advocate*, 389.
[13] Baroja, *World of Witches*, 214. See also reference to 'El libro famoso contra brujas: *Malleus maleficarum*', entry for 13 May 1795 in Jovellanos, *Diarios* (Oviedo, 1954), ii. 62.
[14] Henningsen, *Witches' Advocate*, 389.

'the fashionable late eighteenth-century interest in witchcraft assumed deeper significance among the enlightened minority.' It became a symbol of darkness, of reaction.[15]

It is in such a light that we can understand Francisco Goya's well-known absorption in witch-lore—in his *Caprichos* and later engravings, his paintings for the Osuna family, and, most intriguingly of all, his *Pinturas negras* for the Quinta del Sordo, his house in Madrid. Goya's interest in the diabolical has come to be seen as part of a Romantic gloss on the late Spanish Enlightenment. Demons first appeared in his work in a resolutely *ancien-régime* context, however, in one of the many religious pictures which date from his earlier years as a painter. *St Francis Borgia Attending a Dying Impenitent* dates from the end of the 1780s, a period in which, according to a recent study, Goya was 'eliminating angels and clouds of glory from his religious compositions, and giving them a more naturalistic appearance'. The cherubs and clouds of the charcoal sketch have indeed been left out of the oil sketch and the final canvas. All three versions, however, retain the diabolical. In the charcoal, a winged devil flees from the ministering saint; in the oils, the devil is replaced by groups of monsters lurking behind the penitent's bed. In pictures of succeeding years, the 'monstrueux vraisemblable', as Baudelaire called it, was to become an obsession.[16]

Goya moved in an enlightened milieu in which witchcraft was of great interest. One of his closest friends, the dramatist Moratín, edited an account of the *auto-da-fé* at Logrono in 1610. He saw this work as an opportunity to exorcize the reactionary spirit of the old Spain and it was at moments of liberal success, as Gwyn Williams has noted, that Moratín's work found its publishers: in 1811 Madrid under French control; in 1812 Cádiz with democratic patriotism in full flood; and in 1820, in revolutionary Madrid. Goya's witchcraft engravings in the *Caprichos* were taken straight from his friend's notes to the *Relacion*.[17] Within the context of the *Caprichos*—whose overarching symbol is that of the sleep of reason

---

[15] Williams, *Goya and the Impossible Revolution*, 23.

[16] Juliet Wilson-Bareau, *Goya: Truth and Fantasy* (1994), cat. no. 17 and figs. 118 and 119, text at pp. 150 f. The charcoal sketch is in the Prado; the oil sketch with the Marquesa de Santa Cruz, Madrid; the final painting in Valencia Cathedral.

[17] Edith Helman, 'The Younger Moratín and Goya: On *Duendes* and *Brujas*', *Hispanic Review*, 27 (1959). See also Jutta Held, 'Between Bourgeois Enlightenment and Popular Culture: Goya's Festivals, Old Women, Monsters and Blind Men', *History Workshop Journal*, 23 (1987); Alfonso E. Pérez Sánchez and Eleanor A. Sayre, *Goya and the Spirit of Enlightenment*, (Boston, 1989); Pierre Gassier and Juliet Wilson, *Goya: Life and Work* (Fribourg, 1971); Williams, *Goya and the Impossible Revolution*.

bringing forth monsters, a plate which introduced the scenes of sorcery and demons—engravings like *Devota profesion* ('devout profession') or *Linda Maestra* ('a fine teacher') reflect not only the modish interest in witchcraft among the circles in which Goya moved (reflected also in the subjects of the paintings he made for the Duchess of Osuna's country house[18]), but also a symbolic condemnation, mediated through macabre comedy, of the dark inheritance of the old regime.[19]

Goya continued to be fascinated by the demonic themes of the *Caprichos*. The subjects of his very last drawings include a man mocked by demons (illustration 9), a young witch flying with a rope, a travelling witch, a young woman surrounded by witches, and a scene of union with the Devil.[20] The so-called Black Paintings of Goya's own house, the Quinta del Sordo were executed during his convalescence, 1820 to 1823. Large and technically compelling oil paintings, they are in some senses Goya's testament—pictures which were his indulgence and which dwelt upon those macabre themes which he continued to explore in drawings right to the end of his career. With an anthropophagic nightmare Saturn, a witch-like scene of Judith and her attendant, and the brutality of the duel, as well as the most famous witchcraft scene, *El gran cabròn*, and the demon Asmodée, the viewer is presented with the same sort of fantastical miscellany as the *Caprichos*, bound together by an atmosphere of morbidity, but also by a sense of elusive, personal meaning which lends them the air of a sort of visual *Symphonie fantastique*. These are the progenitors of a Romantic tradition which has the witches' sabbath, as in Berlioz's imagination, as one of its horrific leitmotifs: but Goya's work is at the start of this development, and is striking in its ability to draw on what was still a live concern within Spanish culture, not simply Berlioz's sensationalizing, self-centred *grand guignol*.[21]

[18] Two of the six scenes are drawn from the comedies of Antonio de Zamora ('The Forcibly Bewitched'; and the odd one out, whose theme points to the overarching playfulness of the whole conception, *The Stone Guest*). See Wilson-Bareau, *Goya*, 212–21, six witchcraft subjects (1797–8): *The Witches' Kitchen*, oil on canvas, private collection; *Flying Witches*, oil, Jaime Ortiz-Patiño Collection; *The Witches' Sabbath*, Museo Lázaro Galdiano, Madrid; *The Spell*, same; *Scene from 'El Convidado de Piedra' ('The Stone Guest')*, location unknown since 1896; *Scene from 'El Hechizado por Fuerza' ('The Forcibly Bewitched')*, National Gallery, London.

[19] Francisco Goya, *Los Caprichos* (New York, 1969), pls. 43, 68, and 70; Gassier and Wilson, *Goya*, cat. nos. 536, 587, and 591.

[20] Gassier and Wilson, *Goya*, cat. nos. 1774, 1782, 1789, 1788, 1815, all *c*.1824–8.

[21] Although Goya also has his *idée fixe*; a silhouette of an elegant young woman sitting to the right of the witches' sabbath. Ibid., cat. nos. 1624, 1625, 1616, 1623, 1620, and text 313–19. The arrangement of paintings on the first floor of the Quinta del Sordo also included a painting of witches by Javier Goya, now lost. In the same period see also the apocryphal

Goya's representations of witchcraft and demonology are a trace of what the *ancien régime*, and its sacral state, had left as intellectual remains for the (very late) Spanish enlightenment.[22] There is a tension in all of Goya's occult work, well-expressed for the whole of Spanish society by Gwyn Williams as a 'tension between an imported Enlightenment and an increasingly assertive and xenophobic *costumbrismo*'. This helps to account for the obsession with witchcraft, for sceptics and believers alike, the 'hag-ridden psychology of Spaniards'.[23] Many commentators— Williams, Held, Helman—note this feature of Goya's art, his capacity to propagandize for the Spanish enlightenment with all its political prejudices and panaceas, while also entering into the world of *brujas*, *duendes*, and the *majas*. 'Ya, ya, ya,' Goya wrote to his friend Zapater, 'I'm not afraid of witches, hobgoblins, apparitions, boastful giants, knaves or varlets, etc., nor indeed of any kind of beings except human beings';[24] yet he was haunted, as Murray Kempton has put it, by 'witches half-mocked and half-believed in' (see illustration 9).[25]

From the Spanish lands we now turn to the Protestant, rebellious United Netherlands. The change in political atmosphere is vast: the darkness of the Inquisition yields to the bright birthplace of toleration. One expects progressivism here, if anywhere. Simon van Leeuwen declared as early as the 1660s that 'witchcraft is unknown among us'. Since the Reformation and the banishment of superstition 'all imagined illusions of witchcraft . . . are considered to be curious deception and rejected as a false accusation. Since then nobody has been found to be truly guilty thereof.' The recognition of change was already dawning in the 1630s:

It wouldn't surprise me if most of what has been said during the last hundred years in these lands about spirits, elves, ogres, *kollen*, *kolrijders*, male and female witches, were to have been foolish talk and frightening images. All the more since these days, now that the witchcraft charges are ceasing and are dismissed by the courts, one neither hears nor talks about such whims, nor the calamities and

work on wood, no. 1652, *Execution of a Witch*, *c.*1820–4, a young woman with a rope round her neck; *Carnaval*, no. 1656, *c.*1820–4, which exudes the aura of Sabbath; and the additional design for *Los Disparates* or *Los Proverbios*, no. 1608, 'Démon chutant', *c.*1815–24.

[22] Anthony Pagden, 'The Reception of the "New Philosophy" in Eighteenth-Century Spain', *Journal of the Warburg and Courtauld Institutes*, 51 (1988).

[23] Williams, *Goya and the Impossible Revolution*, 56.

[24] Wilson-Bareau, *Goya*, 212.

[25] Quoted in review of Murray Kempton's *Rebellions, Perversities and Main Events* by Garry Wills in *New York Review of Books*, 41/9 (1994), 3. Compare Goya's attitude to bullfighting, reflected in his *Tauromachia* prints. He was an *aficionado*; his friends, however, disapproved, seeing bullfighting as a vulgar and brutish practice, fit to be rejected by the enlightened.

difficulties accompanying them. Whilst formerly not only houses and hamlets, but whole cities were in bad repute, and the annual felling of all the trees in Holland would scarcely have been enough to burn all those who had a bad name and were talked about in this connection.[26]

This is, in fact, the overdrawn contrast of a progressive, Protestant propagandist. Witchcraft *persecution* was over before it had really started in the northern Netherlands, at the turn of the seventeenth century (though it continued with more virulence in the Catholic, Habsburg south);[27] and one notorious controversy at the end of the century suggests that witchcraft *theory* continued to be important long after the fires had gone out.[28]

Balthasar Bekker published the first two parts of his *De Betoverde Weereld* in 1691.[29] In 1692 he was suspended from office after refusing to retract his noxious opinions, and in the following year parts 3 and 4 of his massive treatise appeared. Most writing about Bekker has missed the point, offering anodyne readings of his work as the embodiment of Cartesian rationalism, arguing about the extent of its influence or its immersion in biblical fundamentalism.[30] There can be no doubt that Bekker was a devoutly religious thinker, his purpose 'to banish the devil from the world and to bind him in hell so that the king Jesus may rule more freely on earth'.[31] The importance of Bekker, however, lies in the response to his work, which clouds the clarity of traditional pictures of free-thinking Dutch society or of the disrepute in which witchcraft belief was held among the European intelligentsia. One hundred and seventy-five books or pamphlets contributed to the Bekker controversy; 131 argued against Bekker. Bekker's own analysis of the strength of witch beliefs in Holland, even among educated people, is significant. Ministers divide into three groups, he wrote: a small group of the credulous, prepared to believe almost any tale of witchcraft; a few sceptics who believe nothing; and the vast majority, who repudiate some vulgar beliefs, but

---

[26] Simon van Leeuwen, *Manieren van Procederen in civile en criminele saaken etc.* (1666); Johan van Heemskerk, *Batavische arcadia* (1637; 2nd edn. 1639). Both cited in Herman Beliën, 'Judicial Views on the Crime of Witchcraft', in Marijke Gijswijt-Hofstra and Willem Frijhoff (eds.) *Witchcraft in the Netherlands from the fourteenth to the twentieth century* (Rotterdam, 1991), 62 f.

[27] Marijke Gijswijt-Hofstra, 'Six Centuries of Witchcraft in the Netherlands: Themes, Outlines, and Interpretations', ibid. 29.

[28] See also ibid. 21 on the Frisian lawyer Huber's affirmation towards the end of the 17th c. that witchcraft remained a capital crime.

[29] See Ch. 4 above.

[30] e.g. R. Attfield, 'Balthasar Bekker and the Decline of the Witch-Craze: The Old Demonology and the New Philosophy', *Annals of Science*, 42 (1985).

[31] Preface, *De Betoverde Weereld*.

believe in the possibility of witchcraft and the veracity of some relations of witchcraft.[32] This is a pattern to be found all over Europe, well into the eighteenth century, after the end of active persecution (which nevertheless continued in some areas even beyond 1750); and it suggests once again that Continental material, French, German, Spanish, and Dutch, far from conflicting with my argument for England, actually strengthens it.

This book has had two overarching points to make: first, theories of witchcraft were far more robust than previous accounts have recognized. We have found witchcraft theory alive and well in England, and in other European countries, well into the eighteenth century. Secondly, the ideological roots of witchcraft theory have been previously underplayed and, consequently, the role of politics in the demise of witchcraft theory has been, until now, obscured. The theories of witchcraft which emerged in the wake of the Reformation were the product of a mentality which saw polity and society as religious entities; a view which placed the sacral state at the centre of ideological concerns, and made the witch, as a compound of anti-social, treasonous, and diabolical threats, highly plausible. The waning of Reformation reflexes throughout Europe was bound to remove these ideological underpinnings, and the ideological function, of witchcraft theory; and, in each political community, political events conspired to remove the issue of witchcraft from the political agenda.

The decline of witchcraft belief in the world at large, the disappearance of witchcraft as a means of ordering the world, and the collapse in the legitimacy of the criminological category of witchcraft: these are developments we can now identify, and which relate to our own conception of witchcraft as an 'irrational' belief. Our twentieth-century world is, without doubt, disenchanted, in Max Weber's sense. Witchcraft makes no sense to us because it has no place in our world; the concepts in which it is grounded do not relate to the world we live and act in; it is an irrelevance and has, consequently, lost whatever explanatory power or useful function it ever had. This does not mean that there is *not* a fact of the matter about witchcraft, its reality or impossibility; only that the fact of the matter has little to do with the demise of witchcraft in history or even our own attitudes. The approximate—very approximate—coincidence in time

---

[32] See G. H. Beckher, *Schediasma critico-literarium de controversis Balthasari Bekkero* (Leipzig, 1721). For Calvinist and Huguenot adherence to witchcraft beliefs across the Atlantic, see also: 'Questions propounded by Joseph Dudley to the Dutch and French Clergymen of witchcraft, in order to procure better direction in future trials of the accused in Massachusetts', at New York, 5 Oct. 1692, printed in *Proceedings of the Massachusetts Historical Society*, Dec. 1884.

between the establishment of certain scientific facts and the demise of witchcraft theory should not tempt us into embracing both under one explanatory framework, however enthusiastically sceptics about witchcraft may have used the fashionable language of the new philosophy.

Witchcraft disappeared, in the first place, piecemeal. Fashion and intellectual communication universalized that disappearance; a domino-effect, comparable in propagation with industrialization or the growth of liberal democracy in the West. The catch-all criterion of correctness cannot be deployed to guarantee the inevitability of these processes and evade, discount, or even disallow nuanced explanation. Moreover, certain sets of political and religious presuppositions could preserve witchcraft as a theory or part of a criminal code long after persecution had effectively ceased. This has not, therefore, been the traditional tale of intellectual revolution and scientific disenchantment followed by intellectual diffusion, but of parallel and interacting ideological developments which, in retrospect, look inevitable but which, at the time (as for Francis Hutchinson in his *Historical Essay*) seemed perilously insecure.

The establishment of the rational canon (by which I mean the body of practices and beliefs constitutive of our idea of rationality) was not achieved by a seamless, monolithic, and singular process, apparently inexorable if only because of its sheer weight. Instead, it was the outcome of a disparate collection of specific battles and debates. It only appears to have had a unity of purpose in retrospect. The rational canon was defined, and redefined, piecemeal. The historian has to start out piecemeal too. This is what it is to write a history of the demise of witchcraft theory, rather than a reconstruction of how it ought to have been if rational criteria had been applied.

Bibliography

BOOKS, ARTICLES, AND ANONYMOUS PRINTED SOURCES

An Account of the Tryal, Examination and Condemnation of Jane Wenham (1712).

ADAMS, GEOFFREY, *The Huguenots and French Opinion, 1685–1787: The Enlightenment Debate on Toleration* (Waterloo, Ontario, 1991).

ADDISON, JOSEPH, *Remarks on . . . Italy &c.*, repr. in *Miscellaneous Works*, ed. A. C. Guthkelch (2 vols.; 1914).

——*The Drummer; Or, the Haunted House. A Comedy* (1716).

——*et al., The Spectator*, ed. D. F. Bond (5 vols.; Oxford, 1965).

ADY, THOMAS, *A Candle in the Dark: Shewing The Divine Cause of the distractions of the whole Nation of ENGLAND, and of the Christian WORLD. That is, the Lord doth Avenge the blood of the Innocent upon the Inhabitants of the Earth* (1656).

ANGLO, SYDNEY (ed.), *The Damned Art: Essays in the Literature of Witchcraft* (1977).

ANKARLOO, BENGT, and HENNINGSEN GUSTAV (eds.), *Early Modern European Witchcraft: Centres and Peripheries* (Oxford, 1990).

Antipas: a solemn appeal to the Archbishops and Bishops with reference to several Bills . . . especially that concerning Witchcraft and Sorcery (1821).

ARCHER, EDMOND, *A Sermon preach'd . . . Before the Reverend Clergy of the Lower House of Convocation: Being the Anniversary of the Martyrdom of King Charles the 1st* (1711).

ARMINIUS, JACOBUS, *Examen Modestum* (Leiden, 1612).

ASHCRAFT, RICHARD, *Revolutionary Politics and Locke's 'Two Treatises of Government'* (Princeton, 1986).

ATTFIELD, R., 'Balthasar Bekker and the Decline of the Witch-Craze: The Old Demonology and the New Philosophy', *Annals of Science*, 42 (1985).

AUBIN, P., *The Humours of the Masqueraders* (1733).

AUBREY, JOHN, 'Remaines of Gentilisme and Judaisme', in *Three Prose Works* (Fontwell, 1972).

AUTUN, JACQUES D' [Jacques Chevanes], *L'Incrédulité savante et la crédulité ignorante au sujet des Magiciens et sorciers. Avecque la response à un livre intitulé Apologie pour tous les grands personnages qui ont esté faussement soupçonnés de Magie* (Lyons, 1671).

BACKSCHEIDER, PAULA, *Daniel Defoe: His Life* (Baltimore, 1989).

BAINE, RODNEY, *Daniel Defoe and the Supernatural* (Athens, Ga., 1968).

BAROJA, JULIO CARO, *The World of the Witches* (1964).

BARROW, HENRY, 'A Refutation of Mr Giffard's Reasons' (1590/1), in *The Writings of Henry Barrow*, ed. L. H. Carlson (1966).

BARROW, ISAAC, *Theological Works* (8 vols.; Oxford, 1830).

BAXTER, RICHARD, *Additional Notes of the Life and Death of Sir Matthew Hale* (1682).

——*Of the Nature of Spirits* (1682).

——*The Certainty of the World of Spirits* (1691).

BAYLE, PIERRE, 'Réponse aux questions d'un provincial' (1703–7) in *Œuvres Diverses*, iii, pt. 2 (The Hague, 1727).

BEAUMONT, JOHN, *An Historical, Physiological and Theological Treatise of Spirits, Apparitions, Witchcrafts, and other Magical Practices* (1705).

BEAUNE, H., 'Les Sorciers de Lyon: épisode judiciaire du XVIIIe siècle', *Mémoires de l'Académie impériale . . . de Dijon*, 2nd ser. 4 (Dijon, 1868).

BECKHER, G. H., *Schediasma critico-literarium de controversis Balthasari Bekkero* (Leipzig, 1721).

BEDFORD, ARTHUR, *A Serious Remonstrance In Behalf of the Christian Religion, Against The Horrid Blasphemies and Impieties which are still used in the English Play-Houses, to the great Dishonour of Almighty God, and in Contempt of the Statutes of this Realm. Shewing their plain Tendency to overthrow all Piety, and advance the Interest and Honour of the Devil in the World* (1719).

BEHRINGER, WOLFGANG, *Hexenverfolgung in Bayern: Volksmagie, Glaubenseifer und Staatsräson in der Frühen Neuzeit* (Munich, 1988).

BEKKER, BALTHASAR, *Engelsch verhaal van ontdekte tovery wederteid door Balthasar Bekker* (Amsterdam, 1689), in Anna E. C. Simoni, 'Balthasar Bekker and the Beckington Witch', *Quaerendo*, 9 (1979).

——*De betoverde weereld* (Amsterdam, 1691–3).

——*Le Monde Enchanté, ou Examen des communs sentimens touchant les esprits* (Amsterdam, 1694).

——*The World Bewitched* (1695).

BELIËN, HERMAN, 'Judicial Views on the Crime of Witchcraft', in Gijswijt-Hofstra and Frijhoff, *Witchcraft in the Netherlands*.

BENNETT, G. V., *The Tory Crisis in Church and State* (Oxford, 1975).

[BENTLEY, RICHARD] (Phileleutherus Lipsiensis), *Remarks upon a late Discourse of Free-Thinking* (1713).

BERKELEY, GEORGE, *Works*, ed. A. A. Luce and T. E. Jessop (9 vols.; Edinburgh, 1948–57).

——*A Treatise Concerning the Principles of Human Knowledge* (Dublin, 1710).

BERNARD, RICHARD, *A Guide to Grand Jurymen* (1627; 1680; 1686).

BERNIER, ABBÉ FRANÇOIS DE, *Histoire de la revolution de l'empire du Mogol* (Paris, 1670).

Bibliothèque Nationale, *Les Sorcières* (Paris, 1973).

BLACKMORE, RICHARD, *Discourses on the Gout, Rheumatism and King's Evil* (1726).

——*Treatise on the King's Evil* (1735).

BLACKSTONE, WILLIAM, *Commentaries on the Laws of England* (4 vols.; Oxford, 1769).

BLUCHE, FRANÇOIS, *Louis XIV* (Oxford, 1990).

BOSWELL, JAMES, *Boswell's Life of Johnson. Together with Boswell's Journal of a Tour to the Hebrides and Johnson's Diary of A Journey into North Wales*, ed. G. B. Hill and L. F. Powell (6 vols.; Oxford, 1934).

BOULTON, RICHARD, *A Treatise of the Reason of Muscular Motion* (1697).

——*Treatise concerning the Heat of the Blood* (1698).

——*An Examination of Mr John Colbatch his Books* (1698).

——*The Works of the Honourable Robert Boyle, Esq. Epitomiz'd* (4 vols.; 1699).

——*A System of Rational and Practical Chirurgy* (1713).

——*Physico-Chyrurgical Treatises* (1714; individual treatises with title-pages dated 1713).

——*A Compleat History of Magick, Sorcery, and Witchcraft* (1715).

——*The Theological Works of the Honourable Robert Boyle, Esq; Epitomiz'd in Three Volumes* (1715).

——*An Essay on the Plague* (Dublin, 1721).

——*The Possibility and Reality of Magick, Sorcery, and Witchcraft, demonstrated. OR A Vindication of a Compleat History of Magick, Sorcery, and Witchcraft. In Answer to Dr Hutchinson's Historical Essay* (1722).

——*Some Thoughts concerning the Unusual Qualities of the Air* (1724).

BOVET, RICHARD, *Pandaemonium* (1684; repr. Aldington, Kent, 1951).

BOWER, EDMOND, *Doctor Lamb Revived, or, Witchcraft condemn'd in Anne Bodenham* (1653).

BOYLE, ROBERT, *Works*, ed. T. Birch (6 vols.; 1772).

——'The Origin of Forms and Qualities', in *Works*, iii.

BRAGGE, FRANCIS, jun., *A Defense of the Proceedings against Jane Wenham, wherein the Possibility and Reality of Witchcraft are Demonstrated from Scripture, and the concurrent Testimonies of all Ages* (1712).

[——], *A Full and Impartial Account of the Discovery of Sorcery and Witchcraft, Practis'd by Jane Wenham* (1712).

[——], *Witchcraft farther displayed* (1712).

BRAMHALL, JOHN, *Works*, ed. A.W.H. (5 vols.; Oxford, 1842–5).

——*Castigations of Mr Hobbes . . . [&] The Catching of Leviathan Or the great Whale* (1658).

BRIGGS, ROBIN, *Communities of Belief: Cultural and Social Tension in Early Modern France* (Oxford, 1989).

BRINSLEY, JOHN, *A Discovery of the Impositions of Witches and Astrologers* (1680).

British Museum, *Catalogue of Prints and Drawings . . . Division 1, Political and Personal Satires* (3 vols.; 1870).

BROWNE, THOMAS, *Religio Medici* (1642; Oxford, 1972).

BUCKLE, H. T., *The History of Civilisation in England* (new ed., 1871).

BURKE, PETER, *The Fabrication of Louis XIV* (New Haven, 1992).

BURNET, GILBERT, *Some Passages of the life and death of . . . John earl of Rochester* (1680).

—— *Life and Death of Sir Matthew Hale* (1682).

BURTHOGGE, RICHARD, *The Nature of Church-Government, Freely Discussed and set out* (1691).

—— *An Essay upon Reason, and the Nature of Spirits* (1694).

BUTLER, SAMUEL, *Hudibras*, ed. Zachary Grey (1663; 1744).

—— *Hudibras*, ed. J. Wilders (1663; Oxford, 1967).

BYFIELD, NICHOLAS, *The Marrow of the Oracles of God* (1640).

Calendar of State Papers, America and West Indies, 1689–1692, ed. J. W. Fortescue (HMSO, 1901).

Calendar of State Papers, Domestic Series, 1682, ed. F. H. Blackburne Daniell (HMSO, 1932).

CARLYLE, ALEXANDER, *The Autobiography of Dr Alexander Carlyle of Inveresk, 1722–1805*, ed. James Kinsley (Oxford, 1973).

CASAUBON, MERIC, *A Treatise of Use and Custome* (1638).

—— *Treatise Concerning Enthusiasme*, 2nd edn. (1656).

—— *A True and Faithful Relation of what passed for many yeers between Dr John Dee (A Mathematician of Great Fame in Q. Eliz. and King James their Reignes) and Some Spirits. With a preface confirming the reality (as to the point of spirits) of this relation: and shewing the several good Uses that a sober christian may make of all* (1659).

—— *A Vindication of the Lord's Prayer* (1660).

—— *Of the Necessity of Reformation, in, and before Luther's time* (1664).

—— *Of Credulity and Incredulity in things Natural, Civil, and Divine* (reissue of 1668 edn., 1672).

—— *Letter . . . to Peter du Moulin . . . Concerning Natural Experimental Philosophy* (1669).

The Case of Mrs Mary Catherine Cadiere, Against the Jesuit Father John Baptist Girard, 10th edn., (1732).

The Case of the Hertfordshire Witchcraft Considered (1712).

CAVENDISH, MARGARET, *The Life of William Cavendish*, ed. C. L. Firth (1886).

CERTEAU, MICHEL DE, *La Possession de Loudun* (Paris, 1990).

CERVANTES, FERNANDO, 'The Devils of Querétaro: Scepticism and Credulity in Late Seventeenth-Century Mexico', *P & P* 130 (1991).

—— *The Devil in the New World: The Impact of Diabolism in New Spain* (New Haven and London, 1994).

CLARK, J. C. D., *English Society 1688–1832* (Cambridge, 1985).

CLARK, STUART, 'King James's *Daemonologie*: Witchcraft and Kingship', in Anglo, *Damned Art*.

——'Protestant Demonology: Sin, Superstition, and Society (*c.*1520–*c.*1630)', in Ankarloo and Henningsen, *Early Modern Witchcraft*.

CLARKE, SAMUEL, *Works* (1738).

CLÉMENT, PIERRE (ed.), *Lettres, instructions et mémoires de Colbert* (6 vols.; Paris, 1861–9).

CLERK, JOHN, *Memoirs of the Life of Sir John Clerk of Penicuik*, ed. J. M. Gray (Publications of the Scottish Historical Society, 13; Edinburgh, 1892).

COBBETT, W., HOWELL, T. B. *et al.* (eds.), *Cobbett's Complete Collection of State Trials, and Proceedings for High-Treason, and Other Crimes and Misdemeanors. With Notes Compiled by T. B. Howell* (33 vols.; 1809–28).

——WRIGHT, J., *et al.* (eds.), *The Parliamentary History of England ... to ... 1803* (36 vols.; 1806–20).

COLLINS, ANTHONY, *A Discourse of Free-Thinking* (1713).

COLLINS, WILKIE, *The Moonstone* (1868; Harmondsworth, 1986).

COOK, HAROLD J., *The Decline of the Old Medical Regime* (Ithaca, NY, 1986).

COOPER, THOMAS, *The Mystery of Witchcraft* (1617).

CORNEILLE, THOMAS, and VIZÉ, DONNEAU DE, *La Devineresse ou les faux enchantements* (1680).

CRAWFURD, RAYMOND, *The King's Evil* (Oxford, 1911).

[CROCKET, GILBERT, and MONRO, JOHN?], *The Scotch Presbyterian Eloquence* (1692).

CROFT, P. J., *Autograph Poetry in the English Language* (1973).

DAMROSCH, JR., LEOPOLD, 'Hobbes as Reformation Theologian: Implications of the Free-Will Controversy', *JHI* 40 (1979).

DAVIES, REGINALD TREVOR, *Four Centuries of Witch-Beliefs, with Special Reference to the Great Rebellion* (1947).

The Defence of F. John Baptist Girard (4th edn., 1732).

DEFOE, DANIEL, *Defoe's 'Review'. Reproduced from the Original Editions with an Introduction and Bibliographical Notes . . .* , ed. A. W. Secord (New York, 1938).

——*Letters of Daniel Defoe*, ed. G. H. Healey (Oxford, 1955).

——*The Advantages of the Present Settlement* (1689).

——*Reflections upon the Late Great Revolution* (1689).

——*The Villainy of stock-jobbers detected* (1701).

——*The Shortest-Way with the Dissenters: Or, Proposals for the Establishment of the Church* (1702).

——*More Short Ways with the Dissenters* (1704).

——*The Storm: or a Collection of the Most Remarkable Casualties and Disasters which Happened in the Late Dreadful Tempest, Both by Sea and Land* (1704), in L. A. Curtis (ed.), *The Versatile Defoe* (1979).

——*The Secret History of the October Club*, 2nd edn. (1711).

——*Robinson Crusoe* (1719; Oxford, 1981).

DEFOE, DANIEL, *The Farther Adventures of Robinson Crusoe* (1719), in *The Life and Adventures of Robinson Crusoe* (2 vols.; 1840).

——*A Journal of the Plague Year* (1722; Harmondsworth, 1966).

——*Moll Flanders* (1722).

——*Roxana, or The Fortunate Mistress* (1724; Oxford, 1981).

——*The Political History of the Devil* (1726).

——*An Essay on the History and Reality of Apparitions* (1727).

——*A System of Magick* (1727).

DENISART, J. B., *Collection de décisions* (Paris, 1756).

Dénonciation des factums de M. Chaudon avocat de la demoiselle Cadière; à messieurs les avocats du parlement de Provence (n.p., 1731).

DESCARTES, RENÉ, *Les Principes de la Philosophie* (Paris, 1647).

DEXTER, FRANKLIN (ed.), *The Literary Diary of Ezra Stiles* (3 vols.; New York, 1910).

DIDEROT, DENIS, et al., *Encyclopédie* (Neufchâtel, 1765).

DODWELL, HENRY, *Separation of Churches from Episcopal Government, as practised by the present Non-Conformists, proved schismatical . . . The Sinfulness and Mischief of Scisme* (1679).

DOWNAME, JOHN, *A Treatise of Securitie* (1622).

——*The Christian Warfare* (1634).

DOWNIE, J. ALAN, *Robert Harley and the Press* (Cambridge, 1979).

D[REWE], P[ATRICK], *The Church of England's Late Conflict with, and Triumph over, the Spirit of Fanaticism* (1710).

DU LUDE, COMTE, *Daimonologia or, a treatise of spirits . . . [with] reflections on Mr Boulton's answer to Dr Hutchinson's 'Historical Essay'* (1723).

DUDLEY, JOSEPH, 'Questions propounded by Joseph Dudley to the Dutch and French Clergymen of witchcraft, in order to procure better direction in future trials of the accused in Massachusetts', at New York, 5 Oct. 1692, in *Proceedings of the Massachusetts Historical Society* (Dec. 1884).

DUGDALE, WILLIAM, *A Short View of the Late Troubles in England* (Oxford, 1681).

DUHEM, PIERRE, *The Aim and Structure of Physical Theory*, tr. Philip P. Wiener (1906; New York, 1962).

DUNN, JOHN, *The Political Thought of John Locke* (1969).

DYKE, DANIEL, *Two Treatises: the one of repentance; the other of Christs Temptations* (1618).

EARLE, PETER, *The World of Defoe* (1976).

EDWARDS, THOMAS, *Gangraena: or a Catalogue and Discovery of many of the Errours, Heresies, Blasphemies and pernicious Practices of the Sectaries of this time* (1646).

ELIAS, NORBERT, *The Court Society* (Oxford, 1983).

ELIOT, GEORGE, *The Mill on the Floss* (1860; Harmondsworth, 1979).

The English Devil: or, Cromwel and his monstrous witch discover'd at White-Hall: with the strange and damnable speech of this hellish monster, by way of revelation, touching king and kingdome; and a narrative of the infernal plots, inhumane actings, and barbarous conspiracies of this grand imposter, and most audacious rebel, that durst aspire from a brew-house to the throne, washing his accursed hands in the blood of his royal soveraign (1660).

ERSKINE, JAMES, *Extracts from the Diary of a Senator of the College of Justice* (Edinburgh, 1843).

——'Letters of Lord Grange', in *The Miscellany of the Spalding Club*, iii (Aberdeen, 1846).

EVELYN, JOHN, *Diary*, ed. E. S. de Beer (6 vols.; Oxford, 1955).

EVERITT, ALAN, *The Community of Kent and the Great Rebellion, 1640–1660* (Leicester, 1966).

EWEN, C. L'E., *Witch Hunting and Witch Trials* (1929).

Factums et arrest du parlement de Paris, contre des bergers sorciers, executez dans la province de Brie (Paris, 1695).

——*Witchcraft and Demonianism* (1933).

FARGE, ARLETTE, *Subversive Words: Public Opinion in Eighteenth-Century France* (Cambridge, 1994).

FIELDING, HENRY, *Jonathan Wild* (1743; Harmondsworth, 1982).

FILMER, ROBERT, *Patriarcha and other political works . . .* , ed. P. Laslett (Oxford, 1949).

[——] *Of the Blasphemie against the Holy Ghost* (1646).

——'Observations on Mr Hobbes's Leviathan' (1652), in *Patriarcha*.

——*An Advertisement to the Jury-Men of England, Touching Witches. Together with a difference between an English and Hebrew witch* (1653).

FIRTH, C. H., assisted by G. Davies, *The Regimental History of Cromwell's Army* (2 vols.; Oxford, 1940).

FLINT, VALERIE I. J., *The Rise of Magic in Early Mediaeval Europe* (Oxford, 1991).

FOSTER, J., *An answer to dr Stebbing's Letter on the subject of heresy, a letter* (1735).

FOSTER, M., *Examination of the Scheme of Church Power laid down in the Codex* (1735).

A Full and Authentic Account of the Strange and Mysterious Affair Between Mary Squires a Gypsy, and Elizabeth Canning, 2nd edn. (1754).

A Full Confutation of Witchcraft: More particularly of the Depositions against Jane Wenham Lately Condemned (1712).

FUNCK-BRENTANO, FRANTZ, *Princes and Poisoners* (London, 1901).

FURBANK, P. N., and OWENS, W. R., *The Canonisation of Daniel Defoe* (New Haven, 1988).

GASCOIGNE, JOHN, 'Politics, Patronage and Newtonianism: The Cambridge Example', *HJ* 27/1 (1984).

GASSIER, PIERRE, and WILSON, JULIET, *Goya: Life and Work* (Fribourg, 1971).

GAULE, JOHN, *Select Cases of Conscience* (1646).

GEE, EDWARD, *The divine right and original of the civill magistrate from God* (1658).

GEIS, GILBERT, 'Lord Hale, Witches, and Rape', *British Journal of Law and Society*, 5 (1978).

GIBSON, EDMUND, *Codex Juris Ecclesiae Anglicanae* (1713).
——*A Sermon Preached to the Societies for the Reformation of Manners* (1723).
GIFFORD, GEORGE, *A Discourse of the Subtill Practises of Devilles by Witches and Sorcerers* (1587).
——*A Dialogue concerning Witches* (1593).
GIJSWIJT-HOFSTRA, MARIJKE, 'Six Centuries of Witchcraft in the Netherlands: Themes, Outlines, and Interpretations', in Gijswijt-Hofstra and Frijhoff, *Witchcraft in the Netherlands*.
——and FRIJHOFF, WILLEM (eds.), *Witchcraft in the Netherlands from the Fourteenth to the Twentieth Century* (Rotterdam, 1991).
[GILBERT, JOHN], *Reflections on Dr Fleetwood's Essay upon Miracles: Shewing the Absurdity, Falshood, and Danger of his Notions. With a Supplement, Wherein is represented the Extent and Strength of the Evidence which Miracles give to Revealed Religion* (1706).
GLANVILL, JOSEPH, *Scepsis Scientifica: or, confest ignorance, the way to science; in an essay of the vanity of dogmatizing, and confident opinion* (1665).
——*Philosophical Considerations touching Witches and Witchcraft* (1666).
——*A Blow at Modern Sadducism* (1668).
——'Antifanatick theologie and free philosophy. [In a continuation of the New Atlantis]', in *Essays on several important subjects in philosophy and religion* (1676).
——*Saducismus Triumphatus: or, full and plain evidence concerning witches and apparitions, the first part thereof containing philosophical considerations which defend their possibility. Whereunto is added, the true and genuine notion, and consistent explication of the nature of a spirit, for the more full confirmation of the possibility of their existence* (1681).
[——], *The Zealous and Impartial Protestant, shewing some great, but less heeded dangers of Popery. In order to thorough and effectual security against it* (1681).
——*Mr J. Glanvil's Full Vindication of the late Reverend, Pious and Learned Mr Richard Baxter* (1691 ?).
GODBEER, RICHARD, *The Devil's Dominion: Magic and Religion in Early New England* (Cambridge, 1992).
GODECHOT, JACQUES, *Les Institutions de la France sous la Révolution et l'Empire*, 3rd edn. (Paris, 1985).
GOLDIE, MARK, 'John Locke, Jonas Proast and Religious Toleration 1688–1692', in John Walsh, Colin Haydon, and Stephen Taylor (eds.), *The Church of England c.1689–c.1833: From Toleration to Tractarianism* (Cambridge, 1993).
GOLDSMITH, OLIVER, *Works*, ed. A. Friedman (5 vols.; Oxford, 1966).
GORDON, GEORGE, LORD BYRON, *The Complete Poetical Works*, ed. J. J. McGann (7 vols.; Oxford, 1986–).
GORDON, THOMAS, *The Humourist: being essays upon several subjects* (2 vols.; 1724–5).
[——], *A Seasonable Apology for Father Dominick, Chaplain to Prince Prettyman the Catholick, But now lying in Durance under the Suspicion of secret Iniquity. In*

which are occasionally inserted some weighty Arguments for calling a General Council of the Nonjuring Doctors, for the further Propagation of Ceremonies, Unity, Dissention, and Anathemas; and for the better Improvement of Exorcism and March-Beer (1723).

GOYA, FRANCISCO, *Los Caprichos* (New York, 1969).

[GRANT, FRANCIS], *Sadducismus Debellatus: Or a True Narrative of the Sorceries and Witchcrafts Exercis'd by the Devil and his Instruments upon Mrs Christian Shaw* (1698).

GREEN, J. B., *John Wesley and William Law* (1945).

GREENE, ROBERT, *Principles of Natural Philosophy* (1712).

GREENFIELD, EDMUND, *The Glorious Exaltation of the Holy Lamb of God, Our Lord and Saviour Jesus Christ, over all the Powers of Darkness* (1820).

GUERRINI, ANITA, 'The Tory Newtonians: Gregory, Pitcairne and their Circle', *JBS* 25 (1986).

GUSKIN, P. J., 'The Context of Witchcraft', *Eighteenth Century Studies*, 15 (1981).

GUYOT, P., *Le Répertoire universel* (Paris, 1784–5).

HALE, MATTHEW, *An Essay Touching the Gravitation or Non-Gravitation of Fluid Bodies* (1673).

——*Difficiles Nugae; Or, Observations Touching the Torricellian Experiment* (1674).

——*Observations touching the principles of natural motions* (1677).

——*The Primitive Origination of Mankind* (1677).

——*The Judgment of the late Lord Chief Justice Hale Of the Nature of True Religion* (1684).

——'A meditation concerning the mercy of God, in preserving us from the malice and power of evil angels' (1682), in *A Collection of modern relations of matter of fact, concerning witches and witchcraft upon the persons of people. To which is prefixed a meditation concerning the mercy of God, in preserving us from the malice and power of evil angels. Written by the late Lord Chief Justice Hale, upon occasion of a tryal of several witches before him* (1693).

——*Magnetismus Magnus* (1695).

——*The History of the Pleas of the Crown* (1734).

——'Reflections by the Lrd. Cheife Justice Hale on Mr Hobbes His Dialogue of the Lawe', in W. S. Holdsworth, *History of English Law* (1903–72), v (1924).

HALICZER, STEPHEN, 'The Jew as Witch: Displaced Aggression and the Myth of Santo Nino de La Guardia', in M. E. Perry and A. J. Cruz (eds.), *Cultural Encounters: The Impact of the Inquisition in Spain and the New World* (Berkeley, 1991).

HANSON, L., *Government and the Press 1695–1763* (Oxford, 1936).

HARE, HUGH, *A Charge Given at the General Quarter Sessions of the Peace for the County of Surrey* (1692).

HÄRTING, U. A., *Studien zu Kabinettmalerei des Frans Francken, ii* (Holz, 1983).

HEARNE, THOMAS, *Remarks and Collections*, iii, ed. C. E. Doble (Oxford, 1889).

HEIMANN, P. M., 'Voluntarism and Immanence', *JHI* 39 (1978).

HELD, JUTTA, 'Between Bourgeois Enlightenment and Popular Culture: Goya's Festivals, Old Women, Monsters and Blind Men', *History Workshop Journal*, 23 (1987).

HELMAN, EDITH, 'The Younger Moratín and Goya: On *Duendes* and *Brujas*', *Hispanic Review*, 27 (1959).

HENNINGSEN, GUSTAV, *The Witches' Advocate: Basque Witchcraft and the Spanish Inquisition, 1609–1614* (Reno, Nev., 1980).

HENRY, JOHN, 'Occult Qualities and the Experimental Philosophy: Active Principles in Pre-Newtonian Matter Theory', *HS* 24 (1986).

HERVEY, JOHN, *Memoirs of the Reign of George II* (2 vols.; 1849).

HEYD, MICHAEL, 'The Reaction to Enthusiasm in the Seventeenth Century: Towards an Integrative Approach', *Journal of Modern History*, 53 (1981).

HILL, BRIAN W., *Robert Harley: Speaker, Secretary of State and Premier Minister* (New Haven, 1988).

HILL, CHRISTOPHER, *The World Turned Upside Down* (1972; Harmondsworth, 1975).

The History and Proceedings of the House of Commons (1742).

HMC, *The Manuscripts of the Duke of Hamilton* (11th report, app., pt. VI, 1887).

HMC, *Report on the Laing Manuscripts* (2 vols.; 1914, 1925).

HMC, *Report on the Manuscripts of the Earl of Mar and Kellie* (3 vols.; 1904, 1930).

HMC, *The Manuscripts of the Earl of Onslow* (14th report, app., pt. IX, 1895).

HOBBES, THOMAS, *English Works*, ed. W. Molesworth (11 vols.; 1839–45).

—— *Opera Philosophica quae Latine scripsit omnia* (*Latin Works*), ed. W. Molesworth (5 vols.; 1839–45).

—— 'Human Nature' (1650; written 1640 as part one of 'The Elements of Law'), in Hobbes, *English Works*, iv.

—— *The Elements of Law, natural and politic* (1640), ed. J. C. A. Gaskin (Oxford, 1994).

—— *De Cive*, English version, ed. H. Warrender (orig. pub. in Latin, 1642; Oxford, 1983).

—— *Leviathan* (1651), ed. Richard Tuck (Cambridge, 1991).

—— 'Six Lessons to the Savilian Professors of the Mathematics' (1656), in Hobbes, *English Works*, vii.

—— 'Dialogus Physicus' (1661), tr. by S. Schaffer, in S. Shapin and S. Schaffer, *Leviathan and the Air-Pump*.

—— 'Considerations upon the Reputation, Loyalty, Manners, and Religion of Thomas Hobbes' (1662) in Hobbes, *English Works*, iv.

—— *A Dialogue between a Philosopher and a Student of the Common Laws of England* (1681; drafted 1666), ed. J. Cropsey (Chicago, 1971).

—— 'An Historical Narration concerning Heresy, and the Punishment thereof' (1668), in Hobbes, *English Works*, iv.

—— 'An Answer to Bishop Bramhall's Book' (1682; drafted *c*.1668), in Hobbes, *English Works*, iv.

—— *Behemoth* (1679; written 1670), in Hobbes, *English Works*, vi.

—— 'Of Liberty and Necessity', in Hobbes, *English Works*, iv.

HOGARTH, WILLIAM, *Hogarth's Graphic Works*, ed. R. Paulson, 3rd rev. edn. (1989).

HOGG, JAMES, *Confessions of a Justified Sinner* (1824; Oxford, 1969).

HOLE, ROBERT, *Pulpits, Politics and Public Order in England 1760–1832* (Cambridge, 1989).

HOLMES, CLIVE, 'Women: Witnesses and Witches', *P & P* 140 (1993).

HORNER, FRANCIS, *Memoirs and Correspondence*, ed. L. Horner (1843).

House of Commons, *Journals*.

House of Lords, *Journals*.

HUME, DAVID, *An Enquiry Concerning the Principles of Morals*, ed. P. H. Nidditch (Oxford, 1975).

HUNTER, MICHAEL, ' "Aikenhead the Atheist": The Context and Consequences of Articulate Irreligion in the Late Seventeenth Century', in Hunter and Wootton, *Atheism from the Reformation to the Enlightenment*.

—— 'The Witchcraft Controversy and the Nature of Free-Thought in Restoration England: John Wagstaffe's *The Question of Witchcraft Debated* (1669)', in *Science and the Shape of Orthodoxy* (Woodbridge, 1995).

—— and WOOTTON, DAVID (eds.), *Atheism from the Reformation to the Enlightenment* (Oxford, 1992).

HUTCHINSON, FRANCIS, *Sermon preached . . . May 1st 1707, being the Day of thanksgiving for the Union of England and Scotland* (1708).

—— *A Short View of the Pretended Spirit of Prophecy* (1708).

—— *A Compassionate Address to those Papists, Who will be prevail'd with to examine the CAUSE for which they Suffer* (1716).

—— *The Life of the Most Reverend Father in GOD, John Tillotson* (1717).

—— *An Historical Essay Concerning Witchcraft* (1718).

—— *A defence of the Antient Historians* (Dublin, 1734).

HUTCHINSON, JOHN, *Moses's Principia* (1724).

HYDE CASSAN, S., *Considerations on the Danger of any Legislative Alteration Respecting the Corporation and Test Acts; and of any Concession to Dissenters or Papists* (1828).

The Impossibility of Witchcraft (1712).

INNES, JOANNA, 'Parliament and the Shaping of Eighteenth-Century English Social Policy', *TRHS* 5th ser. 40 (1990).

ISAMBERT, FRANÇOIS ANDRÉ, *et al.* (eds.), *Recueil général des anciennes lois françaises* (Paris, 1821–33).

ISRAEL, JONATHAN, *The Dutch Republic: Its Rise, Greatness, and Fall 1477–1806* (Oxford, 1995).

JACOB, J. R., *Henry Stubbe, Radical Protestantism and the Early Enlightenment* (Cambridge, 1983).

JACOB, MARGARET, *The Newtonians and the English Revolution* (Ithaca, NY, 1976).

JOVELLANOS, GASPAR MELCHOR DE, *Diarios* (Oviedo, 1954).

JUXON, JOSEPH, *A Sermon upon Witchcraft* (1736).

KEBLE, JOSEPH, *An Assistance to the Justices of the Peace* (1683).

KEEBLE, N. H., and NUTTALL, GEOFFREY F. (eds.), *Calendar of the Correspondence of Richard Baxter* (2 vols.; Oxford, 1991).

KENDALL, R. T., *Calvin and English Calvinism to 1649* (Oxford, 1979).

KENNETT, WHITE, *The Witchcraft of the present Rebellion, A Sermon preach'd . . . On Sunday 25th of September, 1715* (1715).

KENYON, J. P., *Revolution Principles: The Politics of Party 1689–1720* (Cambridge, 1977).

KIRKTON, J., *The Secret and True History of the Church of Scotland from the Restoration to the Year 1678*, ed. C. K. Sharpe (Edinburgh, 1817).

KLANICZAY, G., 'The Decline of Witches and the Rise of Vampires under the 18th-Century Habsburg Monarchy', in *The Uses of Supernatural Power* (Cambridge, 1990).

KUHN, PHILIP A., *Soulstealers: The Chinese Sorcery Scare of 1768* (Cambridge, Mass., 1990).

LABROUSSE, ELISABETH, *Bayle* (Oxford, 1983).

—— '*Une foi, une loi, un roi: essai sur la révocation de l'Édit de Nantes* (Paris, 1985).

LAHONTAN, BARON DE, *Dialogues de monsieur le baron de Lahontan et d'un sauvage de l'Amerique* (Amsterdam, 1704).

LAING, DAVID, note in *Proceedings of the Society of Antiquaries of Scotland*, 11 (1876).

LAMOINE, GEORGES (ed.), *Charges to the Grand Jury, 1689–1803*, Camden 4th ser. 43 (1992).

LANGFORD, PAUL, *A Polite and Commercial Society* (Oxford, 1989).

LARNER, CHRISTINA, *Enemies of God: The Witch-Hunt in Scotland* (1981).

—— *Witchcraft and Religion* (Oxford, 1984).

LASLETT, PETER, 'Sir Robert Filmer: The Man versus the Whig Myth', *William and Mary Quarterly*, 3rd ser. 5/4 (1948).

LATOUR, BRUNO, *Science in Action* (Milton Keynes, 1987).

LAUD, WILLIAM, *Conference with Fisher the Jesuit* (1639; 1901).

LE CLERC, JEAN, *Bibliothèque Universelle et Historique*, xxi (Amsterdam, 1691).

LEA, H. C., *Materials towards a History of Witchcraft*, ed. A. C. Howland (Philadelphia, 1939).

LEIBNIZ, G. W., 'Essais de Theodicée', in *Die Philosophischen Schriften von Gottfried Wilhelm Leibniz* (Berlin, 1885), vi.

[LEIGH, CHARLES], *Remarks on Mr Richard Bolton's piece concerning the Heat of the Blood* (Manchester, 1698).

LEVACK, BRIAN, 'The Great Scottish Witch Hunt of 1661–1662', *Journal of British Studies*, 20 (1980).

—— *The Witch-Hunt in Early Modern Europe* (1993).

LIMBORCH, PHILIP VAN, *Historia Inquisitionis* (Amsterdam, 1692).

LINGARD, JOHN, *The Confessed Intimacy of Luther with Satan, at whose suggestion he abolished the Mass* (1821).

LITTLETON, ADAM, *Sixty One Sermons* (1680).

LOCKE, JOHN, *Epistola de Tolerantia* (1689), ed. R. Klibansky (Oxford, 1968).

——*An Essay Concerning Human Understanding* (1690), ed. P. Nidditch (Oxford, 1975).

——*Two Treatises of Government* (1690), ed. P. Laslett (Cambridge, 1960).

——'Some Thoughts Concerning Education' (1693), in *Works* (10 vols.; 1823), ix.

——'A Discourse of Miracles' (written *c.*1703), in *Works* (10 vols.; 1823), ix.

——'Elements of Natural Philosophy', in *The Works of John Locke*, ed. St John (2 vols., 18).

——*The Correspondence of John Locke*, ed. E. S. de Beer (8 vols., Oxford, 1978–89).

LOUIS XIV, *Mémoires de Louis XIV*, ed. C. Dreyss (2 vols.; Paris, 1860).

MacDONALD, MICHAEL, *Mystical Bedlam* (Cambridge, 1981).

——'Religion, Social Change, and Psychological Healing in England 1600–1800'. *Studies in Church History*, 19 (1982).

McINNES, ANGUS, *Robert Harley: Puritan Politician* (1970).

McKEON, MICHAEL, *The Origins of the English Novel, 1600–1740* (Baltimore, 1987).

McMANNERS, JOHN, *Death and the Enlightenment* (Oxford, 1985).

MAFFEI, SCIPIONE, *Arte Magica dileguata; lettera del Signor Marchese Maffei al Padre I. Ansaldi* (Verona, 1749).

MALCOLM, NOEL, 'Hobbes and the Royal Society', in Rogers and Ryan, *Perspectives on Thomas Hobbes.*

MANDROU, ROBERT, *Magistrats et sorciers en France au XVIIe siècle* (Paris, 1968).

——(ed.), *Possession et sorcellerie au XVIIe siècle: textes inédits* (Paris, 1979).

MARTIN, BENJAMIN, *Supplement containing remarks on a rhapsody of adventures of a modern knight-errant* (Bath, 1746).

MATHER, COTTON, *Memorable providences relating to witchcraft* (1689).

——*The Wonders of the Invisible World* (1692; New York, 1991).

MATTHEWS, WILLIAM (ed.), *Charles II's Escape from Worcester: A Collection of Narratives Assembled by Samuel Pepys* (Berkeley and Los Angeles, 1966).

MAXWELL, T., 'The Scotch Presbyterian Eloquence: A Post-Restoration Pamphlet', *Records of the Scottish Church History Society*, 8 (1944).

METTAM, R., *Government and Society in Louis XIV's France* (1977).

MIDELFORT, H. C. ERIK, *Witch Hunting in Southwestern Germany, 1562–1684* (Stanford, Calif., 1972).

MILL, JOHN STUART, 'Jeremy Bentham's Rationale of Judicial Evidence' (1827), in *Miscellaneous Writings*, vol. xxi of *Collected Works of John Stuart Mill* (1989).

MILLER, JOHN, 'The Late Stuart Monarchy', in J. R. Jones (ed.), *The Restored Monarchy* (1979).

MILLER, LUCASTA, 'The Shattered *Violl*: Print and Textuality in the 1640s', in Nigel Smith (ed.), *Essays and Studies* (1993).

MILLER, PERRY, 'The Marrow of Puritan Divinity', *Publications of the Colonial Society of Massachusetts*, 32 (1937).

MINTZ, SAMUEL, *The Hunting of Leviathan: Seventeenth-Century Reactions to the Materialism and Moral Philosophy of Thomas Hobbes* (Cambridge, 1962).

A Miracle of Miracles: wrought by the Blood of King Charles the First, of happy memory, upon a Mayd at Detford foure miles from London, who . . . by making use of a piece of handkircher dipped in the Kings blood is recovered of her sight, etc. (1649).

MONOD, PAUL, *Jacobitism and the English People, 1688–1788* (Cambridge, 1989).

MONTER, E. W., 'The Historiography of European Witchcraft: Progress and Prospects', *Journal of Interdisciplinary History*, 2 (1972).

——*Witchcraft in France and Switzerland: The Borderlands during the Reformation* (Ithaca, NY, 1976).

——*Frontiers of Heresy: The Spanish Inquisition from the Basque Lands to Sicily* (Cambridge, 1990).

MONTESQUIEU, CHARLES LOUIS DE SECONDAT, BARON DE LA BRÈDE ET DE, 'L'Esprit des Lois', in *Œuvres complètes* , ed. R. Caillois (2 vols.; Paris, 1949–51).

MOORE, JOHN, *Sermons on several Subjects*, ed. S. Clarke (2 vols.; 1715, 1716).

MOORE, HENRY, *The Life of the Reverend John Wesley* (Leeds, 1825).

[MORE, HENRY], *Enthusiasmus Triumphatus, or a Discourse of the Nature, Causes, Kinds, and Cure of Enthusiasme; written by Philophilus Parrasiastes, and prefixed to Alazonomastix his Observations and Reply* (1656).

MORTON, CHARLES, *Compendium Physicae*, ed. S. E. Morison (Boston, 1940).

MOSSIKER, FRANCES, *The Affair of the Poisons: Louis XIV, Madame de Montespan and One of History's Great Unsolved Mysteries* (London, 1970).

MOUSNIER, ROLAND, *The Institutions of France under the Absolute Monarchy 1598–1789* (Chicago, 1979).

MURAT, INES, *Colbert* (Paris, 1980).

NEWTON, ISAAC, *Philosophiae Naturalis Principia Mathematica*, 2nd edn., (1713).

NORTH, ROGER, *The Autobiography of the Hon. Roger North*, ed. A. Jessopp (1887).

——*The Lives of the Norths*, ed. A. Jessopp (3 vols., 1890).

NOTESTEIN, WALLACE, *A History of Witchcraft in England from 1558 to 1718* (Washington, 1911).

NOVAK, MAXIMILLIAN, *Defoe and the Nature of Man* (Oxford, 1963).

Of Plays and Masquerades (1719).

OMOND, G. W. T. (ed.), *Arniston Memoirs: Three Centuries of a Scottish House 1571–1838* (Edinburgh, 1887).

[ORCHARD, NICHOLAS], *The Doctrine of Devils proved to be the grand Apostasy of these later Times. An Essay tending to rectifie those Undue Notions and Apprehensions Men have about Daemons and Evil Spirits* (1676).

OSBORN, FRANCIS, *Advice to a Son* (1656).

PACCHI, ARRIGO, 'Hobbes and the Problem of God', in Rogers and Ryan, *Perspectives on Thomas Hobbes.*

PAGDEN, ANTHONY, 'The Reception of the "New Philosophy" in Eighteenth-Century Spain', *Journal of the Warburg and Courtauld Institutes*, 51 (1988).

The Parliamentary Debates [Hansard], iv (1821).

PAULSON, RONALD, *Hogarth: Art and Politics* (3 vols.; Cambridge, 1993).

PEPYS, SAMUEL, *Private Correspondence and Miscellaneous Papers of Samuel Pepys, 1679–1703*, ed. J. R. Tanner (2 vols.; 1926).

——*The Diary of Samuel Pepys*, ed. R. C. Latham and W. Matthews (10 vols.; 1970–83).

PERKINS, WILLIAM, *A Discourse of the Damned Art of Witchcraft; So farre forth as it is reuealed in the Scriptures, and manifest by true experience* (Cambridge, 1608).

——*Workes* (2 vols.; Cambridge, 1609).

PERRY, T. W., *Public Opinion, Propaganda and Politics in Eighteenth-Century England* (Cambridge, Mass., 1962).

PETITFILS, JEAN-CHRISTIAN, *L'Affaire des poisons: alchimistes et sorciers sous Louis XIV* (Paris, 1977).

PETTO, SAMUEL, *A Faithful Narrative of the Wonderful and Extraordinary Fits under which Mr Tho. Spatchet . . . was under by Witchcraft: Or, A Mysterious Providence in his even Unparallel'd Fits* (1693).

PIERCE, THOMAS, αυτοκατακρισις *or Self-Condemnation* (1658).

PITCAIRN, T., *et al.* (eds.), *Acts of the General Assembly of the Church of Scotland 1638–1842* (Edinburgh, 1843).

PITCAIRNE, ARCHIBALD, *The Assembly, A Comedy, By a Scots Gentleman* (1722).

POCOCK, J. G. A., *The Ancient Constitution and the Feudal Law: A Study of English Historical Thought in the Seventeenth Century. A Reissue with a Retrospect* (Cambridge, 1987).

PRESTON, JOHN, *The Breast-Plate of Faith and Love*, 4th edn. (1634).

PRIOR, MOODY E., 'Joseph Glanvill, Witchcraft, and Seventeenth-Century Science', *Modern Philology*, 30 (1932–3).

PRYNNE, WILLIAM, *The Quakers Unmask'd, and clearly detected to be but the spawn of Romish frogs* (1655).

QUINE, W. V. O., *From a Logical Point of View* (Cambridge, Mass., 1964).

R., G, *The Belief of Witchcraft Vindicated* (1712).

RACK, HENRY D., *Reasonable Enthusiast: John Wesley and the Rise of Methodism* (1990).

RAVAISSON, F. N. N. (ed.), *Archives de la Bastille* (Paris, 1866–1904).

Recueil général des pièces concernant le procez entre la demoiselle Cadière . . . et le père Girard, Jésuite (2 vols.; Marseilles, 1731).

Relation of the Diabolical Practices of above Twenty Wizards and Witches of the Sheriffdom of Renfrew in the Kingdom of Scotland (1697).

The Remarkable Confession, and Last Dying Words of Thomas Colley (1751).

RILEY, P. J., *The Union of England and Scotland* (Manchester, 1978).

ROBBINS, R. H., *Encyclopaedia of Witchcraft and Demonology* (New York, 1959).

ROBERTS, ALEXANDER, *A Treatise of Witchcraft* (1616).

ROBERTS, CLAYTON, 'The Fall of the Godolphin Ministry', *JBS* 22/1 (1982).

ROGERS, G. A. J., and RYAN, A. (eds.), *Perspectives on Thomas Hobbes* (Oxford, 1988).

ROGERS, NICHOLAS, 'Riot and Popular Jacobitism in Early Hanoverian England', in E. Cruickshanks (ed.), *Ideology and Conspiracy: Aspects of Jacobitism, 1689–1759* (Edinburgh, 1982).

Round about our Coal Fire: or Christmas entertainments . . . Adorn'd with many curious cuts (*c.*1730), British Library 12354.d.4. (1).

RUSSELL, CONRAD, *The Causes of the English Civil War* (Oxford, 1990).

SÁNCHEZ, ALFONSO E. PÉREZ, and SAYRE, ELEANOR A., *Goya and the Spirit of Enlightenment* (Boston, 1989).

SCARGILL, DANIEL, *Recantation publickly made before the University of Cambridge (of which he was formerly a member)* (1669).

SCHAFFER, S., 'Godly Men and Mechanical Philosophers: Souls and Spirits in Restoration Natural Philosophy', *Science in Context*, 1 (1987).

——'Defoe's Natural Philosophy and the Worlds of Credit', in J. Christie and S. Shuttleworth (eds.), *Nature Transfigured* (Manchester, 1989).

SCHOCHET, GORDON, 'Sir Robert Filmer: Some New Bibliographical Discoveries', *Transactions of the Bibliographical Society*, 5th ser. 26 (1971).

SCHONHORN, M. (ed.), *Accounts of the Apparition of Mrs Veal* (Los Angeles, 1965).

——*Defoe's Politics: Parliament, Power, Kingship and 'Robinson Crusoe'* (Cambridge, 1991).

SCHWARTZ, HILLEL, *The French Prophets* (Berkeley, 1981).

SCOT, REGINALD, *The Discoverie of Witchcraft* (1584).

The Second Edition of the Conjuror's Repository; or, the whole art and mystery of magic displayed (1809).

SEDGWICK, ROMNEY, *The House of Commons 1715–54* (2 vols.; 1970).

SELDEN, JOHN, *Table Talk* (Oxford, 1892).

SÉVIGNÉ, MARIE DE RABUTIN CHANTAL, MARQUISE DE, *Correspondance* (3 vols.; Paris, 1974).

SHADWELL, THOMAS, *The Lancashire Witches* (1682), in *The Complete Works of Thomas Shadwell*, ed. Montague Summers (1927), iv.

SHAPIN, S. and SCHAFFER, S., *Leviathan and the Air-Pump* (Princeton, 1985).

SHAPIRO, BARBARA, *Probability and Certainty in Seventeenth-Century England* (Princeton, 1983).

[SHERLOCK, WILLIAM], *The Notes of The Church, As Laid down By Cardinal Bellarmin; Examined and Confuted* (1688).

SHIELDS, ALEXANDER, *A Hind let loose* (n.p., 1687).

SIBBES, R., 'Bowels Opened' (1639), in *Works*, ed. A. B. Grosart (Edinburgh, 1862).

SIMON, RICHARD [M. de Sainjore], *Bibliothèque Critique* (Amsterdam, 1708).

SKERRET, R., *Peace and Loyalty, Recommended in a Sermon Preach'd at the Lent-Assizes Holden at Brentwood in Essex* (1720).

SMART, CHRISTOPHER, *The Poetical Works of Christopher Smart, i: 'Jubilate Agno'*, ed. Karina Williamson (Oxford, 1980).

SMITH, JAMES, *An Examination of the Signs of the Times: Or, Seasonable Remarks on Mr Massey's Sermon. Proving That 'tis an Unscriptural, Prevaricating and Seditious Libel* (1722).

SMITH, JOHN, *Select Discourses* (1660).

SMITHERS, PETER, *The Life of Joseph Addison*, 2nd edn. (Oxford, 1968).

SMOLLETT, TOBIAS, *The Adventures of Peregrine Pickle* (1751; Oxford, 1983).

SOMAN, ALFRED, 'The Parlement of Paris and the Great Witch Hunt (1565–1640)', *Sixteenth Century Journal*, 9/2 (July 1978).

——*Sorcellerie et justice criminelle: le Parlement de Paris* (Aldershot, 1992).

SPEE, FRIEDRICH VON, *Cautio Criminalis* (Rinteln, 1631).

SPILLER, M. R. G., *'Concerning Natural Experimental Philosophie': Meric Casaubon and the Royal Society* (The Hague, 1980).

SPURR, JOHN, 'The Church of England, Comprehension and the Toleration Act of 1689', *EHR* 104 (1989).

——*The Restoration Church of England, 1646–1689* (New Haven, 1991).

STALLYBRASS, P., and WHITE, A., *The Politics and Poetics of Transgression* (1986).

STEBBING, H., *A letter to mr Foster on the subject of heresy* (1735).

STEELE, RICHARD, *et al.*, *The Tatler*, ed. D. F. Bond (3 vols.; Oxford, 1987).

[STEWART OF GOODTREES, JAMES], *Jus Populi Vindicatum* (1669).

S[TUBBS], PH[ILIP], *The Witchcraft of the Scriptures: A sermon preach'd on a Special Occasion* (1736).

The Surey Demoniack: or an account of Satan's strange and dreadful actings, in and about the Body of Richard Dugdale of Surey, near Whalley in Lancashire (1697).

SYKES, NORMAN, *Edmund Gibson* (Oxford, 1926).

——*Church and State in the Eighteenth Century* (Cambridge, 1934).

——*From Sheldon to Secker* (Cambridge, 1959).

T., R., *The Opinion of Witchcraft Vindicated. In an Answer to a Book Intituled the Question of WITCHCRAFT Debated. Being a Letter to a Friend* (1670).

TARTAROTTI, GIROLAMO, *Del Congresso Notturno Delle Lamie Libri Tre . . . S'aggiungono due dissertazione epistolari sopra l'arte magica* (Rovereto, 1749).

TAYLOR, STEPHEN, 'Sir Robert Walpole, the Church of England, and the Quakers' Tithe Bill of 1736', *HJ* 28 (1985).

——'William Warburton and the Alliance of Church and State', *JEH* 43 (1992).

TAYLOR, ZACHARY, *The Devil turn'd Casuist; or the Cheats of Rome* (1696).

——*The Surey Impostor: Being an Answer to a Late Fanatical Pamphlet, Entituled The Surey Demoniack* (1697).

TEALL, JOHN L., 'Witchcraft and Calvinism in Elizabethan England: Divine Power and Human Agency', *JHI*, 23 (1962).

TEMPLE, WILLIAM, *Observations upon . . . the Netherlands* (1672).

TENISON, THOMAS, *The Creed of Mr Hobbes Examined; In a feigned conference between him, and a student in divinity* (1670).

THOMAS, KEITH, *Religion and the Decline of Magic* (1971; Harmondsworth, 1973).

THOMASIUS, CHRISTIAN, *Dissertatione de Crimine Magiae* (Halle, 1701).

——*De Origine ac progressu Processus inquisitorii contra Sagas* (Halle, 1712).

THOMPSON, E. P., 'Hunting the Jacobin Fox', *P & P* 142 (1994).

To the Loyal and Religious Hearts in Parliament (1706).

TRENCHARD, JOHN, and GORDON, THOMAS, *Cato's Letters*, 3rd edn. (4 vols.; London, 1733).

TREVOR-ROPER, HUGH, 'Laudianism and Political Power', in *Catholics, Anglicans and Puritans: Seventeenth-Century Essays* (1987).

The Tryal of Thomas Colley (1751).

A Tryal of Witches Held at the Assizes held at Bury St. Edmunds (1691).

TUCK, RICHARD, 'The "Christian Atheism" of Thomas Hobbes', in Hunter and Wootton, *Atheism*.

TWISSE, WILLIAM, *The Riches of Gods Love unto the Vessells of Mercy Consistent with His Absolute Hatred or Reprobation of the Vessells of Wrath* (Oxford, 1653).

TYACKE, NICHOLAS, *Anti-Calvinists: The Rise of English Arminianism* (Oxford, 1987).

VAN HEEMSKERK, JOHAN, *Batavische arcadia*, 2nd edn. (1639).

VAN LEEUWEN, SIMON, *Manieren van Procederen in civile en criminele saaken etc.* (1666).

VENTURI, FRANCO, 'Enlightenment versus the Powers of Darkness', in *Italy and the Enlightenment: Studies in a Cosmopolitan Century* (1972).

VERNON, JAMES, *Letters . . . to the Duke of Shrewsbury by James Vernon Esq., Secretary of State*, ed. G. P. R. James (3 vols.; 1841).

Victoria and Albert Museum, *Catalogue of Foreign Paintings before 1800* (1973).

VIGUERIE, JEAN DE, 'Le Miracle dans la France du XVIIe siècle', *XVIIe Siècle*, 140 (1983).

VILVAIN, ROBERT, *Theoremata Theologica* (1654).

VOLTAIRE [FRANÇOIS-MARIE AROUET], 'Prix de la Justice et de l'Humanité' (1777), in *Œuvres* (Garnier, Paris, 1883), xxx.

VOUGLANS, MUYART DE, *Les Loix Criminelles de France, dans leur ordre naturel* (Paris, 1780).

WAGSTAFFE, JOHN, *Historical Reflections on the Bishop of Rome: chiefly discovering Those Events of Humane Affaires which most advanced THE PAPAL USURPATION* (1660).

[——] *The Question of Witchcraft Debated* (1st edn., 1669; 2nd edn., 1671).

WALKER, D. P., *Unclean Spirits: Possession and Exorcism in France and England in the Late Sixteenth and Early Seventeenth Centuries* (1981).

WEBSTER, CHARLES, 'The Experimental Philosophy of Henry Power', *Ambix*, 14 (1967).

—— *The Great Instauration* (1975).

WEBSTER, JOHN, *The Displaying of Supposed Witchcraft* (1677).

WESLEY, JOHN, *The Journal of Rev. John Wesley* (4 vols.; 1906).

WILDE, C. B., 'Hutchinsonianism, Natural Philosophy and Religious Controversy in Eighteenth Century Britain', *HS* 18 (1980).

—— 'Matter and Spirit as Natural Symbols in Eighteenth-Century British Natural Philosophy', *BJHS* 15 (1982).

WILLIAMS, GWYN A., *Goya and the Impossible Revolution* (1976).

WILLIAMSON, GEORGE, 'The Restoration Revolt against Enthusiasm', *Studies in Philology*, 30 (1933).

WILLS, GARRY, review of Murray Kempton's *Rebellions, Perversities and Main Events, New York Review of Books*, 41/9 (1994).

WILSON, LESLIE, 'Salem's Lot', *London Review of Books*, 17/6 (1995).

WILSON, THOMAS, *The Diaries of Thomas Wilson, DD, 1731–1737 and 1750, Son of Bishop Wilson of Sodor and Man*, ed. C. L. S. Linnell (1964).

WILSON-BAREAU, JULIET, *Goya: Truth and Fantasy* (1994).

The Witch of Endor: Or, a Plea for the Divine Administration By the Agency of Good and Evil Spirits. Written some Years ago, at the Request of a Lady; and now Reprinted with a Prefatory Discourse, Humbly Addressed to the Honourable Members of the House of C—s, who brought in their Bill (Jan. 27) for Repealing the Statute of I Jac. Cap. 12. concerning WITCHCRAFT (1736).

WODROW, ROBERT, *Early Letters of Robert Wodrow 1698–1709* (Publications of the Scottish Historical Society, 3rd ser. 24; Edinburgh, 1937).

—— *Analecta*, ed. M. Leishman (4 vols.; Glasgow, 1842).

—— *The Correspondence of the Rev. Robert Wodrow* (Edinburgh, 1842).

WOOTTON, DAVID, 'Lucien Febvre and the Problem of Unbelief in the Early Modern Period', *Journal of Modern History*, 60 (1988).

WORDEN, BLAIR, 'Toleration and the Cromwellian Protectorate'. *Studies in Church History*, 21; Oxford (1984).

YATES, FRANCES, *Giordano Bruno and the Hermetic Tradition* (1964).

YOLTON, JOHN, *Thinking Matter: Materialism in Eighteenth-Century Britain* (Oxford, 1984).

ZARET, DAVID, *The Heavenly Contract: Ideology and Organization in Pre-Revolutionary Puritanism* (Chicago, 1985).

SEVENTEENTH- AND EIGHTEENTH-CENTURY NEWSPAPERS AND JOURNALS

Censor

Flying Post

Foreign Post

Gentleman's Magazine

Medley

Midwife; Or Old Woman's Magazine

Lloyd's News

Oxford Magazine

Post Boy

Protestant Mercury

Protestant Post-Boy

World

MANUSCRIPTS

Letter of NICHOLAS BERNARD to Meric Casaubon, with statement by John Cotton concerning Dr Dee's relation, Bodleian MS Ashm. 1788 f65 (1658).

Letter of EDMUND BOHUN to William Sancroft, 23 Jan. 1677, Bodleian MS Tanner 40, f 39.

RICHARD BOULTON to Sir Hans Sloane, BL Sloane MS 4058 ff47–9 (1695).

Letter written by MERIC CASAUBON and placed in Earl of Anglesey's copy of Dee's relation, Bodleian MS Rawl. D 923 f 295.

Note in MERIC CASAUBON, *A Treatise of Use and Custome*, Bodleian Vet A2 e 295.

Manuscripts of ROBERT FILMER in the possession of Peter Laslett, Trinity College, Cambridge.

'Rough draught' of MATTHEW HALE's 'Reflections' on Thomas Hobbes's 'Dialogue', BL Add. MS 18235.

MATTHEW HALE, 'The Secondary Origination of Man', BL Add. MS 9001.

EDWARD HARLEY, CUL MS Add. 6851 [Parliamentary Journal for 1734–51].

Letter of FRANCIS HUTCHINSON to Arthur Charlett, Bodleian Ballard MS 38 f 27 (1718).

Letters of FRANCIS HUTCHINSON to Sir Hans Sloane: BL Sloane MS 4040, f 302 (1706); BL Sloane MS 4043, f 38 (1712); BL Sloane MS 4047, f 67 (1723).

LORD NAIRNE, 'Grounds of a true Catholick', Bodleian Carte MS 208 f 224a.

Letter of ROBERT WYLIE to William Hamilton, SRO GD103/2/3/17/1, 16 June 1697, and copy in Bodleian MS Locke b4 f 107.

UNPUBLISHED THESES AND ARTICLES

BOSTRIDGE, IAN, 'Jurisprudence and Natural Philosophy: Matthew Hale and Thomas Hobbes', Cambridge M.Phil. thesis (1987).

MALCOLM, NOEL, 'Thomas Hobbes and Voluntarist Theology', Cambridge Ph.D. thesis (1983).

RIBEIRO, AILEEN, 'The Dress Worn at Masquerades in England 1730–1790', dissertation, Courtauld Institute, University of London (1975).

WOOTTON, DAVID, 'Reginald Scot' (paper at Birkbeck College early modern history seminar, 1993).

Index

DATE DUE